A Companion to the Works of Heinrich Heine

Studies in German Literature, Linguistics, and Culture

Edited by James Hardin
(*South Carolina*)

The Camden House Companions provide well-informed and up-to-date critical commentary on the most significant aspects of major works, periods, or literary figures. The Companions may be read profitably by the reader with a general interest in the subject. For the benefit of student and scholar, quotations are provided in the original language.

A COMPANION
TO THE WORKS OF
Heinrich Heine

Edited by
Roger F. Cook

CAMDEN HOUSE

First published 2002
by Camden House

Camden House is an imprint of Boydell & Brewer Inc.
PO Box 41026, Rochester, NY 14604–4126 USA
and of Boydell & Brewer Limited
PO Box 9, Woodbridge, Suffolk IP12 3DF, UK

ISBN: 1–57113–207–4

Library of Congress Cataloging-in-Publication Data

Cook, Roger F., 1948–
    A companion to the works of Heinrich Heine / Cook, Roger F.
      p. cm. — (Studies in German literature, linguistics, and culture)
    Includes bibliographical references and index.
    ISBN 1–57113–207–4 (alk. paper)
      1. Heine, Heinrich, 1797–1856 — Criticism and interpretation.
    I. Title. II Series.

PT2340 .C66 2002
831'.7—dc21

                                                            2002019455

A catalogue record for this title is available from the British Library.

This publication is printed on acid-free paper.
Printed in the United States of America.

Contents

Acknowledgments

I WOULD LIKE TO THANK both the Research Board of the University of Missouri and the Research Council of the University of Missouri-Columbia for their generous support of this project.

Chronology of Heine's Life

1797   Born in December (probably Dec. 13) in Düsseldorf to Samson and Betty Heine.

1807–1814   Student at Catholic schools and, from 1810 on, the Lyceum in Düsseldorf.

1815–1819   Business and banking apprenticeship; worked in Hamburg bank of his uncle Salomon Heine; ran family textile business.

1819–1825   Study of law (University of Bonn, 1819–1820; University of Göttingen, 1820–1821 and 1824–1825; University of Berlin, 1821–1824); member of *Verein für Cultur und Wissenschaft der Juden,* 1822–1824; doctor of law degree from Göttingen, 1825.

1825–1831   Worked as writer in Lüneberg, Hamburg, Munich, Berlin; co-editor of *Neue Allgemeine Politische Annalen* (Munich, 1827–1828), travels in Italy, 1828.

1831   Moved to Paris in January, where he began writing as a correspondent for German newspapers, most notably the Augsburg *Allgemeine Zeitung.*

1835   Named in Bundestag decree as one of six members of *Junges Deutschland.*

1843–1844   Friendship with Karl Marx in Paris; two journeys to Hamburg to visit his mother and his lifelong publisher, Julius Campe.

1848   Physical collapse in February; subsequent confinement to bed in his Paris "Matratzengruft" (mattress tomb) until his death.

1856   Died in Paris on February 17, buried in Montmarte Cemetery.

Heine's Major Works

(With English title and date of first published English translation in parentheses.)

Gedichte, 1822.

Briefe aus Berlin, 1822.

Tragödien nebst einem lyrischen Intermezzo (includes the plays *Almansor* and *William Ratcliff*), 1823.

Buch der Lieder, 1827 (*Book of Songs*, 1856).

Reisebilder, 4 vols., 1826–1831 (includes *Die Harzreise; Die Heimkehr; Die Nordsee; Ideen: Das Buch Le Grand; Reise von München nach Genua; Die Bäder von Lucca; Die Stadt Lucca; Englische Fragmente*), (*Picture of Travels*, 1855).

Aus den Memoiren des Herrn von Schnabelewopski, 1833 (The Memoirs of Herr von Schnabelewopski, 1892).

Französische Zustände, 1833 (*French Affairs*, 1889).

Französische Maler, 1833 (*French Painters*, 1892).

Zur Geschichte der Religion und Philosophie in Deutschland, 1835 (*On the History of Religion and Philosophy in Germany*, 1882).

Die Romantische Schule, 1836 (originally published as *Zur Geschichte der neueren schönen Literatur in Deutschland*, 1833), (*The Romantic School*, 1882).

Elementargeister, 1836 (*Elementary Spirits*, 1905).

Florentinische Nächte, 1836 (*Florentine Nights*, 1887).

Shakespeares Mädchen und Frauen, 1839 (*Heine on Shakespeare*, 1895).

Der Rabbi von Bacherach, 1840 (*The Rabbi of Bacherach*, 1892).

Ludwig Börne. Eine Denkschrift, 1840 (*Ludwig Börne: Portrait of a Revolutionist*, 1881).

Neue Gedichte, 1844 (*New Poems*, 1859).

Deutschland. Ein Wintermärchen, 1844 (*Germany: A Winter's Tale,* 1859).

Atta Troll. Ein Sommernachtstraum, 1847 (*Atta Troll: A Midsummer Night's Dream,* 1859).

Die Götter im Exil, 1854 (*The Gods in Exile,* 1887).

Romanzero, 1851 (*Romancero,* 1859).

Der Doktor Faust (a ballet scenario), 1851 (*Doctor Faust,* 1905).

Gedichte. 1853 und 1854, 1854 (*Poems: 1853 and 1854,* 1859).

Geständnisse, 1854 (*Confessions,* 1887).

Lutezia, 1854 (*Lutetia,* 1905).

Memoiren, 1884 (*Memoirs,* 1884).

Abbreviations

References to the following editions will be cited parenthetically in the text using these abbreviations:

B   Heinrich Heine. *Sämtliche Schriften*. Ed. Klaus Briegleb. Munich: Hanser, 1968–1976. 6 vols. (in 7).

DHA   Heinrich Heine. *Historisch-kritische Gesamtausgabe der Werke*. Düsseldorfer Ausgabe. Ed. Manfred Windfuhr, et al. Hamburg: Hoffmann und Campe, 1973–1997. 16 vols. (in 23).

HSA   Heinrich Heine. *Werke, Briefwechsel, Lebenszeugnisse. Säkular-ausgabe*. Ed. Nationale Forschungs- und Gedenkstätten der klassischen deutschen Literatur in Weimar and Centre National de la Recherche Scientifique in Paris. Berlin and Paris: Akademie-Verlag and Editions du CNRS, 1970–. 27 vols.

Introduction

Roger F. Cook

HEINRICH HEINE CAME INTO THE world in 1797, at the beginning of Napoleon's rise to power, which would shake the foundations of European society, and by his death in 1856 Heine's life had spanned a transitional period in German history stamped by hope, disillusionment, anticipation, and suspended action. His generation inherited a dying system of social structures and cultural values without possessing a clear vision of either the political or the social order that could replace it. In this state of limbo on the threshold to modernity, the new generation of German *Dichter und Denker* were torn between a turn back to glorified visions of the past and a radical break with even the most revered traditions. No other German writer reflected this ambivalence as deeply as Heine. The richness and diversity of his writings is itself a testament to the vacillations that characterize German culture during his lifetime.

Heine was the oldest of four children born to Samson and Betty Heine in Düsseldorf. His father ran a yard-goods business that slowly deteriorated in the weak economic climate of the early Restoration period, until it finally collapsed in 1819. After two years in a communal Hebrew school, where he learned a smattering of Hebrew, Heine began attending Catholic schools in 1804, which at the time were structured according to the French system. He was a student at the Lyceum in Düsseldorf from 1810 until 1814, when he dropped out before graduation in order to prepare for a career in business.

However, coming of age in a time when Romantic poetry was considered the most genuine form of literary expression, and indeed even the mark of genius, Heine embraced it as his calling in his late teens. He continued to write Romantic verse even while his uncle Salomon, a wealthy Hamburg banker, supported him through half-hearted attempts to help revive the failing family business and then financed his university studies in law. As his poems began to appear in journals and then in a first published collection (entitled simply *Gedichte,* 1821), he established something of a reputation for himself as one of the best young Romantic poets. Throughout his reluctant and prolonged study at three universities (Bonn, Berlin, Göttingen) he devoted more of his energies to writing than to law, trying his hand at drama, literary prose, and journalistic writing while continuing to fashion his own unique poetic voice. As his studies were drawing to a close, Heine wrote the first of what would become a series of satirical "travel pictures" (*Reisebilder*, 1824–1831) that, due in large part to their biting humor and innovative new style, enjoyed immediate success among a large portion of the German reading public. When he moved to Paris in 1831, where he resided for the final twenty-five years of his life in self-declared "exile," this new genre of literary prose served as his chief calling card in the Paris circles of the intellectual and cultural elite. Only after Romantic composers began to set his early lyrical poems to music in the 1830s did his first major poetry anthology, *Buch der Lieder* (1827), enjoy similar success and earn him renown as a major Romantic poet. It is in this regard that he became one of the leading figures in the canon of nineteenth-century German literature and it remains the predominant image of Heine today, even though he pursued primarily other literary interests after the mid-1820s. He did continue to write lyrical verse throughout the first period in France and even published his second major anthology, *Neue Gedichte,* in 1844. However, the majority of his work in these years consisted of: reports on Parisian cultural and social life for German journals (published collectively in various editions, including *Französische Muler* [1833], *Französische Zustände* [1833], and the large collection of articles written in the 1840s for the Augsburg *Allgemeine Zeitung* but published much later as *Lutezia* [1854]); intellectual and belletristic essays (most notably, *Die Romantische Schule* [1836], *Zur Geschichte der Philosophie und Religion in Deutschland* [1835], and *Ludwig Börne. Eine Denkschrift* [1840]); polemical essays; and the two long narrative poems that mounted a barbed attack against the political and cultural tendencies in pre-1848 Germany (*Deutschland. Ein Wintermärchen* [1844] and *Atta Troll* [1847]). Not until he suffered a debilitating physical collapse in 1848 did Heine again train his energies primarily on poetry. Ironically, the onset of the still unknown illness that would confine him to bed in his Paris "Matratzengruft" — as he termed it in a now famous characterization of his plight in 1851 — coincided with the outbreak of the doomed 1848 Revolution, which, in effect, signaled the demise of the revolutionary ideals that had informed much of Heine's writings in the prerevolutionary period (*Vormärz*). The ensuing shift in his poetry away from the predominantly political themes of the *Vormärz* has generated much speculation among critics as to the effect that the failure of political liberalism of 1848–1849 and/or his physical condition had on his thinking. What occurred was not a return to the Romantic poetry of his early period, but a retrospective engagement with Romantic themes in a larger historical context, one that assesses their role within a larger scheme of history that itself is undergoing re-evaluation in this late period, for instance in *Romanzero* (1851) and *Gedichte. 1853 und 1854* (1854). As he strives to depict how the major themes of his writings evolve throughout the diverse phases of his life, Heine also offers ample reflective commentary on his thought in autobiographical texts such as *Geständnisse* (1854) and the posthumously published *Memoiren* and various accompanying pieces, among them "Nachwort zum Romanzero" (1851) and "Vorrede zur zweiten Auflage" of *Zur Geschichte der Religion und Philosophie in Deutschland* (1852).

The effort Heine devoted to constructing a final, definitive account of his thinking suggests one of the challenges facing a Companion volume that seeks to do justice to a writer so diverse and ambivalent in his views, so controversial and fluctuating in his stances, and so varied and rich in his literary production. Any attempt to provide a composite view of this important European literary figure and his significance as a writer must focus on his work as a whole. Although this may be true to some extent of any writer, in Heine's case it has special validity. For he placed particular emphasis on the overall image that his writings would present of him as an author and historical personage. Moreover, as he produced his final texts during the prolonged period of terminal illness and suffering (1848–1856), he became even more attentive to the way they would dovetail with his earlier writings to form an aggregate picture of his life's work. And while his writing had always, with only minor exceptions, presented at least partial views of his own poetic persona, his late, more expressly autobiographical texts take up this task more directly. He openly admitted at times that they were to serve this purpose, and wrote in a letter of August 3, 1854 to his lifelong publisher and friend Julius Campe that his *Geständnisse* "ebenfalls nicht Jedem zugänglich [sind], doch sind sie wichtig, indem die Einheit aller meiner Werke und meines Lebens besser begriffen wird" (HSA 23: 358).

This attempt to combine his oeuvre into a harmonious whole did not suddenly begin when the dying poet became more concerned with the lasting image he would leave for posterity. In the various phases of a career that took many twists and turns, Heine frequently assured the public that he had not abandoned those ideas and principles that had informed his earlier works. Perhaps the first major gap he needed to bridge in this regard came during the first political phase in France in the 1830s. After the success of his early journalistic reports from Paris and his important essay on philosophy and religion (*Zur Geschichte der Religion und Philosophie in Deutschland*, 1835), he had gained fame as a leading opponent of the conservative alliance between nobility and clergy in the German lands. And when he was named in the Bundestag decree of 1835 as one of a band of subversive writers called *Junges Deutschland*, his status as a leading dissident was solidified. But this new image seemed at odds with the idea many had of the poet whose early love songs were also gaining increased recognition as they were set to music by Romantic composers. He addressed this dichotomous image in the preface to the second edition of *Buch der Lieder* (1837), when he declared that he no longer felt the same impulses that had inspired his early Romantic poetry. Nonetheless, Heine was not about to distance himself completely from this Romantic phase. More importantly, he maintained that, as different as the literary products of the early 1820s may be from his present writing, the new phase did not signal a shift in his basic outlook. He cautioned that his poetry was spawned by the same idea that was behind his political, theological, and philosophical writings, and that no one can condemn the one (his poetry) because of the idea behind it, while praising the other (B 1: 11).

In the same passage he defended himself against rumors from the opposite direction, against claims that his more moderate language or even silence, which he attributes to stricter censorship following the 1835 decree, was a sign that he had abandoned the political cause of social justice. Asserting that such a change would be nothing less than "ein Abfall von mir selber" (B 1: 11), he again confirmed the constancy and consistency of his thinking. Given the multifaceted aspects of his personality and his work, it is difficult to accept this self-assessment without certain reservations, or at least provisions for explaining apparent inconsistencies. But for Heine himself his steadfast loyalty to a higher cause was the unshakable foundation for all his writings, no matter how divergent the particular positions he may have chosen at different junctures in his life. Whenever he felt the need to affirm this constancy, he always came back to the struggle for emancipation as the driving force behind his writing. This holds true even for the years of personal despair following the disabling illness of 1848. "Enfant perdu," a poem clearly situated at a point in *Romanzero*, where one might expect a definitive self-characterization, begins with this declaration of his steadfast devotion to the cause:

> Verlorener Posten in dem Freiheitskriege,
> Hielt ich seit dreißig Jahren treulich aus. (B 6.1: 120)

And indeed, scholars have generally supported this effort on Heine's part, frequently citing "Enfant perdu" as evidence of his undying allegiance to liberty.[1]

That he was so intent on presenting this consonant picture of himself and that scholars have often quoted the texts that do so to support their own accounts of him as a consistent champion of freedom is itself evidence of the many ambivalences that characterize his life and work. The essays in this volume address those various different sides of Heine that are difficult to reconcile into a single, harmonious image of a German writer in the first half of the nineteenth century. This introductory essay discusses five authorial personae that, when seen in composite, offer a differentiated and consistent, although by no means complete, image of the individual and writer. Categorizing the different sides of Heine in this way also provides a backdrop against which to place the individual contributions to this Companion volume. However, these figurations are more than just a grid forced onto the wild variability of this complex author. In each case, they represent a literary persona he assumed both in his fictional and autobiographical writings, and about which he offered reflective commentary and assessment.

The Romantic Poet

Without question Heine began his literary career with the express goal of becoming a great German Romantic poet.[2] And while he wavered on the importance of poetry during the height of his political writings in Paris (ca. 1832–1845), much of his work after 1848 was devoted to the question of his own Romantic nature and the ability of poetry to mediate between such Romantic impulses and the collective human progress toward a more enlightened social order. Not only did he proclaim that Romanticism was a passing cultural movement whose viability had already ended, but he claimed for himself the distinction of the poet-herald who first announced its end. In doing so, he did not however claim that he himself had outgrown those subjective tendencies that gave rise to Romanticism. To the contrary, he confessed that his own psyche was a product of its particular cultural heritage, and he conceded that even if he had been the first to declare that this age was over, he himself would never outgrow his Romantic sensibilities. Or, in his own self-characterization, which scholars have so often employed with regard to the problematical ambivalences of his final years, he termed himself a "romantique défroqué," and he acknowledged: "Trotz meiner exterministischen Feldzüge gegen die Romantik, blieb ich doch selbst immer ein Romantiker, und ich war es in einem höhern Grade, als ich selbst ahnte" (*Geständnisse;* B 6.1: 447).

Although Heine attributed this self-awareness to the wisdom of hindsight, he had practiced the same self-critique even as he was gaining fame as a Romantic poet. As early as 1830, he wrote that his age was wrought with psychic frailty, and that healthier future generations would look back on it as a time of sickness (B 2: 490–93). And even though he was aware of this deficiency, he admitted that he belonged to this age. Nor did he contend that his insight into this collective malady would make him immune to it: "Denn ach! Ich gehöre ja selber zu dieser kranken alten Welt, und mit Recht sagt der Dichter: wenn man auch seiner Krücken spottet, so kann man darum doch nicht besser gehen" (B 3: 593–94). As Michael Perraudin points out in this volume, *Buch der Lieder* is not merely a poetic compilation of Heine's personal discontent. What is often lost in the common perception of Heine's love poetry, Perraudin argues, is that it is "a document of generational disillusionment," a reflection of the general pessimism and recognition of both cultural and political postidealist disappointment following the Congress of Vienna.

In some respects, however, Heine's critics, at least more recent ones, have given him more credit for bringing about the end of Romantic poetry and its complicity with "dieser kranken alten Welt" than he himself did. His own claims refer more to his critical prose writings that distance themselves from Romantic poetry and predict its end. Modern scholars have argued that this criticism is already inherent in his early poetry, residing in an irony and poetic idiom that undermines the idealist aesthetic notion of lyrical poetry's power to recover an original, non-alienated mode of expression. To what extent this criticism distinguishes him from the more progressive forms of German Romanticism remains a matter of debate.[3] Heine himself differentiated at times between the self-critical and progressive force of Romantic literature and the literature of the "Kunstperiode," whose end he proclaimed in the 1820s. However, as Perraudin shows convincingly, Heine's early love poems invoke what had become an almost commonplace poetic ideality in order to disrupt the mode of Roman-

tic idealism they embody. Not only do they undermine the very linguistic clichés of Romantic poetry, Perraudin maintains, but they even
parody fashionable modes of emotional and spiritual experience that
had been conditioned by Romantic literature.

To be sure, when the ailing Heine of the final years declares that
he remained a Romantic despite his crusades against Romanticism,
this bon mot applies predominantly to his psychic makeup rather than
to his poetic production. With respect to his literary legacy, he im-
modestly proclaimed for himself the role of an epochal innovator: "ich
bin ihr [der deutschen Romantik] letzter Dichter, mit mir ist die alte
lyrische Schule der Deutschen geschlossen, während zugleich die neue
Schule, die moderne deutsche Lyrik, von mir eröffnet ward" (B 6.1:
447). This assertion is all the more immodest when one considers the
importance Heine ascribed to poetry. Near the end of *Geständnisse*,
after he had given account of his (Romantic) character flaws at length,
he concludes: "Es ist nichts aus mir geworden, nichts als ein Dichter."
But eschewing false modesty as the disingenuous trick of imposters, he
quickly reverses his feigned disregard for poetry: "Man ist viel, wenn
man ein Dichter ist, und gar wenn man ein großer lyrischer Dichter ist
in Deutschland, unter dem Volke, das in zwei Dingen, in der Philosophie und im Liede, all andern Nationen überflügelt hat" (B 6.1: 498).
This estimation of poetry and the coupling of it with philosophy does
not assign any special status to Romanticism. But it does point to a
central thesis that underlies all of Heine's poetry. As Perraudin demonstrates clearly in his analysis of the *Buch der Lieder* poems, there is a
constant oscillation between narratives of "poetic impotence" and
those of "poetic power."

For Heine, Romantic poetry was only the most recent phase in a
young but rich literary tradition that provided an important complement to philosophy in the push toward an enlightened post-Christian
Europe. He saw himself as a product of this transitional period and a
writer whose Romantic poetry was ultimately deconstructing itself as
part of the cultural stride forward.

The Poet-Herald of German Philosophy

In his evaluation of the German intellect and its ability to express itself
in poetry, Heine carefully distanced himself from those nationalists
who advocated an innate superiority of the German mind (*Geist*) and
saw Romantic poetry as a manifestation of a purer, higher spirit. His

allegiance was to a broader German intellectual tradition that champions universal humanist principles applicable to the world community as a whole. At times, particularly when he was taking up the cause of the German masses against their princely and priestly suppressors most avidly, he was accused of betraying his own national heritage. In the foreword to *Deutschland. Ein Wintermärchen* (1844) he defends himself against those who portray him as a friend of the French and a traitor to his homeland. Referring to the territorial dispute over Alsace-Lorraine that had given rise to the most recent nationalistic outcries, Heine offers his own supra-national idea of Germany's special destiny:

> Indessen, die Elsasser und Lothringer werden sich wieder an Deutschland anschließen, wenn wir das vollenden, was die Franzosen begonnen haben, wenn wir diese überflügeln in der Tat, wie wir es schon getan im Gedanken, wenn wir uns bis zu den letzten Folgerungen desselben emporschwingen, . . . wenn wir das arme, glükkenterbte Volk und den verhöhnten Genius und die geschändete Schönheit wieder in ihre Würde einsetzen, wie unsre großen Meister gesagt *und gesungen* [my italics], und wie wir es wollen, wir, die Jünger — ja, nicht bloß Elsaß und Lothringen, sondern ganz Frankreich wird uns alsdann zufallen, ganz Europa, die ganze Welt — die ganze Welt wird deutsch werden! Von dieser Sendung und Universalherrschaft Deutschlands träume ich oft, wenn ich unter Eichen wandle. Das is *mein* Patriotismus. (B 4: 574–75)

This vision of Germany's preeminence is intended as an alternative to the apotheosization of the German spirit common among early nineteenth-century nationalists. With it, Heine also placed himself as poet in a tradition of "great masters" of German poetry and philosophy older and broader than that of Romanticism.[4]

Not only did Heine revere the achievements of German philosophy, he saw its significance extending far beyond the academic discipline. As evidenced in the foreword to the *Wintermärchen,* he ascribed to German critical philosophy a revolutionary import that would radically change Western civilization. His prophecy that the whole world would become German invoked nationalist claims about the German *Geist* that had arisen in the first decades of the nineteenth century in order to reverse their thrust. As opposed to those who suggest that intellectual superiority is based on ethnic heritage, Heine grounded any claim to special destiny in the tradition of critical philosophy. His alternative message is that the irreversible advance of reason as the arbiter of all public discussion had established itself in philosophy, and that the ideas it had produced would inevitably exert their authority in the sociopolitical world as well.

If philosophical discourse is the compelling agent for progressive change, then in what capacity does the poet ("gesagt *und gesungen*") merit a commensurate place in the cultural heritage destined to lead the way? This same passage indicates what the singer's role should be: not until the radical idea that delegates all authority to reason is put into action will the accomplishments of German philosophy find fruition. Heine believed that the cognitive genius of a Kant or Hegel capable of constructing comprehensive, impregnable systems of thought worked best in undisturbed detachment and lacked the rhetorical skills of engagement needed for such a step. The poet, on the other hand, belonged to a tradition in which wit, metaphor, word play, anecdote, allusion, insinuation, and the like had long been employed to smuggle contraband ideas into the mainstream.[5] As one might expect from a writer who touted himself as the initiator of modern German poetry, Heine also envisioned himself as the poet who first took up this mission:

> Ein neues Lied, ein besseres Lied,
> O Freunde, will ich Euch dichten!
> Wir wollen hier auf Erden schon
> Das Himmelreich errichten. (B 4: 578)

But he also envisioned himself as more than just the executor of the philosophical idea. In the early 1840s, as he began to predict the inevitable successes of the nascent communist movement, he also boasted of how he had disclosed the irresistible logic of the Hegelian dialectic and the inevitable results it would engender. Looking back to his essay on *Religion und Philosophie in Deutschland,* he claimed that already at this early stage he had lifted the veil hiding the secret of German philosophy and had revealed it as the driving force behind a dialectical progression toward emancipation and enlightened autonomy. He assigned epochal, almost mythological importance to his own role in this intellectual evolution:

> Man hat mir von mancher Seite gezürnt, daß ich den Vorhang fort-
> riß von dem deutschen Himmel und jedem zeigte, daß alle Gotthei-
> ten des alten Glaubens daraus verschwunden, und daß dort nur eine
> alte Jungfer sitzt mit bleiernen Händen und traurigem Herzen: die
> Notwendigkeit. (B 5: 196)

While the claim that he had understood and revealed the sociopolitical consequence of the Hegelian dialectic in the 1830s is an exaggeration, Heine had indeed adopted a progressive view of history along broad

Hegelian lines even earlier. He had attended Hegel's lectures on the philosophy of history at the University of Berlin in summer 1821 and formed his own poetic approach to historical progress. While the philosopher elaborates a conceptual system that elucidates its dynamics, the poet devises a narrative capable of conveying its essence in terms of the contemporary political and social reality. In a well-known metaphor often cited as exemplary of Heine's synthesis of the political and the poetic, the narrator in the *Die Bäder von Lucca* (1830) laments that a great rift in the world runs straight through the heart of the Romantic poet and that his psychic wounds are also those of the collective soul of alienated modern humanity. For Heine, the poetic articulation of this collective wound not only serves to illuminate the present stage of history but also acts as a force pushing toward revolution. In this sense, he regarded himself as the herald of a progressive dialectic and, eventually, in the 1840s, when he ascribed a universal validity to dialectical philosophy, he claimed that his poetic revelation of the historical process was an integral part of the drumbeat driving history forward.

Even as the author of an introductory essay designed to familiarize the French with German philosophy, Heine never studied philosophical concepts and arguments with any disciplinary rigor. Where he did engage them more critically, it was inevitably in connection with revolutionary change and historical progress. And yet, in this regard perhaps more so than all others, his thoughts remain ambivalent. Gerhard Höhn addresses this issue at length in this volume, asking whether Heine eventually abandons the progressive view of history in the years following his physical collapse of 1848. Höhn establishes a continuity between the dying poet's reflections on the question of history and the ideas he had expressed at various earlier points in his writing. One central question that has occupied scholars in several recent studies is the break with Hegel, which Heine himself adamantly and frequently proclaimed after 1848. For the most part, the attempt has been to contextualize his renunciation of Hegel in such a way as to salvage a progressive (Hegelian) view of history. Following this line of thought, Höhn argues that Heine carefully qualified his vision of the historical dialectic, but ultimately did not discard it altogether. Regardless of how one judges his final stance on both Hegel and the Hegelian dialectic, and the differences on this matter will likely remain, one aspect of his historical reasoning is certain: it harbors a skepticism that is, as Höhn points out, characteristic of modern critical thinking on history.

The Politically Engaged Writer

When Heine began his studies at the newly founded university in Bonn in the fall of 1819, he immediately became involved in the patriotic liberal movement that was an outgrowth of the War of Liberation. For this son of the Rhineland who had come of age in Düsseldorf during the height of its embrace of Napoleonic reform — including civil rights for the Jews — student life entailed political opposition to the conservative forces reinstated at the Congress of Vienna. Early in 1820 he joined a *Burschenschaft,* even though the Carlsbad Decrees had banned them the previous fall. However, shortly after he transferred to the more conservative University of Göttingen in the fall of 1820, Heine was expelled from the student fraternity, quite possibly because he was Jewish. In any case, he experienced at first hand the repression of the Restoration powers that would stifle opposition and leave his generation disillusioned in its hopes for liberal reform.

As he concentrated on his literary career, Heine did not abandon his commitment to political change, and even devised in the satirical anecdotes of his *Reisebilder* an innovative mode of critique that, to some extent, could sidestep the extensive censorship of the 1820s. It was not, however, until the July Revolution of 1830 in France that he began to consider activist political writing a viable alternative. As was always the case when he considered the prospects of revolution, he viewed the events in France and the promise they held for similar up-risings in the German states ambivalently. To be sure, his Helgoland letters that make up book 2 of *Ludwig Börne. Eine Denkschrift* (1840) describe an elated response to the news of the July Revolution, which he received somewhat belatedly while on the island of Helgoland in the summer of 1830. In them he expresses enthusiasm that the French Revolution has now entered its second, more advanced stage and that it will now provide the basis for a broad social revolution throughout Europe. Although dated July-August 1830, these letters were certainly composed later, probably in 1839 when the Börne *Denkschrift* was written. Actual letters to friends at the time reveal a much more skeptical attitude about the movement, and in particular about the various parties rushing to join it.

This skepticism was fueled in no small part by patriotic-nationalist tendencies within the German liberal movement that frequently assumed conservative and, perhaps most important, anti-Semitic points of view. While he considered this a result of inbred nationalist sentiments that would be extremely difficult to root out, he had equally strong reservations about the puritanical attitudes that dominated the opposition on the left. In his political positions as in his philosophical views, he carved out his own unique niche. While he shared the liberal call for social justice and the end of unfair privilege, he rejected what he termed their Nazarene character. In his call for not merely political emancipation, but also for libertine principles that challenge the religious rejection of pleasure (the "Nazarene" element), Heine considered himself an avant-garde thinker opposed to a reactionary moralism that even permeated revolutionary politics, critical philosophy, and aesthetic practice. While he often used this radical stance on the reinstatement of pleasure to excuse questionable political stances, there is no denying that the restoration of the flesh was a central part of his program for social change throughout all phases of his writing. Whether one agrees with his vision or not, there is in this regard some truth to the bold claim that his political allies in the fight against the exploitation of the German people did not understand it: "Auch war ich ihnen [den deutschen Revolutionären der dreißiger Jahre] so weit voraus geschritten, daß sie mich nicht mehr sahen, und in ihrer Kurzsichtigkeit glaubten sie, ich wäre zurückgeblieben" (B 4: 91). His own distinctive synthesis of progressive philosophy (Hegel) and early socialist doctrine (Saint-Simonianism) put him at odds with central tenets of every political program or ideological movement of his times.

In the 1830s and 1840s, when he pursued this vision most avidly — becoming, in his own estimation, "der große Heide Nr. 2" (B 5: 109) — his ideas were perhaps closest to those of the "literary prince" he both admired and challenged, Goethe. Despite his frequent sharp criticism of Goethe's refusal to fight for his Hellenist principles[6] in the political arena, Heine repeatedly embraced the ideas themselves as his own. He saw the free thought and devotion to the sensual world expressed in Goethe's writings as a useful paradigm for that culture which would restore once again "den verhöhnten Genius und die geschändete Schönheit." Heine differed from the poet laureate who withdrew into the protected provincial world of Weimar in that he felt compelled to join the struggle for "das arme, glückenterbte Volk." His involvement with German philosophy revolves largely around this political or, more importantly, social vision, which he saw as a direct consequence of a modern philosophy determined to throw off the shackles of traditional religious authority and submit all ideas to the tribunal of reason. In a bold reading of Spinoza's notions of the divine, Heine argued that Spinoza's philosophical system does not advocate atheism, but rather a pantheism that recognizes the divine presence in all things, in the material as well as in the spiritual world:

> "Gott," welcher von Spinoza die eine Substanz und von den deutschen Philosophen das Absolute genannt wird, "ist alles was da ist," er ist sowohl Materie wie Geist, beides ist gleich göttlich, und wer die heilige Materie beleidigt, ist eben so sündhaft, wie der, welcher sündigt gegen den heiligen Geist. (B 3: 565–66)

Here is the essence of Heine's "political" program: "die Rehabilitation der Materie, die Wiedereinsetzung derselben in ihre Würde, ihre moralische Anerkennung, ihre religiöse Heiligung, ihre Versöhnung mit dem Geiste" (B 3: 568). In his far-reaching analysis of the aesthetic strategies Heine employed to establish the validity of this pantheistic philosophical perspective over and against the dominant idealist discourse, Willi Goetschel shows how Heine's social, political, theoretical, and religious (namely, Jewish) concerns coalesced most forcefully in the pursuit of this primary goal. Much more crucial to revolutionary progress than any change in the institutions of government was the fulfillment of this philosophical idea, which Heine — in a move designed to realign the critical thrust of German philosophy — attributed to Spinoza, whose thinking brought charges of heresy from a coalition of the dominant social, political, and religious authorities of his day. As Goetschel argues, Heine mobilized a vast array of unusual tactics to reveal the material base of all philosophical discourse and the ideological underpinning of idealist conceptions that debase the physical world.

For Heine, the reinstatement of the flesh would not be achieved by political or even social revolution alone, but rather would evolve out of the philosophical idea and the basic human demand for happiness. In an often-cited passage from book 2 of *Religion und Philosophie in Deutschland* Heine differentiates his idea of revolution from those Jacobean republicans who, in his view, preach total sacrifice and devotion to the cause of equality at the cost of pleasure:

> Wir kämpfen nicht für die Menschenrechte des Volks, sondern für die Gottesrechte des Menschen. Hierin, und in noch manchen andern Dingen, unterscheiden wir uns von den Männern der Revolution. Wir wollen keine Sansculotten sein, keine frugale Bürger, keine wohlfeile Präsidenten: wir stiften eine Demokratie gleichherrlicher, gleichheiliger, gleichbeseligter Götter. Ihr verlangt einfache Trachten, enthaltsame Sitten und ungewürzte Genüsse; wir hingegen verlangen Nektar und Ambrosia, Purpurmäntel, kostbare Wohlgerüche, Wollust und Pracht, lachenden Nymphentanz, Musik und Komödien —. (B 3: 570)

It is perhaps in the context of this peculiarly Heinean vision of social and political progress that Paul Peters's essay on the erotic in Heine's poetry adds most cogently to the composite image of his life and work. For the erotic — which, as Peters demonstrates, is either openly manifest or lurking in the shadows of the love poetry — is always part and parcel of Heine's campaign to eliminate the ideological restraints placed on pleasure by the privileged elite for their own advantage. Too seldom have critics emphasized this aspect of the love poetry, focusing rather on it more as Romantic verse on the verge of modernity in the aesthetic sense, but without addressing its political thrust. My own piece on Heine's love poetry focuses more on the pain engendered by the experiences of unfulfilled love, but also argues that the investigation of love's torments in the Romantic poetry always serves, too, as an indictment of the Nazarene renunciation of the flesh.

While the above emphasizes the more visionary and evolutionary aspect of Heine's political thinking, it is also important to note that he often took quite controversial and even dangerous stances on political issues. He did tend at times to exaggerate the danger his critical views may have caused him, but contemporary critics in Germany did in fact face hardships and even received prison sentences for less caustic and less visible attacks than his own. Both in his *Zeitgedichte* and in various prose writings, particular after his move to Paris in 1831, he addressed many of the hot political and social topics of his time, directing at times sharp criticism at the reactionary political governments in Austria, Prussia, and other German states and, more generally, at the Restoration alliance of the nobility and Church.

In *Deutschland. Ein Wintermärchen,* the most famous of his directly political writings, he not only turned all his literary skills against these conservative forces in Germany, but also reflected on the role of the poet as the mediator between the revolutionary idea of critical philosophy and the changes it is to effect in the sociopolitical realm. This epic poem addressing diverse political issues of the day was a new genre, or better yet, a genre unto itself that has yet to find a comparable companion in German literature. He proclaimed it as a new song ("Ein neues Lied, ein besseres Lied" [B 4: 578]) that would replace the old "song" of abstinence and obedience, the centuries-old creed fed to the people by the Church and aristocracy. While the latter creed is a standard refrain that breeds dependency and inaction, the poet depicts his own verses as a call for action against those exploitive forces. In the sixth and seventh chapters he describes "einen vermummten Gast" who lurks behind him furtively as he writes or walks the streets

at night, always appearing in those moments "Wo Weltgefühle sprie-
ßen" (B 4: 591). This shadow figure is cloaked in black, and from beneath his coat, light reflects off what appears to be an executioner's ax.
When the poet confronts him on a moonlit night in Cologne and asks
what he is carrying under his cloak, his mysterious companion reveals
himself:

> Ich bin dein Liktor, und ich geh
> Beständig mit dem blanken
> Richtbeile hinter dir — ich bin
> Die Tat von deinem Gedanken. (B 4: 592)

Here we see Heine at his most confident as a political writer. Buoyed
by the Left-Hegelian idea of an unstoppable dialectic of history, he
entertains a grand notion of his own role in the inevitable revolutionary upheavals that are to come. Not only does his writing attack the
dominant reactionary forces of the Restoration period, but it also conveys to the masses ("das arme, glückenterbte Volk") the revolutionary
import of critical modern philosophy in a form they can understand.
Even as Heine maintains that he himself as a Romantic poet will be
out of place in the new social order, he acclaims the liberty and social
justice that it will bring as unimpeachable advances in the path toward
a higher civilization. George Peters argues in his essay on the reception of Heine during the Weimar Republic that the events of 1918–
1919 came closest to matching the optimistic predictions he had made
in the *Wintermärchen*. However, Peters also chronicles how leftist intellectual supporters of the Weimar Republic on various different fronts all
failed to embrace him as an ally, thus missing an opportunity to find
grounding for the new republic in a part of Germany's literary tradition that otherwise provided little. This failure may also be seen in some
ways as a confirmation of Heine's own growing distrust in the liberal
movement and its ability to bring about effective social revolution.

At this point in the middle of the *Vormärz* years, Heine, like most
of those who shared this liberal vision of emancipation and civil rights,
felt that an end to the repressive Metternich regime was imminent.
While his prophecy that the future belonged to the nascent communist movement was bold for its time (as early as 1843, and before he
met Marx), he harbored serious doubts about the liberal movement
and its ability to effect significant change.[7] When the uprising against
the reactionary regimes in central Europe did finally break out in February and March 1848, it coincided with Heine's collapse in such a
manner that he imagined his illness as an uncanny physical embodi-

ment of the futile political revolution. While he had been skeptical of the liberal political forces throughout the 1830s and 1840s, after 1848 he abandoned the idea that his political writings could act as a catalyst that would transform the ideas of Left-Hegelian philosophy into revolutionary action — at least in his lifetime or in any foreseeable future. However, even if the idea of his own time as a revolutionary epoch in history faded, Heine continued to hold a progressive view of history (see the essay by Gerhard Höhn), maintaining at least in general terms his faith that reason would continue to establish its influence over human affairs.

The German-Jewish Poet: Between History and Religion

Heine's own sense of German identity had its roots in the liberal-patriotic stirrings of the German Rhineland. Not only his strong identification with the blossoming of German culture in the eighteenth century, but also his thinking on history, philosophy, literature, and religion were informed by the enthusiastic embrace of the revolutionary ideals of the French Revolution he had experienced during his youth in Düsseldorf. No small part of his own fervor for the liberal Enlightenment principles of the Revolution must have been fueled by the promise of civil rights for the Jews. But the patriotic uprising against the increasingly tyrannical reign of Napoleon brought with it a backlash against the laws for the emancipation of the Jews he had imposed on the occupied German lands — and also against the Jews themselves. Moreover, the conservative-patriotic resistance to the Napoleonic code, and to the Jews, had deeper cultural roots in the Romantic idealization of the German past and, in particular, in a historicist concept of freedom that clashed with the more universal Enlightenment idea.

When seen in this light, Heine's desire to become a Romantic poet seems almost paradoxical. When he first began to write poetry, however, there was a complex set of factors involved in the intersection of Jewish assimilation and Romanticism. Romanticism was, of course, the leading cultural movement at the time, one that attracted the interest of the French to a German literature long deemed derivative and provincial, and that induced Mme. de Staël to give Germany the proudly embraced epithet: the land of "Dichter und Denker." While this external recognition did much to strengthen the status of the German cultural elite, *Kultur* had already established itself in the late eighteenth century as an important component in the rise of the bourgeoisie. For the Jews, who had to prove their capacity for *Bildung* — both as a people and as individuals — as a prerequisite for emancipation, *Kultur* served as an "entry ticket"[8] into German society on two levels: first for the very possibility of assimilation, and then for inclusion in the privileged sphere of the evolving *Bildungsbürgertum*.

Without question, Heine took up literature in part because of the opportunity it offered for fame, recognition, and simply acceptance. At the same time, he was, as he repeatedly maintained throughout his life, an irrepressible romantic by "nature." But, as he also was quick to point out, this personal character was a culturally produced "Naturell" rooted not only in the German way of life, but also in the historical epoch in which he lived. Not surprisingly, his characterization of this Romantic disposition links it to the Enlightenment vision of a world community grounded in universal principles of reason and moral law. Precisely this understanding of what it meant to be a German Romantic poet put him at odds with the ethnocentric nationalist view of the Romantic soul as an organically evolved spirit whose roots necessarily go back to an early period of the Germanic tribes. In its more radical instances, this romanticized notion of German character excluded Jews from any intimate, authentic participation in Romantic thought and feeling. Thus, even while Heine's poetry established him as a Romantic poet par excellence, he found it necessary to continually affirm that he was a German poet of the highest order, that is, a Romantic poet by "nature." And, as Robert Holub stresses in his analysis of Heine's characterizations of his conversion of 1825, the dichotomous existence as Romantic poet and proponent of Jewish culture resulted in a complex dynamic of displacement that influenced Heine's statements on related issues ranging from his stance toward Judaism and Protestantism to his late renunciation of Hegel.

Heine's initial efforts on behalf of Jewish assimilation already exhibited some of the ambivalence that later surrounded his conversion. Spurred at least in part by his direct contact with anti-Semitic "Teutomaniacs"[9] in the student fraternities in Göttingen, he sought avenues for supporting the civil rights of Jews. As he entered the university system, he certainly became familiar with the debates stirred by conservative-nationalist academics (Jakob Fries, Friedrich Rühs) who, in the wake of the Congress of Vienna, questioned Jewish assimilation. Only weeks after he arrived in Berlin in 1821 Heine gained entry into the salon of Rahel Varnhagen, where he began important associations with some of the leading young minds of the Berlin cultural scene, and in particular, with liberal thinkers who actively supported full Jewish emancipation. The following year he became a member of the *Verein für Cultur und Wissenschaft der Juden,* a society founded by young Jewish intellectuals intent on developing a path for Jewish assimilation that would allow the Jews to maintain their identity and cultural heritage. While he shared his fellow members' call for unconditional rights for all Jews, he differed with them in some important ways as well. First, as Holub argues, he had already adopted at this early stage the critical, even dismissive stance toward all "positive" religions that he would retain throughout his life (even during the so-called "religious return" to God in 1848). At times he singled out the Jewish Reform movement in particular, whose advocates he often ridiculed as social conformists who were abandoning Judaism for the sake of assimilation and their own desire for status. In his contribution to this Companion volume, Jeffrey Grossman examines at some length the textual strategies Heine employed to undermine the dominant assimilationist approach that saw *Bildung,* that is, the abandonment of Jewish culture and consciousness for the ascendant German middle-class values, as a prerequisite for Jewish emancipation. He focuses on, among other writings, the travel essay "Über Polen," in which Heine subtly questions whether the Jews in Poland, despite their squalid living conditions and "regressive" ghetto culture, have not retained a cultural integrity that the German Jew is shedding in the rush to assimilation. Written simultaneously with his admission to the *Culturverein* in fall 1822, *Über Polen* demonstrates a more radical adherence to the idea of Jewish emancipation than that advocated by most of his fellow members. Similarly, Holub shows that from this early point on Heine identified with the Jewish nation's long, collective history of unjust suffering.

The other key difference with the *Culturverein* concerns the always-difficult question of Hegel. Key figures in the *Verein,* whose members belonged to the first generation of university-educated German Jews, were strongly influenced by Hegel, whose philosophy had taken German academia by storm in the preceding years. In their application of the historical dialectic to Jewish history, these Hegelian thinkers — primarily, Eduard Gans and Immanuel Wohlwill — focused on the monotheistic *idea* as the great contribution of Judaism. In its most exacting form, this school of thought held that the particular laws and customs of Judaism had outlived their usefulness in the modern era and could, or even should be jettisoned in their entirety. This placement of the idea over and above life itself — in this case, the living customs, social interactions, and even language of the Jews — upset Heine almost violently. In a letter to Moses Moser in 1823, even as he was most heavily involved in the work of the *Verein,* he raved against this tendency toward abstraction, complaining that Gans and Wohlwill want to turn everything, even Heine himself, into nothing but an idea! (HSA 20: 97; June 18, 1823). In this emotional outburst against the Christian spiritualist dimension of the Hegelian dialectic, we see an early example of that unique synthesis of Hellenic sensualism and Jewish moral pragmatism that will become central to the late Heine.

After his involvement with the *Verein* ended in 1825, at the same time as his practically motivated baptism into the Protestant Church, Heine became less concerned with matters of Jewish emancipation and assimilation. When he moved to Paris in 1831 and became absorbed in the revolutionary import of German philosophy and the dialectical march of history, he accepted, in broad terms, Hegel's relegation of Judaism to a past role in history. Not only Judaism, but all positive religions would, he argued, soon be superseded by that materialistic pantheism he touts in *Religion und Philosophie in Deutschland* as the secret of modern German philosophy. Still, he never stopped fighting for the rights of Jews and the end to all persecution, becoming involved whenever anti-Semitism flared up, most notably as a result of the Damascus affair of 1840.[10]

Not until the collapse of 1848, when he began to re-examine his adoption of the Hegelian dialectic, did Judaism again play an important role in Heine's thinking on human progress. This question is complicated by the often at least apparently contradictory statements he made about a renewed faith in a "personal God" (the so-called "religious return") and about religion in general. One thing, however, remained constant, as he himself stressed in *Geständnisse* in response to rumors flying about an embrace of Protestantism: "Ich weiß nicht, inwieweit ich merken ließ, daß ich weder für ein Dogma noch für irgendeinen Kultus außerordentlich schwärme und ich in dieser Beziehung derselbe geblieben bin, der ich immer war" (B 6.1: 488–89). While the passage to which he referred concerns primarily Protestantism and Catholicism, the reference to dogma and ritual practice also includes the formal practice of the Jewish religion. On the other hand, he displayed a reinvigorated faith in the elemental moral law introduced by the Jews, and even offered a somewhat idealized vision of how it was practiced in the early days of Judaism:

> [D]as Echte, Unvergängliche und Wahre, nämlich die Sittlichkeit des alten Judentums, wird in jenen Ländern ebenso gotterfreulich blühen, wie einst am Jordan und auf den Höhen des Libanons. Man hat keine Palme und Kamele nötig, um gut zu sein, und Gutsein ist besser denn Schönheit. (B 6.1: 486)

Perhaps the essence of Heine's "religious return" — particularly insofar as he depicted his belief in a personal God as a rejection of an atheism he had once adopted along with the *absolute* idea of the historical dialectic — is that this renewed faith in a fundamental moral law, whose validity is established ultimately by intuition rather than by logic, replaced the Hegelian view of history.

However, for the present context, more important than the consistency of Heine's personal stances on God, religion, or even philosophy is his perspective on the role the Jews have played historically in humanity's struggle for progress. The return to Judaism manifests itself in his late poetry, where Jews, as the people of the diaspora, serve dialectically as a critical, corrective Other to their dominant host nations. His autobiographical texts touch on this role marginally, but Heine was cautious in addressing such issues explicitly, always wary of the misconceptions they would be likely to produce. This had happened readily in 1848 even in response to more private and personal utterances he had made about his recent thoughts concerning God. Rumors abounded about a religious "conversion," with the result that he found himself forced to issue a public disclaimer ("Berichtigung" [B 5: 108–10]) in April 1849; and he continued to confront them in the "Nachwort" to *Romanzero,* the "Vorrede" to the second edition of *Religion und Philosophie in Deutschland,* and in *Geständnisse.*

Heine enlisted his late thinking on Judaism more cogently in the poetry, where he assumes the personae of Jewish figures in history who had suffered and been pushed to the margins of society because of, among other things, their ethnic heritage: Moses, the Sephardic poets of "Jehuda ben Halevy," and Lazarus. In one important respect, those Jewish figures of the diaspora (in particular the medieval *poets* in "Jehuda ben Halevy") suffer a fate analogous to Heine's own as the unjustly exiled German-Jewish opponent of Restoration Germany. He also identified with literary (Aristophanes) and religious figures (Job) who had questioned divine authority in their day, much as Heine challenged the "positive" religions of Europe. And even the "personal God" whom he had acknowledged in the autobiographical texts appears in the late poems. It is a conception of God that is open to radical revision; a God whom he can engage in dialogue, openly challenge, and even place before the tribunal of reason that will strip away all those attributes that support unjust privileges or delusions.

Thus, the discourse of Judaism Heine invokes is select, limited largely to those cases that correspond well to his own situation as a German-Jewish writer whose opposition to dominant social and political forces not only made him an arch-enemy of reactionary parties but also alienated him from many of his liberal allies. As his despair at the political situation converged with the futility of his lifelong struggle for the emancipation of the flesh — that is, the restoration of sensual pleasure as a basic human need and right, which he generally termed the Hellenic principle — he reassessed the merits of Judaic tradition. In both cases, the ethical complement to reason that allowed for hope on both fronts was not the Jewish religion, but rather the moral law in its essence,

> nämlich das Gesetz, welches Mose dem Hause Jakob zum Schatz befohlen hat. . . . Daraus der Verstand geflossen ist, wie der Euphrates, wenn er groß ist. . . . Er ist nie gewesen, der es ausgelernt hätte: und wird nimmermehr werden, der es ausgründen möchte. Denn sein Sinn ist reicher, weder kein Meer: und sein Wort tiefer, denn kein Abgrund. (B 3: 512–13)

However, "Hebräische Melodien," the set of three poems that comprise the final section of *Romanzero,* is a sophisticated poetic engagement of Jewish tradition in a critical project whose depths scholars have only recently begun to fathom. The focus on these poems in three of the essays in this volume (Goetschel, Grossman, Phelan) is representative of the present emphasis in Heine scholarship on this theme, which until recently has not received its due attention.

The Dying Poet in His "Matratzengruft"

The contributions to this volume are weighted more heavily in favor of the later period of Heine's life. This stronger focus on the later writings is in keeping with a decided shift in Heine scholarship over the last two decades. In part, it represents a swing of the pendulum back from what had been an overemphasis on the politically engaged writer and critic of an emerging German nationalist ideology in the first half of the nineteenth century. It is not surprising that the reinstatement of Heine as a leading figure of German literature after the Second World War would concentrate on him as an opponent of what at the time, in the aftermath of the Nazi regime, had become suspect elements in German culture. Accordingly, the rather checkered history of the reception his works had received, both in his own lifetime and up through the Nazi period, took on new significance as scholars began to examine the German literary tradition from this new critical perspective. From the vantage point of the present, this emphasis on Heine as political dissident during the period of divided Germany is itself of historical interest. And while it is not possible here to pursue this question further, the difference in approaches in the two German states even became to some extent a matter of political propaganda that reinforced the strong focus on the politically engaged poet.

The need to champion an early opponent of nascent nationalist ideologies in the nineteenth century led scholars in the two Germanys to downplay those sides of the dying poet that are hard to reconcile with the more favored image. This applies in particular to the often ambiguous or puzzling statements found in the important autobiographical texts and reflective commentaries of the late period: primarily, *Geständnisse,* the "Nachwort" to *Romanzero,* the "Vorrede" to the second edition of *Religion und Philosophie in Deutschland,* and the *Memoiren.* The tendency to shy away from the more perplexing views on religion and philosophy carried over to his late poetry as well. Broader and more complex in their thematic scope as well as in their narrative strategies, the late poems require however more comprehensive analysis before they can shed light on Heine's thinking in these final years. This complexity is due in large part to an almost programmatic effort on Heine's part to produce a final, consistent image of his work and thought, and ultimately of himself as a figure of historical significance.[11] Only recently have scholars begun to give the late poetry its due attention. The result has been not only a better insight into Heine's thinking in the "Matratzengruft." Indeed, critics have found that a critical engagement with both the poetry and the prose after 1848 leads to a fuller understanding of the earlier work, from the philosophical and literary essays to even the early Romantic poetry.

If at the beginning of the new millennium Heine scholars can look back and explain the reception of his works in the second half of the twentieth century largely in terms of divided Germany's attempts to come terms with its recent history, then a later generation of scholars will probably see the recent focus on the late period as a function of our own critical (perhaps postmodern or even *posthistoire*) fixations. To the extent that the reception of Heine — not merely after 1945, but from the 1820s on — has served as an effective barometer of the German *Zeitgeist,* this gives a twofold meaning to the title of one of his favored categories of poems, *Zeitgedichte*. Not only do they address social or political issues that were current at the time, but they can also serve in some respects as a foil in which later generations can see reflected their own thinking on similar issues of their time.

This holds, however, not only for his poetry, and in the case of his poetry not only for the actual *Zeitgedichte*. Many, indeed the great majority of the late writings address either directly or indirectly Heine's own situation. Facing an imminent death, or at least a death that he always thought was imminent during the last eight years of his life, Heine reflected back on his life and work, assessing his views and the goals he had set for his writing. However, in doing so he did not slip back into the past; rather he continued even after 1848 to depict an inextricable connection between his own life and the contemporary situation of Europe along its progressive path to a more enlightened social order. Given the failure of the middle European liberal movement in the revolutionary uprisings of 1848–49, and Heine's already totally pessimistic view of these events at their very outset, it is not surprising that his late writings display aspects of a critical thinking that would not dominate mainstream culture until near the end of the nineteenth century. Two factors have caused this affinity to modernism to go largely unheeded until quite recently: first, his own focus on individual, mainly personal parameters within this larger social development; and second, the desire of many to hold onto the image of the directly involved writer whose critical verve was part of an active opposition. As a result, scholars have only recently begun to examine the distinctive form of modern negative aesthetics Heine developed in the late writings.

In his piece on the late poetry, Anthony Phelan points to several such perspectives, or "archetypes of modernity," as he terms them. He analyzes subtle narrative and aesthetic strategies that draw into question not only the specific poetic project of Romanticism, but the whole cultural tradition that informed Heine's literary career. Taking up ideas first postulated in Adorno's well-known short essay "Die Wunde Heine" (albeit one that had rather the effect of curbing further pursuit of the modernity issue), Phelan examines passages (here, primarily from "Jehuda ben Halevy") that reveal how traditional aesthetic values are rendered obsolete as art becomes dominated by the laws of commodity exchange. He locates other, now commonplace perspectives of modernity in Heine's resigned vision of exhausted traditions. They include: the city as an enervating locus for modern culture; a secularized culture that leaves little room for moral consolation;

the ennui of a daily bourgeois life that is as paralyzing as it is plain; and an empty continuity that precludes narrative closure, mythic importance, and heroic action. In his essay on Heine's discursive use of Greek mythology, Paul Reitter also argues that the late writing (and *Die Götter im Exil* in particular) addresses the problem of a traditional mode of cultural enfranchisement that has lost its vibrancy. He emphasizes, however, Heine's attempt to offset the degenerative tendency of modernity and to find an alternative mode by which the "otherness of mythic sensualism" can exert its redemptive powers. While no longer the self-assured prophet of an eventual synthesis of the sensual and the spiritual, the ailing writer continues the "Freiheitskampf" even in his own weakened capacity and against a suffocating modern culture. In his incisive examination of the concept of time in the three poems of "Hebräische Melodien," Goetschel also demonstrates how Heine endeavored to ward off what he saw as a debilitating modernist apprehension of history. In particular, he shows how Heine (in "Disputation") reveals that the derogatory idea of a divided Jewish identity is in actuality the projection of modernity's own split onto a Jewish tradition still vibrant enough to oppose the exhaustion of tradition in the modern world.

This emphasis on Heine's analysis of historical progress at the threshold of modernity should not come at the expense of his reflections on his personal situation and the perspectives they open up on the individual psyche. Joseph Kruse focuses on this aspect of the late writings, while cautioning that even the investigation of his most private thoughts never loses sight of the larger goals of a collective human progress. Moreover, Heine used these more intimate contemplations as a foundation for reassessing his former thinking in a productive fashion, such that the final poetry even expands on the earlier themes. Kruse also explains how the confinement to the "Matratzengruft" necessitated a move away from the social and cultural world Heine had frequented both in person in Paris and intellectually in Germany. It resulted in a journey inward, most notably to the edge of that netherworld that preoccupied him during much of these last eight years. This manifested itself in his writing as a provocative approach to his own death that defied the normal limits of propriety. Working in what one could justifiably describe as a living hell, he was able, in an astonishing feat of will, to maintain a balance between his desire for death and the will to live on, and correspondingly, between total resignation at the human condition and continued commitment to the struggle for social justice.

In this last phase of his life Heine had to relinquish all hope of personally benefiting from the goal he had given the highest priority in his pursuit of freedom — the restoration of sensual pleasure as an important and legitimate part of human existence. Nonetheless, he continued to give it the same importance in his philosophical contemplations. But now his thinking lacked the idealistic fervor that had infused it during the earlier period in Paris, when he had held out more immediate hope for revolutionary change. In exchange, it became more detached and possibly more objective in its ability to determine a practical vision of this goal. Conversely, or even paradoxically, his late writing suggests that the less idealistic the vision, the more complex the literary strategies needed to convey it without lapsing into prefabricated systems of thought that contravene the move toward practical reason. It is this deconstructive aspect that offers a new perspective on Heine's work as a whole and provides the rationale for this Companion volume, which aims to open the main features of Heine's work to contemporary critical approaches that share some of its underlying assumptions.

*   *   *   *   *

Editions of Heine's Works

A few words here about the standard critical editions of Heine's works and a few selected reference works may prove useful to those who are not actively involved in Heine scholarship. As the list of abbreviations of frequently cited works in this volume indicates, there are only three editions now commonly cited by scholars. With the exception of an occasional reference to the accompanying notes or critical essays in the earlier editions, there is seldom reason to cite another edition, except when comparing the state of knowledge about the manuscripts or documenting the history of the editorial work. The definitive critical edition is the *Historisch-kritische Gesamtausgabe der Werke* (16 volumes in 23, commonly known as the Düsseldorfer Ausgabe) which, under the general editorship of Manfred Windfuhr, was compiled and published in collaboration with the Heinrich-Heine-Institut in Düsseldorf and completed in 1997, just in time for the bicentennial celebration. Its volumes 1–15 — seven of which have the notes and critical apparatus under separate cover, while volume 16 is an *Ergänzungs- und Registerband* — contain all of Heine's writings, including both those published in his lifetime under his consultation, and those left in unpublished manuscript form. The edition follows meticulously

the spellings in the original publications and in the unpublished manuscripts retaining all the gaps, omissions, and misspellings of the handwritten texts. The critical work is thorough, scholarly, and precise
throughout. Quality or completeness was obviously not sacrificed for
the sake of speed during the twenty-four years of work on this edition.

Now that the Düsseldorfer Ausgabe is finished, there would be no
need to cite another edition of Heine's works if the volumes of this
definitive collection were more widely available and less cumbersome.
The widely used alternative is the six-volume (in seven) *Sämtliche
Schriften* edited by Klaus Briegleb and published in the years 1968–
1976. Complemented by the first complete edition of Heine's letters
(edited by Friedrich Hirth and published originally in six volumes
from 1950 to 1957, and then in two volumes in 1965), Briegleb's
edition was the West German rival to Hans Kaufmann's *Werke und
Briefe in 10 Bänden,* published by the Aufbau Verlag (East Germany)
between 1961 and 1964. Bolstered by hefty but uneven critical commentary, the Briegleb edition eventually left the combined East German collection of works and letters in its wake, probably more as a
result of the successful publishing industry behind it than because of
the editorial work. The commentary and critical apparatus of the
Sämtliche Schriften lacks the thoroughness and precision of the Düsseldorfer Ausgabe, at times obscuring the most helpful knowledge
with an overabundance of references and related quotations, and in
other cases presenting notes so thin that the reader is likely to ignore
them altogether. As frustrating as this can be, the commentary does
often prove helpful, particularly for those reading a work for the first
time. But as the first critical edition in the West since the Oskar Walzel
expansion and reworking (1910–1920) of Ernst Elster's first definitive
Sämtliche Werke (1887–1890), the Briegleb edition has had great success and has appeared in several reprints, including even a quite af-
fordable twelve-volume paperback *Kassette* that put the commentary
for each volume into a separate book, and more recently in a seven-
volume *Kassette.* One feature that has frustrated this Heine enthusiast
often, and probably many other readers of the most widely circulated
issues of the *Sämtliche Schriften* as well, is the tiny print of the commentary — a sure source of eye strain for anyone who uses it at length.
Still, this edition will likely remain for some time the standard edition
needed to complement the complete, but unwieldy and expensive
historical-critical collection.

While the East German editions have in both these instances been
dwarfed by their Western counterparts, there is one niche where they

maintain their own monopoly — Heine's correspondence. The *Säkularausgabe* of *Werke, Briefwechsel, Lebenszeugnisse* was begun in 1970 as a joint French-East German effort to produce the first complete historical-critical edition of Heine's writings. However, it lacked the central focus, organization, and financial support that contributed to the success of the Düsseldorfer Ausgabe. And while work continues on the remaining, uncompleted volumes of this edition, there seems to be little expectation that they will have any better circulation than those already out. There is one major exception: the eight volumes 20–27 comprise the only complete and annotated collection of letters written both *by* and *to* Heine — and in the case of those letters written to Heine, it is the *only* published collection. As evidenced by the fact that all the essays in this Companion volume cite letters to and from Heine from this edition, it has become the standard edition that scholars use almost exclusively in citing either set of letters. And even though the edition is not as widely available as one would like, it will almost certainly remain the definitive collection of letters for the foreseeable future.

With the completion of the Düsseldorfer Ausgabe there is little need, even for the most dedicated Heine scholar, to do archival research. All the handwritten manuscripts of his writings have now been published with painstaking attention given to possible variations. Also, almost all of the known letters written by Heine and most of those written to him are included in the *Säkularausgabe*. Thus, although the Heinrich Heine Institute possesses an extensive collection of the handwritten manuscripts for both those published in Heine's lifetime and those published posthumously, neither they nor the smaller number of manuscripts housed in other collections offer new insights into his work.

For those seeking Heine's works in English there are a number of options, none of which will satisfy in every regard. However, together they enable one to become familiar with his writing as a whole, even if much of the nuance and enjoyment is lost in the translation. This is true of course primarily for the poetry, whose charm depends on subtleties of meter and rhythm that can only be approximated at best in translation. Also the ironic shifts between cultural registers, the constant wordplays that depend on multiple meanings, the allusions to specific social or cultural contexts, and the minute but striking prosodic variations are all difficult to render into English, particularly when they appear in còncert. The two most complete collections of the poems are Hal Draper's *The Complete Poems of Heinrich Heine: A*

Modern English Version, which includes all of Heine's work in verse, and the translations by Louis Untermeyer and Aaron Kramer in *The Poetry and Prose of Heinrich Heine* edited by Frederic Ewen. The latter is the most extensive single volume in English, but the prose selections are taken out of their context and arranged by thematic categories, with the result that important contexts and connections are often lost or distorted. Other useful recent volumes with more modest selections are: the volume *Selected Prose* in the Penguin Classics series (1993), translated by Ritchie Robertson; and the two volumes titled *Poetry and Prose,* edited by Jost Hermand and Robert Holub in the German Library series — the latter include almost exclusively works that highlight the progressive political writer and social critic.

In addition to these editions and translations, a few other reference works will probably prove helpful to those who want to familiarize themselves with Heine. Michael Werner's two-volume *Begegnungen mit Heine: Berichte der Zeitgenossen* (an expanded continuation of H. H. Houben's *Gespräche mit Heine*) is a well-organized and pleasantly presented work that is also thoroughly researched and dependable in its information. It offers valuable insights into Heine's thinking during all periods of his life. Fritz Mende's extensive chronicle of events in Heine's life, including detailed information on the various publications during his lifetime, is a good reference for information on the publishing history and the chronology of his life and work. However, some patience is required to sort through the somewhat confusing structure of the listings.

Bibliographies documenting the immense amount of scholarship on Heine are available and necessary for anyone who needs an overview of the secondary literature on a particular topic. The standard ones, with the years of the period they cover, are: Wilhelm and Galley (to 1953); Seifert (1954–1964); Sammons (1956–1980); Seifert and Volgina (1965–1982); and Wilamowitz-Moellendorff and Mühlpfordt (1983–1995). Also, each year the *Heine-Jahrbuch* presents a complete list of new publications of Heine's works and of all new secondary literature on him — including even works that discuss Heine or his works as a partial or secondary topic and reviews of scholarly works on Heine.

Among the numerous works offering an overview of the reception of Heine, two stand out as frequently cited standard works. The project undertaken by Eberhard Galley and Alfred Estermann of presenting all the critical commentary on him published during his lifetime (*Heinrich Heines Werk im Urteil seiner Zeitgenossen*) stalled in 1992 after the sixth volume appeared, bringing the collection up to the year

1841. Whether it will ever be continued or completed remains to be seen. A more modest anthology is Karl Theodor Kleinknecht's *Heine in Deutschland: Dokumente seiner Rezeption 1834–1956*. A quite useful recent work, particularly for native speakers of English who are looking for an initial overview of the reception and critical literature, is George Peters's *The Poet as Provocateur: Heinrich Heine and His Critics* (2000).

Gerhard Höhn's *Heine-Handbuch: Zeit, Person, Werk* also deserves mention here because it gives in one volume important background information and an evenhanded introductory commentary on all Heine's works. In each case, Höhn first explains the origins and history of the text and its variants in a section called "Entstehung, Druck, Text" before offering a concise "Analyse und Deutung" that consistently hits the main points in a moderate and reasonable manner. Where appropriate, he also discusses the "Aufnahme und Wirkung"; and in all cases, he gives a short list of significant critical literature on the work. The *Heine-Handbuch* first appeared in 1987, and a second updated and expanded edition was published ten years later. This in itself is an indication of the value of this volume for both Heine scholars and newcomers alike.

And finally, there is a recent CD-ROM containing almost all of Heine's works, published by Directmedia as part of the *Digitale Bibliothek* series. It also includes a digital version of the Rowohlt biography by Christian Liedtke and some visual images of people and places from his life. But the most attractive feature of the disk is the versatile search engine that enables the reader to search quickly through all the works (or any part of them) for a phrase or combination of words. Given the dispersion of interesting and pithy Heine passages throughout the diverse multiplicity of his writings, this capability is as valuable to the experienced Heine scholar as it is to those who are only interested in his statements on a particular topic. It is also possible to cut and paste passages from the disk directly to word processing files. However, caution is warranted here. The disk draws from earlier editions of the writings for which the copyright has expired, and the transcription onto the disk includes many typing mistakes. Nonetheless, the search engine makes this CD-ROM edition a very helpful tool indeed.

Notes

[1] For two examples, which however understand the nature of his continued participation in the "Freiheitskriege" somewhat differently, see the final arguments of the essays by Gerhard Höhn and Anthony Phelan in this volume.

[2] For a more comprehensive discussion of this see the beginning of my own essay in this volume.

[3] Jürgen Habermas has argued that what "chafes German readers, the thing for which they have not forgiven Heine" is that he restores the liberal, progressive force to Romanticism: "they have not forgiven Heine the *Romantic* for rescuing their romantic heritage from a deadly nationalistic idealization, from false historicizing, from a transfiguring sentimentality, and restoring it to its own radical origins" ("Heinrich Heine and the Role of the Intellectual in Germany," *The New Conservatism: Cultural Criticism and the Historians' Debate,* trans. Shierry Weber Nicholson [Cambridge, MA: MIT Press, 1989], 83).

[4] This aspect of Heine's identification with Germany's intellectual traditions has often not received enough recognition from scholars. See, however, the more recent contribution (first published in 1994) by Manfred Windfuhr, "'Unsere großen Meister.' Materialien zu Heines intellektuellem Deutschlandbild," *Rätsel Heine: Autorprofil — Werk — Wirkung* (Heidelberg: C. Winter, 1997), 185–209.

[5] Heine used this metaphor himself in a well-known passage in the *Wintermärchen.* As he crosses the border into Prussian territory in his fictional account of his 1843 journey to Hamburg, he describes how the customs officials search through his belongings, and then he remarks:

> Ihr Toren, die Ihr im Koffer sucht!
> Hier werdet Ihr nichts entdecken!
> Die Contrebande, die mit mir reist,
> Die hab ich im Kopfe stecken. (B 4: 579)

[6] For an extensive account of Heine's conception of what he perceived as the two fundamental and diametrically opposed tendencies in European civilization, which he called Nazarene and Hellenist, see the essay by Paul Reitter in this volume.

[7] See his article of June 15, 1843 for the Augsburg *Allgemeine Zeitung* entitled "Kommunismus, Philosophie und Klerisei" (B 5: 496–513). For a discussion of the development of this idea about the political import of the Hegelian dialectic see Cook, *By the Rivers of Babylon: Heinrich Heine's Late Songs and Reflections* (Detroit: Wayne State UP, 1998), 68–75.

[8] Heine's comment that the baptismal certificate is "das Entréebillett zur europäischen Kultur" (B 6.1: 622) referred to his conversion to Protestantism. But the religious conversion, and most importantly the abandonment of the Jewish religion and culture, was an important, often necessary first step — hotly contested by Jews and German Christians alike — for those Jews seeking acceptance into the German social and cultural world.

[9] He used this term when referring to those elements — and specifically the followers of Friedrich Ludwig Jahn — who envisioned a German greatness rooted in the early Germanic tribes (and showed a corresponding animosity toward the French). See B 3: 290; B 4: 104–5; B 5: 33, 40–41, 233.

[10] In 1840 the Jewish community in Damascus was charged with murdering a Capuchin monk and using his blood in a ritual. This reversion to charges of blood-libel that were common in Europe in the Middle Ages resulted in the torture of Jews in Damascus in an attempt to gain confessions from them. The French government, which had political interests in Syria at the time, refused to denounce the practice, and the French consul in Damascus even aided the authorities in their action against the Jewish community. For more on the incident and Heine's response, see S. S. Prawer, *Heine's Jewish Comedy: A Study of His Portraits of Jews and Judaism* (Oxford: Clarendon, 1983), 297–310.

[11] It should be cautioned here that this attempt to produce a consistent image does not mean that Heine tried to eliminate contradictory aspects in the self-image projected in his works. To the contrary, the poetic persona of the late writings reveals a synthesis of seemingly incompatible sides of its character that is more confounding than ever. Recent scholarship has, wisely, been more willing to forego attempts to force them into a single, unchanging figure. With respect to the poem "Der Apollogott," Norbert Altenhofer writes: "Jüdisches, Hellenisches, Christliches überlagern sich in diesem irritierenden Vexierspiel, das . . . das — uneindeutige, nie zu 'Charakter' sich verfestigende — Künstlersubjekt in seinem Reichtum und in seiner Fragwürdigkeit konstituiert. Nach der 'echten,' der 'wahren' Identität zu fragen, is legitim, aber vergeblich, wenn die Frage nicht an das Werk gerichtet wird" ("Rabbi Faibisch Apollo. Zum Spiel der Identitäten in Leben und Werk Heinrich Heines," *Die verlorene Augensprache: Über Heinrich Heine* [Frankfurt am Main and Leipzig: Insel, 1993], 231).

Works Cited

Altenhofer, Norbert. "Rabbi Faibisch Apollo. Zum Spiel der Identitäten in Leben und Werk Heinrich Heines." *Die verlorene Augensprache: Über Heinrich Heine*. Frankfurt am Main and Leipzig: Insel, 1993. 207–32.

Cook, Roger F. *By the Rivers of Babylon: Heinrich Heine's Late Songs and Reflections*. Detroit: Wayne State UP, 1998.

Galley, Eberhard, and Alfred Estermann, eds. *Heinrich Heines Werk im Urteil seiner Zeitgenossen*. Hamburg: Hoffmann und Campe, 1981–. 6 vols. to date.

Habermas, Jürgen. "Heinrich Heine and the Role of the Intellectual in Germany." *The New Conservatism: Cultural Criticism and the Historians' Debate*. Trans. Shierry Weber Nicholson. Cambridge, MA: MIT Press, 1989. 71–99.

Heine, Heinrich. *Historisch-kritische Gesamtausgabe der Werke*. Düsseldorfer Ausgabe. Ed. Manfred Windfuhr, et al. Hamburg: Hoffmann und Campe, 1973–1997. 16 vols. (in 23).

————. *Poetry and Prose*. Ed. Jost Hermand and Robert C. Holub. The German Library 32. Trans. Gilbert Cannan, Frederic Ewen, Robert C. Holub, and Helen Mustard. New York: Continuum, 1982.

————. *The Poetry and Prose of Heinrich Heine*. Ed. Frederic Ewen. Trans. Louis Untermeyer, Aaron Kramer, Frederic Ewen, et al. New York: Citadel, 1948.

————. *The Romantic School and Other Essays*. Ed. Jost Hermand and Robert C. Holub. Trans. Gilbert Cannan, Frederic Ewen, Robert C. Holub, and Helen Mustard. The German Library 33. New York: Continuum, 1985.

————. *Sämtliche Schriften*. Ed. Klaus Briegleb. Munich: Hanser, 1968–1976. 6 vols. (in 7).

————. *Sämtliche Werke*. Ed. Ernst Elster. Leipzig: Bibliographisches Institut, 1887–1890. 7 vols.

————. *Sämtliche Werke*. Ed. Oskar Walzel, et al. Leipzig: Insel, 1910–1920. 10 vols.

————. *Selected Prose*. Ed. and Trans. Ritchie Robertson. London: Penguin, 1993.

————. *Werke*. CD-ROM. Ed. Mathias Bertram. With illustrations and a copy of Christian Liedtke, *Heinrich Heine* (Reinbek bei Hamburg: Rowohlt, 1997), and a recording of *Die Harzreise*. Digitale Bibliothek. Berlin: Directmedia, 1998.

————. *Werke, Briefwechsel, Lebenszeugnisse. Säkularausgabe*. Ed. Nationale Forschungs- und Gedenkstätten der klassischen deutschen Literatur in Weimar and Centre National de la Recherche Scientifique in Paris. Berlin and Paris: Akademie-Verlag and Editions du CNRS, 1970–. 27 vols.

Höhn, Gerhard. *Heine-Handbuch: Zeit, Person, Werk*. Stuttgart: Metzler, 1987. 2nd rev. ed., 1997.

Houben, Hans Hubert. *Gespräche mit Heine*. Frankfurt am Main: n.p., 1926.

Kleinknecht, Karl Theodor, ed. *Heine in Deutschland: Dokumente seiner Rezeption 1834–1956*. Tübingen and Munich: Deutscher Taschenbuch Verlag and Niemeyer, 1976.

Mende, Fritz. *Heinrich Heine: Chronik seines Lebens und Werkes*. Berlin: Akademie, 1970.

Peters, George F. *The Poet as Provocateur: Heinrich Heine and His Critics*. Rochester, NY: Camden House, 2000.

Prawer, S. S. *Heine's Jewish Comedy: A Study of His Portraits of Jews and Judaism*. Oxford: Clarendon, 1983.

Sammons, Jeffrey L. *Heinrich Heine: A Selected Critical Bibliography, 1956–1980.* New York and London: Garland, 1982.

Seifert, Siegfried. *Heine-Bibliographie 1954–1964.* Berlin and Weimar: Aufbau, 1968.

Seifert, Siegfried, and Albina A. Volgina. *Heine-Bibliographie 1965–1982.* Berlin and Weimar: Aufbau, 1986.

Werner, Michael, ed. *Begegnungen mit Heine: Berichte der Zeitgenossen, in Fortführung von H. H. Houbens "Gespräche mit Heine."* Hamburg: Hoffmann und Campe, 1973. 2 vols.

Wilamowitz-Moellendorff, Erdmann, and Günther Mühlpfordt. *Heine-Bibliographie 1983–1995.* Stuttgart and Weimar: Metzler, 1998.

Wilhelm, Gottfried, and Eberhard Galley. *Heine Bibliographie.* Weimar: Arion, 1960. 2 vols.

Windfuhr, Manfred. "'Unsere großen Meister.' Materialien zu Heines intellektuellem Deutschlandbild." *Rätsel Heine: Autorprofil — Werk — Wirkung.* Heidelberg: C. Winter, 1997. 185–209.

The Romantic Poet

Illusions Lost and Found: The Experiential World of Heine's *Buch der Lieder*

Michael Perraudin

I

THE GREAT LITERARY-HISTORICAL importance of Heine's *Buch der Lieder* of 1827 is as a document of generational disillusion. It articulates as no other work in German does the combination of disappointment, skepticism, irony, and self-pity that was the prevailing mood of the first post-Romantic generation, those born around 1800 and coming to maturity at the beginning of the 1820s. Such other German-language authors as Mörike, Grillparzer, Immermann, and Nestroy in their different ways also represent this spirit. But *Buch der Lieder* is its classic document.

In the widest sense what is at issue is the demise of idealism — political, philosophical, emotional, aesthetic. In the German states — and elsewhere — the fifteen years after 1815 seemed politically an insipid and unheroic time. Depending on political allegiance, the grandeur of the previous age might be found in the Napoleonic principle, in national self-affirmation and the resistance to Napoleon, in the striving for bourgeois democracy, or in social revolution; but from all of these points of view the regressive politics of the 1820s were ignoble and prosaic. At the same time, the cultural world of the Classical/Romantic era was collapsing, as its representatives came to look old and foolish and its precepts began to seem irreconcilable with modern reality. Philosophies that held that truth lay within the human mind, of which the world of phenomena was merely an invention, or that the cultivation of the subjective, irrational, unconscious self was the path to fulfillment, lost their credibility; literature that sought its aesthetic and ideological models in a primitive past, or that considered the empirical present the least worthy object of representation, began to seem absurd. Such reactions were themselves a necessary effect of the wider changes taking place in the intellectual and physical world: specifically, the predominance of a materialist outlook, which came with the development of modern empirical science and its industrial exploitation, with the rise to economic power and social dominance of the class of capital, and with the emergence of an urban mass society. The socioeconomic changes may have happened more slowly in the German states than elsewhere, but the shift in outlook — to the sense of what Büchner in the 1830s called a "material age"[1] — was profound in Germany, too.

These were the processes which, inter alia, lay at the root of European realism, including its peculiar German forms, namely the sense of a moral and intellectual need for literature to render present reality with maximum transparency. That is certainly part of the context in which we should view *Buch der Lieder*. We have key texts in other European literatures that straddle the historical gap between Romantic worlds of the imagination and skeptical social and psychological realism: *La chartreuse de Parme* by Stendhal, Jane Austen's *Sense and Sensibility*, perhaps *Illusions perdues* of Balzac. Heine's *Buch der Lieder* can be viewed as the German equivalent, as the text that articulated his and his generation's sense of the breakdown of idealist patterns of experience, before he passed on to his own answers to the realist impulse, that is, political journalism, quasi-fictitious travelogue and satirical verse. So it can be seen, at any rate, and so Heine himself in a certain sense saw it.

The characteristic gesture of the *Buch der Lieder* is the invoking of an ideal domain that loses credibility in collision with material reality — social, psychological, emotional — and then an implication of regret at the loss. Even the cyclical groupings into which the poems of the anthology are organized do this in various ways. The historicizing titles "Junge Leiden" and "Die Heimkehr" signal a now superseded world of experience. The title of "Lyrisches Intermezzo" tells the reader to regard its contents as of secondary importance. The prologue and epilogue poems accompanying several of the cycles and sub-cycles are similarly relativizing statements. And the narrative arrangement of one at least of the central cycles, the "Lyrisches Intermezzo," is designed to chart, at any rate approximately, a progress from optimistic naiveté:

> Im wunderschönen Monat Mai,
> Als alle Knospen sprangen, (B 1: 75)

toward gloomy disabusement:

> Da brachen auf die Wunden,
> Da stürzt' mit wilder Macht
> Aus Kopf und Brust der Blutstrom,
> Und sieh! — ich bin erwacht. (B 1: 103).

Aside from such cyclical effects, however, the individual poems of the anthology also perform this gesture in a large variety of ways. Mostly the ideal domain is an ideal of love as an uplifting spiritual force, unending, asocial, asexual, and conflict-free, with the beloved herself as a saint. To begin with an obvious example: in the famous poem "Sie saßen und tranken am Teetisch" (B 1: 95–96), such an ideal of love is relativized as the discourse of a social world that belies the ideal in its own behavior. The beloved in this world is class-conscious, faithless, and trivial; love in this world is prurient and adulterous, both sexual and sexually repressed. Many other poems similarly signal the beloved's un-ideal defectiveness — as heartless, indifferent, spiteful, deceitful, hypocritical and stupid, even if she is physically desirable: "schön und bissig," "falsch [und] fromm," "holde Törin," "Schlange," "Herzchen so süß und so falsch und so klein," "das Herzchen ist verdorrt" (B 1: 81, 83, 87, 96). She is not a poet's idealizing construct, but the reality of amorous relations:

> Aber dich und deine Tücke,
> Und dein holdes Angesicht,
> Und die falschen frommen Blicke —
> Das erschafft der Dichter nicht. (B 1: 81)

She belongs to — and has even married into (B 1: 86) — a social world inimical to the poet. And as the object of the poet's obsession she is in a sense gratuitous: if not her, then someone else:

> Und doch möcht ich im Grabe liegen,
> Und mich an *ein* totes Liebchen schmiegen.
> (B 1: 87; my emphasis)

The poet's own emotion claims or seeks a kind of heroic grandeur, but there is fatuity in the grandeur:

> Lehn deine Wang an meine Wang,
> Dann fließen die Tränen zusammen;
> Und an mein Herz drück fest dein Herz,
> Dann schlagen zusammen die Flammen!
> (B 1: 76–77)

There is also an elaborate mythology of love accompanying the ideal domain, a mythology into which the poet seeks to project himself, but which collapses on him. This includes the poet as knight-at-arms from medieval romance:

> Die Hunde bellen, die Diener
> Erscheinen mit Kerzengeflirr;
> Die Wendeltreppe stürm ich
> Hinauf mit Sporengeklirr. (B 1: 99)

It also includes mythical India:

> Die Lotosblume ängstigt
> Sich vor der Sonne Pracht. (B 1: 78)

and Avalon, the isle of love:

> Die Geisterinsel, die schöne,
> Lag dämmrig im Mondenglanz;
> Dort klangen liebe Töne,
> Und wogte der Nebeltanz.
>
> Dort klang es lieb und lieber,
> Und wogt' es hin und her;
> Wir aber schwammen vorüber
> Trostlos auf weitem Meer. (B 1: 92)

as well as other "Zauberländer":

> Ach! jenes Land der Wonne,
> Das seh ich oft im Traum;
> Doch kommt die Morgensonne,
> Zerfließts wie eitel Schaum. (B 1: 93)

Even unhappy love — uncomplicated, unadulterated unhappy love — is part of the lost, ideal domain. Thus in the "Doppelgänger" poem ("Heimkehr" 20) the pure, poetic misery of the lover wringing his hands beneath the beloved's window has become a painfully inaccessible — because no longer credible — experience:

> Du Doppeltgänger! du bleicher Geselle!
> Was äffst du nach mein Liebesleid,
> Das mich gequält auf dieser Stelle,
> So manche Nacht, in alter Zeit? (B 1: 118)

Or there is the poem:

> Wenn zwei von einander scheiden,
> So geben sie sich die Händ,
> Und fangen an zu weinen,
> Und seufzen ohne End.
>
> Wir haben nicht geweinet,
> Wir seufzten nicht Weh und Ach!
> Die Tränen und die Seufzer,
> Die kamen hintennach. (B 1: 95)

Here, past emotional simplicity[2] is replaced by a world of non-communication, confusion, misunderstanding, and repression, that is, the psychology of real human interaction. As Heine wrote to one of the previous generation of Romantic poets, Wilhelm Müller, in 1826: "Wie rein, wie klar sind Ihre Lieder und sämmtlich sind es Volkslieder. In meinen Gedichten hingegen . . . [gehört] der Inhalt . . . der conventionnellen Gesellschaft" (HSA 20: 250).

The ideal domain is indeed very much bound up with the world of poetry. These last two poems ("Heimkehr" 20 and "Intermezzo" 49), and also many others in the anthology, speak — or at any rate spoke to the initiated contemporary reader — through prior poetic utterance, through earlier, implicitly more naive texts. Thus "Der Doppelgänger" ("Heimkehr" 20) comes at the end of a long line of Romantic pseudo-folk songs — Uhland, Eichendorff, Kerner, Arnim, et al. — around the folk motifs of the homecoming and the lover's nighttime vigil. "Wenn zwei von einander scheiden, / So geben sie sich die Händ," or versions of it, was a standard and familiar folk song couplet. The beginning of the Isle of Avalon poem, "Mein Liebchen, wir saßen beisammen, / Traulich im leichten Kahn" (B 1: 92), is an echo of Wilhelm Müller's popular *Schöne Müllerin* cycle of 1821.[3] And there are numerous other examples. Such allusions are designed to signal that the models belonged to a world of poetic ideality that is no longer feasible. Heine's adaptations entail a systematic reduction of the model's supposed harmony to disharmony, beauty to ugliness, and illusion to disillusion.

In a sense what the anthology registers is the collapse of poetry; and certainly it registers a collapse of poetic imagery. That is what the poem "Wahrhaftig" says most emphatically, with its dismissive list of the routine building blocks of love poetry:

> Doch Lieder und Sterne und Blümelein,
> Und Äuglein und Mondglanz und Sonnenschein,
> Wie sehr das Zeug auch gefällt,
> So machts doch noch lang keine Welt. (B 1: 64)

— or, in its earlier version in a letter of Heine's: "'. . . Ist es doch noch lang nicht die Welt!' . . . Ja, die Welt besteht noch aus andern Ingredienzen" (February 5, 1821; HSA 20: 39). There is a real world to which such material is entirely inadequate. Innumerable other poems operate equivalently. Many are designed to undermine themselves with the over-formulaic character of their imagery and rhetorical structure:

> Die blauen Veilchen der Äugelein,
> Die roten Rosen der Wängelein,
> Die weißen Liljen der Händchen klein, (B 1: 87);

> Die Welt ist so schön und der Himmel so blau,
> Und die Lüfte die wehen so lind und so lau,
> Und die Blumen winken auf blühender Au, (B 1: 87);

> Die Rose, die Lilje, die Taube, die Sonne,
> Die liebt ich einst alle in Liebeswonne, (B 1: 76);

> Warum sind denn die Rosen so blaß,
> O sprich, mein Lieb, warum?
> Warum sind denn im grünen Gras
> Die blauen Veilchen so stumm?

> Warum singt denn mit so kläglichem Laut
> Die Lerche in der Luft (B 1: 83–84).

Others, such as the "Lorelei" poem or "Mein Herz, mein Herz ist traurig" ("Heimkehr" 3), have a final gesture that breaks the poetic illusion, breaks out of the poem's image world, and signals sudden boredom with it:

> Ich glaube, die Wellen verschlingen
> Am Ende Schiffer und Kahn;
> Und das hat mit ihrem Singen
> Die Lore-Ley getan. (B 1: 107)

These are familiar poems, often used as illustrations of Heine's poetic processes. But it is important to establish precisely what is taking place in them. It is customary to say that they register a discrediting of poetic language, a devaluation of the common currency of poetic speaking that previous generations had handed down. So indeed they do. They represent a problem of linguistic cliché, forms of expression that have grown stale and unoriginal through overuse. The clichés are not only linguistic, however, but also experiential. The poems speak of forms of emotional and spiritual experience that are losing credibility. The vigil beneath the beloved's window in the "Doppelgänger" poem is not just a literary topos, it is also a perfectly possible experiential reality, at least for someone who is able to undertake such behavior without skepticism. One may think of Heine's contemporaneous imaginative travelogue *Die Harzreise* and the poet's and his companions' worshipful contemplation of nature on the Brocken, the mood of which is broken by the enthusiastically fatuous cry, "Wie ist die Natur im allgemeinen so schön!" (B 2: 145), from one of those present (a traveling salesman). In the correspondence of some of Heine's contemporaries — for instance, Mörike's extraordinary letters to his fiancée, Luise Rau (146–215) — one finds accounts of quasi-mystical emotional experiences, with such behavioral accompaniment as heavy weeping, which for the writers were evidently real events, not fictions. Romantic idealism had conditioned not only literary writing, but also the way people felt and acted, or felt that they acted. In Heine's writing of the 1820s, however, this experiential world was collapsing too: the lover's nocturnal vigil, or his noble embrace, or his floods of tears, or the loving self's mystic union with nature and the divine, were themselves turning into clichés, contrived and self-conscious.

Implicit in the *Buch der Lieder* is always a contrary reality against which these experiential and poetic-linguistic patterns are measured and which exposes their insufficiency. It is, as was suggested earlier, the world of political conflict, class divisions, and other forms of prejudice, economic interest and a skeptical, more or less deterministic view of human interaction and motivation. Against this reality Heine's collection measures Romantic subjective idealism and the poetic language associated with it. Thus, in a poem such as "Ich grolle nicht, und wenn das Herz auch bricht, / Ewig verlornes Lieb! Ich grolle nicht" (B 1: 81–82), what we hear is a voice entirely deluded about the un-ideal reality of human sexual nature and relationships, including its own: inconstancy, betrayal, embitterment, and ignobility. And "Wahrhaftig" and the many other poems whose poetic imagery corroborate it amount to a confession (and an expression of frustration) that the given language of poetry is incapable of rendering the world as it is.

II

Such an admission of the delusory character of the ideal domain, of the inadequacy of poetry to the real world, and in effect of the impotence of the lyric poet, is certainly, as was indicated at the outset, the primary meaning of *Buch der Lieder* and what has given the work its epochal significance as a proto-realist, post-Romantic statement: "jene romantische Schule, wo ich meine angenehmsten Jugendjahre verlebt und zuletzt den Schulmeister geprügelt habe" ("Vorrede" to *Atta Troll*, B 4: 495). However, there is another thread in the collection that makes its position on the cusp of a historical change even more acute. This is the strand of utterance that suggests, not that the ideal domain is illusion or falsehood, but that the fault lies with modern man, who in his materialism and rationality has lost his capacity to experience such ideality. The poem "Gespräch auf der Paderborner Heide" is a step toward such a position, in which the philistine and the "fantasist" argue whether the sounds they hear are farmyard noises or the songs of spirits. The poem's conclusion seems to edge in a materialist direction:

> Nun, mein Freund, so magst du lachen
> Über des Phantasten Frage!
> Wirst du auch zur Täuschung machen,
> Was ich fest im Busen trage? (B 1: 63)

— a regretful suggestion that the speaker's perceptions are beautiful imaginings. However, though the ambiguity is perhaps less thoroughly maintained than, for example, in the poem's most famous precursor, Goethe's "Erlkönig," an element of ambivalence nonetheless remains. Heine's ballad "Die Grenadiere" (B 1: 47–48) presents an equivalent dialogue, between a realist and a Bonapartist idealist, but with a stronger sense of the correctness — at least the moral correctness — of the idealist position. The most subtle presentation of the desolate inadequacy of a realist consciousness, however, is the poem from "Heimkehr," "Wir saßen am Fischerhause," in which tourists by the seashore at dusk reflect wistfully on the "seltsame Völker" of distant lands across the sea, the mythical inhabitants of ancient India and the real fisher-folk of the far North, before lapsing into empty and bereft silence:

Die Mädchen horchten ernsthaft,
Und endlich sprach niemand mehr;
Das Schiff war nicht mehr sichtbar,
Es dunkelte gar zu sehr. (B 1: 111)

This poem must be seen in the context of Heine's other writings of the time about premodern, prerational peoples in *Die Harzreise* and *Nordsee III*. Both these texts are preoccupied with the notion of a sort of supra-rational consciousness that integrates the individual with himself, his community and his natural environment, permits immediate and intuitive knowledge of truths that the fragmented, rational, analytical consciousness of modern man can only labor toward, and in the end represents a kind of liberating force. Primitive peoples, even when they are ignorant and downtrodden, as are the Harz miners and the fisher-folk of the North Sea, possess a form of such consciousness, a "tiefes Anschauungsleben" (*Die Harzreise*, B 2: 119). This is also the consciousness of children:

Unser Leben in der Kindheit [ist] so unendlich bedeutend, in jener Zeit ist uns alles gleich wichtig, wir hören alles, wir sehen alles, bei allen Eindrücken ist Gleichmäßigkeit, statt daß wir später absichtlicher werden, uns mit dem Einzelnen ausschließlicher beschäftigen, das klare Gold der Anschauung für das Papiergeld der Bücherdefinitionen mühsam einwechseln, und an Lebensbreite gewinnen, was wir an Lebenstiefe verlieren. (B 2: 119)

And it, or a form of it, is the consciousness of the Great Men of History, according to *Die Nordsee III*, who "in einer mystischen Gemeinschaft . . . über die Jahrtausende hinweg einander zu[nicken]" (B 2: 234). Theirs is

[ein] Verstand . . ., der, weil er nicht wie der unsrige diskursiv, sondern intuitiv ist, vom synthetisch Allgemeinen, der Anschauung eines Ganzen als eines solchen zum Besonderen geht, das ist, von dem Ganzen zu den Teilen. Ja, was wir durch langsames analytisches Nachdenken und lange Schlußfolgen erkennen, das hatte jener Geist im selben Momente angeschaut und tief begriffen. (B 2: 234–35)

Finally and crucially, both these works also articulate the belief that the poet himself in the flights of his Romantic-poetic imagination may attain such a consciousness, escaping the limits of the modern mind. The poet of *Die Harzreise*, high up in the mountains and inspired by love, can talk to the trees and meet the elemental spirits (B 2: 125–26, 130, 158–60). And the poet of *Die Nordsee III*, wandering by the shore, observes how: "[Es] dehnt sich meine Seele so weltenweit . . .”; “allerlei Ahnung und Erinnerung [erwacht] in mir. . . . Wie aus der Tiefe eines Jahrtausends kommen mir . . . allerlei Gedanken in den Sinn, Gedanken uralter Weisheit” (B 2: 225, 227). This highly (and consciously) Romantic claim for the power of poetry and the poetic imagination is purposely left with a hint of ambivalence: “Es ist der erste Mai, der lumpigste Ladenschwengel hat heute das Recht, sentimental zu werden, und dem Dichter wolltest du es verwehren?” (*Die Harzreise*, B 2: 166). But it is nonetheless strongly present, as an important and, for Heine, substantially serious idea.

In the poems of *Buch der Lieder* that, as it were, lead up to these prose texts, there is accordingly a kind of secondary, countervailing thread, antithetical to the anti-idealist narrative that was traced above, a narrative concerned not with poetic impotence in the face of empirical reality, but with poetry's and the poet's sovereign power to move and mold the world. It begins with an extraordinary poem that Heine wrote around the end of 1816 (therefore at the age of 18 or 19), and subsequently excluded from *Buch der Lieder,* named “Die Weihe” (B 1: 219–21)[4] — where the consecrating referred to in the title is inter alia of himself as poet. In his letters of that time he announced how, from his emotional distress (at being spurned in love by his cousin), he would make poetry: “Und wenn der Mensch in seiner Qual verstummt, / Gab mir ein Gott, zu sagen wie ich leide” (October 27– November 20, 1816; HSA 20: 21), he said, echoing Goethe's Tasso; and:

> Wenn die Stunde kommt wo das Herz mir schwillt,
> Und blühender Zauber dem Busen entquillt,
> Dann greif ich zum Griffel rasch und wild,
> Und mahle mit Worten das Zaubergebild.
> (July 6, 1816; HSA 20: 18).

And “Die Weihe” itself charts — somewhat obscurely — a journey that his amorously stimulated poetic imagination takes through a range of poetic forms and image incarnations: via folk ballad, *Marienlied, Minnesang,* Spanish romance, and the Italy of Goethe's heroine Mignon, “west-east” to the Persian orientalism of Goethe's *West-östlicher Divan* and also to Heine's own Jewish spiritual home by the Jordan:

> Knabe hat es wohl verstanden,
> Was mit Sehnsuchtglut ihn ziehet
> Fort und fort nach jenen Landen,
> Wo die Myrte ewig blühet. (B 1: 221)

Love, including unfortunate love, will inspire the gifted poet to great leaps of the imagination and displays of creative power.[5]

In the poems of the next few years the realization of such self-assertion shows itself in various ways: for example, in the multiple identities into which the poet projects himself in the "Romanzen" in "Junge Leiden"; in the generic variety of the "Junge Leiden," asserting his technical mastery; and similarly with the attempt he makes in the "Romanzen" to establish a personal balladesque style or signature of his own.[6] The ultimate power-poem in the early sub-cycles is the eighth of the "Traumbilder," "Ich kam von meiner Herrin Haus," in which the rejected poet's imagination, incarnated as a spectral *Spielmann*, summons up from the graveyard a series of further ghostly incarnations of himself, each a different character, with a different story, and in a different, skillfully managed verse form (B 1: 30–35). From emotional prostration comes artistic might.

The subsequent sections, "Lyrisches Intermezzo" and "Die Heimkehr," especially the generally optimistic early part of the "Intermezzo," offer in the more lyrical and subjective idiom of those cycles further moments of poetic self-assertion. In "Intermezzo" 2 —

> Aus meinen Tränen sprießen
> Viel blühende Blumen hervor,
> Und meine Seufzer werden
> Ein Nachtigallenchor. (B 1: 75)

— subjugation in love is accompanied and balanced by the poet's imaginative power to create his own world: his tears blossom into flowers, to be presented as a bouquet to the beloved; his sighs become nightingales, to be made to sing beneath her window. In "Heimkehr" 40 ("Wie der Mond sich leuchtend dränget") a whole magic world from medieval romance is conjured out of the beloved's gaze:

> Märchenhaft vorüberzogen
> Berg und Burgen, Wald und Au; —
> Und das alles sah ich glänzen
> In dem Aug der schönen Frau. (B 1: 128)

In "Intermezzo" 9 —

> Auf Flügeln des Gesanges,
> Herzliebchen, trag ich dich fort,
> Fort nach den Fluren des Ganges,
> Dort weiß ich den schönsten Ort. (B 1: 78)

— his imagination performs exactly the kind of journey to exotic and mystic domains that "Die Weihe" had signaled. And in "Intermezzo" 8, love and the beloved's face open the poet's mind to the mystic language of the stars:

> Sie sprechen eine Sprache,
> Die ist so reich, so schön;
> Doch keiner der Philologen
> Kann diese Sprache verstehn.
>
> Ich aber hab sie gelernet,
> Und ich vergesse sie nicht;
> Mir diente als Grammatik
> Der Herzallerliebsten Gesicht. (B 1: 77)

These poems are nearly, but not quite, jokes. The same is true of such poems in "Die Heimkehr" as the "Wunschlied" folk song, "Mir träumt': ich bin der liebe Gott / Und sitz im Himmel droben" (B 1: 139), and the similarly self-deifying "Heimkehr" 24:

> Ich unglückselger Atlas! eine Welt,
> Die ganze Welt der Schmerzen, muß ich tragen,
> Ich trage Unerträgliches, und brechen
> Will mir das Herz im Leibe. (B 1: 120)

The poet is indeed a kind of god in his own creation. In the end, his subjugation before the beloved even becomes a kind of vampiric or incubus-like power over her:

> Jegliche Gestalt bekleidend,
> Bin ich stets in deiner Nähe,
> Aber immer bin ich leidend,
> Und du tust mir immer wehe.
>   . . .
> Wenn du eine Rose pflückest,
> Und mit kindischem Behagen
> Sie entblätterst und zerstückest —
> Hörst du mich nicht leise klagen?
>   . . .
> Hörst du nicht die Klagetöne
> Selbst im Ton der eignen Kehle?
> In der Nacht seufz ich und stöhne
> Aus der Tiefe deiner Seele. (B 1: 267–68)

And in the end too, the poet's tendency to repeat the pattern of miserable love affairs is likewise a token of power:

> Und wie viel ist dir geblieben!
> Und wie schön ist noch die Welt!
> Und, mein Herz, was dir gefällt,
> Alles, alles darfst du lieben! (B 1: 131)

The prose works *Die Nordsee III* and *Ideen. Das Buch Le Grand,* published as Heine was assembling his *Buch der Lieder* anthology in 1827, are an extension of the principle of these poems — extended by the same process of free, imaginative, poetic (that is, Romantic) thought-association that all these texts more or less explicitly extol. In *Die Nordsee III,* the poet in quasi-mystic mood by the seashore approaches in himself the kind of "synthetic consciousness" he has idealized:

> Wenn ich des Nachts am Meere wandelnd, den Wellengesang höre, und allerlei Ahnung und Erinnerung in mir erwacht, so ist mir, als habe ich einst . . . von oben herabgesehen . . .; es ist mir dann auch, als seien meine Augen so teleskopisch scharf gewesen, daß ich die Sterne in Lebensgröße am Himmel wandeln gesehen. . . . Wie aus der Tiefe eines Jahrtausends kommen mir dann allerlei Gedanken in den Sinn, Gedanken uralter Weisheit. (B 2: 227)

And in the same context he remarks: "die Metempsychose ist oft der Gegenstand meines Nachdenkens" (B 2: 226). *Das Buch Le Grand* then puts these notions into poetic practice, for the text is constructed around a series of transmigratory reincarnations of the soul of poet and beloved back through factual and mythical history, a process of metempsychosis which is a hyperbole of the poet-lover's utter subjugation — the curse of love — but also a token of the free-flying power of his imagination, able to leap across time and space in an instant with his "Siebenmeilenstiefel-Gedanken" (B 2: 275).[7]

A good deal of the two cycles of *Nordsee* poems at the end of *Buch der Lieder* is also concerned with this complex, with the idea of the poet-lover's titanic imaginative power. In "Krönung" he anoints the beloved, his latest beloved, as queen of his heart, with precious materials wrenched from the heavens:

> Von der Sonne droben
> Reiß ich das strahlend rote Gold,
> Und webe draus ein Diadem
> Für dein geweihtes Haupt.

> Von der flatternd blauseidnen Himmelsdecke,
> Worin die Nachtdiamanten blitzen,
> Schneid ich ein kostbar Stück,
> Und häng es dir, als Krönungsmantel,
> Um deine königliche Schulter. (B 1: 180)

In "Die Nacht am Strande" (B 1: 183–85) he is implicitly Odysseus, "Fremdling am Gestade," as well as one of the "sons of God [who] came in unto the daughters of men" in chapter 6 of Genesis (v. 4) and engendered with them "Helden, Wunder der Welt."[8] In "Poseidon" he is again in his imagination Odysseus (B 1: 185–87). In "Erklärung" he is specifically a titan:

> Der Himmel wird dunkler, mein Herz wird wilder,
> Und mit starker Hand, aus Norwegs Wäldern,
> Reiß ich die höchste Tanne,
> Und tauche sie ein
> In des Ätnas glühenden Schlund, und mit solcher
> Feuergetränkten Riesenfeder
> Schreib ich an die dunkle Himmelsdecke:
> "Agnes, ich liebe Dich!" (B 1: 187)[9]

— as he emblazons the beloved's name in giant letters upon the firmament. This is the titanism that he repeats and also names in *Die Nordsee III:* "meine Seele mit ihrem alten Titangebet" (B 2: 226), and repeats again in *Das Buch Le Grand* (B 2: 300–301). Moreover, it is an imagery that persists in Heine's writings in various contexts (especially contexts concerning the role of the political poet) over the next two decades, from *Die Stadt Lucca* to *Deutschland. Ein Wintermärchen.*[10]

III

Of course, there is a problem with all this. The imaginative titanism of the *Buch Le Grand* is also termed in the text "Narrheit" (B 2: 300), in the same way as the outburst of imaginative power at the end of *Die Harzreise* is perhaps just the sentimentality of a shop-boy, a "lumpiger Ladenschwengel" (B 2: 166). The poet's imaginative soaring among the stars in *Die Nordsee III* is accompanied by an element of panic and weakness — "als . . . sei [ich] vor schwindelndem Schrecken zur Erde heruntergefallen"; "durch all den wirbelnden Glanz geblendet worden" (B 1: 227). The poet-hero-god of "Die Nacht am Strande" ends up unheroically chilled, asking for tea with rum to ward off a cold (B 1: 185). Altogether the heroic utterances in the *Nordsee* cycles alternate with expressions of the poet's frailty, impotence, and ridiculousness: "O Tor, du Tor, du prahlender Tor!" says "Der Gesang der Okeaniden" (B 1: 204); in "Poseidon," the god mocks his insignificance:

> Da schäumte das Meer,
> Und aus den weißen Wellen stieg
> Das schilfbekränzte Haupt des Meergotts,
> Und höhnisch rief er:
>
> Fürchte dich nicht, Poetlein!
> Ich will nicht im gringsten gefährden
> Dein armes Schiffchen,
>
> . . .
>
> Denn du, Poetlein, hast nie mich erzürnt,
> Du hast kein einziges Türmchen verletzt
> An Priamos' heiliger Feste,
> Kein einziges Härchen hast du versengt
> Am Aug meines Sohns Polyphemos,
> Und dich hat niemals ratend beschützt
> Die Göttin der Klugheit, Pallas Athene;
>
> (B 1: 186)

and in "Fragen," he is again a "fool," helplessly perplexed by the mystery of existence:

> Am Meer, am wüsten, nächtlichen Meer
> Steht ein Jüngling-Mann,
> Die Brust voll Wehmut, das Haupt voll Zweifel,
> Und mit düstern Lippen fragt er die Wogen:
>
> "O löst mir das Rätsel des Lebens,"
>
> . . .
>
> Es murmeln die Wogen ihr ewges Gemurmel,
> Es wehet der Wind, es fliehen die Wolken,
> Es blinken die Sterne, gleichgültig und kalt,
> Und ein Narr wartet auf Antwort. (B 1: 208)

In the end this is also the paradox — the intended paradox — of the *Buch der Lieder* as a whole. The reality of *Buch der Lieder* is a tension between the two narratives I have traced, between poetic impotence and poetic power, between ideality lost and ideality found, between a sense of the demise of Romantic experience in its collision with the material world and a reaffirmation of the validity and potency of a version of Romantic experience. Ambiguity and contradictoriness underlie this poetry, as they underlie much of Heine's work:[11] by the time of *Die Harzreise, Die Nordsee I, II* and *III* and *Ideen. Das Buch Le Grand* this particular contradiction had developed into a theme and a strategy, to be seen as part of the world-dissonance ("große Weltzerrissenheit") that Heine liked to claim he reflected in his own soul (B 2: 215, 405; B 3: 568). But it began, as we have seen, as the fact of contrary tendencies in his artistic disposition, a subtle and unresolved battle between idealist and post-idealist impulses, difficult for the reader both of our own and of Heine's time to grasp, but fundamental to his mind and writing.

Notes

[1] "Unsere Zeit ist rein *materiell.*" Georg Büchner in a letter of June (?) 1836 to Karl Gutzkow (319). See Büchner, *Werke und Briefe. Münchner Ausgabe,* ed. Karl Pörnbacher, Gerhard Schaub, Hans-Joachim Simm, and Edda Ziegler (Munich: Hanser, 1988).

[2] Siegbert Prawer speaks memorably of "grief over the lost simplicity of grief" as the characteristic mood of such poems (37). Prawer's short book *Heine: "Buch der Lieder"* (London: Arnold, 1960) remains the most serviceable survey of the collection.

[3] See Perraudin, *Heinrich Heine: Poetry in Context. A Study of "Buch der Lieder"* (Oxford: Berg, 1989), 46, 72–80, 158.

[4] See also DHA 1: 1074–77, and Perraudin, *Poetry in Context,* 119–31.

[5] Older writing on *Buch der Lieder* was much preoccupied with whether or how this poetry was autobiographical. Notably, Ernst Elster's two editions (vol. 1 of each) reduced it to direct articulations of pain at his rejection by successive cousins. Then William Rose in 1962 produced an influential antidote, purporting — not absolutely credibly — to disprove all the evidence on which such approaches were based (*The Early Love Poetry of Heinrich Heine: An Inquiry into Poetic Inspiration* [Oxford: Clarendon, 1962]). The solution to the matter is as suggested here: Heine himself saw factual amorous rejection as an inspirational basis for his love lyrics, but regarded it as the essentially trivial stimulus for the exercise of great imaginative energy.

[6] See Perraudin, "'Der schöne Heros der früh dahinsinkt. . . .' Poesie, Mythos und Politik in Heines *Die Grenadiere,*" *Interpretationen: Gedichte von Heinrich Heine,* ed. Bernd Kortländer (Stuttgart: Reclam, 1995), 32–50.

[7] In its context in *Buch Le Grand,* this word applies to the figure of Napoleon; but Heine's intention in his text is that the term should also attach analogically to the poet himself.

[8] See Margarita Pazi, "Die biblischen und jüdischen Einflüsse in Heines 'Nordsee-Gedichten,'" *Heine-Jahrbuch* 12 (1973): 3–19, especially 14–15; and Lydia Baer, "Anklaenge an Homer (nach Voss) in der *Nordsee* Heinrich Heines," *Journal of English and Germanic Philology* 29 (1930): 1–17, especially 9–10.

[9] See also the poem "Die Götter Griechenlands" (poem 6 of *Die Nordsee. Zweiter Zyklus*), in which the poet appears momentarily as titan-cum-messiah (B 1: 207).

[10] He repeats it too, in an explicitly political context, in his "Spätere Nachschrift" to *Die Stadt Lucca* — addressing "uns . . . Titanen," who are the agents of the Revolution (B 2: 529).

[11] It seems to me, in particular, that quite similar patterns of contradiction are discernible in the most personal of his later collections of poetry. Thus, the cycle "Verschiedene" in *Neue Gedichte* presents a theoretical glorification of the emancipation of the flesh (especially with the poem "Auf diesem Felsen bauen wir" [B 4: 325]), but combines it with articulations of practical sexual ennui and nausea. And equivalently, the late verse from Heine's "Matratzengruft" presents in the poet's response to the physical sufferings of the end of his life a purposely elusive balance between countervailing moods of embitterment and acquiescence, and skepticism and faith.

Works Cited

Baer, Lydia. "Anklaenge an Homer (nach Voss) in der *Nordsee* Heinrich Heines." *Journal of English and Germanic Philology* 29 (1930): 1–17.

Büchner, Georg. *Werke und Briefe. Münchner Ausgabe*. Ed. Karl Pörnbacher, Gerhard Schaub, Hans-Joachim Simm, and Edda Ziegler. Munich: Hanser, 1988.

Heine, Heinrich. *Sämtliche Werke*. Ed. Ernst Elster. Leipzig: Bibliographisches Institut, 1887–1890. 7 vols.

———. *Werke*. Ed. Ernst Elster. Leipzig: Bibliographisches Institut, 1925. 4 vols. (incomplete).

Mörike, Eduard. *Briefe*. Ed. Werner Zemp. Zurich: Manesse, 1949.

Pazi, Margarita. "Die biblischen und jüdischen Einflüsse in Heines 'Nordsee-Gedichten.'" *Heine-Jahrbuch* 12 (1973): 3–19.

Perraudin, Michael. *Heinrich Heine: Poetry in Context. A Study of "Buch der Lieder."* Oxford: Berg, 1989

———. "'Der schöne Heros, der früh dahinsinkt. . . .' Poesie, Mythos und Politik in Heines *Die Grenadiere*." *Interpretationen. Gedichte von Heinrich Heine*. Ed. Bernd Kortländer. Stuttgart: Reclam, 1995. 32–50.

Prawer, Siegbert. *Heine: "Buch der Lieder."* London: Arnold, 1960.

Rose, William. The Early Love Poetry of *Heinrich Heine: An Inquiry into Poetic Inspiration*. Oxford: Clarendon, 1962.

A Walk on the Wild Side: Heine's Eroticism[1]

Paul Peters

Für S.

I

"SIE LIEBT MICH *NICHT*" (HSA 20:19). Heine's exile is tradition-ally dated from 1831, the year of his move from Germany to Paris. In a certain sense, however, one might almost be tempted to date it from 1816, the year of his move from Düsseldorf to Hamburg. For from that year date the beginnings of his fateful, unrequited love for his cousin Amalie, whose initial yet lasting imprint is faithfully recorded here in Heine's letter to the friend and confidante of his youth, Christian Sethe. And even twelve years later, in Heine's *Buch le Grand,* we read: "Sie war liebenswürdig, und Er liebte Sie. Er war aber nicht liebenswürdig, und Sie liebte Ihn nicht" (DHA 6: 173). For the story, if fateful and enduring in its effects, is nonetheless quickly, almost too quickly told; and of such elemental simplicity as to make it an appropriate linguistic vehicle for the teaching of the sparest rudiments of German grammar: two bald statements, pronouns of the masculine and feminine, cases of the nominative and accusative, of subject and of object. The poor relation Heine, more tolerated than welcome in the home of his millionaire uncle Salomon, never had a chance with his alluring *haute-bourgeoise* cousin, a fact he was soon given unmistakably to feel. In his vicissitudes, he consoled himself, as so many before and after him, with verses: "Aber solltest Du es wohl glauben, die Muse ist mir demohngeachtet lieber als je . . . Ich dichte viel" (HSA 20: 21).

Indeed, it was this experience of jilted and unhappy love that was to make of Heine the poet of the *Buch der Lieder* (1827), to this day his most celebrated work, a book of European impact and reputation, and, throughout the nineteenth century, the lyric companion for several generations of German youth. For if the experience — of unrequited love — was commonplace enough, the poetry was not. And indeed, some subsequent critics have doubted whether the "Amalienerlebnis," as some of Heine's first biographers were to rather extravagantly call it, was even an "experience" at all; and thus, whether the poetry of Heine's most celebrated volume can be said to have arisen from anything really felt or lived (Rose 15). "Den Talmudkommentar dazu her!" as Franz Kafka once exclaimed in a similar Heine context.[2] For the question is indeed as delicate as it is moot, and incapable of resolution. As we immediately shall see, however, it also hangs over, if not the Talmud, then certainly the better part of the classic love poetry of the Western canon; and its real usefulness perhaps consists in confronting us with this fundamental fact. At the same time, it may serve to reveal some unexpected and more hidden dimensions of Heine's "outsider" status, which was to make of him such a searing, telling critic of contemporary society and its mores. For his critique is nowhere more searing and more telling than in his critique of love; a critique which ultimately led Heine to stake out a poetic territory — and unleash forms of imagination and expressiveness — in realms quite beyond the habitual pale of literary convention and middle-class propriety, realms that helped disclose new dimensions of the erotic to the European artistic imagination, and that may, in their brazen violations of sexual-political correctness, indeed still shock today.[3]

What may well have initially impelled Heine into these realms, however, was all that happened between him and his adored upper-middle-class Amalie. Or rather: all that didn't happen. And here we encounter the first instructive difficulty of accounting for the emergence of Heine's distinctive language of love. For his "experience" was indeed, in any commonly understood sense of the term, not an experience at all. The poet's excesses and torments of feeling in fact left their object quite cold, if indeed she was ever more than dimly aware of them; no emotional contact or intimacy of any kind ever ensued between the two, not to mention the fact that the poet's first real erotic-sexual experiences, which presumably took place at this time, were undoubtedly also made elsewhere. In short, "nothing happened": and the critic must first come to terms with the fact that this impalpable, intangible "nothing" stands at the very generative heart of Heine's early poetry, which then so reverberated in the European imagination, and, "on wings of song," around the world.

It is perhaps, however, the very same "nothing" which, in different ways, stands at the heart of most of the great love poetry in the

European tradition; and indeed, not only the European one. For if we examine that tradition more closely, what do we find? "Nothing happened" between Dante and Beatrice, Petrarch and Laura, Shakespeare and the "dark lady" of the sonnets, to name but three of the most imposing and classic paradigms of the love lyric in the Western canon. And even the most imposing and paradigmatic model for Heine's own time — Goethe — is only an apparent exception to the rule. True, Goethe's spontaneous and immediate poetry of feeling stands in many important senses markedly apart from the tradition we have just mentioned, in directly addressing, and indeed, dialoguing with the beloved, being so intimately linked to her individuality and person, as well as to her direct and interlocutive role in the poet's own emotional and personal development. At the same time, it has come to form what readers, and particularly German readers, naturally expect when they hear the words "love poetry." Goethe's "Erlebnislyrik" — poetry rooted in lived, singular, individual experience — came to be the implicit norm by which all subsequent poetry, including Heine's, was judged, and indeed perceived.

Yet, more recent biographers of Goethe have been forced to rather shamefacedly conclude that, in matters erotic, up until the Italian sojourn the actual experiential basis of this poetry is shockingly, even scandalously, slight. That, in other words, "nothing happened" with Frederike, Lily, Charlotte, Marianne, i tutti quanti.[4] Similarly, the remarkable, even heroic efforts of Pierre Bertaux, the biographer of Hölderlin, have led to equally sobering results. Bertaux went to unheard-of lengths to establish that at least one "Liebesnacht," one tryst, one act of physical union must have taken place between the poet and Susette Gontard, the "Diotima" of his poetry (465–72). Bertaux's exertions in this regard have been at least as desperate as any measures undertaken by the man and woman in question — who did, beyond doubt, love each other — and are perhaps doomed to similar frustration. Indeed, in the light of this whole tradition, the fact that Bertolt Brecht wrote love poetry to women with whom he actually slept, may be taken as one further proof of his remarkable originality as a poet.[5] In this context, it could be plausibly asserted that the fact that "nothing happened" might be better understood as a traditional prerequisite for the writing of great love poetry, rather than as that circumstance that would somehow definitively preclude it.

For indeed, as the popular wisdom has it: "nothing happened — and everything happened." And Heine's, like any great poet's, is a very particular form of this "everything" and "nothing." "Ich fühle tiefer, wie andre Menschen," Heine records in a tone of dry and sober self-assessment, in a letter that redounds with genuine amazement at the staggering phenomenon of normalcy, at the capacity of other mortals to so easily overcome their traumas and catastrophes of feeling and simply get on with their lives (HSA 20: 343). For Heine there could be no question of simply going on to the next, perhaps less ill-starred venture, in a type of sexual-political business as usual. The poet rather plunged himself, with monomaniacal fervor, into his torment: "Ich lechze nach ewiger Nacht" (HSA 20: 104).

"Love is intensity," writes Octavio Paz,[6] and the intensity of re-jection is no less than the intensity of fulfillment. Heine's early lyric plumbs this intensity; in it a dread void, a terrifying absence plays the same determining role as does in Goethe an affirming and fulfilling presence. And the scores and scores of lyrics of the *Buch der Lieder,* with their obsessive recurring single theme, are as it were flung into that void, to somehow fill it. It might at first glance be tempting to debunk all of this as a veritable festival of disappointed masculine pro-jection, of self-indulgent narcissism; and to see woman here in her — since Petrarch's, and indeed, since Catullus's day — traditional role as mere *Auslöser,* catalyst, for the male protagonist to explore and culti-vate his own inner world. In other words, if not as the time-honored positive, then as the equally venerable negative "source of inspira-tion," that energizing and dynamizing charge of suffering needed to shape the male subject into a poet; since, as Heine was once tempted to say, "die glückliche Liebe schreibt gar keine Verse" (HSA 21: 246). And undoubtedly, this is all true; but it is perhaps not the most inter-esting or compelling truth. For the fact remains that Heine's early love poetry reverberates with a shock not simply of rejection, but also of cognition. Like all great poetry, the *Buch der Lieder* is pre-eminently a book of revelation: and what it reveals above all are not simply the agonizings of a male protagonist, but some of the deepest mysteries of the female subject.

II

The first of these mysteries is that, paradoxically, the female subject of the *Buch der Lieder* is not, in the habitual sense, a subject at all. For if, as Queen Victoria put it, "Mother was not a person," neither is the female beloved of Heine's poetry. Theodor Adorno once interestingly observed that the fleeting moment of freedom for women in a patriar-chal society is the brief instant when they can still say "no."[7] In a cer-tain sense, Heine's *Buch der Lieder* is a monument to that moment; in

its shock and terror, for the individual male subject, as in its ultimate
fleetingness and untenability, vis-à-vis patriarchal society as a whole.
For truly, the "love object" of Heine's early poetry manifests her subjectivity in the at once most terrifying and convincing way: by inflict-
ing pain. "Und Schlag auf Schlag, und sonder Weil / Summt sie ein
Lied und schwingt das Beil," as we read in the "Traumbilder" (DHA
1.1: 20) — a most unladylike activity! But she manifests this freedom
only in order to better fulfill a chilling program of compulsion: not to
embark on an autonomous program of life or fulfillment, but to simply marry, and thus definitively give her life over to a more socially
and economically established, and therefore alluring and acceptable
male. In that sense, in a truly unhappy triangle, the dominating force
of the *Buch der Lieder* is neither feeling nor desire, but the sheer
power of convention:

> Die Linde blühte, die Nachtigall sang,
> Die Sonne lachte mit freundlicher Lust;
> Da küßtest du mich, und dein Arm mich umschlang,
> Da preßtest du mich an die schwellende Brust.
>
> Die Blätter fielen, der Rabe schrie hohl,
> Die Sonne grüßte verdrossenen Blicks;
> Da sagten wir frostig einander: "Lebwohl!"
> Da knixtest du höflich den höflichsten Knix.
>
> (DHA 1.1: 157)

"Und das Band, das uns verbindet, sei kein schwaches Rosen-
band." It has been well observed how, in Goethe's "Auf einem ge-
malten Band," the lyric successfully breaks through a mere outward
convention to infuse it with authentic feeling and individuality (Goethe 1: 25–26, 424–25). In Heine's lyric, however, the iron reign of
convention remains unbroken, and the female subject is more Pavlov-
ian than Goethean. In that sense, here neither lover nor beloved, but
the curtsey is the "hero" of the poem. Its impersonal and implacable
power will effortlessly break the subjective, human inclinations of both
man and woman, so that the preprogrammed and inalterable agenda
of the bourgeois mating ritual may be inexorably fulfilled. "Du leblo-
ses, verdammtes Automat!" as E. T. A. Hoffmann's Nathanael cries
when he makes a similar discovery about his betrothed Clara in *Der
Sandmann*.[8] And when we read of the beloved in the "Lyrisches Intermezzo," "Und schüttelst das blonde Köpfchen" (DHA 1.1: 189),
we have the uncanny feeling that that lovely blonde head is being

pulled on a string. Indeed, there is a moment of dread discovery in the *Buch der Lieder* not unlike that in certain North American "B" science fiction films and television series. There, the unsuspecting male protagonist goes to embrace some delectable blonde succuba and detects the telltale metallic glint under her scalp, or the green, reptilian scales protruding from beneath her skin, fatally revealing the robot, cyborg, or alien invader. And the "einziger Angstschrey" at this discovery, which Heine once remarked in Hoffmann, also echoes throughout the *Buch der Lieder:*

> Liebste, sollst mir heute sagen:
> Bist du nicht ein Traumgebild',
> Wie's in schwülen Sommertagen
> Aus dem Hirn des Dichters quillt?

> Aber nein, ein solches Mündchen,
> Solcher Augen Zauberlicht,
> Solch ein liebes, süßes Kindchen,
> Das erschafft der Dichter nicht.

> Basilisken und Vampyre,
> Lindenwürm' und Ungeheu'r,
> Solche schlimme Fabelthiere,
> Die erschafft des Dichters Feu'r.

> Aber dich und deine Tücke,
> Und dein holdes Angesicht,
> Und die falschen frommen Blicke —
> Das erschafft der Dichter nicht.
> (DHA 1.1: 149)

The *Bürgertochter* as succuba — that is the primal shock, and, as it were, the "primal scream" of Heine's *Buch der Lieder:* it is, however, also a shock and scream at the discovery of another, unheard-of form of subject.

III

A further double-edged and paradoxical discovery of the female subject in the *Buch der Lieder* is that of feminine sensuality; double-edged and paradoxical in that the exhilarating *promesse de bonheur* emanating from it is at once proffered and withheld: the revelation of sexuality, of the Paradisiacal forbidden fruit, is thus simultaneous with the revelation of all the prohibitions and taboos, of the complex and ultimately — within conventional bourgeois society — impenetrable system of rules and signs regulating it. Riveted, transfixed, fascinated by female corporeality, the male persona of Heine's lyric will embark on the vain effort to unravel these baffling and deceptive signs, still in the hope and expectation of fulfillment;[9] their decoding will, however, demonstrate that, for him, there is in fact to be no fulfillment at all within the existing system. For it finally and cruelly shows itself to be a system of renunciation and deferment, of endless canalizations, banishments, constraints, and sublimations.

And characteristic for Heine, even at this early stage, is his utter refusal of this system; a refusal that marks a perilous, yet resolute heterodoxy of the poetic subject both within society as a whole, and within the dominant literary tradition. Indeed, Heine's path remains the obverse of the successful, "well-adjusted" path of socialization, be it in poetry or life: namely, acceptance of the system of renunciation and deferment, or of what Herbert Marcuse once called "affirmative culture" (56–101). This is nowhere more evident than in the fact that Heine, in his poetry, refuses that very task which affirmative culture, and its classic paradigm in this instance, Petrarch, would have demanded of him: namely to, in Freud's words, "sublimate," and to use his lyric as a medium to refine and overcome his "base" sensual desires, to purify and transform them into feats of an ideal love, of intellect and culture.[10] With an epigrammatic shrug — self-censoriously suppressed in the contemporary editions of the *Buch der Lieder* — Heine cheekily dismisses this entire cultural legacy with a single memorable quatrain:

> Himmlisch war's, wenn ich bezwang
> Meine sündige Begier,
> Aber wenn es mir nicht gelang,
> So hatt' ich doch ein groß Plaisir.
> (DHA 1.1: 485)

Heine's emphatic rejection of the whole "sublimating," "spiritualizing," and "soulful" tradition in love is further immortalized in lines he addresses directly to the beloved, lines he later also deemed too *risqué* for the "tugendhafte Ausgabe" of his early poetry. Even today they retain something of their sting:

> Ich kann es nicht vergessen,
> Geliebtes, holdes Weib,
> Daß ich dich einst besessen,
> Die Seele und den Leib.

Den Leib möcht' ich noch haben,
Den Leib so zart und jung;
Die Seele könnt Ihr begraben,
Hab' selber Seele genung.

Ich will meine Seele zerschneiden,
Und hauche die Hälfte dir ein,
Und will dich umschlingen, wir müssen
Ganz Leib und Seele seyn. (DHA 1.1: 462)

Heine recoils before the revealed "soul" of woman and *Bürgertochter;*
her body, however, continues to fascinate him. He loves "Woman,"
not as person, but as sheer corporeality, a love that will only deepen,
also in its capacity to provoke, throughout his poetic career. Indeed,
though Heine may use his poetry to refine his sensuality, he will never
do so to officially renounce or "overcome" it: in fact, poetry becomes — in a singular affront to the whole affirmative and Petrarchan
tradition — the very medium through which the claims of sensuality
are to be upheld. Caught between two breathtaking disclosures —
that of sexuality and the female body, and the particular use to which
bourgeois society then puts them — Heine's fundamental loyalty will
always be to the first, and not the second discovery: the discovery of
the fruit, rather than its prohibition.

This primordial decision condemns the poet to a perpetual outsider status. He is not alone, however, but finds himself in his powerlessness and exclusion in some rather interesting company. For like
him, sensuality and authentic feeling too are the outcasts of bourgeois
society, doomed to a shadowy existence on its fringes — unseen, unspoken, the uninvited, if ubiquitous and unwanted guests at its decorous table. As in the unforgettable vignette:

Sie saßen und tranken am Theetisch,
Und sprachen von Liebe viel.
Die Herren, die waren ästhetisch,
Die Damen von zartem Gefühl.

Die Liebe muß seyn platonisch,
Der dürre Hofrath sprach.
Die Hofräthin lächelt ironisch,
Und dennoch seufzet sie: Ach!

Der Domherr öffnet den Mund weit:
Die Liebe sey nicht zu roh,
Sie schadet sonst der Gesundheit.
Das Fräulein lispelt: wie so?

Die Gräfin spricht wehmütig:
Die Liebe ist eine Passion!
Und präsentiret gütig
Die Tasse dem Herren Baron.

Am Tische war noch ein Plätzchen;
Mein Liebchen, da hast du gefehlt.
Du hättest so hübsch, mein Schätzchen,
Von deiner Liebe erzählt. (DHA 1.1: 183)

Cant, appearances, *sous-entendre, Doppelmoral,* and, above all, sexual misery mark the company that the beloved too is soon to keep: if Heine is among the first to use the theatrical term "Charaktermaske" for a social setting, then it is only as such masks, as pure social titles and functions, that the *personae* are here allowed to interact. At the same time, Freud's unspeakable, forbidden "Es" is already palpably lurking behind all of what they say, and forms, in a certain sense, the single underlying theme of conversation. Here, though, in this "dialogue" of male and female, in every instance it is the often mute, unspoken female action and reaction that reveals the hidden truth. Thus, the involuntary sigh and ironic smile of the Hofrätin is a devastating counterpoint to the disquisition of the Hofrat on the merits of the platonic, the well-nigh "official" discourse on love in the nineteenth century, the age of Victoria and Biedermeier. The Domherr's all-too-emphatic statement about the possible crude excesses of love, and their potential menace to health, is a corresponding reference to the dark side of sexual underworlds quite incomprehensible to the still wide-eyed and clueless Fräulein; while the ceremonious presentation of the teacup by the Baronin is the admission of a doomed, secret passion for the Graf. It is this company to which the beloved too is soon to be admitted, presumably to then participate in their chorus of hypocrisy and frustration.

It is not a chorus that the poet himself is about to join. As he was the first to admit, Heine was later to plunge himself into many rather quixotic ventures, which pitted him against some vast, forbidding powers: the opposition to Prussia and the Restoration, for example, or to the rise of German nationalism. But no venture is perhaps more quixotic than the enterprise in which the poetic persona of the *Buch der Lieder* is engaged: the quest for sensual fulfillment on the hostile terrain of conventional society. If it is not quite like drawing water from a stone, then it is certainly reminiscent of the extraction, in the middle of the desert, of one or two drops of water from a cactus by some parched and expiring traveler. At first glance, the straitlaced Biedermeier is certainly no school of *voluptatis,* or a natural habitat for sybarites: "Besaß eine schöne Seele gewiß / Doch war das Fleisch sehr zähe" (DHA 4: 112). But like those animals and organisms that have adapted to the harsh conditions of the desert landscape, and can actually draw their sustenance from it, the poet too makes an extraordinary, if temporary, adjustment to his inhospitable surroundings. And if, according to a standard pedagogical precept of the period, hardship molds character, then this period of denial served paradoxically only to further mold, form, and deepen Heine's inveterately sensualist nature:

> Jedes Weib ist mir eine geschenkte Welt, ich schwelge in den Melodien ihres Antlitzes, und mit einem einzigen Blick meines Auges kann ich mehr genießen als Andre, mit ihren sämmtlichen Gliedmassen, Zeit ihres Lebens. (DHA 6: 176)

Here, as so often for Heine, the paucity of fulfillment is thus at least momentarily more than made up for by a corresponding intensity, when it does occur. And this circumstance, as well as the underlying tension of lust and sentiment, of body and soul, in the *Buch der Lieder,* is perhaps nowhere better illustrated than in the metamorphoses of that singular meeting of feeling and desire, in the career of the kiss:

> Ich will meine Seele tauchen
> In den Kelch der Lilje hinein;
> Die Lilje soll klingend hauchen
> Ein Lied von der Liebsten mein.
>
> Das Lied soll schauern und beben,
> Wie der Kuß von ihrem Mund',
> Den sie mir einst gegeben
> In wunderbar süßer Stund'.
> (DHA 1.1: 139)

In this poem, positioned at an early and precarious stage of the "Lyrisches Intermezzo," the kiss still seems all that which, according to the ideology of love, it is supposed to be: the seal of inwardness, of spiritual and physical union, of emotional and corporeal harmony: the very fleeting moment of fulfillment. But its quick passing will instantly predominate over its brief joy. For soon, too soon, the grand disillusionment comes: a disillusionment, though, with the soul of the beloved — and not the body.

For if the soul betrays, might not the body yet keep its part of the kiss's promise? Much like a guerilla fighter, who knows he cannot win a conventional military confrontation, but engages in a series of countless raids and ambushes to manifest his continuing resistance, the poetic persona of Heine's *Buch der Lieder* clings to the kiss as a type of defiant guerilla action. He still desperately holds out in the war of the body, where he has long since lost the battle of the soul:

> O schwöre nicht und küsse nur,
> Ich glaube keinem Weiberschwur!
> Dein Wort ist süß, doch süßer ist
> Der Kuß, den ich dir abgeküßt!
> (DHA 1.1: 145)

Or in the poem that follows:

> Die Welt ist dumm, die Welt ist blind.
> Wird täglich abgeschmackter!
> Sie spricht von dir, mein schönes Kind,
> Du hast keinen guten Charakter.
>
> Die Welt ist dumm, die Welt ist blind.
> Und dich wird sie immer verkennen;
> Sie weiß nicht wie süß deine Küsse sind,
> Und wie sie beseligend brennen.
> (DHA 1.1: 147)

Unlike the world, the poet is undeceived by the beloved: not because the world's assessment of her soul was in any sense mistaken, but because he has, nonetheless, and, as it were, miraculously extracted from her love's real and lasting revelation: the sensual promise of her body. Rarely, by the way, has the corporeal, the acoustic base of a poem been so fused with its abstract meaning: the text initially denies us "poesy," the pleasure, the fulfillment of lush sound and rhyme, through its harsh discordant clash of "abgeschmackter" and "Charakter." The "prose of life," indeed! This prosaic triumph is then, however, unexpectedly reversed with the delicious, delectably ambiguous rhyme on "verkennen," at a later stage then even alliteratively heightened by the poet.[11] It is as if the lost soul of the beloved has been wondrously recovered in her body — and the elixir of poesy and sensuality somehow drawn forth from the thorns and thickets of conventional society.

If this redemption takes place against all odds and in extremis, such miraculous resurrections take on, in some later moments of the "Intermezzo," an even more drastic form. For if the language of gallantry knows *la petite mort,* Heine will, through the overwhelmingly negative amorous constellation governing the *Buch der Lieder,* be compelled to give this metaphor a decidedly new twist. And from the very start, commencing with the sepulchral "Traumbilder," his male protagonist must go through a hundred-fold *petite mort* not of erotic fulfillment, but of erotic rejection, appropriately symbolized through the superabundant imagery of the tomb.[12] He will somehow survive them all, however, to be ultimately reunited with his beloved when she too has "gone the way of all flesh":

> Mein süßes Lieb, wenn du im Grab,
> Im dunklen Grab wirst liegen,
> Dann will ich steigen zu dir hinab,
> Und will mich an dich schmiegen.
>
> Ich küsse, umschlinge und presse dich wild,
> Du Stille, du Kalte, du Bleiche!
> Ich jauchze, ich zitt're, ich weine mild,
> Ich werde selber zur Leiche.
>
> Die Todten stehn auf, die Mitternacht ruft,
> Sie tanzen im luftigen Schwarme;
> Wir beide bleiben in der Gruft,
> Ich liege in deinem Arme.
>
> Die Todten stehn auf, der Tag des Gerichts
> Ruft sie zu Qual und Vergnügen;
> Wir beide bekümmern uns um nichts,
> Und bleiben umschlungen liegen.
>
> (DHA 1.1: 163–65)

"Body and soul": the grave is here less the fearsome repository of the departed or the transcendent gateway of the immortal spirit than the secret passage to a longed-for other life where the poet, disencumbered of society and its strictures, finally has free, untrammeled access to the beloved's adored physis, to her ever enticing "earthly remains." Death is here less of an obstacle than convention, as the poet unhesitatingly "robs the grave" of bourgeois sexuality.

This necrophilic beyond is however not the only sexual underworld available to the protagonist of the *Buch der Lieder*. He will have recourse to another, more readily accessible, if no less forbidding than the grave: the world of prostitution. This integral if unmentionable part of many a young man's "sentimental education" in the nineteenth century also hovers furtively at the edges of that "book of songs" routinely given to the German youth of the period as a confirmation or engagement present. In his description of contemporary London in the *Reisebilder*, Heine describes the scene:

> Nur hie und da, am Eingange eines dunklen Gäßchens, steht schweigend ein zersetztes Weib. . . . Die Armuth in Gesellschaft des Lasters und des Verbrechens schleicht erst des Abends aus ihren Schlupfwinkeln. . . . Arme Armuth! wie peinigend muß dein Hunger seyn, dort wo Andere im höhnenden Ueberfluße schwelgen! . . . Wohl hast du Recht, wenn du dich zu dem Laster und dem Verbrechen gesellst. Ausgestoßene Verbrecher tragen oft mehr Menschlichkeit im Herzen, als jene kühlen, untadelhaften Staatsbürger der Tugend, in deren bleichen Herzen die Kraft des Bösen erloschen ist, aber auch die Kraft des Guten. Und gar das Laster ist nicht immer Laster. Ich habe Weiber gesehen, auf deren Wangen das rothe Laster gemalt war und in ihrem Herzen wohnte himmlische Reinheit. Ich habe Weiber gesehen — ich wollt ich sähe sie wieder! (DHA 7.1: 217–18)

This culminates, in the original version of the "Heimkehr," in the most notorious of its suppressed quatrains:

> Blamir' mich nicht, mein schönes Kind,
> Und grüß' mich nicht unter den Linden;
> Wenn wir nachher zu Hause sind,
> Wird sich schon Alles finden. (DHA 1.1: 485)

The scabrous poem marked the trajectory that Heine was to take in his Parisian period, in life as well as poetry: the path to the *grisettes* and the *demimondaines*. Again, it is perhaps useful to recall how this development embodies the very inverse of the characteristic course of "successful" male socialization for Heine's class and period: in youth, an ephemeral sexual initiation through prostitution, followed in maturity by the lasting emotional and institutional matrimonial bond to the wife and mother of one's children. Instead, through the dynamics of mutual repulsion obtaining between himself and conventional society, Heine was impelled along a course that increasingly took him from what Marilyn French has termed the "in-law," the domesticated, safe, "good," wife-and-mother side of femininity, to the "outlaw," or wild, uncontrolled, unbounded, sensuous and threatening side (23–24). The effects on his erotic imagination were incalculable.

IV

In 1839, already established in Paris, but called upon to write a preface to his youthful work *Buch der Lieder,* Heine authored a remarkable poem that not only links the love poetry of his earlier with the frank eroticism of his later period, but perhaps sums up what was indeed for him the ultimate revelation of the feminine. It is a poem on the sphinx-like character of woman:

> Dort vor dem Thor lag ein Sphynx,
> Ein Zwitter von Schrecken und Lüsten,
> Der Leib und die Tatzen wie ein Löw',
> Ein Weib an Haupt und Brüsten.
>
> Ein schönes Weib! Der weiße Blick,
> Er sprach von wildem Begehren;
> Die stummen Lippen wölbten sich
> Und lächelten stilles Gewähren.
>
> Die Nachtigall, sie sang so süß —
> Ich konnt nicht widerstehen —
> Und als ich küßte das holde Gesicht,
> Da war's um mich geschehen.
>
> Lebendig ward das Marmorbild,
> Der Stein begann zu ächzen —
> Sie trank meiner Küsse lodernde Glut,
> Mit Dürsten und mit Lechzen.
>
> Sie trank mir fast den Odem aus —
> Und endlich, wollustheischend,
> Umschlang sie mich, meinen armen Leib
> Mit den Löwentatzen zerfleischend.
>
> Entzückende Marter und wonniges Weh!
> Der Schmerz wie die Lust unermeßlich!
> Derweilen des Mundes Kuß mich beglückt,
> Verwunden die Tatzen mich gräßlich.

Die Nachtigall sang: "O schöne Sphynx!
O Liebe! was soll es bedeuten,
Daß du vermischest mit Todesqual
All' deine Seligkeiten?

"O schöne Sphynx! O löse mir
Das Räthsel, das wunderbare!
Ich hab' darüber nachgedacht
Schon manche tausend Jahre."

(DHA 1.1: 11–13)

For the ultimate shock of the female and the feminine may reside in depths that can only be accessed by peeling back the established regulatory norms that govern and canalize, tame, "domesticate," and bind them, and thus shield us from their power.

Heine was to resolutely engage himself in the peeling away of all such norms: be they the norms of the "person" and the "soul," of idealized love and matrimony, of the taboos and strictures governing the practice of sexuality and sensuality. What this opened him up to in his poetry was the as it were "unprotected," unsafe encounter not simply with woman as slippery, elusive, and dangerous prey in the "game of love," nor even with woman as the source and goal of sexual desire, who in turn rendered Heine's male protagonist into her captive and tormented object. Rather it set free woman in his poetry as a type of lasting "metaphysical" shock of pure alterity, of radical difference, a difference, however, that he is as impelled to incorporate as he is to be incorporated by it. The philosopher Hegel summed up this metaphysical shock of love by pointing out that the very fulfillment of the subject — in the attainment of his erotic wish — must mean his death, the end of all he was before.[13] Freud too repeatedly emphasized the ontological revolution it signified in the life of each human being to so drastically admit another into the sphere of physical and psychic intimacy. Indeed, perhaps it is the Freudian interpretation of the "Medusenhaupt," as the riveted male gaze upon the sheer otherness of woman, that also best accounts for Heine's "Sphinx":[14] a sphinx before which the poet does not simply recoil or stand paralyzed, however, but to which he is constantly and irresistibly drawn.

V

In a letter written in halting but eloquent French not many years after his arrival in Paris, Heine, staying on the French coast, recorded the strange effects of the shipwreck of a British vessel carrying condemned prostitutes off to deportation in Australia:

> C'étoient presque toutes des jeunes créatures condamnées à la De-portation, pour mauvais moeurs, et parmi lesquelles il-y-en avoient d'une rare beauté. J'ai vu une femme sortir de l'écume de la mer, qui étoit une veritable Aphrodite, mais une Aphrodite morte. Ces pau-vres malheureuses, avant de mourir, elles avoient passé deux long heures entières dans l'angoise la plus horrible. Leurs cris percoient le bruit de l'orage. Lorsqu'elles ne voyoient pas venir du secours, beau-coup d'entre elles se desabilloient pour se sauver à la nage; mais la mer fut aussi impitoyable que la Legislation de l'Angleterre, elle ne leur fit pas grâce, et les immolat froidement. (HSA 21: 64)

> [They were almost all young creatures condemned to deportation for bad morals, and among whom there were some of a rare beauty. I saw a woman rising from the foam who was a true Aphrodite, but a dead Aphrodite. Before dying, these poor unfortunates spent two whole hours in the most horrible anguish. Their cries pierced the roar of the storm. When they saw that no help was coming, many of them un-dressed in the attempt to save themselves by swimming; but the sea proved as pitiless as the English legislature, it showed them no mercy, and sacrificed them coldly.[15]]

The letter speaks volumes, not only about Heine's sympathies for these social outcasts, but also for the role of the feminine in his imagi-nation: the messengers of other worlds, of the night, the unbounded sea, shipwreck, death, and the mysterious beyond, are the floating bodies of beautiful, illicit women.

It is equally characteristic that these fascinating women are, if not quite faceless, then anonymous and nameless. For despite all the things that woman is, what she nevertheless is not — and here Heine and Queen Victoria agree — is a person. In speaking about Heine, the prominent German critic Marcel Reich-Ranicki once made the inter-esting observation that, unlike almost all other great poets of love in world literature, it is, with few exceptions, quite impossible to biographi-cally determine the identity of the woman, sexual partner or beloved, about whom Heine is speaking in any given poem; Reich-Ranicki at-tributed this circumstance to a quality one does not always spontane-ously associate with Heine: his perfect gentlemanliness! (18). It may perhaps be more plausibly attributed to the fact that — much as strong female personalities, such as Rahel Varnhagen and George Sand, al-ways intrigued Heine — in the areas of eros and poetic fantasy, women existed for him as a transpersonal, amoral sexual power. They thus were a source of countless daring archetypes and *imagines* of an arresting and compelling alterity that broke all bounds of convention.

In a revealing letter, Heine writes to Karl August Varnhagen von Ense about Frederike Robert, a very striking and spirited Jewess and mentor of one of Berlin's leading salons: he pays the usual comple-ments to her intellect, to then significantly add: corresponding with a beautiful woman is like writing letters to a *pâté de foie:*

> Unter uns gesagt, einer schönen Frau schreiben scheint mir eben so thörigt als wenn ich mit einer straßburger Pastete in Correspondenz treten wollte. Jedes Ding in der Welt will auf seine eigne Weise ge-nossen seyn. Jene schönen Augen deren Glanz unser Herz erfreut, und jene Trüffelpastete deren Duft uns begeistert — sie verlieren gar sehr in der Ferne. (HSA 20: 287)

In so demonstratively saying this, Heine is also, as a poet, and a poet of love, unmistakably demarcating his poetic territory.[16] For as a poet, he is simply not interested in the personhood of woman; he is inter-ested in the "Trüffelpastete." And there can be no doubt that this stands in such flagrant apparent contradiction to his overall program of emancipation as to give pause to all who hold that program dear.[17] Indeed, this "facelessness" of woman in Heine is such a monstrous and profound disfigurement that his erotic poetry can often arouse in us a similar unease and discomfiture as the sight of the Sphinx or the Medusa: "Die Gestalt der wahren Sphinx / Weicht nicht ab von der des Weibes" (DHA 3.1: 203). But that is its very purpose. Heine's greatness as an erotic poet stems in large measure from this terrible act of effacement and limitation.

For woman as personality — in the singularity, forcefulness, or depth of her individual psyche, is certainly an elemental and primal force in much love poetry, including, of course, the canonical love po-etry of Goethe: but for Heine, for that very reason, she would only be a fatal encumbrance. And in this, as in so much, Heine is the exact counterpoint to his Weimar *Übervater:* for we have already seen how the warm, affirming presence of the beloved's person in Goethe be-came, for the early Heine, chilling absence and negation; and the later Heine extrapolates this absence, this de-personalization, into unprece-dented dimensions. This is because in the conflict of Eros and Sexus, to which Walter Benjamin once alludes (1: 648), Heine consistently opts for the latter: not the play of personality in love, but the elemen-tal play of suprapersonal, libidinous, and archetypal forces. That makes of woman's personhood for Heine something like the restraining seal on a veritable Pandora's box, enclosing all the teeming sexual and imaginary energies associated with the feminine. To free those energies, Heine breaks the seal of personhood. And all those volatile, incalculable energies are then explosively released.

Indeed, the force of this explosion is such as to radically put in question received notions of subject and object, of fulfillment or pain, affirmation and negation, as well as all our notions of that which might denigrate or heighten, affirm or negate, empower or disempower the female and the feminine. For the inherited, sententious discourse of respect and admiration for woman as person is also a repressive and confining one. It affords woman an official "honored" place in the predominantly male world at the cost of her straitening and domestication; and Heine's suspension of this discourse is also the suspension of such gilded confinement. Heine's women are not nice; and, as every woman knows, female self-assertion in whatever sphere most often begins with the end of niceness. Two poems, both of them pointedly devoted to "Weib" and not "Frau" — as it were, "woman," not "lady" — may be cited to illustrate this far-reaching confusion of signs:

> Du sollst mich liebend umschließen,
> Geliebtes, schönes Weib!
> Umschling' mich mit Armen und Füßen,
> Und mit dem geschmeidigen Leib.
>
> *   *   *
>
> Gewaltig hat umfangen,
> Umwunden, umschlungen schon,
> Die allerschönste der Schlangen
> Den glücklichsten Laokoon. (DHA 1.1: 461)

Interestingly enough, this poem was also considered by its author to be of too strong stuff to find its place in the official version of his *Buch der Lieder*. In it, woman as pure body — one need only point to the rhyme of "Leib" and "Weib" — instantaneously undergoes an even more shocking metamorphosis: that from sexual object into sexual subject. She then threatens, in classic fulfillment of the age-old male anxiety about female sexual prowess and insatiability, to fatally entwine and crush the male protagonist. "Lebendig ward das Marmorbild / Der Stein begann zu ächzen —"; as in the "Sphinx" poem, the petrification and fixation of woman by the desirous male gaze is but the prelude to her rebirth as an all-consuming sexual creature, threatening to crush the poet.

And yet, in a further deepening of the confusion of signs, he willingly, even ecstatically accedes to this embrace. The invocation of the Laocoon legend from Virgil is another striking example of how, in this instance, the inherited order of things is stood on its head through the power of eros. For the original Virgilian scene — also celebrated because of its privileged position in German aesthetics in the writings of Winckelmann and Lessing — was regarded, in poetry as in sculpture, as the classic depiction of agony, of physical pain and anguish.[18] Yet here it is a veritable mimesis of passion, an image of the sheer physical ambiguity and transport of the sexual embrace, and as such, the acme of fulfillment. And it is woman as shape-shifter, as polyvalent serpent — the snakes of the Laocoon legend, the snakes of the "Medusenhaupt," but also and above all the serpent of Eve, the seductive snake of the Garden of Eden — who is at its source. For here, the wrenching, irresistible embrace of Eve is indeed the symbol of disaster; but a disaster of delight, of pleasure and ecstatic transport, and as such, in a turn which Heine will later make explicit, a token less of the Fall than of the readmission into paradise. The "snake" is "beautiful."

Similarly, in the first poem of the Parisian cycle "Romanzen," the reader is also immediately taken to the perilous frontier marking the end of woman's domesticated, sanctioned status, and the beginning of her wild and "outlaw" being:

> Sie hatten sich beide so herzlich lieb,
> Spitzbübin war sie, er war ein Dieb.
> Wenn er Schelmenstreiche machte,
> So warf sie sich auf's Bett und lachte.
>
> Der Tag verging in Freud und Lust,
> Des Nachts lag sie an seiner Brust
> Als man ihn in's Gefängnis brachte,
> Sie stand am Fenster und lachte.
>
> Er ließ ihr sagen: O komm zu mir,
> Ich sehne mich so sehr nach dir,
> Ich rufe nach dir, ich schmachte —
> Sie schüttelt' das Haupt und lachte.
>
> Um sechse des Morgens ward er gehenkt,
> Um sieben ward er in's Grab gesenkt;
> Sie aber schon um achte
> Trank rothen Wein und lachte. (DHA 2: 75)

In this poem of two outlaws, the woman is significantly more "outlaw" than the man: and his roguery only serves to demonstrate to what remarkable degree her roguery exceeds his. For if the long arm of the law reaches him, she remains utterly beyond its grasp. This law, however, is not simply the criminal code; instead, it may be fairly taken to be the law of patriarchy itself. "Der Tag verging in Freud und Lust" — and this would seem to be the most evident transgression of the couple: that they live entirely for the day, for their transitory, spontaneous pleasures, and not by the code of work, deferment, or prescribed morality.

The man, though, ultimately remains entrapped in the patriarchal code. For the law takes double hold of him: firstly, of course, through his imprisonment and execution; but secondly, by having him make a last appeal from the jailer's cell to the fealty of his companion. This appeal, however, clad in all the ritual pathos and rhetoric of love, is nonetheless one for abandonment of her inmost law — carefree and autonomous pleasure — to one of duty, fidelity, and, in the final analysis, subjugation and compulsion. "Was wir Mädchen alles sollen!" as Brecht has his heroine Jenny say at a similar decisive moment in *Mahagonny,* when she too is dramatically summoned to stand by her man (373). At such a juncture, where loyalty and subjection to the male will, and be it an "outlaw" will, are imperiously demanded of her, Heine's rogue woman can, for her part, only laugh. For she — as natural body, sheer impulsiveness, lust, enjoyment — is well beyond the bounds and limits of all male discourse, as all male law. In this way, a poem traditionally taken to be "misogynist" in its depiction of the amorality of woman may well support a diametrically opposite reading:[19] as an affirmation, an ode, a celebration of the anarchic, irrepressible difference of the feminine in the face of all patriarchal codes. After all, woman here embodies the law of freedom and life-giving forces, whereas the patriarchal law, which even her outlaw mate, in all his desperation, cannot escape, is one of constraint, confinement, and, ultimately, death.

VI

> Es war ein alter König,
> Sein Herz war schwer, sein Haupt war grau;
> Der arme alte König,
> Er nahm eine junge Frau.

Es war ein schöner Page,
Blond war sein Haupt, leicht war sein Sinn;
Er trug die seidne Schleppe
Der jungen Königinn.

Kennst du das alte Liedchen?
Es klingt so süß, es klingt so trüb!
Sie mußten beide sterben,
Sie hatten sich viel zu lieb. (DHA 2: 23–24)

In his essay on *La llama doble,* Octavio Paz has emphasized that in its classic manifestations, love and eros are always rupture and transgression, a perilous violation and subversion of the social order. For they break all rules, and accept none of the established constraints or strictures of society; rather, they question and destabilize not only mores of morality or decorum, but attack the very roots of the social hierarchy itself. Love, which enslaves, itself is free, and can be given only by volition: as such, it imposes its own system of mastery and subjugation as a type of "parallel power," a countervailing force to the existing order of the world; a kind of fiercely democratizing logic from which even empresses and kings are not exempt.[20] In the poetry of the "plebian" Heine, this power of love to overthrow, however momentarily, the order of the world, constitutes one of its greatest and most abiding fascinations. In his ballad of the *Ritter Olaf,* the account of this deadly and delectable transgression assumes almost cosmological proportions: the ephemeral "overpowering" of the world through love becomes the very redeeming quality of existence. In this poem, as so often, Heine conjoins forbidden sexual union and death, as the holy institute of matrimony paradoxically becomes the tie that links the two indissolubly together. Ritter Olaf has deflowered the king's daughter; he must first marry her to restore her honor, to then, as punishment for having violated it, be executed immediately thereafter:

Herr Olaf es ist Mitternacht,
Dein Leben ist verflossen!
Du hattest eines Fürstenkinds
In freyer Lust genossen. (DHA 2: 84)

In the moment before his execution, as he takes his leave from the world, the hero pronounces this unexpected paean to Creation:

"Ich segne die Sonne, ich segne den Mond,
Und die Stern', die am Himmel schweifen.
Ich segne auch die Vögelein,
Die in den Lüften pfeifen.

Ich segne das Meer, ich segne das Land
Und die Blumen auf der Aue.
Ich segne die Veilchen, sie sind so sanft
Wie die Augen meiner Fraue.

Ihr Veilchenaugen meiner Frau,
Durch euch verlier' ich mein Leben!
Ich segne auch den Holunderbaum,
Wo du dich mir ergeben." (DHA 2: 84)

This last speech only assumes its full meaning when viewed in polemical dialogue with another, more celebrated *Segensspruch* over all Creation, the "Lied des Türmers" from Goethe's *Faust:*

Zum Sehen geboren,
Zum Schauen bestellt,
Dem Turme geschworen,
Gefällt mir die Welt.
Ich blick' in die Ferne,
Ich seh' in der Näh'
Den Mond und die Sterne,
Den Wald und das Reh.
So seh' ich in allen
Die ewige Zier,
Und wie mir's gefallen,
Gefall' ich auch mir.
Ihr glücklichen Augen,
Was je ihr gesehen,
Es sei wie es wolle,
Es war doch so schön! (3: 340)

Through the mouth of his character Lynkeus, the patrician and *Dichterfürst* Goethe would seem to be speaking his contented retrospective blessing of Creation as his assured and rightful possession. Characteristically, it appears to him only as Nature, upon which he casts a benign and grateful gaze of pure and serene contemplation, his only apparent wish being to assure that his song disturb as little as possible its eternal, decorous order. But in Heine, Creation and the Cosmos are not an assured, but a forbidden fruit, watched over by a vigilant and despotic social system. And they are to be enjoyed only through dangerous acts of transgression, rendered all the more intense and thrilling by their fleetingness and daring. The preeminent incarnation of such ultimate earthly enjoyment, "der berauschendste Lebensgenuß," is, however, eros:

> Täglich ging die wunderschöne
> Sultanstochter auf und nieder
> Um die Abendzeit am Springbrunn,
> Wo die weißen Wasser plätschern.
>
> Täglich stand der junge Sklave
> Um die Abendzeit am Springbrunn,
> Wo die weißen Wasser plätschern;
> Täglich ward er bleich und bleicher.
>
> Eines Abends trat die Fürstin
> Auf ihn zu mit raschen Worten:
> Deinen Namen will ich wissen,
> Deine Heimath, deine Sippschaft!
>
> Und der Sklave sprach: ich heiße
> Mohamet, ich bin aus Yemmen,
> Und mein Stamm sind jene Asra,
> Welche sterben wenn sie lieben.
>   ("Der Asra"; DHA 3.1: 41–42)

Mohamet — here the prophetic medium of the divine law of love and desire — is doubly enslaved by the sight of the Sultan's daughter. The enjambement at "wunderschön" is expressive of this fateful split and doubling in the nature of his absolute submission. Yet, she, for all her exponential power over him, is also caught up in the play of eros, the sudden swings and role reversals of domination and submission. Her preemptory address to the slave is thus symbolic both of power and of powerlessness, of an imperious capitulation. For now she must know, and what she must know is the great and single question of love — the "¿Quién eres?" "Who are you?" of which Paz writes.[21] And so she demands of him his name and identity. In disclosing it, as he must, the Asra at the same time reveals his fate, which is also hers; for when he dies, she too will perish, will wither and pine of love and its mysterious, incurable affliction. No crowned head is safe from its ineluctable power; and if the royal metaphor is the symbolic heightening of all the "splendor and misery," all the grandeur and limitations of earthly, human existence, it cannot surprise that the plebian poet Heine has a particular fondness for the royal metaphor in love:

> Verstummt sind Pauken, Posaunen und Zinken.
> An Salomos Lager Wache halten
> Die schwertgegürteten Engelgestalten,
> Sechstausend zur Rechten, sechstausend zur Linken.
>
> Sie schützen den König vor träumendem Leide,
> Und er zieht finster die Brauen zusammen,
> Da fahren sogleich die stählernen Flammen,
> Zwölftausend Schwerter, hervor aus der Scheide.
>
> Doch wieder zurück in die Scheide fallen
> Die Schwerter der Engel. Das nächtliche Grauen
> Verschwindet, es glätten sich wieder die Brauen
> Des Schläfers, und seine Lippen lallen:
>
> O Sulamith! das Reich ist mein Erbe,
> Die Lande sind mir unterthänig,
> Bin über Juda und Israel König —
> Doch liebst du mich nicht, so welk' ich und sterbe.
>
> ("Salomo"; DIIA 3.1: 112)

Solomon, greatest king of the Judaic tradition, resplendent and un-surpassed in power, wealth, and wisdom, is helpless before Sulamith and his own passion, from which not even his host of guardian angels can protect him. His desperate outcry is at the same time the call of love's egalitarian and democratizing triumph. Before its leveling pow-ers, as before death itself, all mortals are shown to be equal, and equally susceptible. That is the revenge of love on the social order, a vengeance Heine is only too happy to exact.

VII

That the prime locale of such forays of eros against the established so-cial order should be Paris, in those instances where Heine chooses to adopt a contemporary setting, is, of course, anything but mere bio-graphical happenstance. For Paris, often called the capital of the nine-teenth century was the metropolis not only of politics, art, society, and literature, but also of sin.[22] And the first act of Heine as a Parisian poet would indeed be to articulate his own highly original poetic contribution to the myth of Paris as the Sodom of the nineteenth century. His first explicitly Parisian collection, "Verschiedene," is devoted exclusively to this theme.

No collection of Heine's — not even his most incendiary political poetry — aroused such scandal in his own day, and the poetry of "Verschiedene" has remained largely inassimilable even in our own. And quite apart from the question whether one is in sympathy with Heine's sensualist program or not — or whether one finds these texts, to a feminist sensibility, offensive — one still does not quite know what to make of them. This is because their real interest, the question that they fundamentally raise, perhaps does not ultimately reside there where Heine himself identified it, and where the *Nachwelt* has been concerned to judge his relative failure or success: namely whether or not the poet here indeed evokes that world of untroubled, joyful sensual fulfillment that he had adopted as his political-erotic program.[23] Instead, one might almost be tempted to say that Heine, despite his protests to the contrary, is still here engaged in fulfilling — and be it for the purposes of frivolity — "Thaten der Notwendigkeit" (DHA 2: 43). For leaving aside the question of what the "Versuch freien Verkehrs mit unfreier Weiblichkeit," as one critic put it, actually meant for Heine's own biographical "education sentimentale," its significance in his development as a poet may be identified: for by so demonstratively steeping himself in a "wild" femininity he emancipated himself, if not as a biographical, then as a poetic subject; he definitively broke, in his poetry, the mold of official sexual-political discourses and middle-class conventions.[24] This was perhaps the primary significance of the poet's encounter with Paris, which was in the first instance an erotic one. Or as he attempted to explain in a letter to an appalled Karl Gutzkow, a German colleague and editor who then promptly did everything he could to suppress Heine's verses:

> Ein eigentliches Urtheil können nur wenige Deutsche über diese Gedichte aussprechen, da ihnen der Stoff selbst, die abnormen Amouren in einem Welttollhaus, wie Paris ist, unbekannt sind. Nicht die Moralbedürfnisse irgend eines verheuratheten Bürgers in einem Winkel Deutschlands, sondern die Autonomie der Kunst kommt hier in Frage. (HSA 21: 292)

In that sense, Heine's "Verschiedene" is fundamentally a festival of the polymorphous: of a libidinous energy allowed free range to roam the untamed sexual frontiers of the *Vie parisienne,* of the infamous and legendary *Sündenbabel* on the Seine:

> Auf dem Fauxbourg Saint-Marceau
> Lag der Nebel heute Morgen,
> Spätherbstnebel, dicht und schwer,
> Einer weißen Nacht vergleichbar.
>
> Wandelnd durch die weiße Nacht,
> Schaut' ich mir vorübergleiten
> Eine weibliche Gestalt,
> Die dem Mondenlicht vergleichbar.
>
> Ja, sie war wie Mondenlicht
> Leichthinschwebend, zart und zierlich;
> Solchen schlanken Gliederbau
> Sah ich hier in Frankreich niemals.
>
> War es Luna selbst vielleicht,
> Die sich heut bey einem schönen,
> Zärtlichen Endymion
> Des Quartier Latin verspätet?
>
> Auf dem Heimweg dacht ich nach:
> Warum floh' sie meinen Anblick?
> Hielt die Göttinn mich vielleicht
> Für den Sonnenlenker Phöbus?
> ("In der Frühe"; DHA 2: 81–82)

"Der Nebel als Trost der Einsamkeit," wrote Walter Benjamin of the erotic Parisian cityscape in the poetry of Baudelaire (Benjamin 1: 679): Bathed in a white night both of the desirous male gaze and of the eerie reflections of the gaslight in the fog, the unknown female passerby has her everyday identity both transfigured and effaced, thus rendering the notorious anonymity of the big city not oppressive, but exhilarating. For the anonymity of the nocturnal Parisian cityscape affords, much like the Venetian carnival, the opportunity for an erotic *perpetuum mobile,* a never-ending *masque gallante* of charged encounter and endangerment, through the bold assumption of new and unprecedented personae, as evinced by Heine's quote of the Endymion myth. Through it, the woman now takes on the identity of Luna, while he, as poet, is Apollo: and both protagonists, male and female, become wrapped in a mutual pull of erotic tension and symbolic heightening, opened up by the very fact of their being, for each other, so manifestly and utterly unknown: no pre-cast bourgeois mold, no mundane, established quotidian identity intercedes to dampen or foreclose this process of deepening erotic mystery. In the Parisian landscape, the battle of the sexes has become not a war of position, proceeding from fixed identities, but a war of movement, where identities are fluid. The lithe, svelte body of woman in the poem is the incarnation of such motion; motion is however a property of the free and the living, the unconfined and the unfettered, and the male gaze that moves with it must now surrender its traditional impulse to hold such beauty fast. Or as Heine writes, with unmistakably far-reaching consequences both for received notions of female beauty, and for its male appropriation:

> Sind die Pariserinnen schön? Wer kann das wissen! . . . Sind ihre Gesichter schön? Auch dieses wäre schwierig zu ermitteln. Denn alle ihre Gesichtszüge sind in beständiger Bewegung, jede Pariserinn hat tausend Gesichter, eins lachender, geistreicher, holdseliger als das andere, und setzt denjenigen in Verlegenheit, der darunter das schönste Gesicht auswählen oder gar das wahre Gesicht errathen will . . .

And Heine then goes on to describe the novel and unprecedented aesthetic problem of this war of movement:

> Damit ein richtiges Urtheil gefällt werde, muß der Beurtheilende und der Gegenstand der Beurtheilung sich im Zustande der Ruhe befinden. Aber wer kann ruhig bey einer Pariserinn seyn und welche Pariserinn ist jemals ruhig? Es giebt Leute, welche glauben, sie können den Schmetterling ganz genau betrachten, wenn sie ihn mit einer Nadel aufs Papier festgestochen haben. Das ist eben so thörigt wie grausam. Der angeheftete, ruhige Schmetterling ist kein Schmetterling mehr! Den Schmetterling muß man betrachten wenn er um die Blumen gaukelt . . . (DHA 5: 236–37)

In his seminal and groundbreaking poem, Heine, in the phrase of a contemporary French critic the "most Parisian of poets," attempts to capture this new female beauty while still in motion, and at the same time prefigures Baudelaire's "Heroism of Modern Life" (949–52) by endowing mythic dimensions to a chance urban encounter. His poem, however, in some ways offers a marked contrast to its more well-known Baudelairean pendant, "À une passante" (88). For, however we may choose to understand the veiled secret of Baudelaire's female protagonist in that celebrated text, there can be no doubt that the poem itself is tragic, the elegy of a fearful loss and closure: of the "unlived," in Volker Braun's telling phrase, of a possibility forever lost, eternally not realized. Heine's is more a poem of the "not yet," of still open, untapped possibility, of thrilling expectation; and — the chords of Wagner's *Tristan* prelude are not at a far historical remove — this high expectancy itself here indeed takes on something of the very aspect of fulfillment.

There can thus be no doubt that it is a genuine and arresting historical reality and possibility of the *Großstadt* that finds expression in these lyrics. The metropolis, in its very multiplicity and anonymity, gave its inhabitants (and visitors) the chance to abandon a sexual identity dictated by tradition, and to assume and experiment with a plurality of others; it was teeming with enticing and forbidden forms much like the uncensored "Es" or unconscious of Freud's later theory. The sense of the "Verschiedene" poems is this bold experiment with the megapolitan libido. It is only through the uncertainties of this experimental process itself that something new, an original, unprecedented, undoubtedly still patriarchal, yet re-formed male sexual identity begins to take form and emerge, beyond the established codes of virtue, matrimony, monogamy, and propriety. And the force of the resulting poetry resides perhaps less in any fulfillment reached than in the experiment itself: the bold exploration of new sentiments and sensations, the all-encompassing carnivalesque affront to a host of interdictions, the transgression and travesty of stifling mores and conventions. As in the poem *Yolante und Marie:*

> In welche soll ich mich verlieben,
> Da beide liebenswürdig sind?
> Ein schönes Weib ist noch die Mutter,
> Die Tochter ist ein schönes Kind.
>
> Die weißen, unerfahrnen Glieder,
> Sie sind so rührend anzusehen!
> Doch reitzend sind geniale Augen,
> Die unsre Zärtlichkeit verstehn. (DHA 2: 49)

Needless to specify the countless taboos that this poem suspends in such short order, with this image of an embarrassment of sensual riches: for in the vision of the polygamy with mother and daughter, not only sexual propriety, but the sanctities of motherhood and daughterhood themselves are here abruptly dispatched. But the male fantasies engaged in the "Verschiedene" poems are not simply the seductive ones of such forbidden sexual plenty; they also offer this sur-

prising (not least considering the manic jealousy of the biographical
subject Heine!) dismissal of one of the most fundamental laws of patriarchy — the possession of the female object:

> Während ich nach andrer Leute
> Andrer Leute Schätze spähe,
> Und vor fremden Liebesthüren
> Schmachtend auf und nieder gehe:
>
> Treibt's vielleicht die andren Leute
> Hin und her an andrem Platze,
> Und vor meinen eignen Fenstern
> Aeugeln sie mit meinem Schatze. (DHA 2: 40)

"Das ist menschlich!," enjoins the poet, with true *weltmännische*
tolerance, thus casually reducing a host of classic novels of adultery,
from the nineteenth century to our own day, from *Effi Briest* to *Madame Bovary* to *Anna Karenina,* if not to the dustbin, then to the old
curiosity shop of sexual-political history. Similarly, the ideal of mutual,
reciprocal love, culminating in the form of a stable, institutionalized
man-woman relationship, in the successful transfer of the female into
the safe harbor of holy matrimony, and thus into the realm of the
male law, is for the new male subject of the "Verschiedene" poems no
longer the sought-for goal, but the dreaded end of all romantic attraction:

> Wie rasch du auch vorüberschrittest
> Noch einmal schautest du zurück,
> Der Mund, wie fragend, kühngeöffnet,
> Stürmischer Hochmuth in dem Blick.
>
> O, daß ich nie zu fassen suchte
> Das weiße flüchtige Gewand!
> Die holde Spur der kleinen Füße,
> O, daß ich nie sie wiederfand!
>
> Verschwunden ist ja deine Wildheit,
> Bist wie die Andern zahm und klar,
> Und sanft und unerträglich gütig,
> Und ach! nun liebst du mich sogar!
>
> (DHA 2: 38)

In the suppressed "Laokoon" poem of the *Buch der Lieder,* catastrophe was fulfillment. But here, fulfillment is catastrophe. The traditional domestication of female desirability no longer interests the male subject of the "Verschiedene" poems; "Ich treibe jetzt Monogamie," Heine significantly writes in a letter about his "wilde Ehe" with the *grisette* Crescene Mirat, who was later indeed to become his lawful wife and to go into literary history as "Mathilde" (HSA 23: 50). Similarly, the puritanical *Sittenrichter* Ludwig Börne, who engaged in a famous series of polemics against Heine, provoked the poet with his hypocritical *menage à trois* with Jeanette Wohl and Salomon Strauss, as with his tireless campaign of innuendo against Heine's own choice of sexual and life partner. Under such duress, Heine saw himself driven to some rather excessive, but also revealing utterances. Thus the telling witticism of Heine's on the subject of Madame Wohl, that one did not know if she were Börne's lover or "only" his wife — "wovon man nicht wußte, zu welchem Titel ihr Verhältniß zu Börne sie berechtige, ob sie seine Geliebte oder bloß seine Gattinn" (DHA 5: 89). In all of these inversions of the standard usages and hierarchies of the sexual order, Heine established the new primacy of the outlaw and untamed versus the domesticated side of female partnership and sexuality.

VIII

And yet all of these relentless generalized affronts almost pale in comparison to the following poem, which would seem to render them, for all their violation of existing sexual-political mores, into mere preparatory exercises for this truly defining and anarchic blow: the frank decapitation, the brutal excising of the soul of woman:

> Diese schönen Gliedermassen
> Kolossaler Weiblichkeit
> Sind jetzt, ohne Widerstreit,
> Meinen Wünschen überlassen.
>
> Wär' ich, leidenschaftentzügelt,
> Eigenkräftig ihr genaht,
> Ich bereu'te solche That!
> Ja, sie hätte mich geprügelt.

Welcher Busen, Hals und Kehle!
(Höher seh' ich nicht genau.)
Eh' ich mich ihr anvertrau,
Gott empfehl' ich meine Seele.

("Diana"; DHA 2: 42)

This is the true *coup de grace* to the personhood, to the soul of woman. A few years ago, geologists spoke of having possibly uncovered, in a vast, submerged crater in the wilds and jungles of Central America, the smoking gun of astrophysics and earth history: the telltale trace of the meteor strike that ended the reign of the sauropods and created new conditions for life on earth, by wiping out all existing preconditions of life before it. In terms of *Kulturgeschichte* and sexual-political history, Heine's "Diana" is, if not a geophysical smoking gun, then a kind of scalpel or circumcision knife, an at once delicate, gruesome, and defining cultural-political surgical instrument, and the "colossal" body of Diana a true *corpus delecti:* it is the glorious physis of woman finally and definitively liberated and cut loose from the bonds of personhood and soul. Freed of such baleful and inimical distractions, the male protagonist can devote himself to his enjoyment with a single-mindedness of purpose resembling that — to use the metaphor employed by Kafka in *Der Process* — of a feeding animal.[25]

Yet it is important that the reader, and, one is almost tempted to say, the erotic initiate of the "Verschiedene" poems, withstand, and not merely recoil from or simply succumb to, the shock that this may indeed provoke: for he — and she — are indeed being put to the test. And upon second glance, we can see that, not only does woman here, far from being merely reduced to an object, continue to wield a terrible, impressive power of sexual attraction and subjectivity, retaining above all that telltale mark of the subject, the capacity to inflict pain — here again, the rhyme of "geprügelt" on "entzügelt" saying all. But even more importantly and mysteriously, as befits the subtle laws of reciprocity, analogy, and correspondence that govern the erotic, it is not simply the female, but also the male subject who is here wondrously decapitated, and happily gives up his soul ("Gott empfehle ich meine Seele"), first willingly consigning to the spirit that which is the spirit's, before then eagerly giving to the flesh that which is the flesh. We have seen how, in the first erotic *Lehrjahre* of the *Buch der Lieder,* the beloved's head seemed to be attached to strings; in a later, more advanced Parisian stage of his erotic apprenticeship, Heine's poetic persona finally cut those strings by unceremoniously lopping off first his female partner's, and then his very own head and soul. For the body is not to be had for less; and that is the lesson of "Verschiedene"; the daring, dangerous operation conducted in its pages. In the plays and novellas of the great German Romantic most admired by Heine, Heinrich von Kleist, it is only through natural and social catastrophes, earthquakes, insurrections, trance, and hypnosis, that love and passion become realizable, through their suspension of the dread power of convention. And so it is too with Heine's rehabilitation of the flesh. It is only possible through a similar liberating catastrophe, and an equally drastic, devastating blow against seemingly sacrosanct, inviolable structures — be they chastity, abstinence, morality, holy wedlock, or indeed, the timeworn shibboleth of the soul itself.

IX

And what emerges, or, as it were, resurfaces through all of this is indeed the lost continent of woman, as the lost continent of the body. In a poem of an appropriately continental sweep and vastness, Heine celebrates this recovery:

> Des Weibes Leib ist ein Gedicht,
> Das Gott der Herr geschrieben
> Ins große Stammbuch der Natur,
> Als ihn der Geist getrieben.
>
> Ja, günstig war die Stunde ihm,
> Der Gott war hoch begeistert;
> Er hat den spröden, rebellischen Stoff
> Ganz künstlerisch bemeistert.
>
> Fürwahr, der Leib des Weibes ist
> Das Hohelied der Lieder;
> Gar wunderbare Strophen sind
> Die schlanken, weißen Glieder.
>
> O, welche göttliche Idee
> Ist dieser Hals, der blanke,
> Worauf sich wiegt der kleine Kopf,
> Der lockige Hauptgedanke.
>
> Der Brüstchen Rosenknospen sind
> Epigrammatisch gefeilet;
> Unsäglich entzückend ist die Cäsur
> Die streng den Busen theilet.

Den plastischen Schöpfer offenbart
Der Hüften Parallele;
Der Zwischensatz mit dem Feigenblatt
Ist auch eine schöne Stelle.

Das ist kein abstraktes Begriffspoem!
Das Lied hat Fleisch und Rippen,
Hat Hand und Fuß; es lacht und küßt
Mit schöngereimten Lippen.

Hier athmet wahre Poesie!
Anmuth in jeder Wendung!
Und auf der Stirne trägt das Lied
Den Stempel der Vollendung.

Lobsingen will ich dir, o Herr,
Und dich im Staub anbeten!
Wir sind nur Stümper gegen dich,
Den himmlischen Poeten.

Versenken will ich mich, o Herr,
In deines Liedes Prächten;
Ich widme seinem Studium
Den Tag mitsammt den Nächten.

Ja, Tag und Nacht studier ich dran,
Will keine Zeit verlieren;
Die Beine werden mir so dünn —
Das kommt vom vielen Studieren.
("Das Hohelied"; DHA 3.1: 283–84)

The *shir ha-shirim asher li-shelomo,* the "Song of Songs," the *Canticle canticlorum,* from which this poem draws not only its title, but its whole subject matter and rapturous, hymnic tone, is a text *sui generis* in the biblical canon: its ardent, passionate verses of unbridled sexual desire soon became an embarrassment to the official priestly guardians of the Judeo-Christian tradition, and were promptly allegorized into the search of the soul for God, the relationship of Israel to Yahweh, or indeed the unstinting quest of the faithful for the One True Chruch.[26] For Heine's sensualist critique of religion this is perhaps the prime example of the baleful, sublimating effects of spiritualism on the natural, physical impulses of love and sexuality; and in this instance one may even argue that Heine, intimate connoisseur of the Bible that he was,

was right. That is, his title and poem are less a travesty than a restitution or rehabilitation of the authentic original impulse of the *Canticle canticlorum,* in head-on and direct confrontation with the whole Nazarene tradition. What is of most compelling interest in the present context is, however, the biblical element of Creation and re-Creation also present in the poem. Heine's return to the source, the Bible, is here also a return to Genesis; to the primal act of generation and re-generation. In this sense, it is of interest to note that the creation of this poem itself is linked to the *Schöpfungslieder,* which have the Creation as their explicit theme. In one of those poems we read:

> Der Stoff, das Material des Gedichts,
> Das saugt sich nicht aus dem Finger;
> Kein Gott erschafft die Welt aus Nichts,
> So wenig wie irdische Singer.
>
> Aus vorgefundenem Urweltsdreck
> Erschuf ich die Männerleiber,
> Und aus dem Männerrippenspeck
> Erschuf ich die schönen Weiber.
>
> Den Himmel erschuf ich aus der Erd'
> Und Engel aus Weiberentfaltung;
> Der Stoff gewinnt erst seinen Werth
> Durch künstlerische Gestaltung. (DHA 2: 63)

In the discussion of its *Entstehungsgeschichte,* the creation of "Das Hohelied" was traditionally placed in the 1840s, roughly parallel to "Verschiedene"; later it was fixed in Heine's latest period, around 1853.[27] One is tempted to say, however, that this poem as presence and idea must have accompanied the poet throughout these years, ultimately crystallizing at this late stage, much as he only wrote the culminating poem of the *Schöpfungslieder,* also begun in the 1840s, at this time. "Erschaffend konnte ich genesen, / Erschaffend wurde ich gesund" (DHA 2: 63). In this sense, the prostrate and, as it were, momentarily lifeless body of woman in "Das Hohelied" is indeed stretched out, in T. S. Eliot's phrase, "like a patient etherized upon a table"; for she is to be put into a condition in which she can be safely operated upon, an operation through which the poet promises healing not only for her, but for himself. What, though, is the terrible sickness, "Krankheit," that afflicts them both? It is that same legacy of spiritualism, what Heine called the Nazarene teachings of miserablism and abnegation, against whose deformations he seeks to rehabilitate and recover the lost, primal "Song of Songs" of human eros and sexuality. "To love is to sing," and Heine here returns this song to its natural source.[28] Or as the poet wrote in his critique of the spiritualist legacy:

> Die nächste Aufgabe ist: gesund zu werden; denn wir fühlen uns noch sehr schwach in den Gliedern. Die heiligen Vampire des Mittelalters haben uns so viel Lebensblut ausgesaugt . . . Denn das Christenthum, unfähig die Materie zu vernichten, hat sie überall fletrirt, es hat die edelsten Genüsse herabgewürdigt, und die Sinne mußten heucheln und es entstand Lüge und Sünde. Wir müssen unseren Weibern neue Hemde und neue Gedanken anziehen, und alle unsere Gefühle müssen wir durchräuchern, wie nach einer überstandenen Pest . . . (DHA 8.1: 59)

Heine's drastic statements on the scope of the Christian interdiction of beauty and of sensuality might at first glance seem more polemical than real; they are in fact, however, based on a close study of the sources. And from what epochal depths of catacombic and sepulchral exile the female body and female beauty, as a veritable *ecclesia pressa,* are here to be recovered, is perhaps best expressed in two episodes drawn from the early history of the Church that fatefully branded beauty together with sexuality as damnable excess and sin. Women were rather to "become male," and suppress their sexual attributes and physical attractiveness.[29] This sometimes took on extreme if characteristic forms, such as the following, drawn from the exemplary hagiographic lives of Pelagia and Alexandra. The former is celebrated by her biographer because:

> she had lost those good looks I used to know; her astounding beauty had all faded away, her laughing and bright face . . . had become ugly, her pretty eyes had become hollow and cavernous . . . The joints of her holy bones, all fleshless, were visible beneath her skin though emaciation brought about by ascetic practices. Indeed the whole complexion of her skin was coarse and dark like sackcloth, as the result of her strenuous penance.

The good Alexandra went even further in wishing to avoid the sin of beauty; she let herself be confined in a tomb, allowing only a small opening for food to be passed to her, for, as she stated:

> A man was distressed in mind because of me and, lest I seem to afflict or disparage him, I chose to betake myself alive into the tomb rather than cause a soul, made in the image of God, to stumble.

It is precisely from this millennial, sunken tomb of beauty that, in "Das Hohelied," the body of woman has been rescued. And thus, it is not only in new sentiments and raiment, but in a resurrected body, a new physis that woman is now to be clad; as in the Jewish creation myth, the divine transfiguring *ruach hakodash* or holy breath is now breathed into her, this time by the poet, her earthly re-Creator.

Again, one might well say: woman as object.[30] Were not, as so characteristic for love and eros, the lines between subject and object, exaltation and abasement, powerlessness and empowering, here so hopelessly confused. For in thus re-creating woman, the poet re-creates himself; he issues forth from her no less than she from him. If she is momentarily abased, then it is only to be subsequently exalted, restituted as that "körperliche Offenbarung Gottes," in the words of that frank and disarming confession Ludwig Börne elicited from Heine when he summoned the poet to defend and justify his intimate and scandalous life choices (DHA 5: 90). And if she is, like the patient stretched out on the table, still weak and vulnerable after her thousand-year ordeal, and for a moment lifeless and defenseless before the life-giving ministrations of the poet, it is only to subsequently emerge and re-emerge from them like a true convalescent, miraculously reconstituted, revived, resuscitated, in an exponential heightening of her power. For there can be no doubt that the poet feeds on her, not only as the lover feasts upon his beloved's beauty, but as the infant nourishes itself from its mother's physical being. And if in one moment the poet is exalted over her, as that creative breath infusing her with new form and life, in the end he is reduced and helpless before the sublime, sustaining, and engulfing vastness of his own creation, from which he draws his sustenance, and through which he is then ultimately, and self-ironically, overwhelmed. And indeed, if we are to regard this poem, at the macrocosmic level of "universal history," as the gloriously resurfaced and reconstituted body of woman, after a millennial burial and confinement in beauty's tomb, it may also correspondingly be viewed, within the microcosmos of Heine's own creative process, as the late disclosure and ultimate surfacing of the "mother ground" of Heine's Parisian period, that generative presence from which the other erotic poems, or "bodies," issued forth.

X

As in the following poem, the programmatic *summa* of the "Verschiedene," as of Heine's entire project of the "rehabilitation of the flesh":

Auf diesem Felsen bauen wir
Die Kirche von dem dritten,
Dem dritten neuen Testament;
Das Leid ist ausgelitten.

Vernichtet ist das Zweyerley,
Das uns so lang bethöret;
Die dumme Leiberquälerey
Hat endlich aufgehöret.

Hörst du den Gott im finstern Meer?
Mit tausend Stimmen spricht er.
Und siehst du über unserm Haupt
Die tausend Gotteslichter?

Der heilge Gott der ist im Licht
Wie in den Finsternissen;
Und Gott ist alles was da ist;
Er ist in unsern Küssen.
            ("Seraphine" 7; DHA 2: 34)

This singular poem is in some sense the sacral and sanctifying space of the otherwise so profane and worldly terrain of the "Verschiedene." As Heine moved back to the "mother ground," the primal act of Creation in reconstituting the female (and with it the male) body in *Das Hohelied,* here too he reaches back into the fundamental founding myths of Western civilization, the myths of "Schöpfung und Er-lösung," Creation and Redemption, Genesis and Golgotha, to write them anew: and if we may speak of the Bible, particularly in these two great founding myths, as representing a kind of genetic "basic row" of all of Occidental culture, then we have some type of measure for scope of Heine's erotic experiment, of his daring surgical incision into the cultural history of Western sexuality.[31]

For Heine's text does not simply consist of a further variation of this "basic row," but is an intervention into that row itself. Heine takes with an almost frightening seriousness the eschatological motifs in which the Saint-Simonian doctrines of the period, as the *Nouveau Christianisme,* liked to clad themselves. The Saint-Simonian Third Testament — of the rehabilitation of the flesh — appears here less as the continuation, than as the supersession of the first two Testaments, above all in the poetic sphere, in the dimension of their most suggestive and compelling imagery. Returning them to their *degré zero,* their *incipit,* the stories of Genesis and Golgotha are here recast under the sign of sensualism, the corporeal union of the — unmarried — lovers' kiss. It is now a — in the biblical context highly numinous — "rock" of kisses upon which the new faith is based, the, as it were, true and corporeal Resurrection; and the human couple in its sensuality, regarded in post-Pauline Christianity as the sign, if not indeed as the source of the Fall, is here nothing less than the medium of the return of the Earth to Paradise, to its original Edenic state.

In his autobiography, not without some boastful stylizing of his erotic career on Paris streets, calculated to arouse the prurient interest of his prim and proper Biedermeier public, Heine concludes his account with this dramatic reversal of the usual codifications of purity and sin, virtue and defilement, by representing his dalliances as one great, redemptive expedition:

> Ich war die Ursittlichkeit, ich war unsündbar, ich war die incarnirte Reinheit; die anrüchigsten Magdalenen wurden purifizirt durch die läuternde und sühnende Macht meiner Liebesflammen, und . . . mit einer ganz neuen Jungfräulichkeit gingen sie hervor aus den Umarmungen des Gottes. (DHA 15: 35–36)

If here, at least for Heine's confident and thoroughly unrepentant persona, the case seems clear, the jury is still out on the "Verschiedene" as a poetic chronicle of such redemption: indeed, its particular drama, tension, and quality as a cycle may well also reside in the fact that with each encounter, the redemptive project is once more very much at stake; that it indeed may fail — be it through guilt, estrangement, lassitude, "dailiness," *tristia,* or indeed ennui. As befits, perhaps, its very sanctity, sensual fulfillment — "Glück" — in the profane world is never assured, but remains aleatory, a type of epiphany, or, if we may use the term, a state of grace. It is, in Heine's verses, then all the more luminous when it does occur, as in these lines, which in their spontaneity and freshness can rival in beauty the numinous quality of the lovers in "Seraphine" 7, affording a human and immediately accessible dimension to the archetypal heroism of that primal pairing:

> Nimmer glaub ich, junge Schöne,
> Was die spröde Lippe spricht;
> Solche große schwarze Augen,
> Solche hat die Tugend nicht.

Diese braungestreifte Lüge,
Streif sie ab; ich liebe dich.
Laß dein weißes Herz mich küssen —
Weißes Herz, verstehst du mich? (DHA 2: 38)

In the marvelous conceit of color which underlies the poem, the polarity of white and black are set against the middle hue of brown.
Again, the body does not lie: the blackness of the beloved's eyes speak
a different, truer language than her official discourse of virtue. "Black"
is the stereotypical color of vice, sin, and perdition, but in the Heinean
reversal of values, it is the path of "blackness" that the poet follows.
That path leads to an unexpected turn, and unimaginable alliance: for
black conjoins with white, the color of purity. But white is also, for
Heine, the color of desire, just as it is — if we choose for a moment to
disregard such wayward facts of cultural history as Jeanne Duval, the
Creole mistress of Charles Baudelaire — the color, in a European,
Caucasian context, of the revealed body of the beloved. It is, thus,
paradoxically the path of "blackness" and supposed vice that leads to
this whiteness of purity and revelation, in casting off the distorting
prism of the "brown-striped lie" that throws its darkening shadow on
desire. The poles of vice and purity thus meet: and the shared abso-
luteness of whiteness and blackness is upheld as the predominant element joining them against the compromising false admixture, the
interceding masking layer of the "brown."

But more than this: not only our preconceived notions of the attributes of white and black are here confounded, but also our ideas of
body and soul. For here the revealed body of woman is at once her
"heart" — and her "white," or pure, luminous heart at that. In an
understanding reminiscent of the indissoluble unity of bodily presence
and personhood once present in the Middle High German word *lîp*,
later to become the New High German *Leib,* the two aspects are here
again conjoined.[32] For Heine, body is the soul of woman, and to love
a woman is to love her body. To *love;* not merely to desire. For in
love, as Elias Canetti has written, "es geht um Körper" (28), and it
may safely be said that in Heine this physicality of love is taken into
another dimension. For one will not be able to deny this love its own
astonishing depths of constancy and heroism, the ability to withstand
trial and travails at least as desperate as those confronted by more traditional, sublimated, and "spiritual" attachments.

In this context, it is perhaps useful to recall Freud's daring speculation about the invention of the soul as the first *Doppelgänger* of the

human being, as the double of his body: a double at a safe remove from time and physicality and not subject to the manifold and even disfiguring assaults they cause our physical being (12: 247). In other words, to love a soul is, in the long run, just simply safer than to love a body; and the love of the body, is, as opposed to the consoling protective subterfuges of the soul, the true tough love. And it is indeed a measure of the depths and force of Heine's love of woman's physicality that it will yet withstand the cruelest trials to which disease, time, death, disfigurement could possibly expose it. As in the following poem, found among the poet's posthumous papers:

> Für eine Grille — keckes Wagen! —
> Hab ich das Leben eingesetzt
> Und nun das Spiel verloren jetzt,
> Mein Herz du darfst dich nicht beklagen.
>
> Die Sachsen sagen: "Minschenwille
> Ist Minschen-Himmelrik" — Ich gab
> Das Leben hin, jedoch ich hab
> Verwirklicht meines Lebens Grille!
>
> Die Seeligkeit die ich empfunden
> Darob war nur von kurzer Frist
> Doch wer von Wonne trunken ist,
> Der rechnet nicht nach eitel Stunden
>
> Wo Seligkeit ist Ewigkeit
> Hier lodern alle Liebesflammen
> In eine einzge Glut zusammen;
> Hier giebt es weder Raum noch Zeit
> (DHA 3.1: 353)

It is to the social and political scientist Dolf Sternberger that we owe a remarkable piece of philological detective work that has enabled an understanding of this poem that would make it unique in the annals of world literature (241–58). Reading the correspondence of Heine's youth in Göttingen, Sternberger discovered a passage in a letter that speaks of the "Doppelliebe" of the poet — to the statue of Venus in the university library and to a "veneric" kitchen maid of his acquaintance (HSA 20: 145) — and linked it to the much later and posthumous text. Is this poem in fact the late, retrospective, and elegiac record of that youthful dalliance? The quotation of the well-known

German folk proverb in the dialect of Lower Saxony would indeed seem to definitively localize the poem; and the explicit reference to the fatality of that encounter — "ich gab mein Leben hin" — also creates a plausible link to the "schöne" — and venereally infected — "Köchinn" of that early letter.

Heine himself always remained convinced that the malady that paralyzed and ultimately caused his death was a syphilitic infection he had contracted in his youth. As indeed, he may have.[33] The scourge was one of the main killers of men in the nineteenth century, and "le plaisir qui tue" — the pleasure that kills — was for Baudelaire and Heine therefore not simply metaphor for the all the *grandes* and *petites morts* of eros, but a frank reference to their own impending physical demise through the medium of sex, in the form of that sexually communicable disease which at the time was as fatal, incurable, and epidemic as is AIDS in our own day (Gilman 252). If this be so, however, then what we have before us in this poem is nothing less than the *non plus ultra* of male sexual gratitude, a commemorative ode to the woman and the moment through which the poet himself believed to have contracted the disease which crippled and then killed him. This would afford a harrowing and impressive background of biographical authenticity to the passionate statement once elicited from Heine in his book on Börne:

> ich kann aber . . . die Versicherung geben, daß ich, selbst in meiner tollsten Jugendzeit, nie ein Weib erkannt habe, wenn ich nicht dazu begeistert ward durch ihre Schönheit, die körperliche Offenbarung Gottes, oder durch die große Passion, jene große Passion, die ebenfalls göttlicher Art, weil sie uns von allen selbstsüchtigen Kleingefühlen befreyt und die eitlen Güter des Lebens, ja das Leben selbst, hinopfern läßt! (DHA 11: 90)

It would be difficult indeed to surpass such a declaration of abiding love to the female body.

Yet perhaps there is a moment in which Heine will yet surpass it: in a moment where the embrace of woman, in its destructive fatality and transporting passion, becomes the universal symbol, the central metaphor for the poet's relation to "the last things," to life and death itself. We have seen how in the "Laokoon" poem he had still willingly acceded to that paradoxical female embrace, which brought both ecstasy and torment. In the "Sphinx" poem of 1839 woman herself had become a "Zwitter von Schrecken und Lüsten," whose attraction, though fearful, was not to be resisted. In the Lazarus cycle in *Ro-*

manzero, where the languishing invalid poet bemoans his fate upon the "Matratzengruft," he offers us the final, and, as it were, ultimate extension of this image:

> Es hatte mein Haupt die schwarze Frau
> Zärtlich ans Herz geschlossen;
> Ach! meine Haare wurden grau,
> Wo ihre Thränen geflossen.
>
> Sie küßte mich lahm, sie küßte mich krank,
> sie küßte mir blind die Augen;
> Das Mark aus meinem Rückgrat trank
> Ihr Mund mit wildem Saugen. (DHA 3:1: 198)

In one of the grand texts of the spiritualist tradition, in his "Frô welt, ir sult dem wirte sagen," Walther von der Vogelweide had bid farewell to the blandishments of Dame World, that feminized allegory of earthly existence, whose transient and illusory charms were of course embodied by woman in her time-honored role as temptress. Seeing through her, the medieval poet catches the glimpse of the chilling world of fleshly decay behind her alluring mask, and opts for Christian transcendence (198). The anti-spiritualist poet Heine inhabits a cosmos quite without such consolations; his exposure to the world is absolute, and its image is that of woman. He has no alternative to the agonizing, ineluctable grip of mortality, disease, and suffering, the paradoxical vampire grip of the female Sphinx "of terrors and pleasures" that offers both boundless joy and pain, transport and annihilation, and which has here been, through its very boundlessness, extrapolated to an image of the cosmos, as of life itself. Again, however, we observe that here as always the poet, even in expiring from it, does not attempt to escape this wrenching grasp. Even in death, his attachment to it is undying. And that its image should be that of woman is, with this poet, the signum not of a sphere of ephemeral illusion, but of a truth that is at once irresistible, ultimate, and compelling. Indeed, one might almost say that Heine, in his agony, not only succumbs, but still clings to her; and that even here, before the "last things" and the finality of death, the tones of an all-consuming earthly passion, sounding forth from this embrace, still easily overpower and engulf the lament over its effects of doom and devastation.

XI

Ich weiß nicht, was soll es bedeuten,
Daß ich so traurig bin;
Ein Mährchen aus alten Zeiten,
Das kommt mir nicht aus dem Sinn.

Die Luft ist kühl und es dunkelt,
Und ruhig fließt der Rhein;
Der Gipfel des Berges funkelt
Im Abendsonnenschein.

Die schönste Jungfrau sitzet
Dort oben wunderbar,
Ihr gold'nes Geschmeide blitzet,
Sie kämmt ihr goldenes Haar.

Sie kämmt es mit goldenem Kamme,
Und singt ein Lied dabei;
Das hat eine wundersame,
Gewaltige Melodei.

Den Schiffer im kleinen Schiffe
Ergreift es mit wildem Weh;
Er schaut nicht die Felsenriffe,
Er schaut nur hinauf in die Höh'.

Ich glaube, die Wellen verschlingen
Am Ende Schiffer und Kahn;
Und das hat mit ihrem Singen
Die Lore-Ley gethan. (DHA 1.1: 207–9)

It is not the moment here to probe all the reverberations of this youthful stroke of poetic genius:[34] of Heine's complex, effortless crossover and fusion of Homeric and of Rhenish myth, of the call of the Sirens and the echo of the *Lurlei* cliff. It must suffice to point out the following aspects: from the heights of gold and beauty, it is not the witch, the vamp, or sorceress who looks down upon the boatsman and, with the force of all the elements, draws him to his doom: it is the maid, the virgin, the "Jungfrau," the very symbol of female purity, but, at an even more archaic, deeper level, the symbol too of autonomous, magical, and unbounded female power.[35] From this perspective, the German male choirs who, at the turn of the century, in black frock coats and top hats, traditionally sang this song do seem a worthy object of ethnological study. For beyond all specific social settings in which this story may and must be encased, it remains the tale of a true *rite de passage,* of the perilous libidinous journey of the male subject to the sheer alterity of woman. And in the strange doubling of perspective in the poem, where the boatsman inevitably perishes and the poetic voice miraculously survives, Heine gives us the very image of the stakes of life and death, of extinction and becoming, involved in such a journey.

Notes

[1] In writing this essay I was much indebted to my discussions with my doctoral candidate Sophie Boyer, who was writing her dissertation on the discourse of love in the poetry of Heine and Baudelaire at the time, and who will hopefully soon be presenting the results of her research to the learned public.

[2] Quoted in Karl Theodor Kleinknecht, ed., *Heine in Deutschland: Dokumente seiner Rezeption 1834–1956* (Tübingen and Munich: Deutscher Taschenbuch Verlag and Niemeyer, 1976), xxvi.

[3] On the career and aftershocks of some of these Heinean motifs in French and European literature see Mario Praz, *The Romantic Agony* (London: Oxford UP, 1933); Kurt Weinberg, *Henri Heine "romantique défroqué": Héraut du symbolisme français* (Paris: Presses universitaires de France, 1954); Oliver Boeck, *Heines Nachwirkung and Heine-Parallelen in der französischen Dichtung* (Göppingen: Alfred Kümmerle, 1972).

[4] For a detailed discussion of Goethe's sexual pyschopathology see K. R. Eissler, *Goethe: Eine psychoanalytische Studie* (Frankfurt am Main: Stroemfeld/Roter Stern, 1985/1988), 2 vols. Indeed, in the light of the most recent findings of Goethe research, one might be tempted to ask oneself if, in addition to Goethe's undoubted psychological need for female stewardship and mentorship, all this *Liebeslyrik* was not at the same time just an elaborate hoax to deceive his contemporaries and posterity as to the real nature of his sexual preferences. On this, compare the material assembled in Alice Kuzniar, ed., *Outing Goethe and His Age* (Stanford: Stanford UP, 1996).

[5] On Brecht's special place in the history of love and love poetry see Sabine Kebir, *Ein akzeptabler Mann?* (Berlin: Buchverlag Der Morgen, 1987).

[6] Octavio Paz, *La llama doble: Amor y erotismo* (Barcelona: Seix Barral, 1993); here quoted according to the English language edition: *The Double Flame: Love and Eroticism* (New York and London: Harcourt Brace, 1995), 160.

[7] Theodor W. Adorno, *Minima Moralia* (Frankfurt am Main: Suhrkamp, 1951), 113: "Kein Mann, der einem armen Mädchen zuredet, mit ihm zu gehen, wird,

solange er sich nicht ganz stumpf macht, das leise Moment des Rechts in ihrem Widerstreben verkennen, dem einzigen Prärogativ, welches die patriarchale Gesellschaft der Frau läßt, die, einmal überredet, nach dem kurzen Triumph des Nein sogleich die Zeche zu bezahlen hat." What Heine's *Buch der Lieder* presents us with is both this momentary female triumph and its cost, its instantaneous and permanent revocation.

[8] Hoffmann, *Sämtliche Werke*. Vol. 1 (Munich: Winkler, 1960), 348. On this aspect of Hoffmann's work — thematically very close to Heine's in the *Buch der Lieder* — see also Franz Fühmann, *Fräulein Veronika Paulmann aus der Pirnaer Vorstadt oder etwas über das Schauerliche bei E. T. A. Hoffmann* (Hamburg: Hoffmann und Campe, 1980).

[9] On Heine's authoritative role for the articulation of a semiotics of love see Roland Barthes, *Fragments d'un discours amoureux* (Paris: Seuil, 1977); English language edition *A Lover's Discourse* (New York: Hill and Wang, 1978); see also Bernd Kortländer, ed., *Interpretationen von Heines Gedichten* (Stuttgart: Reclam, 1995), 200.

[10] On Heine and Petrarch, see Manfred Windfuhr, "Heine und der Petrarkismus," *Jahrbuch der deutschen Schillergesellschaft* 10 (1966): 266–85. His seminal essay remains indispensable reading for any account of Heine's poetic language of love. On the main point, however, Heine's affirmation of corporeality in his break with Petrarchism, Windfuhr is much more reserved than was the poet himself. Compare DHA 2: 89 or DHA 5: 91; also the bitter denunciation of the "christliche Lüge" in love, HSA 21: 170.

[11] Cp. DHA 1.1: 146; DHA 1.2: 793.

[12] Windfuhr, in "Heine und der Petrarkismus" (275), refers to the distressingly high level of fatalities in Heine's first major volume of verse: "Über achtzigmal im *Buch der Lieder* . . . ist vom metaphorischen oder wirklichen Verbluten und Sterben des Liebhabers die Rede."

[13] Hegel, *Werke,* ed. Eva Moldauer and Karl Markus Michel (Frankfurt am Main: Suhrkamp, 1970), 3: 270–72, under the revealing heading "Die Lust und die Notwendigkeit."

[14] Freud, *Gesammelte Werke* (Frankfurt am Main: S. Fischer, 1968–1978), 17: 45–49. Freud himself referred to Heine's characterizations to help clinch his own argument on the "Rätselhaftigkeit des Weibes" (10: 120). Indeed, there is reason to believe that Heine's theory of the "Exile of Gods," of the phantom afterlife of the sensuous deities of antiquity who had, as it were, "gone underground" to become forbidden, enticing demons and devils in the Christian imagination, had a considerable role in the articulation of Freud's own view of the libido and the sexual unconscious in general (12: 248).

[15] The translation is mine.

[16] Above, we have left the statement in its provocative baldness. We should add, however, that in the same letter Heine also writes about Friederike, referring to her in her capacity as the life partner of Ludwig Robert: "Auch gestehe ich, daß ich, wie sehr seine Frau auch geistig ausgezeichnet ist, sie doch lieber sprechen sehe, als auf dem Papiere lese." What the plebian Heine detests are all forms of

"disembodied" discourse, all the more so when they deny him the body of woman — which to him, however, is an integral part of her very "soulfulness." For here the separation of script and speech is already suggestive of that separation of "body" and "soul" that Heine rejects, and that may ultimately in fact be patriarchal in origin. As we shall see in the further course of this essay, Heine's interest in the interlocking of female body and psyche converges surprisingly with that of contemporary feminism, much as his interest in an unbridled female sexuality is anything but typically "patriarchal."

[17] Cp. Hans Kaufmann, *Heinrich Heine: Geistige Entwicklung und künstlerisches Werk* (Berlin and Weimar: Aufbau Verlag, 1976), 172–78.

[18] The original description occurs in Virgil, *Aeneidos,* Liber II, V. 212–24.

[19] For a good description of the traditional view of this poem as misogynist see Kaufmann, *Heinrich Heine,* 176–77. Another possible view is offered by Marilyn French in her *Shakespeare's Division of Experience* (New York: Summit, 1981), 24: "Pleasure of all sorts, but especially sexual pleasure, is a threat to the masculine principle, the energies of which must be directed towards transcendent goals . . . The outlaw feminine principle is a rebellion against any permanency except the cyclic permanence of nature. These two principles comprise a dichotomy of their own: the masculine principle, the pole of power, is the pole of the individual who dedicates his life to a supra-personal goal; the outlaw feminine principle, the pole of sex and pleasure, is the pole of people destined for oblivion who dedicate their lives to personal satisfaction." There can be little doubt that Heine's "Weib" is such an "outlaw."

[20] Paz, *The Double Flame,* 160 and *passim.*

[21] Paz, *La llama doble,* 10; *The Double Flame,* 2.

[22] On the myth of Paris see Benjamin's *Passagenwerk* (vol. 5); Pierre Citron, *La poésie de Paris dans la littérature française de Rousseau à Baudelaire* (Paris: Minuit, 1961); Karlheinz Stierle, *Der Mythos von Paris* (Munich: Hanser, 1993).

[23] See on this my first attempt at approaching these texts: Paul Peters, "Der Fels der Küsse," in *Interpretationen: Gedichte von Heinrich Heine,* ed. Bernd Kortländer (Stuttgart: Reclam, 1995), 86–104, particularly 100–102.

[24] On Heine and the "anti-bourgeois" Paris avant-garde, see Dolf Oehler, *Pariser Bilder I/II* (Frankfurt am Main: Suhrkamp, 1979/1988).

[25] "K . . . fasste, küsste sie auf den Mund und dann über das ganze Gesicht, wie ein durstiges Tier mit der Zunge über das endlich gefundene Quellwasser jagt" (Kafka, *Der Process,* Heft #11, 97).

[26] Compare the commentaries in the *Encylopedia Judaica* 15: 144–52, and Julian Obermann, Introduction and commentary to the "Song of Songs," *The Interpreter's Bible,* vol. 5., ed. George Allan Buttrick (New York: Abingdon, 1956), 91–143.

[27] On the textual history see DHA 3.2: 1316.

[28] Cp. Obermann, "Introduction," 105.

[29] Margaret R. Miles, *Carnal Knowing* (New York: Vintage, 1991), 54–72, from which the following two examples have been drawn. It is Miles who refers to the

recent interest of feminist theory, and particularly of Frigga Haug, in reformulating the relationship of female subjectivity and identity — the female soul and body.

[30] In that subterranean dialogue in which great poems, even inadvertently, sometimes find themselves, Heine's German-Jewish compatriot Gertrud Kolmar has authored a poem of woman's body — "Die Unerschlossene" — of a similar continental scope and vastness, in which that mute body as it were "talks back" (*Das lyrische Werk* [Heidelberg and Darmstadt: Lambert Schneider, 1955], 12).

[31] For a more detailed interpretation of this poem see Peters, "Der Fels der Küsse," 86–104.

[32] Lexer's classic dictionary gives two essential definitions: "leben, Leib, körper," to then add: "häufig bezeichnet *líp* geradezu Person" (1930–31).

[33] That the disease that killed Heine may indeed, as with Baudelaire, have been syphilis, is considered a serious possibility in the most recent and exhaustive study. See Henner Montanus, *Der kranke Heine,* Heine-Studien (Stuttgart and Weimar: Metzler, 1995).

[34] For an attempt at a more detailed interpretation see Paul Peters, "Die Frau auf dem Felsen: Besuch bei Heines Loreley," *Heine-Jahrbuch* 36 (1997): 1–21.

[35] Cp. Freud 12: 159–80.

Works Cited

Adorno, Theodor W. *Minima Moralia*. Frankfurt am Main: Suhrkamp, 1951.

Baudelaire, Charles. *Oeuvres Complètes*. Paris: Gallimard, 1961.

Barthes, Roland. *Fragments d'un discours amoureux*. Paris: Seuil, 1977. English language edition: *A Lover's Discourse*. New York: Hill and Wang, 1978.

Benjamin, Walter. *Gesammelte Schriften*. Ed. Rolf Tiedemann. Frankfurt am Main: Suhrkamp, 1998. 13 vols. 1972–.

Bertaux, Pierre. *Friedrich Hölderlin*. Frankfurt am Main: Suhrkamp, 1978.

Boeck, Oliver. *Heines Nachwirkung and Heine-Parallelen in der französichen Dichtung*. Göppingen: Alfred Kümmerle, 1972.

Brecht, Bertolt. *Werke*. Große kommentierte Berliner und Frankfurter Ausgabe. Vol. 2. Frankfurt am Main and Berlin: Suhrkamp/Aufbau, 1988. 32 vols. 1988–1998.

Canetti, Elias. *Der andere Prozeß*. Munich: Hanser, 1969.

Citron, Pierre. *La poésie de Paris dans la littérature française de Rousseau à Baudelaire*. Paris: Minuit, 1961.

Eissler, K. R. *Goethe: Eine psychoanalytische Studie*. Frankfurt am Main: Stroemfeld/Roter Stern, 1985/1988. 2 vols.

Encyclopedia Judaica. New York: Macmillan, 1971.

French, Marilyn. *Shakespeare's Division of Experience.* New York: Summit, 1981.

Freud, Sigmund. *Gesammelte Werke.* Frankfurt am Main: S. Fischer, 1968–1978. 18 vols.

Fühmann, Franz. *Fräulein Veronika Paulmann aus der Pirnaer Vorstadt oder etwas über das Schauerliche bei E. T. A. Hoffmann.* Hamburg: Hoffmann und Campe, 1980.

Gilman, Sander L. *Disease and Representation: Images of Illness from Madness to AIDS.* Ithaca and London: Cornell UP, 1988.

Goethe, Johann Wolfgang von. *Werke.* Hamburg: Christian Wegner, 1948. 14 vols.

Hegel, Georg Wilhelm Friedrich. *Werke.* Ed. Eva Moldauer and Karl Markus Michel. Vol. 3. Frankfurt am Main: Suhrkamp, 1970. 20 vols. 1969–1971.

Hoffmann, E. T. A. *Sämtliche Werke.* Vol. 1. Munich: Winkler, 1960.

Kafka, Franz. *Der Process.* Frankfurt am Main: Stroemfeld/Roter Stern, 1995.

Kaufmann, Hans. *Heinrich Heine: Geistige Entwicklung und künstlerisches Werk.* Berlin and Weimar: Aufbau Verlag, 1976.

Kebir, Sabine. *Ein akzeptabler Mann?* Berlin: Buchverlag Der Morgen, 1987.

Kleinknecht, Karl Theodor, ed. *Heine in Deutschland: Dokumente seiner Rezeption 1834–1956.* Tübingen and Munich: Deutscher Taschenbuch Verlag and Niemeyer, 1976.

Kolmar, Gertrud. *Das lyrische Werk.* Heidelberg and Darmstadt: Lambert Schneider, 1955.

Kortländer, Bernd. "Poesie der Lüge: zur Liebeslyrik des Buchs der Lieder." *Heinrich Heine: Ästhetisch-politische Profile.* Ed. Gerhard Höhn. Frankfurt am Main: Suhrkamp, 1991. 195–213.

Kuzniar, Alice, ed. *Outing Goethe and His Age.* Stanford: Stanford UP, 1996.

Lexer, Matthias. *Mittelhochdeutsches Handwörterbuch.* Leipzig: Hirzel, 1872.

Marcuse, Herbert. *Kultur und Gesellschaft.* Vol. 1. Frankfurt am Main: Suhrkamp, 1965.

Mayer, Hans. "Heinrich Heine, German Ideology and Ideologists." *New German Critique* 1 (1973): 2–18.

Miles, Margaret R. *Carnal Knowing.* New York: Vintage, 1991.

Montanus, Henner. *Der kranke Heine.* Heine-Studien. Stuttgart and Weimar: Metzler, 1995.

Obermann, Julian. Introduction and commentary to the "Song of Songs." *The Interpreter's Bible.* Vol. 5. Ed. George Allan Buttrick. New York: Abingdon, 1956. 91–143.

Oehler, Dolf. *Pariser Bilder I/II*. Frankfurt am Main: Suhrkamp, 1979/1988.

Paz, Octavio. *La llama doble: Amor y erotismo*. Barcelona: Seix Barral, 1993. English language edition: *The Double Flame: Love and Eroticism*. New York and London: Harcourt Brace, 1995.

Peters, Paul. "Der Fels der Küsse." *Interpretationen: Gedichte von Heinrich Heine*. Ed. Bernd Kortländer. Stuttgart: Reclam, 1995. 86–104.

———. "Die Frau auf dem Felsen: Besuch bei Heines Loreley." *Heine-Jahrbuch* 36 (1997): 1–21.

Praz, Mario. *The Romantic Agony*. London: Oxford UP, 1933.

Reich-Ranicki, Marcel. *Heine und die Liebe*. Augsburg: Schriften der Philosophischen Fakultät, 1992.

Rose, William. *The Early Love Poetry of Heinrich Heine: An Inquiry into Poetic Inspiration*. Oxford: Clarendon, 1962.

Sternberger, Dolf. *Heinrich Heine und die Abschaffung der Sünde*. Hamburg: Claassen, 1972.

Stierle, Karlheinz. *Der Mythos von Paris*. Munich: Hanser, 1993.

Virgil. *Opera*. Oxford: Oxford UP, 1959.

Walther von der Vogelweide. *Werke*. Darmstadt: Wissenschaftliche Buchgesellschaft, 1972.

Weinberg, Kurt. *Henri Heine "romantique défroqué": Héraut du symbolisme français*. Paris: Presses universitaires de France, 1954.

Windfuhr, Manfred. "Heine und der Petrarkismus." *Jahrbuch der deutschen Schillergesellschaft* 10 (1966): 266–85.

The Riddle of Love:
Romantic Poetry and Historical Progress

Roger F. Cook

I T IS NOT EASY TO SAY why Heine wrote Romantic poetry. On the
face of it, there are some factors that seem obvious. When he first
began to pursue or at least envision for himself a career as a literary
writer (sometime around 1816), Romanticism was at its peak in terms
of the broad public perception of it as the cutting edge of cultural innovation and visionary insight, but was already in decline as a revolutionary cultural movement that was challenging the status quo in German literature. As is perhaps the case for most aspiring writers, Heine
wanted to stake his claim to creative genius and win the grand psychic
boost, as well as ambivalent social promotion, that accompany it. There
is probably no better marker of the status granted to a German poet at
the time than the wide and lasting fame gained by Mde. de Staël's assertion that Germany is a land of (romantically inspired) "Dichter und
Denker." Without doubt, "Heine wanted to *be* a poet" (Sammons 60),
and at that time to be a German poet meant to be a Romantic poet.
Regardless of how one resolves the question "Why?," he became a
German Romantic poet and persisted in this identity, in one form or another, until the end.

Consequently, Romantic poetry became a key discourse for his in-
quiries into human existence and his medium for contributing to
European culture's collective pursuit of self-knowledge. This remains
true for Heine even after Romanticism had ceased to be the dominant
force in German culture. Even when he saw himself, in his own never
modest estimation of his place in German poetry, as the initiator of a
modern German lyric that had supplanted Romantic poetry,[1] he declared himself to be nothing other than a "romantique défroqué" (B
6.1: 447). But one could also claim that he already considered the poetic idiom of Romanticism antiquated at the time of his first great successes in the Romantic manner in the early 1820s. As Heine scholars
have argued frequently,[2] his own harsh form of irony in *Buch der Lie-*

der undermines the very essence of the Romantic ideal and draws into question the language, the vision, the voice, and ultimately the viability itself of Romantic poetry as a literary discourse.

Still, Heine continued to engage the poetic ideality of Romanticism up until his death in 1856, employing its outworn tropes, images, language, and themes in ever-changing poetic contexts and modes of self-reflection. As he did so, one particular theme took central stage — the poetic lament and incrimination of frustrated love. This in itself may seem odd, for Heine had abandoned the *minne* ideal of unrequited love even as he was first developing his own mode of Romantic love poetry. And yet, the frustrations of love endured as the central, unifying topic in his periodic returns to Romantic poetry. Each time he revisits this poetic trope the incrimination grows stronger, the accusations become harsher, until one senses that they are no longer, if indeed they ever had been, directed at an actual love interest. For all that has been made of his own amorous misfortunes that may have inspired this relentless litany of unhappy love, from the Amalie affair to other speculations, it might reflect more the frustrations of a German Jew trying to attain the status of Romantic poet at a time when this calling was increasingly being attributed to an organicist national disposition. That this was one salient element in his expression of frustrated love can hardly be questioned when one considers how the poet formulates his bitterness at rejection in "Wenn ich an deinem Hause":

> "Ich bin ein deutscher Dichter,
> Bekannt im deutschen Land;
> Nennt man die besten Namen,
> So wird auch der meine genannt.
>
> Und was mir fehlt, du Kleine,
> Fehlt manchem im deutschen Land;
> Nennt man die schlimmsten Schmerzen,
> So wird auch der meine genannt." (B 1: 115)

Similarly, his anachronistic clinging to the Romantic theme of unrequited love could be part of a tenacious resistance to the increasing tendency to deny that a Jew could ever really be a "German poet."[3]

Whatever reasons Heine may have had for continuing to employ this vision of love, he considered Romanticism a phase in European culture that would pass once reason had established itself as the final arbiter of all social questions. When exactly he adopted this view is unclear, but it must have occurred not long after he visited Hegel's

lectures on the philosophy of history in Berlin during the summer se-
mester 1821. At the height of his production of the early love songs
he had already expressed concern that the Romantic dream vision was
a pathological fixation on an imaginary realm. Even in the best known
and arguably most captivating of his Romantic poems he speculated
whether the German nation would be able to free itself from its com-
pulsive attraction to the Romantic world of fantasy:

> Ich glaube die Wellen verschlingen
> Am Ende Schiffer und Kahn; (B 1: 107)

Will Germany [*der Kahn*], under the steerage of its Romantic "Dichter und Denker" [*der Schiffer*], work through this obsession with its
own lack and longing and set about addressing its needs in the real
world? While in the Loreley poem the poet seems uncertain about
Germany's fate, by the time of *Die Stadt Lucca* (1830) Heine had
adopted the Hegelian faith in history more expressly, and thus con-
jectures that at a future point in time a healthy civilization will look
back on the Romantic period as an age of collective neurosis.[4]

Even as he asserts this view of progressive history most confi-
dently, his own Romantic engagement with questions of love, passion,
and desire remains the most troublesome test of that faith. The focus
here will be on his later poetic investigations — that is, after *Buch der
Lieder* — into the complications and mysteries posed by love. Two
related motifs that were present in his early Romantic poetry, but take
on more explicit thematic form in the period following the *Reisebilder,*
will serve as guideposts that mark developments in his analysis right
through his final poems. Following them through his various returns
to the question of love will lead to the recurrence of dilemmas posed
already in the early love songs, but also to a continually deepening
level of critical reflection on the attendant issues. The first is the ever-
present trope of the unresponsive beloved, which Heine employs repeatedly to pursue an almost formulaic engagement with the theme of
love's thorns. In particular, the figure of woman as a cold, heartless
statue serves within this thematic complex as a metaphorical hub for
the most bedeviling questions. Closely related to this image is the
trope of woman as the sphinx of Greek mythology, posing the age-old
riddle of love, which if not solved, will destroy the inflamed lover.
Here too woman is figured as the resistant object of the poet's desire
and the source of his intense psychic pain, as embodied in the claws
on the lion's body.

The following section examines Heine's thoughts on Romantic poetry and its investigations into the questions of love (particularly in relation to these two motifs) from the time he left Germany in 1831 until he published his second poetry anthology in 1844 (*Neue Gedichte*). Then the focus shifts to the changes in his poetic discourse on love, first in this second collection of 1844, and then in his final anthology *Gedichte. 1853 und 1854.* The last section looks at his final reflections on (Romantic) love and death, specifically as they are expressed in one of his last, posthumously published poems on the topic: "Es träumte mir von einer Sommernacht."

Love's Torments — Inevitable or Extinguishable?

As is typical of Heine, one of the most explicit statements he makes about Romantic sensibilities and historical progress appears in a context where, on the face of it, one would least expect it. In the fragmentary memoirs of the fictitious young wanderer Herr von Schnabelewopski, the protagonist describes a dream he had about love and Romantic poetry. It is in the dream itself that the question of Romantic love surfaces, but the narrator prefaces the description with a brief reflection on dreams and death. At the heart of these thoughts lies Heine's faith in humankind's development toward a restored psychic health, which, when attained, will cause dreams to lose their power, if not disappear altogether:

> Das rechte Träumen beginnt erst bei den Juden, dem Volke des Geistes, und erreichte seine höchste Blüte bei den Christen, dem Geistervolk. Unsere Nachkommen werden schaudern, wenn sie einst lesen, welch ein gespentisches Dasein wir geführt, wie der Mensch in uns gespalten war und nur die eine Hälfte ein eigentliches Leben geführt. Unsere Zeit — und sie beginnt am Kreuze Christi — wird als eine große Krankheitsperiode der Menschheit betrachtet werden. (B 1: 545)

The cause of this split ("jener Scheidung, die wir eben zwischen Leib und Geist gestiftet"), Schnabelewopski contends, is the Judeo-Christian renunciation of the flesh, the abstinence from life on earth for the sake of the hereafter. He depicts his own age as a late stage in this long period of human pathology, and Romanticism as both a cultural product of it and as a corrective reflex that points to a healthier future, "wenn einst . . . beide [Leib und Geist] wieder in unserem Bewußtsein vereinigt sind" (B 1: 545).[5]

What Schnabelewopski says about the world of dreams as a refuge for sensual pleasure that was banished during the long centuries of repression also holds true for the Romantic soul:

> Um uns her verschwanden alle Herrlichkeiten der Welt, und wir fanden sie wieder in unserer inneren Seele — in unsere Seele flüchtete sich der Duft der zertretenen Rosen und der lieblichste Gesang der verscheuchten Nachtigallen —. (B 1: 545)

The young romantic's dream then stages an allegorical scene representing the role Romantic love poetry plays within the historical context just described. The setting is one of Heine's most familiar topoi for the Romantic poet: he sits in a boat on the still surface of the water under a cloud-free blue sky, at the feet of his beloved Jadviga. He recites his love poems ("schwärmerische Liebeslieder") to her even as he writes them onto rose-colored slips of paper, which she then rips out of his hand and tosses into the sea as she smiles longingly at him. But even before they reach the water, nixies grab them from the air and bring them to a small gathering at the bottom of the sea, where a young sprite stands and recites them to a circle of nixies seated around him. Their enthusiastic reception of the love poems offers a distanced perspective onto the human world of love, passion, and Romantic poetry:

> Welche sonderbare Wesen sind die Menschen! Wie sonderbar ist ihr Leben! Wie tragisch ihr ganzes Schicksal! Sie lieben sich und dürfen es meistens nicht sagen, und dürfen sie es einmal sagen, so können sie doch einander selten verstehn! Und dabei leben sie nicht ewig wie wir, sie sind sterblich, nur eine kurze Spanne Zeit ist ihnen vergönnt das Glück zu suchen, sie müssen es schnell erhaschen, hastig ans Herz drücken, ehe es entflieht — deshalb sind ihre Liebeslieder auch so zart, so innig, so süßängstlich, so verzweiflungsvoll lustig, ein so seltsames Gemisch von Freude und Schmerz. (B 1: 546)

While the tragedy of human existence is defined here from the Hellenic perspective on mortality, with the nixies providing their own version of the Olympic point of view, the thrust of the passage is not on cathartic acceptance. Rather, the narrator's comments points the finger at the Nazarene (to use Heine's favored term) rejection of life in the here and now:

> Was ist Traum? Was ist Tod? Ist dieser nur eine Unterbrechung des Lebens? Oder gänzliches Aufhören desselben? Ja, für Leute, die nur Vergangenheit und Zukunft kennen und nicht in jedem Momente der Gegenwart eine Ewigkeit leben können, ja für solche muß der Tod schrecklich sein! Wenn ihnen die beiden Krücken, Raum und Zeit, entfallen, dann sinken sie ins ewige Nichts. (B 1: 545)

In a passage that foreshadows Nietzsche's *Die Geburt der Tragödie* almost a half century later, Romantic ecstasy, the modern equivalent of Dionysian *Rausch,* is offered as a counterforce not only to Nazarene renunciation of the physical world, but to despotic scientific rationalism as well. Thus the notion presented by Schnabelewopski — that Romantic indulgence in the fullness of the moment can subvert a rational construction of time (and space) that calls for deferment of pleasure in an ephemeral material world until an eternal, spiritual hereafter — becomes a pivotal point in all Heine's assessments of Romanticism, and of historical progress.

In another context, one in which he addresses German culture in the age of political fragmentation and social inequality, Heine declares impassioned, subjective Romantic art as the most genuine form of cultural expression. Citing his own celebrated proclamation of the "Ende der Kunstperiode,"[6] he looks forward to a future period when art and life will blend harmoniously. But until sociopolitical reality can enable individual freedom and fulfillment, Romantic enthusiasm must give irrepressible voice to this basic right to life: "Bis dahin möge, mit Farben und Klängen, die selbsttrunkenste Subjektivität, die weltentzügelte Individualität, die gottfreie Persönlichkeit, all ihrer Lebenslust sich geltend machen" (B 3: 72–73). This passage from *Französische Maler,* written in 1831 only shortly after the *Schnabelewopski* fragment, comes at a time when Heine was beginning to look on his own Romantic poetry less favorably and see himself more as a politically engaged writer of satirical prose whose true calling was to be the herald of an imminent social revolution that would eventually lead to a new culture ("die neue Zeit wird auch eine neue Kunst gebären" [B 3: 72]).

These feelings reach their zenith at the end of the 1830s, after Heine had published *Zur Geschichte der Religion und Philosophie in Deutschland,* in which he proclaims the role of modern German philosophy in the path to emancipation; and after he had gained notoriety as one of the writers named in the Bundestag decree against the concocted *Junges Deutschland* movement. In the preface to the second edition of *Buch der Lieder* (1837), he writes that for some time something within him had been opposing any urges he might have to write in verse. Here Heine is distancing himself both from his early poems, which he says had lost their "süßesten, jungfräulichen Reizsüßesten, jungfräulichen Reiz" (B 1: 9), as well as from the youthful exuberance he felt during those early years when he composed the poems of *Buch der Lieder.* At the time this is not surprising. This was after all only the second edition of *Buch der Lieder,* while his *Reisebilder* had made him famous among the Germans and was also the first of his writings to be translated into French. Moreover, he stood at the height of his fame as a political writer at a time when the literary left seemed destined to lead Germany to the awaited emancipation from its reactionary leaders.[7]

Despite all this, Heine was not about to distance himself completely from poetry. He cautions that his poetry was spawned by the same idea that was behind his political, theological, and philosophical writings, and that one cannot condemn the one (his poetry) because of the idea behind it, while at the same time praising the other. Two years later, in the preface to the third edition of *Buch der Lieder,* his stance had changed considerably, perhaps in part because by then his fame was already based more on his poems and the attention they had garnered from Romantic composers. Here the preface itself begins with a poem, one that depicts the work on the third edition as a return to that Romantic dream world he had largely abandoned over the last decade:

> Das ist der alte Märchenwald!
> Es duftet die Lindenblüte!
> Der wunderbare Mondenglanz
> Bezaubert mein Gemüte. (B 1: 14)

In a short passage following the poem, he explains his long hiatus from poetry. Declaring that the flame which had inspired his poetry must now be used in the important social and political battles of the day ("zu weit ernsteren Bränden, verwendet werden mußte" [B 1: 16]), he assures that the poet-god Apollo will understand and forgive him. But the poem itself provides unusual insight into that world of love and passion explored in his love poems, offering an overview of the strange mixture of joy and pain that comprises love. In fact, he underscores the analytical character of the poem, when immediately after it he writes: "Das hätte ich alles sehr gut in Prosa sagen können" (B 1: 15).

As the poet wanders through the fragrant moonlit landscape of the poem, Heine's prolific symbol of Romantic song, the nightingale, begins a song with the dominant theme of his own love poetry: "Sie singt von Lieb und Liebesweh / Von Tränen und von Lachen." As the song awakens forgotten dreams of Romantic passion in the poet, he comes upon a forlorn castle with a marble sphinx figure in front of the gate. Overcome by the sweetness of the nightingale's song, he kisses the sphinx passionately, bringing it to life and arousing in himself the old familiar combination of glowing desire and unbearable pain:[8]

> Entzückende Marter und wonniges Weh!
> Der Schmerz wie die Lust unermeßlich!
> Derweilen des Mundes Kuß mich beglückt,
> Verwunden die Tatzen mich gräßlich. (B 1: 15)

Here the mystery of love explored in *Buch der Lieder* becomes the riddle of the sphinx:

> Die Nachtigall sang: "O schöne Sphinx!
> O Liebe! Was soll es bedeuten,
> Daß du vermischest mit Todesqual
> All deine Seligkeiten?
>
> O schöne Sphinx! O löse mir
> Das Rätsel, das wunderbare!
> Ich hab darüber nachgedacht
> Schon manche tausend Jahre." (B 1: 15)

But the preface seems ambivalent about the mystery. The following comment, Heine's assurance that he could have said the same thing in "good prose," suggests rather that the mystery itself is an ideological beguilement, one that diverts attention away from the real cause of unfulfilled love. In fact, he had already stated as much in "good prose" six years earlier in *Die Romantische Schule:*

> Was war aber Die Romantische Schule in Deutschland?
>
> Sie war nichts anders als die Wiedererweckung der Poesie des Mittelalters, wie sie sich in dessen Liedern, Bild- und Bauwerken, in Kunst und Leben manifestiert hatte. Diese Poesie war aber aus dem Christentume hervorgegangen, . . .
>
> Ich spreche von jener Religion [dem römischen Katholizismus] in deren ersten Dogmen eine Verdammnis alles Fleisches enthalten ist, . . . durch deren unnatürliche Aufgabe ganz eigentlich die Sünde und die Hypokrisie in die Welt gekommen, indem eben, durch die Verdammnis des Fleisches, die unschuldigsten Sinnenfreuden eine Sünde geworden, . . . die ebenfalls durch die Lehre von der Verwerflichkeit aller irdischen Güter, von der auferlegten Hundedemut und Engelsgeduld, die erprobteste Stütze des Depotismus geworden. . . . Eben weil wir alle Konsequenzen jenes absoluten Spiritualismus jetzt so ganz begreifen, dürfen wir auch glauben, daß die christkatholische Weltansicht ihre Endschaft erreicht. Denn jede Zeit ist eine Sphinx,

die sich in den Abgrund stürzt, sobald man ihr Rätsel gelöst hat. (B 3: 361–62)

Here it seems that Heine's main consideration in issuing the third edition of *Buch der Lieder* and expressing the sphinxian riddle in the preface in verse form had less to do with a return to Romantic poetry and its engagement of the themes of love, and may well have been financial interest. However, he continued writing Romantic poetry over these years, apparently even keeping it somewhat concealed until the publication of *Neue Gedichte* in 1844. This might suggest that he never considered the mystery of the sphinx's riddle as clearly solved as he implies in those statements that associate his early poetry with his political writings.

When the sphinx topos surfaces again much later in *Gedichte. 1853 und 1854,* the ready solution offered during the years of faith in the inevitable progress of reason is no longer an option:

> Die Gestalt der wahren Sphinx
> Weicht nicht ab von der des Weibes;
> Faselei ist jener Zusatz
> Des betatzten Löwenleibes.
>
> Todesdunkel ist das Rätsel
> Dieser wahren Sphinx. Es hatte
> Kein so schweres zu erraten
> Frau Jokastens Sohn und Gatte.
>
> Doch zum Glücke kennt sein eignes
> Rätsel nicht das Frauenzimmer;
> Spräch es aus das Lösungswort,
> Fiele diese Welt in Trümmer.
>
> (B 6.1: 206–7)

Clearly, at this later point in time the oversimplified relationship between Romantic love (poetry) and the sociopolitical suppression of sensuality no longer suffices as the answer to this sphinx-like riddle of beloved woman. Leaving aside the more speculative question of possible reasons why Heine suggested such an uncomplicated causal connection in the 1830s, the following discussion examines his continued poetic treatment of the theme after 1840. Beginning with *Neue Gedichte,* aspects of love's mysteries addressed in the early poems resurface in a somewhat more reflective thematic context.

Neue Gedichte

In the poems published during the 1840s the topos of a sphinxian riddle gives way to the motif of a highly charged secret, one that the poet divulges selectively and guardedly. In this case too, the mystery of love's torments is bound up with the progressive cause of freedom and social justice. Now, however, Heine sees this social revolution as a necessary and inevitable result of modern critical philosophy. And more specifically, he envisions himself as the poet-herald who understood and revealed the hidden revolutionary import of the Hegelian dialectic. Because of this double frame of reference the treatment of the *Geheimnis* topos in *Neue Gedichte* is clouded in ambiguity.[9] Even in those poems where the "secret" is clearly connected to the mysteries of love there are implied allusions to ideological forces at work in both the religious and secular idealization of unfulfilled love.

A good example of this is "Sorge nie, daß ich verrate." In the poem's explicit address to the female lover the poet assures her that his poetry will never betray the secret of their passionate, consummated love:

> Sorge nie, daß ich verrate
> Meine Liebe vor der Welt,
> Wenn mein Mund ob deiner Schönheit
> Von Metaphern überquellt.
>
> Unter einem Wald von Blumen
> Liegt, in still verborgner Hut,
> Jenes glühende Geheimnis,
> Jene tief geheime Glut.
>
> Sprühn einmal verdächtge Funken
> Aus den Rosen — sorge nie!
> Diese Welt glaubt nicht an Flammen,
> Und sie nimmts für Poesie. (B 4: 314–15)

The metaphors here are consistently divided between those that stand for his love poetry (Metaphern, Wald von Blumen, Rosen) and those that stand for the love affair that inspired the verses (glühende[s] Geheimnis, Glut, Funken, Flammen). The last stanza captures the irony that results when poetry is actually able to express the passion generated by consummated love. The more strongly it appears in poetry the more likely the public will take it to be heightened, sublimated love nourished by frustrations in the real world. This reversal of the "natural" order of things points to the social repression of desire, *and* to the way it has become ingrained in the aesthetic discourse of love. In turn, the secret divulged by the poem is that consummated, physical love is in fact one of the constituent experiences of Romantic love poetry.

The ambiguity surrounding the "secret" motif is most obvious in the poem that actually bears the title "Geheimnis." Its placement in the "Zeitgedichte" section of the anthology points away from the Romantic theme of love's torments, although this theme is clearly dominant in the first two stanzas:

> Wir seufzen nicht, das Aug ist trocken,
> Wir lächeln oft, wir lachen gar!
> In keinem Blick, in keiner Miene,
> Wird das Geheimnis offenbar.
>
> Mit seinen stummen Qualen liegt es
> In unsrer Seele blutgem Grund;
> Wird es auch laut im wilden Herzen,
> Krampfhaft verschlossen bleibt der Mund.
>
> Frag du den Säugling in der Wiege,
> Frag du die Toten in dem Grab,
> Vielleicht daß diese dir entdecken
> Was ich dir stets verschwiegen hab.
>
> (B 4: 414–15)

At the time of *Neue Gedichte* Heine was boasting that he had unveiled the secret of a "demonic necessity" in Hegelian thought, a dialectic of inevitable social and political revolution that the young communist movement would eventually set into motion. The labeling of "Geheimnis" (1838) as a *Zeitgedicht* serves to support two claims Heine was making that would bolster his image as a consistent and even prophetic political writer. One, that he had recognized the radical revolutionary import of German philosophy as early as the 1830s; and two, the claim made in the preface to the second edition of *Buch der Lieder,* that his poetry stemmed from the same basic social thinking as his political and philosophical writings. If "Geheimnis" is indeed read as a *Zeitgedicht,* then the conclusion would be that the deep torment undisclosed by the poet will be eliminated once reason has fully established its influence and the ideological suppression of the flesh is overcome.

Still, the poetic idiom and the persons inscribed in the poem ("wir," "du," "ich") intimate a happy love relationship that is threatened only by the inherent dual nature of love itself. In this more obvious reading, the secret indicated in the title is kin to the riddle of the sphinx both in "Das ist der alte Märchenwald" and in poem 9 of "Zum Lazarus" ("Die Gestalt der wahren Sphinx") in *Gedichte. 1853 und 1854.* The poet guards against disclosing — through even the slightest glance or gesture — this secret to his love companion, with whom he can, at least for the time being, still smile and laugh without crying or sighing. However, even in the happiest love relationships this other, more intrinsically tragic aspect of love, a part of the human condition that cannot be corrected through social evolution, lies barely beneath the surface, known to all in the depths of the soul. But even when repressed with great effort ("Krampfhaft verschlossen bleibt der Mund"), the painful, passionate burning of desire reveals it ("Es wird auch laut im wilden Herzen"). It is this sublime mixture of joy and pain that the Romantic poet expresses in his *Liebeslieder* as a guarded mystery, unrevealed in its stark reality and yet manifest in the sweet pain of longing that would induce the nixie to exclaim "Welch Poesie in einer Menschenträne!"

Heine thematizes his *Neue Gedichte* as a return to the thorny world of Romantic love poetry. In "Neuer Frühling," the opening cycle of the anthology, as he returns to that "alte Märchenwald" he had left behind (biographically, when he left for Paris in 1831), he yearns as well for the combination of pain and joy associated with it:

> Ach, ich sehne mich nach Tränen,
> Liebestränen, schmerzenmild,
> Und ich fürchte, dieses Sehnen
> Wird am Ende noch erfüllt. (B 4: 303–4)

On one hand, this is an acceptance of the poet's privileged knowledge that love always comes at this price. It is also the special commitment made in the choice of Romantic poetry, the knowledge that love is worthy of poetic formulation only when desire outstrips fulfillment.

In *Neue Gedichte* Heine also analyzes anew, with a more distanced and reflective eye, the torturous pain he had expressed in his earlier love songs — and perhaps experienced in the amorous adventures that may have inspired them. Employing the desire that leads him back to Romantic poetry as an analogous model, he describes how the cyclical return of desire constitutes love:

> Die holden Wünsche blühen,
> Und welken wieder ab,
> Und blühen und welken wieder —
> So geht es bis ans Grab.
>
> Das weiß ich, und das vertrübet
> Mir alle Lieb und Lust;
> Mein Herz ist so klug und witzig,
> Und verblutet in meiner Brust. (B 4: 317)

Here he laments that all passionate, enrapturing love — the kind of love that, according to Schnabelewopski, enables one to live in the present moment for an eternity — is subject to the recurring pain of withdrawal. The poet who understands at least this much about the mysteries of love is too clever for his own good. For this reason, he guards against disclosing this knowledge and gives voice to the pain indirectly, serving thus a therapeutic purpose. The therapy functions in a twofold manner. Through artistic engagement it ennobles love, giving it significance beyond its physical or social incarnation. It does so, however, while concealing the blatant truth behind the pain of love. In this respect, the mystification and even glorification of love build an important bulwark against its secrets leaking out with potentially disastrous results ("Fiele diese Welt in Trümmer"). Looking back to the 1839 preface to *Buch der Lieder,* one can conjecture that this may have also been one reason, if not indeed the primary reason why Heine expressed the ideas of "Das ist der alte Märchenwald" in verse rather than in "good prose," as he claimed he could have. For *poetic* inquiry into the hidden truth is defensible — and apparently even integral to the success of the Romantic project; and the flames that the poet claims will remain a secret in "Sorge nie, daß ich verrate,"

> Diese Welt glaubt nicht an Flammen,
> Und sie nimmts für Poesie. (B 4: 315)

refer not only to the real love affair, but also to the deep pain that always accompanies love.

Even as the poet revisits and re-examines the questions of love that had once dominated his poetic world, the ambiguity concerning love in the real world remains. Regardless of how torturous it may be, the poet deplores any missed opportunity to experience it in the fullest. In *Buch der Lieder* he frequently laments the pain incurred when

his beloved spurns his advances (for example, in "Sie haben mich ge-
quälet" or "Die Jahre kommen und vergehen"), or even proclaims the
cruelty of the woman who would inflict such torture on him (for example, in "Das Meer erglänzte weit hinaus" or "Du hast Diamanten
und Perlen"). In *Neue Gedichte* the poet not only expresses his own
suffering over unfulfilled love, but also charges at times that the
woman who rejected his love will regret the missed opportunity and
share in the pain:

> Es kommt zu spät, was du mir lächelst,
> Was du mir seufzest, kommt zu spät!
> Längst sind gestorben die Gefühle,
> Die du so grausam einst verschmäht.
>
> Zu spät kommt deine Gegenliebe!
> Es fallen auf mein Herz herab
> All deine heißen Liebesblicke,
> Wie Sonnenstrahlen auf ein Grab.
>   (B 4: 341–42)

Not only does the woman share in the suffering because she failed to
accept his passionate love; she is also attributed more blame here than
in the earlier poems. But even where this is not the case, poems with
this theme in *Neue Gedichte* convey quite explicitly the idea that these
lost opportunities are part of the human tragedy, regardless of what
exquisite poetry they may serve to generate:

> Wir standen an der Straßeneck
> Wohl über eine Stunde;
> Wir sprachen voller Zärtlichkeit
> Von unsrem Seelenbunde.
>
> Wir sagten uns viel hundertmal,
> Daß wir einander lieben;
> Wir standen an der Straßeneck,
> Und sind da stehn geblieben.
>
> Die Göttin der Gelegenheit,
> Wie 'n Zöfchen, flink und heiter,
> Kam sie vorbei und sah uns stehn,
> Und lachend ging sie weiter. (B 4: 337)

In poem 4 of the same "Hortense" group of "Verschiedene," Heine presents a brief exchange between Eve and the serpent about the forbidden fruit in the Garden of Eden. When Eve, caught up in the enticing lure of the apple and the serpent's bewitching eyes, remarks how it promises "holdes Glück," her temptress replies:

> Dieses ist die Frucht des Lebens,
> Koste ihre Süßigkeit,
> Daß du nicht so ganz vergebens
> Lebtest deine Lebenszeit! (B 4: 338)

And there is little doubt that in this context Heine stands on the side of this female sage ("die kluge Muhme"), reversing the doctrine of abstinence drawn from the traditional Judeo-Christian reading of original sin.

The final word on the return to love poetry and its relationship to actual love experiences comes perhaps in the final poem of the "Katharina" group of "Verschiedene." In the first stanza, the poet depicts his return to love poetry after a long hiatus,

> Gesanglos war ich und beklommen
> So lange Zeit — nun dicht ich wieder!
> Wie Tränen, die uns plötzlich kommen,
> So kommen plötzlich auch die Lieder. (B 4: 367)

and claims that he can sing again of the old themes of love, conflict, separation, and, ultimately, suffering. With the revival of his Romantic poetry he hears again the whispering of the German oaks above his head and the singing of the German nightingales. But they are only dreams that fade away: "Das sind nur Träume — sie verhallen." Now that the love relationships themselves are a thing of the past, the images and tropes of the poems appear like ghosts that haunt him rather than capture the original enchantment of their love:

> Wo sind die Rosen, deren Liebe
> Mich einst beglückt? — All ihre Blüte
> Ist längst verwelkt! — Gespentisch trübe
> Spukt noch ihr Duft mir im Gemüte. (B 4: 368)

Here the roses stand not only for the expression of love in Romantic poetry, but also for the women he had loved and his love itself, both of which provided the material for his early love poetry. Time has passed, and those flowers have now wilted. This is not to say that the poems have lost their ability to speak of love, but rather that the relationship between them and the earlier experience that inspired them has withered. Now the poetic voice examines more this alienation (*Entfremdung*) from those vibrant love experiences than the experiences themselves.

The poet Heine is removed from these poetic images and their referents not only by time. Also distance, both spatial and cultural, separates him from the love that he once enjoyed. As the last poem of the "Katharina" cycle, "Gesanglos war ich und beklommen" stands just before "In der Fremde," and in it the poet stresses that they are *German* oaks ("die deutschen Eichen") and *German* nightingales ("die alten, deutschen Nachtigallen") that return to him like dreams and stir up haunting memories of a fresh, young love that he can now revive poetically but not experientially. Thus cut off from real experience by time and space, the roses as poetic tropes exude a ghostly aura. They are no longer able to engender the sweet dreams ("Es war ein süßer, lieber, sonniger Traum" [B 1: 546]) of a Schnabelewopski drifting along the still surface of the water in the boat with his beloved Jadviga. At this point, the alienation from the world of Romantic imagination (and the Romanticized love situations that had given rise to it) is still far removed from the crisis level that it will reach in the "Matratzengruft." Here it is the years of exile from the homeland that have cast a gloomy shadow over the return to Romantic poetry:

> Das küßte mich auf deutsch, und sprach auf deutsch
> (Man glaubt es kaum
> Wie gut es klang) das Wort: "ich liebe dich!"
> Es war ein Traum. (B 4: 370)

Now I would like to turn my attention to the escalation of this crisis after 1848, when Heine's physical decline renders any further experience of passionate love only a pale shadow of those earlier adventures. In turn, the poetic analysis of Romantic love becomes both more distanced and more embittered. Some of the poetic motifs for this loss employed in *Neue Gedichte* — such as the reappearance of early Romantic tropes as ghosts — return in more drastic figuration. Also, completely new metaphors appear, introducing possible alternative modes of love into what becomes a more complex mix.

Gedichte. 1853 und 1854

When Heine (in the "Nachwort" to *Romanzero*) refers to his Paris apartment as his "Matratzengruft" this is his figurative description for the physical confinement caused by his illness, but it also alludes to a central motif that runs throughout much of his late poetry. Assuming at times the New Testament persona of Lazarus, he takes up a perspective beyond life from which to reflect on the great questions of human existence. This is not the exalted standpoint of a great thinker who has achieved a distance and objectivity that might provide new insights into life. To the contrary, they are the tones of a prostrate and frustrated individual who has, in his own view, fought the good fight, only to be rewarded with prolonged agony and misery.

The Lazarus poems constitute a distinct group of Heine's late poetry, a set of poems that address the themes of unjust suffering, pending death, lost hope for this life, and a retrospective assessment of those Romantic dreams that had underpinned his sense of the value of life. Perhaps the best known of them are found among the final twenty poems of the "Lamentationen" section in *Romanzero,* which appear under the subheading "Lazarus." Here my focus is on the subsequent poems that belong to this circle, and in particular on the eleven poems in a section of *Gedichte. 1853 und 1854* entitled "Zum Lazarus." Although the title suggests that they might be only supplementary poems that complement the ideas presented in the *Romanzero* group, this later cycle of Lazarus poems pushes the questioning from the assumed perspective of the poet-Lazarus persona a step further into an even more radical standpoint, one figured around the central trope of the grave.

Heine does not employ this voice from the tomb to rail disconsolately at the injustices of the world. Rather he employs the grave as an innovative standpoint that opens up new vistas on important questions of human existence, including quite prominently the question of love. The grave, as the poetic parallel to his real Paris "Matratzengruft," is perhaps the most productive of the metaphors for this viewpoint from beyond life. When he showed some of the most powerful of these later poems to Alfred Meissner during a visit to his apartment in 1854, Meissner expressed shock at the almost gruesome anguish and openly blasphemous stance displayed in some of the poems. But Heine, showing an enthusiastic satisfaction at his visitor's reaction, said of their novel poetic tone: "Ja, ich weiß es wohl, das ist schön, entsetzlich schön! Es ist eine Klage wie aus einem Grabe, da schreit ein Lebendigbegrabener durch die Nacht, oder gar eine Leiche, oder gar das Grab selbst" (Werner 2: 351).

One of the poems Meissner saw was the first poem in the "Zum Lazarus" cycle of *Gedichte. 1853 und 1854.* In this group of eleven numbered poems Heine adopts the poetic perspective of the grave in order to investigate once again the theme of Romantic love. As was always the case with his anthologies, Heine arranged the sequence of poems in ways that supplemented each poem's own immanent message. This is particularly true for the Lazarus poems, which stand as an integrated cycle among the otherwise individually sorted poems in the collection. The opening poem of "Zum Lazarus" immediately establishes the poet's defiant and exasperated search for answers to the enigmatic questions of life:

> Laß die heilgen Parabolen,
> Laß die frommen Hypothesen —
> Suche die verdammten Fragen
> Ohne Umschweif uns zu lösen. (B 6.1: 201)

The middle two stanzas then identify as the sore point the same theme that appeared throughout the "Historien" section of *Romanzero:* why do the just suffer ignominious defeat while the evil prevail? The last stanza then pinpoints the grave as the only remaining venue from which these questions can be raised afresh:

> Also fragen wir beständig,
> Bis man uns mit einer Handvoll
> Erde endlich stopft die Mäuler —
> Aber ist das eine Antwort? (B 6.1: 202)

As prelude to the cycle, "Laß die heilgen Parabolen" apprises the reader that the poet is removing that handful of dirt from his mouth and speaking now from this final resting place, which may offer new insight into these bewitching questions.

However, the central theme of the cycle turns out to be not the question of social justice expressed in the middle two stanzas, but rather the riddle of love guarded by the sphinx-like figure of woman. Poem 2 shifts the focus from the general question of the ill-rewards meted out to the just and good on earth to the poet's own specific situation. Making the biographical link to Heine's belief that he was suffering from a venereal disease, the poet laments his relationship with "die schwarze Frau," a metaphorical figure representing both the woman from whom he may have contracted syphilis and the disease itself:

> Sie küßte mich lahm, sie küßte mich krank,
> Sie küßte mir blind die Augen; (B 6.1: 202).

Regardless of the cause of his physical afflictions, the poet evaluates his situation,

> Mein Leib ist jetzt ein Leichnam, worin
> Der Geist ist eingekerkert — (B 6.1: 202),

and then concludes that his wild cursing will not change his fate, and that he should bear it rather with gentle weeping and prayer. Notwithstanding, in poem 3 the poet employs the just introduced image of his *Geist* trapped within a corpse to devise another way of coping with his helplessness. He describes how fantasies parade about in his mind during the night, speculating that he may actually be deceased and that they are ghosts who have sought out his skull for their nightly romp:

> Es mögen wohl Gespenster sein,
> Altheidnisch göttlichen Gelichters;
> Sie wählen gern zum Tummelplatz
> Den Schädel eines toten Dichters. —
>
> (B 6.1: 203)

As the image of his body as corpse reveals itself to be only a metaphor, the poet utilizes these nightly visions as material for his poetry:

> Die schaurig süßen Orgia,
> Das nächtlich tolle Geistertreiben,
> Sucht des Poeten Leichenhand
> Manchmal am Morgen aufzuschreiben.
>
> (B 6.1: 203)

Here Heine engages the theme of the banished Greek gods that he had frequently enlisted in his campaign against the Nazarene renunciation of sensuality and the body.[10] "Orgia" refers literally of course to the nocturnal Bacchanalia celebrating intoxication and sexual revelry. By labeling them "die schaurig süßen Orgia," the poet shifts the context from the original Hellenic festivities to the Romantic celebration of love — and in particular one might recall Heine's own account in the *Schnabelewopski* dream, where the nixies praise the poet's love songs as a combination of the sweetest feelings mixed with accompa-

nying dread of bitter pain, "so zart, so innig, so süßängstlich, so verzweiflungsvoll lustig" (B 1: 546). These expressions of love are now
one more step removed from the immediate, unadulterated experience
of passion as it was represented, even if only one-sidedly, in the Bacchanalia. The poet, a corpse in the sense that he can no longer participate in the physical culmination of love, is haunted by the ghosts of
his former escapades and desires. As in his early Romantic songs, they
form the basis for his poetry, but they return here as displaced memories, themselves only shadows ("Spukgestalten") of the earlier visions that
were inspired in some way by his own romantic adventures. This recalls the return of his poetic love tropes in *Neue Gedichte,* which also
appear as ghastly shadows of the original figures. But now the poet takes
these nocturnal visions as the "material" for his poetic production.

The "Zum Lazarus" poems are, then, products of "des Poeten
Leichenhand." In their now double remove from *Buch der Lieder* they
provide more distance to the poetic engagement with love and a
stronger sense of resignation. Poems 4 through 8 present a retrospective mourning of lost opportunities for love, now made more bitter by
the finality of the poet's physical debility. Poem 4 seemingly refers to
real life experiences in a direct fashion unusual for Heine's love poetry.
The poet regrets how he once rode his proud mount past many flowers, not bothering to stoop and pick them. In this allusion to missed
opportunities for romance, one specific "flower" he passed over ("eine
feuergelbe Viole") preys on his mind.

The next four poems all focus on one female figure, but in this
case the poet places the blame for unfulfilled love on her. Poem 5 begins by declaring that there were a host of unresponsive love interests — well documented in *Buch der Lieder* and *Neue Gedichte* — all
of whom he eventually accompanied to their graves in the smug belief
that they had in the end only deprived themselves:

> Leidtragend folgt ich ihren Särgen,
> Und bis zum Kirchhof ging ich mit;
> Hernach, ich will es nicht verbergen,
> Speist ich zu Mittag mit Apptit. (B 6.1: 204)

But mired in his dismal plight, he suddenly becomes distressed by the
memory of this "längstverstorbenen Schar." One in particular among
this crowd, Julchen, haunts his memory and eventually inhabits the
feverish dreams that he had likened to old pagan gods rumbling
around in the skull of a dead poet:

> Oft kommt zu mir die tote Blume
> Im Fiebertraum; alsdann zumut
> Ist mir, als böte sie posthume
> Gewährung meiner Liebesglut. (B 6.1: 204)

Again, this belated response to his offers of love is two stages removed from the original experience, returning as a ghostly reminder of the burning desire to which he had once given sublimated form in his love poetry, but which he now — "posthumously" — wants to fulfill in the real world. Poem 6 recalls their happy times together, beautiful summer days along the Rhine when they shared each other's enthusiasm for such splendor, only to end with the sour remembrance of Julchen's inability to give herself over totally to the moment: "Ein Herzchen im Korsett wie'n kleiner Gletscher" (B 6.1: 205). Then, in poem 7, the poet takes her to court for this icy resistance, only to admit in the end that, according to the dictates of reason, there is no basis for the charges:

> Vom Schöppenstuhle der Vernunft
> Bist du vollständig freigesprochen. (B 6.1: 205)

Only in his nightly dreams does a voice speak against her, presenting reams of documents that support his claim, "Du habest mich zugrund gerichtet." When he awakes the next morning, this accuser, together with all the evidence, has disappeared, and only his status as victim remains from the proceedings:

> Nur eins bleibt im Gedächtnis mir,
> Das ist: ich bin zugrund gerichtet. (B 6.1: 206)

The actual cause of the poet's misery — as determined by all rational judgment — is not the cold-hearted beloved who shunned his passionate desires but, to the contrary, "die schwarze Frau" of poem 2, who joined in the revelries of love and inflicted him with the fatal disease. The accusations made against Julchen in his dreams are, like the other nightly fantasies of "Zum Lazarus," remnants of his earlier Romantic poetry that have returned as the poet delves into the mysteries of love once again. They are the charges he made against unwilling lovers in his love songs; but for the infirm and dying poet they have another meaning. This is borne out in the next poem, when the poet tells of a letter he has received from Julchen expressing her sadness about his misery. If this most unfeeling object of his affection is now moved by his suffering, then, he surmises, his situation must be even worse than he had imagined:

> O Gott, wie muß ich elend sein!
> Denn sie sogar beginnt zu sprechen,
> Aus ihrem Auge Tränen brechen,
> Der Stein sogar erbarmt sich mein! (B 6.1: 206)

This vision of his beautiful beloved, cold as a marble statue ("marmor-schön und marmorkühl"), shedding tears is also taken from his Romantic writings on love — not from the love poetry, but from Schnabelewopski's dream. When the poet-hero of the dream hears the nixies exclaim how death casts its melancholy shadow over even the happiest moments of human love, he urges Jadviga to join him in an embrace that will prove them wrong:

> Hörst du, sagte ich zu Jadviga, wie die da unten über uns urteilen? — wir wollen uns umarmen, damit sie uns nicht mehr bemitleiden, damit sie sogar neidisch werden! Sie aber, die Geliebte, sah mich an mit unendlicher Liebe, und ohne ein Wort zu reden. Ich hatte sie stumm geküßt. Sie erblich, und ein kalter Schauer überflog die holde Gestalt. Sie lag endlich starr, wie weißer Marmor, in meinen Armen, und ich hätte sie für tot gehalten, wenn sich nicht zwei große Tränenströme unaufhaltsam aus ihren Augen ergossen — und diese Tränen überfluteten mich, während ich das holde Bild immer gewaltiger mit meinen Armen umschlag —. (B 1: 547)

This grotesquely humorous image of the weeping Jadviga offers ironical distance to Schnabelewopski's Romantic vision of transcendent love, his bidding that one must "in jedem Momente der Gegenwart eine Ewigkeit leben" (B 1: 545). For the bedridden, grotesquely suffering poet Heine, it is a ghostly legatee of his early poetic persona that continues to advocate this ideal vision — and the appeal has legitimate grounds in his feverish dreams, only to dissipate with the light of day.

Where does all this leave us with respect to the question of love? Has Heine returned to (or has he always maintained) the vision of love as an inherently bittersweet emotion ultimately doomed to unhappiness? Poem 9, his revisiting of the sphinxian riddle presented in "Das ist der alte Märchenwald," provides an answer, of sorts. Quoted in full earlier, it asserts that the mystery of love is "Todesdunkel": that is, only when lovers can avoid or repress the truth of love's ephemeral nature and enjoy the moment with no regard to the inevitable future can it deter reality and sustain life. Heine's sphinxian figure of Woman is not Woman per se, but the unresponsive beloved of his Romantic love songs. It is Schnabelewopski's Jadviga, who becomes cold and rigid like a marble statue when her poet-lover invokes her to share with him the passion of love. And the dark secret that she conceals unknowingly is the truth exclaimed by the nixies — the sublimated beauty and ecstasy that they adore in humankind is one born of the pain of unattainable pleasure and fulfilled in poetry only: "Welche Poesie in so einer Menschenträne!" But the grotesque double stream of tears flowing from Jadviga's eyes attests to the illusion on which love rests. And not only love. According to the dying poet, revisiting his own poetry of unrequited love, if this self-deception were revealed, if sphinxian Woman knew the answer to the riddle she poses with her unyielding resistance to love, then life, culture, and civilization would not be sustainable and the world would fall into ruins.

"Es träumte mir von einer Sommernacht"

When Heine offers insights into the mysteries of love in his late poetry he does not present them as universal truths, but rather as personal conclusions that are strongly colored by his own dismal situation. In fact, the grave as the locus from which to pursue these reflections is itself introduced as a wish projection, or the narrative enactment of that wish in dreams. Frequently in his late writings, both in his poetry and his autobiographical texts, he expresses the desire to exchange his Paris tomb for the real grave and his decrepit body for a corpse. This desire then constitutes a psychological context in which the poet can bypass the self-deception guarding the abysmal ("Todesdunkel") secret of sphinxian Woman. The opening poem of *Gedichte. 1853 und 1854*, "Ruhelechzend," establishes this framework with its final stanza:

> O Grab, du bist das Paradies
> Für pöbelscheue, zarte Ohren —
> Der Tod ist gut, doch besser wärs,
> Die Mutter hätt uns nie geboren. (B 6.1: 189)

And in poem 8 of "Zum Lazarus," when Julchen's letter of sympathy cuts through the darkness of his "tomb" like a flash of lightning, he realizes how deep his misery actually is and he asks God to spare him more such torture:

> Auch du erbarm dich mein und spende
> Die Ruhe mir, o Gott, und ende
> Die schreckliche Tragödia. (B 6.1: 206)

When these poetically captured fantasies of feverish nights disappear in the morning light, the sick poet entertains less radical alternatives and resorts to a more mundane language. Both the concluding poem of the "Zum Lazarus" cycle,

> Gesundheit nur und Geldzulage
> Verlang ich, Herr! O laß mich froh
> Hinleben noch viel schöne Tage
> Bei meiner Frau im statu quo! (B 6.1: 208)

and the final poem of the anthology,

> Unser Grab erwärmt der Ruhm.
> Torenworte! Narrentum! (B 6.1: 239)

mark the return from the frenzied dream world of his death wish to the more common human desire to hold on to life. These two poems counteract his own poetically inscribed myth of the welcome grave and the Hellenic ideal of heroic death as forms of resignation that he had steadfastly resisted throughout his life. But the wish to live out his days free of the tumult created by desire is also discarded as fanciful. The last poem of "Zum Lazarus" undermines the desire to live on in domestic contentment,

> In Schlafrock und Pantoffeln bleibe
> Ich gern bei meiner Frau zu Haus (B 6.1: 208)

with ironic awareness that such a mundane life will never still the thirst for fullness of life that drives the noble of this world — and until the end Heine always held to the belief that his literary efforts were united if by nothing else, then by this singular sense of purpose: to make a life dedicated to noble pleasure and fulfillment a possibility for all. The rigidity and sterility of the poem's last line,

> Bei meiner Frau im statu quo! (B 6.1: 208)

resound in the ensuing silence and betray the wish as a momentary lapse from which he will immediately recover and then demand again not mere existence, but rather enraptured life.

And thus the bewildering questions raised by human desire remain — and the final, posthumous poems continue to pursue them. His last word on the mysteries of love and life offers, of course, no answers, and even, I would argue, suggests that the riddle posed by sphinxian Woman remains more enigmatic than ever. In what may be the last poem he wrote, Heine revisits many of the issues that informed his lifelong poetic quest into these questions.[11] "Es träumte mir von einer Sommernacht" describes an arabesque-like dream in which the poet finds himself amidst the ruins of splendid Renaissance palaces. The arabesque style of Romantic aesthetics permeates the dream vision on various levels: visually, from the interspersed pattern of statue and building fragments, to the ivy that has intertwined itself ("in Arabeskenart") around those broken figures; narratively, in the dream subject's dizzying oscillation between narrating observer and entranced dream-within-a-dream figure; and thematically, in an entangled web of those grand analytical questions that Heine had pursued throughout his life. On all levels the mesh is intricately fashioned to the extent that the poem ultimately defies exegesis. Even the two sets of opposing figures in the ruins, those from Greek mythology and those from the Bible, begin to argue against one another in a clamor of competing voices that confuse the senses:

> O, dieser Streit wird endgen nimmermehr,
> Stets wird die Wahrheit hadern mit dem Schönen,
> Stets wird geschieden sein der Menschheit Heer
> In zwei Partein: Barbaren und Hellenen. (B 6.1: 349)

The familiar opposition between Nazarenism and Hellenism that Heine considered to be at the heart of humankind's striving for a more enlightened civilization resurfaces here. However, now the central issue under debate (moral abstention versus sensuous pleasure) appears both irresolvable and irrepressible, leading only to the poet's despairing disavowal of dualistic thought.

The conflict between Nazarenism and Hellenism is not the only familiar dichotomy the poem addresses. In this final installment of Heine's lifelong attachment to Romantic poetry, those dualities that inevitably thwart any unencumbered experience of love seem to be overcome. The contradictory impulses of love take different forms in the recumbent poet's encounter with the flower of passion. The episode retains that mixture of desire and terror ("gewebt aus Lust und Schauder") that had always accompanied intense, passionate love in

Heine's poetry. The beloved even appears as "die Blume der Passion," a flower that arouses wild and passionate desire but whose internal parts are replicas of the instruments used to torture Christ on Calvary: the whip, rope, hammer, nails, chalice, and crown of thorns. This highly charged figure of the beloved is able to inspire at the same time both idealized, sublimated love and passionate, erotic experience. Its strange combination of colors indicate this:

> Die Blätter schwefelgelb und violett,
> Doch wilder Liebreiz in der Blume waltet.
>
> (B 6.1: 347)

"Schwefelgelb" — related to the "feuergelb" of the flower the poet regretted not having "picked" in poem 4 of "Zum Lazarus" — represents erotic passion, while "violett" stands for the ideal vision of love.

However, the ultimate representation of the encounter's combination of these two mutually exclusive forms of experience is found in the simultaneous presence of language and silence. As the poet finally enjoys with his beloved — "du geliebtes Kind" who embodies all the women in his love poetry — the blissful moment of fulfillment that he had long sought as an eternity in and of itself, he describes it paradoxically as both speech and silence:

> Wir sprachen nicht, jedoch mein Herz vernahm,
> Was du verschwiegen dachtest im Gemüte —
> Das ausgesprochene Wort ist ohne Scham,
> Das Schweigen ist der Liebe keusche Blüte.
>
> Und wie beredsam dieses Schweigen ist!
> Man sagt sich alles ohne Metaphoren,
> Ganz ohne Feigenblatt, ganz ohne List
> Des Silbenfalls, des Wohllauts der Rhetoren.
>
> Lautloses Zwiegespräch! man glaubt es kaum,
> Wie bei dem stummen, zärtlichen Geplauder
> So schnell die Zeit verstreicht im schönen Traum
> Der Sommernacht, gewebt aus Lust und Schauder.
>
> (B 6.1: 348)

The love encounter between the dead poet lying in a sarcophagus amidst the broken statues and his beloved, who appears as "die Blume der Passion," combines passion, physical love ("An deine Küssen"), and an exchange that at least simulates verbal communication ("bei dem stummen, zärtlichen Geplauder"). And the language describing their interaction also intertwines expressions for verbal communication with acts of physical intimacy:

> Doch frage nie, *wovon* im Mondenschein
> Die Marterblume und ihr Toter kosen!
> (B 6.1: 348; my italics)

In the context of the poem's dream vision, the culprit responsible for the impossible expectation placed on love — that is, that it fulfill both ideal visions and physical desires — appears to be language, or at least that crafted, poetic language ("Metaphoren"; "List des Silbenfalls"; "Wohlaut des Rhetoren") that heightens human sensibilities, but sublimates ("der Liebe keusche Blüte"; "Feigenblatt") sexual urges. Conversely, the antidote that enables the poet to enjoy this moment of pure bliss with his truest love ("die Liebste") is a language that confounds its own logical structures and produces words as silence and intimate physical contact as silent verbal communication.

Paradoxically, however, all this occurs in a dream (and a poem), and moreover, in a doubly removed dream world in which the dreaming subject perceives itself (as if in a dream) as a dead man lying in his grave. The silence of the grave, or rather the dream vision of the grave, enables the encounter to defy physical logic and overcome the dualities that frustrate human love:

> O Tod! Mit deiner Grabesstille, du,
> Nur du kannst uns die beste Wollust geben;
> Den Krampf der Leidenschaft, Lust ohne Ruh,
> Gibt uns für Glück das albern rohe Leben! (B 6.1: 348)

The poet enjoys this beautiful dream of a quietude that coexists with the most blissful pleasures of earthly love ("den schönen Friedenstraum"). However, this desire is fulfilled in direct contradiction to the nature of desire itself. Only when the desiring subject disappears, lost in the "Grabesstille" that is devoid of language and thus human life itself, can a truly fulfilling love be realized. The inscription of the poetic subject in the poem highlights this paradox. As the Judeo-Christian and Hellenic figures on the sarcophagus interrupt the dream-bliss with their never-ending debate, the donkey of Baal finally drowns out their disputation with his grating hee-haw, hee-haw!—restoring, in the final verse, the poetic subject to (self-)consciousness:

> Ich selbst zuletzt schrie auf — und ich erwachte. (B 6.1: 349)

This complex layering of subject identity enhances the arabesque patterns that baffle logic and enable the cryptic (sphinxian) episode of love. Is the "ich" that cries out in exasperation at the donkey's braying the dream subject or the waking poet-author, or even the man in the sarcophagus shaken out of his blissful love scene? The same questions apply to the "ich" that awakens. And even if one takes the final "ich" to be a settling return to the authorial poetic subject, the closure is not complete. For the "ich" that awakens is not strictly identical with the poetic subject at the beginning of the poem: "Es träumte *mir* von einer Sommernacht"! The confusion, much like that surrounding the two sets of relief figures carved into the sarcophagus or the rhetorical intermixing of silence and language, inhibits linguistic competence and feigns the forgetting that the poem suggests is requisite for "die beste Wollust."

In the end, what answers do Heine's late reflections on the discourse of Romantic poetry give to those central questions about love that run throughout his writing? Does the envisioned bliss of love in his final poem overcome in any way the restrictions of time and space (or of the human psyche, if one will) that Schnabelewopski had tried to defy in his challenge to Jadviga? Is the riddle of sphinxian Woman ultimately answered, and if so, does the answer offer any hope — for the future of humanity, if not for the dying poet — or at least new insight? One thesis — already argued in the analysis of the "Zum Lazarus" poems — remains intact. Heine abandons his earlier notion of an inevitable historical progress that will lead eventually, with the ascendance of reason and the restoration of the flesh, to a stage where Romantic love simply dissipates. Once this utopian idea had waned, he plays with alternative notions of overcoming the torments of desire in a series of late poems from *Romanzero* to *Gedichte. 1853 und 1854* and related unpublished pieces.[12] One such an alternative was impassioned love without the cycle of desire and frustration, a "schwärmen . . . ohne Lärmen" as he phrases it in one such poem.[13] This vision had appeared in the earlier period as well, but always in a more positive context, such as where the narrator of the *Reisebilder* declares the actual heroic element in the art of ancient Greece to be — in a reversal of the famous Winckelmann formula — "ewige Leidenschaft ohne Unruhe" (B 2: 498). The late poems reveal this to be a wish fantasy, equating it with the desire for death and an escape from the cycle of desire. Thus the same riddle of the sphinx remains in "die Blume der Passion," "rätselhaft gestaltet" with the torture instruments of Christ's crucifixion. And Heine occasionally even alludes, although usually playfully and never fully in earnest, to a parallel between himself and the divine paradigm of self-abnegation.[14] But if he does indeed share with Christ a similar inclination to revel in the pain and passion of love as a path to transcendental experience, as Heine suggests, then he was also careful to make the distinction when it came to the final temptation: to find release in a sublime acceptance of death. Even when confined to bed in protracted suffering, he plays with this alternative only to reject it in favor of life in this world.

If indeed Heine suggests an alternative to the idealist lure of the transcendental, then it is perhaps an overly simplistic solution that lacks viability without the "Wohllaut des Rhetoren." In a plain-spoken formulation, it might go something like this: understanding the convoluted dynamic of human desire, one should enjoy life to the fullest, accepting the pain of cyclical frustration and finitude with a stoically Epicurean attitude. Those who discuss the philosophical possibilities and moral ramifications ad infinitum or who accept the sublimation of Romantic poetry as a replacement for the experiences of love miss the boat, partaking in an endless braying of the donkey of Baal. The much ado about nothing of "Es träumte mir von einer Sommernacht" may be nothing more than the poet's play that conceals the answers to the "final questions" while not failing to ask them or to demand answers to them from the highest authority, all the while knowing the outcome. Thus the challenge issued in the opening poem of "Zum Lazarus," "Suche die verdammten Fragen / Ohne Umschweif uns zu lösen," usually seen as an almost blasphemous demand on God, is perhaps more applicable to those "Dichter und Denker" — the Romantic poet Heine included — who participate in elaborately constructed discourses devised as much for concealment as for revelation.

Notes

1 He makes this claim at the beginning of his *Geständnisse:* "ich bin ihr [der deutschen Romantik] letzter Dichter, mit mir ist die alte lyrische Schule der Deutschen geschlossen, während zugleich die neue Schule, die moderne deutsche Lyrik, von mir eröffnet ward" (B 6.1: 447).

2 A list of scholars who have argued this point would be much too extensive to include here. One exemplary instance is Preisendanz.

3 For a more extensive discussion of this tension between his Jewish heritage and emerging nineteenth-century concepts of German nationalism see Jost Hermand, "Der 'deutsche' Jude H. Heine," *Dichter und ihre Nation,* ed. Helmut Scheuer (Frankfurt am Main: Suhrkamp, 1993), 257–72; see also my "*Vaterlandsliebe* in

Exile: Heinrich Heine and German-Jewish National Identity," *Zur deutsch-jüdischen Literaturgeschichte im 19. Jahrhundert,* ed. Mark Gelber (Tübingen: Niemeyer, forthcoming).

[4] In chapter 5 of *Die Stadt Lucca,* he declares "[j]eder ist selbst krank genug in diesem großen Lazarett [der Welt]" (B 2: 492). This motif of the world as one great hospital surfaces in a more extensive form again at the beginning of book 3 of *Religion und Philosophie in Deutschland* (B 3: 592–94).

[5] For a discussion of more specific allusions to modern, bourgeois aspects of this split see Gerhard Höhn, *Heine-Handbuch: Zeit, Person, Werk* (Stuttgart: Metzler, 1987), 277.

[6] Heine first introduced this, at the time, quite bold idea that Goethe's artistic vision was already a thing of the past in his 1828 review of Wolfgang Menzel's *Die deutsche Literatur:* "Ist doch die Idee der Kunst zugleich der Mittelpunkt jener ganzen Literaturperiode, die mit dem Erscheinen Goethes anfängt und erst jetzt ihr Ende erreicht hat, ist sie doch der eigentliche Mittelpunkt in Goethe selbst, dem großen Repräsentanten dieser Period —" (B 1: 445). The better known phrase "das Ende der Kunsperiode" first appears when he cites the earlier passage three years later, after it had already become quite well known (B 3: 72).

[7] For an extended discussion of this issue as in connection to his return to Romantic poetry after 1848, see chapter 6 of my *By the Rivers of Babylon: Heinrich Heine's Late Songs and Reflections* (Detroit: Wayne State UP, 1998), and in particular, 273–81.

[8] For an overview of this theme in *Buch der Lieder,* including the connection to the sphinx metaphor, see Höhn, *Heine-Handbuch,* 52–54.

[9] For a discussion of the *Geheimnis* motif, which does more perhaps to intensify the ambiguity than to resolve it, see Briegleb's commentary on it in connection with the Börne *Denkschrift* (B 4: 753–54).

[10] For a detailed discussion of this use of mythology see the essay by Paul Reitter in this volume.

[11] For a recent account of the poem as it relates to his attempts to integrate his world of poetic imagination with the questions of world history see Albrecht Betz, "Der letzte Sommernachtstraum. Heines Gedicht 'An die Mouche,'" *Aufklärung und Skepsis: Internationaler Heine-Kongreß 1997 zum 200. Geburtstag,* ed. Joseph A. Kruse, Bernd Witte, and Karin Füllner (Stuttgart and Weimar: Metzler, 1999), 811–18.

[12] For a study of one of Heine's final unpublished poems that provides a complex, and almost cryptic analysis of desire see my "'Citronia': 'Kennst du das Land . . .?': A Riddle of Sexuality and Desire," *Heine-Jahrbuch* 35 (1996): 81–112.

[13] This formulation appears in "Der Abgekühlte" (B 6.1: 110–11); analogous ideas play a prominent role as well in "Für eine Grille — keckes Wagen!" (B 6.1: 322) and "Worte! Worte! Keine Taten!" (B 6.1: 343–44).

[14] Four examples, each quite distinct in their approach, can be found in: *Die Stadt Lucca* (B 2: 499–500); poem 7 of the "Katharina" cycle in *Neue Gedichte* (B 4: 365–67); *Deutschland. Ein Wintermärchen* (B 4: 605–6); and "Nächtliche Fahrt" in *Romanzero* (B 6.1: 54–55).

Works Cited

Betz, Albrecht. "Der letzte Sommernachtstraum. Heines Gedicht 'An die Mouche.'" *Aufklärung und Skepsis: Internationaler Heine-Kongreß 1997 zum 200. Geburtstag.* Ed. Joseph A. Kruse, Bernd Witte, and Karin Füllner. Stuttgart and Weimar: Metzler, 1999. 811–18.

Cook, Roger F. *By the Rivers of Babylon: Heinrich Heine's Late Songs and Reflections.* Detroit: Wayne State UP, 1998.

———. "'Citronia': 'Kennst du das Land . . .?': A Riddle of Sexuality and Desire." *Heine-Jahrbuch* 35 (1996): 81–112.

———. "*Vaterlandsliebe* in Exile: Heinrich Heine and German-Jewish National Identity." *Zur deutsch-jüdischen Literaturgeschichte im 19. Jahrhundert.* Ed. Mark Gelber. Tübingen: Niemeyer, forthcoming.

Hermand, Jost. "Der 'deutsche' Jude H. Heine." *Dichter und ihre Nation.* Ed. Helmut Scheuer. Frankfurt am Main: Suhrkamp, 1993. 257–72.

Höhn, Gerhard. *Heine-Handbuch: Zeit, Person, Werk.* Stuttgart: Metzler, 1987.

Pistiak, Arnold. *"Ich will das rote Sefchen küssen." Nachdenken über Heines letzten Gedichtzyklus.* Heine-Studien. Stuttgart and Weimar: Metzler, 1999.

Preisendanz, Wolfgang. "Der Ironiker Heine. Ambivalenzerfahrung und kommunikative Ambiguität." *Heinrich Heine: Ästhetisch-politische Profile.* Ed. Gerhard Höhn. Frankfurt am Main: Suhrkamp, 1991. 101–15.

Sammons, Jeffrey. *Heinrich Heine: A Modern Biography.* Princeton: Princeton UP, 1979.

Werner, Michael, ed. *Begegnungen mit Heine: Berichte der Zeitgenossen, in Fortführung von H. H. Houbens "Gespräche mit Heine."* Hamburg: Hoffmann und Campe, 1973. 2 vols.

Philosophy, History, Mythology

Nightingales Instead of Owls: Heine's Joyous Philosophy

Willi Goetschel

WHETHER IT HAS BEEN the result of the unquestioned hold of convention or the consequence of the division of labor between the academic disciplines dictated by the institutional organization of research, Heine's prose and poetry are still widely viewed as two distinctly different literary projects. But the separation of the aesthetic from the political significance of his work has limited the comprehension of the critical scope of Heine's writing. Almost exclusive focus on the aesthetic and political implications has led many critics to the assumption that there are two neatly disjunctive spheres, which, in turn, can be equally neatly integrated into one unproblematic, whole Heine. However, Heine challenges precisely such dichotomy. Whereas much of Heine criticism argues as if the aesthetic and political presented two separate, but complementary halves, Heine's work seems, on the contrary, to call for readings more attuned to the problem of their intricate interdependence. Gesturing to a principal questioning of the conceptual grasp of distinctions such as the one between the aesthetic and the political, his writing alerts to the need to reach beyond the constraints of conventional poetics and, instead, to critically refashion and rewrite the author as publicist; as an author whose poetics reflects the problem of tackling the precarious border between reason and imagination that separates but also conjoins thought and the creative forces of the subconscious, the two crucial agents of philosophy and literature.[1] However, the divided reception of Heine as the lyrical genius who would inspire the musical imagination of scores of Romantic composers and even make a Metternich shed a tear, on the one hand, and as an invidious "shadow image of the German intellectual" and provocative scare of the bourgeoisie, as Habermas so succinctly put it (96), on the other hand, has produced a deeply split image of the poet. As a consequence, the philosophically critical impulse at the heart of Heine's work has been lost on most readers.

Certainly, Heine's comments on philosophy and intellectual history have received, if not necessarily their deserved theoretical attention, at least praise for their spirited eloquence. But his writing on religion has also presented some hermeneutic challenges. Yet, the recognition of the importance of philosophy in Heine has remained limited to sporadic acknowledgments of the passages in which he addresses philosophy in explicit terms. Exploited as a gold mine for style and rhetoric, it seemed as if Heine, at best, provided the linguistic savvy and stylistic model for the philosophical projects of Marx, Nietzsche, and the militant activism of the Young Hegelians. The striking power of his metaphors and images was seen to have sprung from the magic black box of poetic talent — if not genius — the result of a fortuitous hand and sharp pen rather than the work of conceptually critical thinking.

But for Heine, philosophy was a much too important matter to be left to philosophers. His playful appropriation of philosophical discourse exposes the presuppositions, hidden claims, implications, and limits of philosophy as his prose and poetry opens up a self-reflective space in which philosophy's language games are rehearsed with a critical purpose. Simply scanning Heine for philosophical relevance is not sufficient, for his texts force the critical review of philosophy's aims, claims, and, purpose, motioning for an imaginative reconception of philosophy itself. Heine's philosophical impetus manifests itself often most profoundly where professional philosophers might least suspect it.[2] Giving voice to the non-conceptual dimension that lies beneath but also defines the conceptual, he stages the limits and constraints of philosophy with a consistency that amounts to philosophically challenging critique.

It would therefore seem peculiar indeed if the texts of a poet whose import can be traced in Marx, Nietzsche, Freud and whose family resemblance with the critical theory of the Frankfurt School makes one wonder about his curious absence from the canon of critical theory[3] would not draw the reader's attention to their insistently overt but also covert philosophical consequences. Heine's persistent resistance to the claims of philosophy's authority suggests more than simply poetry's autonomy and independence from reason. Invoking a concept of philosophy directly opposed to (though in critical dialogue with) Hegel's, Heine argues for an activist understanding of philosophy as critical thinking with a sharp, cutting edge. While according to Hegel, Minerva's Owl takes its flight at the end of the day, Heine has his party of nightingales sing jubilantly as the early messengers not only of liberation, emancipation, and social justice, but also of free-spirited thinking that has broken out of the conceptual cage that the oppositions between sensualism and spiritualism, materialism and idealism had so irrefutably imposed.

Heine's anti-idealist reinstatement of the flesh, of sensualism, and individualism in its irreducible particularity exerts a recalcitrant reticence against normative prescriptions of philosophy of a Hegelian — or for that matter — any other high-flying persuasion, including the clandestine claims of the religious right that had begun to emerge since the days of Jacobi. In the face of philosophy's contested claims and counterclaims, Heine had long realized that its overbearing title to legitimacy was no longer to be kept in check by common sense alone. The claims of philosophy could only be scaled back if its own self-legitimation was scrutinized and exposed as spurious. With the advent of Hegel, philosophy, and, consequently, its prescriptions, seemed to have assumed irrefutable legitimacy. So philosophy had to be challenged from within but at the same time in a manner that remained free from philosophy's own constraints.

Supplementing the epistemological subject that had come under severe attack with a distinctly poetic one, Heine carefully steers between the pitfalls of epistemological formalism and the new metaphysics that sought to trace the subject in its divine nature. Instead, by reasserting the rightful claim of the individual to humanity, his poetic subject reaffirms the critical. At the same time, this poetic subject reflects itself as a self-conscious product of a historical constellation it never fully transcends, but always represents.

Heine's poetic voice — so stirringly lyrical and yet so defiantly resistant against any form of sublation or transfiguration — articulates a critique that is underpinned by a "pantheism of the joyous sort."[4] Heine's form of Spinozism reclaims and reasserts the powerful legacy of philosophy's counterhistory, which had so effectively been eclipsed by the Kantian and Hegelian projects. His persistently critical gesture prefigures in its insistence on a critically conceived recourse to individuality the decisive turn critical theory will come to take in Benjamin, Horkheimer, Marcuse, and Adorno.

Moving between cultures, discourses, and literary *genres*, Heine's poetics figures writing at the interstices, as it were, reflecting the parameters of the normative implications of cultural and sociopolitical constructions. Performing an ever-changing repositioning, this strategic move shakes up the epistemic sedimentations that have for so long imposed their unquestioned authority. Calling into question philosophy's epistemic arrangements and pointing toward alternatives that no longer require erasure of reason's recognition of its other, Heine's writing reveals the glitches and failures of philosophical discourse not just for the sake of aesthetic pleasure or polemical effect. Rather, this enables the aesthetic play of autonomy to highlight the contingent, historically determined character of reason and its other. As a result, the discourse of philosophy emerges in Heine as a historically contingent construct in need of renegotiation and re-invention. Such critical exposure and challenge of philosophy's basic assumptions takes place on different levels but always in a theoretically consistent fashion. Instead of celebrating some kind of uncommitted skepticism, Heine's poetics offers alternative possibilities of imagining and realigning the boundaries of conceptual thought. As a consequence, he reconfigures philosophy as critical force. Consequently, style no longer functions as a frivolous act of *l'art pour l'art* aestheticism but emerges as a powerful agent liquefying the sedimentations of reified thought. In this way, Heine breaks new ground for re-imagining Hegel's project of conceptual work (*Arbeit am Begriff*).

Indeed, Heine's playful exhibition of the contradictions of real life brings home the non-identity between concepts and what they seek to comprehend, thus prefiguring the critical insights of Adorno's *Negative Dialectics*.[5] Celebrating the productive force of contradictions, Heine's writing scrutinizes key philosophical concepts for their soundness and consistency. Releasing their hidden dialectics, his texts highlight the contingency involved in philosophy's construction of its own foundation.

While Heine's ample use of the conventional stock of poetic imagery and the seductively smooth organization of his narratives feign naive compliance with the status quo, he constantly undermines this illusion through the constant use of breaks, interruptions, and displacements of those conventions. Heine's language and style have often been criticized for their uncritical mimetic suppleness. But a closer look reveals behind the pleasant display a keen sense for the brittle fragility of mimetic beauty. Heine casts the mimetic spell to bring out the hidden assumptions that direct the way in which we see and understand the world and according to which we act. This allows him to demonstrate the deep gap separating concepts from the reality they pretend to grasp.

The Signifying Lizard

In the figure of the philosophical lizard that the narrator meets in the opening scene of *Die Stadt Lucca,* Heine captures the profound interlocking of language, hermeneutics, and philosophy. The lizard's philosophy of language may sound strangely familiar to modern readers acquainted with Walter Benjamin's views on language. Half in jest, the lizard proposes a theory that despite — even possibly because of — its ironic presentation, spells out central tenets of Heine's post-Romantic, post-idealist philosophy of language; a philosophy that does not shy away from making use of the best of Romantic insights to which it, however, adds its resolutely anti-idealist twist:

> Die Eidechsen haben mir erzählt, es gehe eine Sage unter den Steinen, daß Gott einst Stein werden wolle, um sie aus ihrer Starrheit zu erlösen. Eine alte Eidechse meinte aber, diese Steinwerdung würde nur dann stattfinden, wenn Gott bereits in alle Tier- und Pflanzenarten sich verwandelt und sie erlöst habe.
>
> Nur wenige Steine haben Gefühl, und nur im Mondschein atmen sie. Aber diese wenige Steine, die ihren Zustand fühlen, sind schrecklich elend. Die Bäume sind viel besser daran, sie können weinen. Die Tiere aber sind am meisten begünstigt, denn sie können sprechen, jedes nach seiner Art und die Menschen am besten. Einst, wenn die ganze Welt erlöst ist, werden alle anderen Erschaffnisse ebenfalls sprechen können, wie in jenen uralten Zeiten, wovon die Dichter singen. (B 2: 477–78)

But not only do the roots of language reach deeper than the surface of human consciousness, or so the lizard argues, but thought itself springs from sources beneath the surface of the conscious. What the human mind likes to call thinking, the lizard points out, is just what accidentally affects the mind. Such occasional moments of innocent conception, he observes, we call ideas; the concatenation of them is then, in turn, called thinking. In short, "kein Mensch denkt, kein Philosoph denkt, weder Schelling noch Hegel denkt, und was gar ihre Philosophie betrifft, so ist sie eitel Luft und Wasser, wie die Wolken des Himmels" (480). But there is one single true philosophy, the lizard reassures the narrator, and this one "steht, in ewigen Hieroglyphen, auf meinem eigenen Schwanze" (480). As capricious as the lizard's philosophy might sound, the practical joke of the philosopher become signifier carrying the truth on his tail points to more profound implications. With the hieroglyphic signs, Heine introduces a striking allegory of allegory. As a living sign, the lizard captures some of the intricate complexity of the connection between language, semiotics, and discursive thought. The hieroglyph is the sign that represents the magic of the confluence of overt and covert meaning, and thus serves as an allegory of the process of constituting meaning. In an ironic turn, Heine's allegoric use of the hieroglyph reworks Romantic and

idealist conceptions of hermeneutics into a theory of "depth hermeneutics" that attends to the power of the unconscious as the constitutive force of human consciousness, and consequently, of language and
thought.[6] Understood as a compromise formation of contradictory
tendencies, Heine conceives writing as the site where the clash between the unconscious and the conscious is given aesthetic expression.
In Heine, the shining brightness of daylight thoughts and the discursive clarity of concepts are always matched by the poetry of dreams
and fantastic imagery, reminding the reader of an ever-different world,
inaccessible to the powers of reason alone. Poetic language, as a semiotic system formed on the basis of a historical repository of experienced illnesses, as Altenhofer puts it ("Chiffre" 150), grasps a reality
that has been repressed by conscious thinking, whose discursive system of concepts is incapable of fully representing this reality.

Ten years later, in *Ludwig Börne. Eine Denkschrift,* Heine returns
to the hieroglyph as the sign language of the repressed. Here, the
metaphorical use of an Egyptian obelisk, transplanted to a Paris
square, serves more than one purpose. In a cruel joke on Börne and
his likes, Heine notes that just as the erection of an obelisk may bring
with it the release of scorpions that had been caught up in the packing
materials, the erection of great cultural obelisks (*Geistesobelisken*) may
also lead to the release of "little poisonous bugs" (*kleinliche Gifttier-
chen*). While this passage might appear to serve the sole purpose of
putting Börne in his place, albeit posthumously, it also links the cultural monument and its hieroglyphic inscription to its history; an ever-
present history that reminds the reader that the accompanying refuse
is part of the message (B 4: 139). But be this complicated double en-
tendre of the economy of semiotics as it may, the obelisk's hieroglyphs
still await the day of decipherment by those sensitive to its hidden
messages: "Wer enträtselt diese Stimme der Vorzeit, diese uralten
Hieroglyphen? Sie enthalten vielleicht keinen Fluch, sondern ein Re-
zept für die Wunde unserer Zeit! O wer lesen könnte!" (B 4: 140).

The inscription on the obelisk erected on the Square Louis XVI
and waiting for its message to be read by those who understand its
script (B 4: 139) serves to visualize the poet's challenge to express
what refuses to be contained in conceptually determinate speech: "In
greller Bilderschrift zeigt mir der Traum das große Leid, das ich mir
gern verhehlen möchte, und das ich kaum auszusprechen wage in den
nüchternen Begriffslauten des hellen Tages —" (B 4: 141). This pictorial script is the coded form into which culture and tradition have
locked the contentious forces of life's antagonisms. The poet's task,

this passage suggests, consists in giving voice to what eludes the grasp of discursive reason. As representants of a submerged consciousness, the relics and ruins of the past world are hieroglyphs of a particular kind. Viewing them as palimpsests whose different layers of inscriptions and meanings attest to the irreducibility of the whole of reality to the narrow scope of rationality, Heine casts his writing as a reading that redeems language from its hieroglyphic petrification.[7]

In the light of this conception of the poet's hermeneutic practice, the philosopher lizard on the road to Lucca is more than just a parodic impersonation of nature's version of Schelling's philosophy. Rather, this speaking hieroglyph representing speech-endowed nature short-circuits conventional views on language in a profound way. Signs cannot speak, or else they would not be signs. What would a self-interpreting sign look like, what would it say? But far from short-circuiting the philosophy of language, the cheerfully lecturing lizard has, at this crucial junction of the *Reisebilder,* a theoretically important message to share: meaning lies inextricably buried in the sign, and the sign, as a consequence, necessitates ever-new readings. For signs can proliferate meaning only if, just like the signs inscribed on the lizard's body, they are grounded in the experience of life itself. But a second point implied in the image of the signifying lizard is that the site of the production of meaning is always located in the reader's — that is, philosopher's — mind. The lizard represents thus not only a clownish performance of the sign that interprets itself but also stands as a reminder that while consciousness may be a key factor in the production of meaning, it does not by itself account for the whole process. For as the other to the unconscious, consciousness remains inseparably tied to the reptile, that is, to ossified animal forces from which it springs.

If the philosopher's stone, if found at all, may never speak, it is an altogether different story with the hieroglyphs on the lizard's tail. They "speak," but only for those who know how to read them. As the encoded, enigmatic, silent sign — though rich in meaning — that awaits hermeneutic redemption, the hieroglyph works as Heine's telling metaphor for allegory. In Heine, the function of allegory works much the way Benjamin describes it in his *Ursprung des bürgerlichen Trauerspiels:* "Allegory . . . is no playful pictorial technique but expression, just like language is expression, indeed just like writing."[8] Heine's play of allegory has no self-serving purpose but — read with the lizard's comments in mind — exhibits the critical impulse of Benjamin's approach to the function of allegory. The pulsating dialectics that, in Benjamin, drives the semiotic movement of allegory is prefigured in Heine's shuttle-like movement between the ever continuous projection of images and their equally perpetual revocation, an oscillation that results in the release of an unrestrained play of language. Benjamin's comment that allegory presents the Hippocratic face of history as petrified primal landscape to the eye of the spectator (343), helps flesh out the moment of radical critique of philosophy in Heine's seemingly innocuous proliferation of the play of allegories.

Read in the light of Benjamin's comments on allegory, the apparently curious connection between history and philosophy of nature that Heine's lizard invokes appears as the precise moment of interlocking where allegory arises.[9] Benjamin's account of the role of the hieroglyphic discourse from the Renaissance to the nineteenth century provides us with a further clue. For, in this tradition, hieroglyphs are the symbols that enable the mystical philosophy of nature to access the esoteric truth of the Absolute. "Hieroglyphs as the image of divine ideas!" as Benjamin (346) quotes his source Giehlow. As the allegorical gaze transforms everything into pulsating writing — represented as fragment, ruins, runes (352) — thus bringing home the deeply seated antinomies of the allegorical (350), the illusion (*der falsche Schein*) of totality fades away: "Denn das Eidos verlischt, das Gleichnis geht ein, der Kosmos darinnen vertrocknet" (352). What better visualization of this phenomenon than Heine's disappearing *Eidechs:* the eidos in retreat.

But if for Heine the original prelapsarian unity of the sign and the referent have long disappeared, that is, if this departure was made explicit, at the latest, in Heine's *Reisebilder,* the consciously allegoric use of language can be traced even farther back. Even the early poems of *Buch der Lieder* display an unusually developed sense of the urgency of the problem. Celebrated for their melodious suaveness, synesthetic effects, and Romantic magic, even the most popular of Heine's poems, which have inspired scores of musical compositions and become icons of shameless exploitation by the culture industry, do not conceal their traces of critical encoding. Their continuous play with rupture and challenge undermines and breaks the Romantic spell it ever so joyfully conjures, adding to the illusively Romantic the deeper countertone of disenchantment.

If poem 9 of "Intermezzo," better known as "Auf Flügeln des Gesanges" (first published 1823) seems an unlikely candidate for such a reading, a closer look confirms that behind the dreamlike narrative of a fantastic escape to the Orient there looms a more critical note. Felix Mendelssohn's enchanting melody has had such an inspiring effect that its tune still rings in the reader's ear, recalling the opening lines:

> Auf Flügeln des Gesanges,
> Herzliebchen, trag ich dich fort,
> Fort nach den Fluren des Ganges,
> Dort weiß ich den schönsten Ort. (B 1: 78)

The poem's highly-charged use of metonymic language conjures a dream world whose fairy-tale-like other-worldliness plays on the Romantic theme of eternal longing. But this dream world clearly steers toward its own collapse, only to be averted, or rather, delayed by the poem's constant metonymic shifting. Once "beneath the palm tree," nothing is left of the dream but to drink love and tranquility and to dream on the blessed dream. The escape from the world is sustained only — as Mendelssohn's captivating music so beautifully expresses it — by continuing the dream, whose content becomes, in turn, a dream itself, ever delaying realization of the dream's desires. There is no other message or point. Brought to its poetological conclusion, the poem carries along with its charm an unspoken, unsung message. This is the message that difference is irrepressible and cannot be contained in a world of dreams that only would produce an infinite series of deferments; a message that brings home the point of urgency that much more strongly. Mendelssohn's hauntingly alluring tune teases the audience's unfulfilled desires as much as does Heine's poetry. Enthrallingly beautiful, its lyric returns the listener at the end of the song to her or his world. Sweet and promising as the poem might appear, the fragility of the other world it conjures underscores the this-worldly urgency to acknowledge difference and its legitimate, even constitutive role.

For in Heine's poetic world, where lovers are flowers in remote exotic gardens, floral metaphors represent more than just beauty, poetry, immaculate innocence, and transcendence, as they did for the Romantics. Rather, for Heine, flowers also express the particular in its irreducible difference. They remind us — as a passage in the *Harzreise* illustrates — that beyond the rationality of the Linnean system of taxonomy, which dissects and categorizes the unique phenomenon of a living flower by subjecting it to the heartless logic of science, there always remains a stubborn rest that resists subsumption to the general. In the *Harzreise,* an anxious mother finds it inappropriate that her daughter has affixed to her dress the strange and unknown flower ("eine fremde, unbekannte Blume") presented to her by an admirer. But the admirer also happens to be the narrator, who indignantly notes: "Es ärgert mich jedesmal, wenn ich sehe, daß man auch Gottes liebe

Blumen, eben so wie uns, in Kasten geteilt hat, und nach ähnlichen Äußerlichkeiten, nämlich nach Staubfäden-Verschiedenheit" (B 2: 156).

"Auf Flügeln des Gesanges," displays the predicament of singularity and otherness in modernity as an issue only permitted to return in the costume of a dubious orientalism. Exported to a dreamlike orient, the revelry of floral love and dream life become the metonymic reminder that it only seems as if particularity and difference must be represented in the exotic costume of faraway places. In actuality, they are the wellspring of life depicted as an exterritorialization that will come to haunt us as long as we fail to recognize them as the very moment of modernity itself.

Gérard de Nerval identified the poetics at work here in no ambiguous terms, describing the moment of beauty in Heine as the ever-present revocation of illusion:

> Ce qu'il y a de beau dans Heinrich Heine, c'est qu'il ne se fait pas illusion . . . aussi règne-t-il dans toutes ces jolies strophes une terreur secrète. Les roses sentent trop bon, le gazon est trop frais, le rossignol trop harmonieux! — Tout cela est fatal; le parfum asphyxie, l'herbe fraîche recouvre une fosse, l'oiseau meurt avec sa dernière note. . . . (B 6.2: 267)[10]

"A pantheism of the joyous sort"

Heine's aesthetic play with the conventions of poetic imagery thus critically engages in a challenge of the limits of reason and intuition. His refusal to allow for a premature resolution of the dialectics of reason and imagination complicates the problem of theory and praxis that emerges as a crucial issue of his day in a challenging way. Heine's approach to the problem of theory and praxis takes its cue from a sophisticated, yet uncompromisingly resolute transformation of the conception of philosophy as it is articulated in his prose and poetry. This issue is further interconnected with Heine's project of "reinstatement of the flesh" and his way of exposing the traditional oppositions between mind and matter, between spiritualism and sensualism, as based on the false premise that the world and its phenomena lend themselves to a legitimate distinction between mind and matter. Heine responds to the deadlock which the juxtaposition of the realm of the senses and the realm of the mind has created with a bold new pantheism. His early attraction to Saint-Simonianism certainly played an important role, and left many traces in his writings.[11] But the conception of Heine's pantheism points to a more sophisticated understanding than the grandiose speculations of the Saint-Simonian school of thought. Heine's pantheism streamlines his social, political, theoretical, and aesthetic concerns and provides a theoretical foregrounding that unifies his project. Heine's defiantly daring injection of Spinoza at the heart of his *Zur Geschichte der Religion und Philosophie in Deutschland* displays his radically modern approach to the problems and politics inherent in the project of national intellectual historiography.[12]

Zur Geschichte der Religion und Philosophie in Deutschland formulates a sophisticated reflection on the theoretical implications of writing history and, in particular, the history of philosophy. Cautious not to read intentionality too quickly into the scheme of history,[13] Heine's interest consists primarily in bringing to the fore the hidden socio-historical forces that guide actors on the stage of world history. Against the conventional approach to history, which casts its protagonists as autonomous subjects in charge of their actions, Heine conceives history in a way that enables exposure of the deeper currents of these socio-historical forces. In a remarkable fashion, Heine prefigures the critical move to theorizing history as a juncture of constellational moments at which the antagonism of social forces crystallizes into figures, actions, and events. One such instance Heine remarks on is the construction of the church of Saint Paul under Pope Leo X. Pointing out that this venture was financed through the church's aggressive sale of letters of indulgence, Heine's comment "daß die Sünde ganz eigentlich das Geld hergab zum Bau dieser Kirche, die dadurch gleichsam ein Monument sinnlicher Lust wurde" (B 3: 532) is more profound than its sharp witted sarcasm might suggest. For if it could be argued that, indeed, the devil built this house of God, it is, on the other hand, not the least of the triumphs of spiritualism that it had sensualism erect its own most beautiful temple (B 3: 532). For Heine, then, works of architecture, like actions and events, reflect a historical dialectic of competing forces. In the case of European history, the defining moment is thus the deep-running antagonism between spiritualism and sensualism.

In Spinoza, Heine finds a theoretically consistent approach to this predicament that — unlike Hegel, Schelling, and other philosophers — allows him to integrate his Jewish identity without being forced to submit to any sort of compromise. Through his unconventional reading of Spinoza, Heine not only breaks new ground for modern Spinoza reception but also clears the way for the philosophical radicalism of Young Hegelians like Moses Hess and Karl Marx.[14]

But Heine's original appropriation of Spinozist thought takes its most creative turn in the insistence that religion, history, identity, and even such complex notions as time are ultimately inseparable from the material base from which they originate. The permanent, often comic, reminder of the material reality behind the lofty notions and their often not so lofty rationale that inform everyday life points to the critical resistance against philosophy's seductive urge to shut out the ugly face of reality. Far from debasing and trivializing the material base of life, Heine's joke is never on life's base materiality but, more piercingly, on the high-strung forms of idealism that ignore its sanctity. Insisting that body and soul, mind and matter, cannot be separated, and that such a split cannot legitimize any hierarchical order, Spinozist ontology resolutely reclaims everyone's equal right to exist in freedom and self-determination.[15] This view inspires Heine's re-examination of how history, identity, and representation are constructed and how their narratives are presented.

In the 1852 preface to the second edition of *Zur Geschichte der Religion und Philosophie in Deutschland,* Heine plants a telling signpost that deserves critical attention. Written in retrospect, close to the end of his career, two decades after the first version had appeared, the notion of auto-deconstructive writing introduced in this preface articulates a central motif in Heine. Establishing the parameters for his own "religious return," which he never discusses without self-conscious irony, Heine notes:

> Es stehen überhaupt noch viel schöne und merkwürdige Erzählungen in der Bibel, die ihrer Beachtung wert wären, z. B. gleich im Anfang die Geschichte von dem verbotenen Baume im Paradiese und von der Schlange, der kleinen Privatdozentin, die schon sechstausend Jahre vor Hegels Geburt die ganze Hegelsche Philosophie vortrug. Dieser Blaustrumpf ohne Füße zeigt sehr scharfsinnig, wie das Absolute in der Identität von Sein und Wissen besteht, wie der Mensch zum Gotte werde durch die Erkenntnis, oder was dasselbe ist, wie Gott im Menschen zum Bewußtsein seiner selbst gelange — Diese Formel ist nicht so klar wie die ursprünglichen Worte: Wenn ihr vom Baume der Erkenntnis genossen, werdet ihr wie Gott sein! ... o Paradies! Sonderbar, so wie das Weib zum denkenden Selbstbewußtsein kommt, ist ihr erster Gedanke ein neues Kleid! Auch diese biblische Geschichte, zumal die Rede der Schlange, kommt mir nicht aus dem Sinn, und ich möchte sie als Motto diesem Buche voransetzen, in derselben Weise, wie man oft vor fürstlichen Gärten eine Tafel sieht mit der warnenden Aufschrift: Hier liegen Fußangeln und Selbstschüsse. (B 3: 510–11)

This warning sign at the opening of the book points to the poetic snare within the text that so artfully auto-deconstructs its own images much in the way Abraham in *Der Rabbi von Bacherach* destroys in Sara's dream the idols of the gods, which, in turn, constantly recompose themselves. This text, as so many of Heine's, alternates between enchantment and disenchantment, and between composition and decomposition, in a manner that foreshadows crucial motifs of Adorno's negative dialectics.

Time's Paradox:
The Moment of the Non/Contemporary

An instructive example of this move toward negative dialectics can be found in the way Heine addresses the question of the paradox of time and the issue of the relationship between the contemporary and the non-contemporary. In "Hebräische Melodien," Heine's reworking of the concepts of time, history, and identity reflects the instance of the non/contemporary as the critical moment for understanding modernity. Building on Heine's approach to philosophy as a project that requires ever-new reconstructive efforts, this cycle of poems calls for a rethinking of the question of the relationship between the contemporary and the non-contemporary. In the remainder of this essay I argue that the sequential order of the three poems "Prinzessin Sabbat," "Jehuda ben Halevy," and "Disputation" articulates a pointed comment on the problem of the contemporary and the non-contemporary. The way in which Heine shapes here the relationship between the contemporary and the non-contemporary stresses the provocative note of "Hebräische Melodien" as one which, in the disguise of the historical, confronts the present with its past and future. Cast as past and future, the non-contemporary emerges as contemporary, while what poses as the contemporary is exposed in repressing its own aspect of the non-contemporary. The philosophical implications of this move warrant a brief discussion of the basic notions at play in "Hebräische Melodien."

In a short text that was originally to open *Zur Geschichte der Religion und Philosophie in Deutschland,* Heine narrates how on a winter's night in Berlin he falls asleep in the theater while attending a performance of a new tragedy. After everyone has left and the lights have gone out, Heine wakes up in the deserted building. He has decided to go back to sleep when he hears noises coming from the orchestra pit. There, a whole group of mice is engaged in a conversation that soon catches Heine's attention. From his seat, he overhears an old mouse commenting on what the young mice folk saw, that is, the tragedy that had put him to sleep. The party of mice had taken the play to be reality, and the whole of reality at that. The old mouse reprimands them for jumping to such a fast conclusion. Having seen many more plays than just that night's performance, his lifelong experience has taught him that "Die ganze Geschichte der Menschheit, die man gern in verschiedene Stücke, Perioden, Epochen und Phasen eintheilen möchte, ist doch immer eine und dieselbe; es ist eine nur maskirte Wiederkehr derselben Naturen und Ereignisse, ein organischer Kreislauf, der immer von vorne wieder anfängt."[16] But this piece of wisdom does not remain uncontested. A giggling voice, coming from a little mouse that has done its research too, makes itself heard. This one had left the orchestra, venturing into the universe that lies *behind* the scene/stage, where it made "some rather curious discoveries." Recognizing that the world is all just illusion, this mouse quickly concludes that all is based on self-interest, selfishness, and materialism. But against such a view, another mouse raises its voice, arguing that things have to be seen in their proper perspective. For this mouse has discovered what lies *before* the scene: the prompter's box. There, this more philosophical mouse explains, sits a thin, gray little man with a script in his hands reciting with a monotonous little voice all those dialogues that are enacted so loudly and passionately on the stage. With a mystical shiver to have glanced at the secret of it all, this mouse arrives at the strikingly idealist or, rather, Hegelian conclusion that this old man, the stage, and the old man's words are one, or in other words, the true trinity.

At this point, Heine cuts off this *Theatervision* to make his point somewhat more explicit. This parable, he observes, rehearses the three main viewpoints according to which his contemporaries explain the divine comedies performed on the great stage called world history. What the parable highlights in Heine's view is that these three viewpoints, which he now calls the fatalistic, the skeptical, and the spiritualistic view, are all relatively true, although none of them taken by itself represents the whole of truth. In a short fragment that dates from the same period, "Verschiedenartige Geschichtsauffassung," Heine distinguishes in almost identical fashion the cyclical, fatalistic view from a progressive viewpoint. But here, too, both attitudes lack resonance with the most vital feelings of life, that is, the desire to think that the meaning of human life transcends its role as a bit part in the scheme of world history.

The challenge to imagine the past, present, and future critically emerges thus as a never-ending proposition, one that plays itself out throughout Heine's work in ever-changing facets. Rather than attempting to press for a resolution of the problem of historiography, Heine stages the constellation of past/present/future in a way that exposes the present as a complex weave of renegotiated past and future.

At a moment when historical thinking and the exigencies of the growing speed of modernization posed a new urgency to rethink the problem of time and history, Heine's writing presents a radically new attempt to reconceptualize their relationship. With the ascendance of Young Germany and the Young Hegelians, time became the political slogan of the day, the watchword for progress, change, even revolution. This fundamental shift in the perception of time replaced a notion of time based on homogeneous temporal continuity with one that privileges the present over the past. This semantic shift had conceptual as well as aesthetic consequences. With regard to the literary project of the post-classical and post-Romantic generation, there was a shift to a new aesthetic program: the young poets and writers saw themselves primarily as publicists. Their aspiration consisted in becoming writers of and for the time, *Zeitschriftsteller*.[17]

Heine was one of the few who were fully aware of the profound implications of this shift. While he acknowledged the timeliness of this move toward the contemporary, he at the same time recognized the problematic position in which this development threatened to transfix the poetic project in modernity. His relentless polemics against many contemporary poets and publicists were motivated by his sensitivity to the fact that the well-intended battle cry of the present, which he joined, might ironically negate critical attention to the dialectic of tradition. For in Heine's view, such overemphasis on the present diverts attention away from time's dynamic dialectic with the past, which alone enables our full, creative, and critical participation in the present; a present that Heine figured as a transitory moment of the constellation of past and future. Heine saw the avalanche of writings by his time-obsessed contemporaries as a result of a conceptual rift performed in the name of time, a move whose reductionist, sanitary attitude toward the past would relegate it to the dustbin of history. Heine feared, in other words, the tendency of these *Zeitschriftsteller* to refashion the past in the image of their own present uncritically.

It is no coincidence that Heine was one of the first critics to address modernity, that is, his own period, with a term that locks progress and the present in a dramatic manner in one composite noun:

Neuzeit.[18] Heine had already coined the term *Modernität* in 1826, a creation that was introduced into French usage with the translation of the *Reisebilder* a few years later.[19] But *Neuzeit* and *Modernität* represented for Heine anything but a totally new beginning oblivious of the past. Rather than understanding the new as disconnected from its past, he embraced the antagonism between the old and the new early on as the constitutive moment that defines modernity. This view opens the way to rethink history in a radically emancipatory manner. As a consequence, the concept of modernity assumes a critical force whose philosophical significance has been curiously overlooked.

Heine's finely developed sense for the paradox of time and the problem of representation of time and history manifested itself early on in the sophisticated manner in which he represented time's contradictory aspects. Time emerges in Heine as a highly mediated construct that is predicated on a dynamic understanding of the past and the future. The insight that time can only be represented through refraction in time, and that history can only be grasped through a poetics that reflects the problematic of representing temporality, defines the innovative form and content of Heine's writing. Both his poetry and prose bring out and, at times, openly address the split that inheres in the notion of time itself. Imagined as both continuity and discontinuity time emerges as an intrinsically dialectical concept that defies and resists ideological inscription.

In typical fashion, Heine addressed this conundrum by celebrating it. Rather than containing it, his texts play it out. This is what makes Heine so radically contemporary, a *Zeitdichter* in the sense that he self-consciously reflected on the temporality of his own poetics. Heine's writing casts the present and its "now" as the literary event informed by the remembrance of the past that the present calls forth. Heine's poetic grammar of the "now" reminds the today that while there was and always will be a yesterday, this yesterday is produced ever anew by the today. As early as in 1832 (in *Französische Zustände*), Heine spells out the critical difference that separates him from the historical thought of the nation-building project of his contemporaries when he observes: "indem man die Geschichte durch die Vergangenheit zu erklären sucht, [wird] zu gleicher Zeit offenbar, wie diese Vergangenheit, erst durch jene, die Gegenwart, ihr eigentlichstes Verständnis findet, und jeder neue Tag ein neues Licht auf sie wirft, wovon unsere bisherigen Handbuchschreiber keine Ahnung hatten" (B 3: 167). This critical turn informs Heine's writing in a programmatic manner. Its affinity with Benjamin's project of a redemptive approach to history seems striking. As the dynamic force of the past is only realized in the present, understood as an ever-new present, time emerges as constant movement, that which mediates past and future but never comes to rest. History can thus only be represented by way of a never-ending reappropriation of the past through a present that reflects itself as originating in this past it reconstructs. Heine responds to this challenge by dislodging conventional notions of the past, confronting them with a self-consciously contemporary mode of imagination. In opposition to the usual approach to draw a clean-cut distinction between the contemporary and the non-contemporary, Heine's writing highlights the impossibility of simply dividing the present into old and new. Rather, the dialectics of the contemporary and non-contemporary suggests a critical notion of the non/contemporary. In Heine, this non/contemporary — that which cannot simply be reduced to a past gone and rendered irrelevant — appears as what returns in the present as its valid, because future-oriented, critique.

In the *Harzreise,* the evasive yet so central problem of time is given a remarkable exposition. It is in Goslar — and where else, one could ask — where Heine situates his dream about the appearance of the ghost (revenant of the old time) that stages the resurfacing of the non-contemporary in an illuminating manner. In the figure of the spectral apparition of the loyal Kantian Saul Ascher, Heine has this ghost argue against the existence of ghosts, a witty and original variation of Hegel's Kant critique. But what is important in our context is that Ascher in his distraction retrieves from his pocket not his golden watch but, instead, a handful of worms. This haunting dream image, a literary precursor of Dali's warped watches, serves as a critical reminder that time — and here Heine plays Kant out against his followers — represents a never quite stable referent which one cannot not just pull out of one's pocket like a trusty old timepiece, securing one's position in the present once and for all. Instead, time literally — in the image of worms — emerges in lieu of the golden watch of the enlightenment philosopher as that amorphous, subversive life that defies mastery and control, even by ghosts. Linked to the image of the absent golden watch, Heine stages the split notion of time as a metonymic shift whose image, produced from the ghost's pocket, signals the intrinsic impossibility to grasp time except as some impure inner form of intuition.

In *Ideen. Das Buch Le Grand,* we find another watch. This, the narrator's own watch, he confides, has advanced much further in mastering the Hebrew language than the narrator himself. For his watch had gotten into some more intimate relationship with pawn-brokers and has thus acquired some Jewish habits, including resting on the Sabbath, or rehearsing Hebrew grammar, ticking irregularly: "katal, katalta, katalti — kittel, kittalta, kittalti — — pokat, pokade-ti — pikat — pik — pik — —" (B 2: 268). Heine's Hebrew time, the watch indicates, obviously has a different rhythm than standard time. Time, as the Hebrew ticking of the narrator's watch signals, is not simply universal, but has its own particular grammar. Announcing its own form of chronometric pace, this watch "kills" but also "criticizes" time ("katal, katalta . . ."). Pawned as collateral for cash ("time is money"), this Jewish chronometer is figuratively, and literally, "doing time" awaiting its release or redemption from the sphere of mone-tary — and temporal — circulation. But it also "orders" or "com-mands" time ("pokat, pokadeti . . ."), a reminder that while "time" dictates, the question remains which time exactly that would be.

Exposing the split inherent in the experience of time, this talking watch gives voice to the constitutive significance of temporal differ-ence that lies at the heart of the experience of time. Heine's Hebrew-speaking timepiece signals that the pulse of time can be heard only if the dialectics of the contemporary and the non-contemporary is al-lowed to be played out. Change of time, to be sure, and radical inno-vation can only be represented as a break with conventional time, not as its continuation. Yet, Heine's imagery brings home the inescapable fact that change can only be imagined in and through time itself. This point finds its most mature expression in Heine's "Hebräische Melodi-en," a poetic cycle that addresses the paradox of time as the constitutive problem of modernity.

Less interested in the exposition of invidiously particular forms of repression and the negation of emancipation's rightful claims, "Prin-zessin Sabbat" addresses the problem of time in modernity as an issue that calls for critical attention to its intrinsically paradox nature. For ignoring this, the poem suggests, would lock us into a time concep-tion that would not only mistake Jewish identity for a divided form of consciousness but view such an assumed split as the predicament of modernity. Instead, "Prinzessin Sabbat" demonstrates that the unre-lenting grip of the conventional notion of time and its tyranny can only be successfully overcome if the paradox at the heart of moder-nity, the paradox of time, is understood as what constitutes it in the first place. History emerges then no longer as the nemesis of time, but as the renegotiated temporality of existence here and now. Time, in turn, can then be understood as the pacemaker of history, as that differential impulse that defines history ever anew, impregnating it with the past at every moment.

On the Jewish Sabbath, time comes to a standstill, or so it seems. Behind the traditional scene of a clear-cut dichotomy between the temporal sphere of everyday life and messianic time, "Prinzessin Sabbat" comments on the subtle twist characteristic of the way modernity constructs the experience of time. The traditional scheme is worth remembering: the Sabbath celebrates the wonder of the creation of the world, a day set aside to meditate on the creation of life, and on creation's completion and perfection as a divine effort of eternal duration. Reflecting on creation and the creator's respite on the day of rest, the Sabbath recalls the moment of the emergence of time as it is described in Genesis. Cast as the division of light and darkness, time comes into being there through division and repetition: day following night, time emerges through the distinctions between before and after.

But while the distinction between continuity and its interruption seems unproblematic, "Prinzessin Sabbath" challenges the dichotomous neatness of the split that informs it. In a resolute countermove to the Romantic practice of stabilizing the anxiety over the loss of a clear boundary between reality and imagination by deploying the concept of the uncanny, Heine addresses this recurring problem of the fantastic by exposing reality, and its time conceptions, as themselves fantastic constructions. Unlike the Romantics, Heine no longer seeks to stabilize the conventional notion of time through simple reversal — the "infinity" of Romantic irony — but exposes the constructedness of time directly.

"Prinzessin Sabbat" gives this problem subtle expression in the way it portrays the repetitive return of the weekly cycle. Citing the *Arabian Nights,* the poem opens with a fairy-tale cue that recalls a world inhabited by enchanted princes who at times regain their original appearance. Israel, the poem informs us, is just such a prince whose deformed features were the result of a witch's curse. While life in the diaspora seems like a curse that has reduced the Jewish people to a dog-like existence, "Prinzessin Sabbat" refuses any simple reversal of time leading to a triumphant Jewish restoration, a return to glory that would at bottom underwrite a circular movement, and historical stasis. Instead, "Prinzessin Sabbat" highlights the tensions that define the existential predicament of temporal existence itself. Sheer repetition, the poem suggests, is no longer simply repetition, but a sign of the repressed opportunities for contemporary Jewish emancipation. As a celebration of discontinuity, time's coming to halt on the Sabbath no longer represents submission to the grinding force of the eternal return of the same, but rather a powerful pause, the space in which repetition can be re-imagined as the doorway to difference, and to the quite political and contemporary imagination of a different and transformed future.

The Jewish Sabbath emerges thus from the poem as a perpetually recurring moment, the temporal gap in which the Jew metamorphoses from a dog-like existence to sovereignty, if only for the short span of a holiday. The time of the Sabbath represents the moment where the dialectics of temporality assumes its own critical voice, the chance for a break in which the imprisoning image of the past is doubled, and at the same time broken through. In turn, time itself is no longer imagined as an unproblematically objective entity, but as a socially and historically constituted construction, almost mythologically inscribed in the deep structure of human existence.

"Prinzessin Sabbat" both accentuates this emphatic standstill punctuating the flow of time and, at the same time, underscores how such a break energizes time's course and gives it direction. The Sabbath — a day of repose, peace, and reflection — interrupts the dog-like daily routine and marks off time in weekly units. Celebrated as the interruption that arrests and breaks the spell of the even flow of time, the Sabbath brings about a pause in time (and of time itself), that opens the perspective to transcendence, revealing the moment of time as that which evades discursive grasp but infuses time with the pulsating moment of messianic hope.

The magic cycle of transformation back into humanity and then, again, back into dog-like existence is thus addressed as an experience of time that is both circular and linear, repetitive and progressive. Tradition is here represented as that which is eminently present, a safe haven from an external, antagonistic world which, however, mirrors that external world point for point. As a consequence, progress is here inscribed in the religious return of the same that never is quite the same, because the interval between one Sabbath and the next spans the open-ended continuum of human agency. Heine's description of repetition suggests not the inescapability of the return of the same but, on the contrary, the chance that what appears to be a return to the past is in fact the radically emancipatory prospect of a different present, and future. Emancipation is thus articulated as something else than simply adjusting one's watch to standard time.

Staging past and present in a reciprocal embrace, "Prinzessin Sabbat" reveals the messianic promise of the future that allows us to imagine the present as more than merely transfixed by the past. Instead, the present appears as that moment which changes, re-invents, transcends, but also retrospectively transforms that past through the promise of an open future. While the dog-like existence seems restored to its humanity, a return to the doggish world, that is, the world in which emancipation is frustrated, appears inevitable so long as emancipation can only be staged as the granting of civil and political rights to those considered to be non-contemporary. In Heine's parlance, this means that the promise of emancipation remains in question as long as a creative Jewish appropriation of Beethoven's composition of Schiller's "Hymn to Joy" can only be figured comically as "Schalet, schöner Götterfunken, / Tochter aus Elysium!" (B 6.1: 128).

Such a Jewish effort at fashioning contemporaneity appears comical as long as it is perceived as present without future or past. Instead, the poem insists that the non-contemporary can never be contained, but shapes the contemporary in crucial ways. Heine's play of the fundamental dialectic of the contemporary and its other reasserts modernity as the site that figures time's paradox as chance rather than a limit of modernity, a site that allows time's paradox to play itself out as a notion in motion.

"Prinzessin Sabbat" exposes the view that casts the Jews as "divided selves," forever locked into their split relationship to time as a curious projection that superimposes modernity's paradox of time onto Jewish existence. Rehearsing this quid pro quo of mistaking modernity's split for an attribute of Jewish identity, "Prinzessin Sabbat"'s phantasmagoric enactment of the drama of enchantment and transformation exposes this split as modernity's own. Returning the criticism of Judaism's non-contemporaneity as split consciousness to modernity rather than internalizing it as a "Jewish question," Heine's poem proposes a radically emancipatory understanding of Judaism's continuing role in modernity. This stand points philosophy toward a critical agenda whose constant threat of erasure Heine's poetics so eloquently counters.

History and Counterhistory

In "Jehuda ben Halevy," Heine offers the alternative of chronicle versus imaginary genealogy, addressing the constructivist aspect of history and the need for historical counter-images. This "skeptical view," as the mice parable would call it, points to another paradox of time and history. "Jehuda ben Halevy" insists that no construction of history can ever be stable and secure but will always remain a dynamic, open-ended process of re-inscription. The poem demonstrates that any attempt at representing time as an even and uninterrupted flow, even when presented as a construction, only reasserts the paradox of time. Placed at the center of the trilogy of "Hebräische Melodien," "Jehuda ben Halevy" stresses the mutable, transformative aspect of time that interferes with any attempt to stabilize the notion of time.

In a tour de force of revisiting the past by creatively re-imagining it, "Jehuda ben Halevy" advances the notion of tradition as an ever-reconstituted reconstruction that figures continuity and innovation as one and the same process through which both past and present emerge as appropriations of never-ending negotiations. Halevi's key import for rethinking Jewish tradition, the poem suggests with an eloquent enchantment based on poetic chant, consists in his sovereign attitude toward tradition that allows him to bring it into play in a free and creative fashion. This notion of poetic freedom returns at the conclusion of the first part of the poem. There, Heine reclaims the poet's sovereignty, proclaiming that, like a king, he answers to God alone. Here, as throughout the poem, aesthetic, cultural, religious, and political themes merge into a contrastive web that highlights the constitutive function of art in the transmission and cultivation of tradition.[20]

Halevi's artistic mastery finds its melodious image in the description of the beautiful manner in which he would recite scripture. For Halevi possessed the gift of singing the cantillation called *Schalscheleth,* a flourish in the recitation, like a bird's.[21] *Schalscheleth,* though a rarely used flourish, may nonetheless have once been sung by Heine himself, if indeed he did sing the parsha on his bar mizvah.[22] But more interesting than such potential self-reference,[23] *Schalscheleth* signals a profoundly gripping semantic field of meaning. The primary meaning of the Hebrew word *Schalscheleth* is "chain," but it can also mean either "tradition" or the kind of necklace described in part 3 of the poem.

Making use of the image and sound, or rather sound image of *Schalscheleth,* Heine illustrates the connection of tradition and innovation as different aspects of one and the same historical process.[24] The poem's use of *Schalscheleth* thus condenses both the meaning of space of experience (*Erfahrungsraum*) and horizon of expectation (*Erwartungshorizont*) into a single word.[25] This move not only brings tradition's and art's autonomy into a new and productive relation, but also opens the door to a principal reconsideration of the function of tradition. Moving beyond a stale concept of secularism, Heine's poetry attends to the full complexity surrounding the issue of tradition, repetition, and transmission in modernity. The poem's performative use of *Schalscheleth* provides insight into the process of recovery, repetition, and continuity that produces tradition.

Once this poetic, yet at the same time critical reconceptualization of tradition and the poetics of its transmission is recognized, the signal import of the poem's central metaphor, or rather, to be precise, metonymy of *Schalscheleth* becomes clear: the artistic flourish and embellishment of the free singer's voice represents a position that rejects both frivolous *l'art pour l'art* symbolism and the notion that art needs to serve a purpose. Heine's *Schalscheleth* denotes the unbound freedom of art that brings life to tradition in the first place as it links the past with the future. It imagines a tradition that makes the new possible as it reconnects it, that is, anchors or roots it in the past it critically re-imagines.

Concluding "Hebräische Melodien" with the controversial poem "Disputation," Heine rehearses the fallacy of historical explanations. Historicism, the poem suggests, is doomed to misconstrue the problem of the paradox of time and the construction of history just as much as fatalist and skeptical models of history were. This "spiritualist view," as the mice parable wittily calls it, may well wish to take a peek behind the stage to see the forces that pull the ropes. But as in the mice parable, the "Hebräische Melodien" suggest that none of these viewpoints is in a position to resolve the paradox of time and history. Instead, the arrangement of the three poems in "Hebräische Melodien" reasserts the paradox of time as one that challenges conventional conceptions of the present.

But read with the theory of the three explanatory models of world history in mind, which the mice parable had introduced, the order of the three poems seems to express an additional point. Heine chooses to conclude "Hebräische Melodien" with "Disputation," thus ending on a strikingly polemical note. "Disputation" is a provocatively feisty account of a theological disputation set during the reign of Pedro in fourteenth-century Spain (Castile). The poem stages the exchange between Christians and Jews like a theological version of a wrestling match. While the Christian party brandishes frankincense and the holy water for baptism, its opponent is busy sharpening knives for circumcision. The spectacle begins as the parties attack with alternating success, though the poem does not seem to leave much doubt about the "home" advantage. The asymmetry in the power relations between the two opponents does, therefore, render problematic readings that reduce the poem to a leveling critique of the ludicrous claims of theology, whatever religion it might support. Such an interpretation ignores not only the asymmetry in the power relation between the opponents, but also the specificity of the differences in religion and tradition that the poem takes great care to illustrate.

Despite this, the final lines are often cited as proof that Heine exposes both sides to be equally wrong. Asked by King Pedro to decide which party has won, Queen Blanca replies:

> Welcher recht hat, weiß ich nicht —
> Doch es will mich schier bedünken,
> Daß der Rabbi und der Mönch,
> Daß sie alle beide stinken. (B 6.1: 172)

No question, this statement is quite abrupt and does not seem to admit much room for qualification, not to mention contradiction. But coming from royalty like the Queen Blanche de Bourbon, whose little French snub nose had been described earlier in the poem as one more accustomed to the Parisian world of perfumes, this final verdict should be seen for what it is: the statement of a historical character.[26] There are no textual pointers that would allow one to construe it as the poet's own voice. On the contrary, my reading suggests that the queen's words represent the arrogation of judgment by a representative of power. To interpret the abrupt ending of the poem as the poet's underwriting of the Queen's verdict would, then, rather appear as an unwarranted closure curiously at odds with the poem's otherwise so resolutely critical tenor.

This note of suspense on which "Hebräische Melodien" concludes emphasizes the poet's concern about a fatal confusion of aesthetics with ethics, as it will assume programmatic significance two decades later in Nietzsche's famous pronunciation in the *Birth of Tragedy:* that only as an aesthetic product can the world be justified for all eternity.[27]

Given the historical circumstances that pitted the Spanish faction loyal to the philosemitic King Pedro, including the entire Castilian Jewry, against the faction loyal to the French-born Queen — a faction that was feared to import anti-Jewish opinions to the Spanish court — her words, too, are the result of a historical constellation.[28] While an ahistorical approach to interpretation has often led critics to ignore this point, the poem's intertextual connection to the theme of the fatalistic, cyclic view of history in "Prinzessin Sabbat" and the skeptical, progressive view of history in "Jehuda ben Halevy" raises the question which view of history the concluding poem proposes.

If "Prinzessin Sabbat" exposes the future as constituted through the past that remains present, and "Jehuda ben Halevy" reads the past through the present, the polemical edge of "Disputation" consists in its critique of the present through the past; a past that betrays a different story than the one German historians and politicians of the nineteenth century were inclined to portray. Seen in this light, "Disputation" emerges as the lasting sting of the "Hebräische Melodien," one that marks Heine's radical critique of a present defined by the past that haunts it.

While the significance of Heine as philosopher or critic of philosophy has repeatedly been questioned and even proved negligible by critics, both his prose and poetry suggest otherwise. Heine's writing articulates an urgent need for a critique that does not shy away from challenging philosophy's dearest held assumptions. Even if Heine remains an unlikely candidate for a place in the hall of philosophers, he stands as a powerful reminder of the contingent grounds on which the foundation of such halls are built.

Notes

[1] Peter Uwe Hohendahl points out that "[i]n this context the figure of the poet and that of the philosopher begin to merge into that of the politically active intellectual." "Heine's Critical Intervention: The Intellectual as Poet," *Heinrich Heine's Contested Identities: Politics, Religion, and Nationalism in Nineteenth-Century Germany,* ed. Jost Hermand and Robert C. Holub (New York: Peter Lang, 1999), 182.

[2] For some examples in the long tradition of disavowal of Heine's relevance as philosopher see Henri Lichtenberger, *Heinrich Heine als Denker* (Dresden: C. Reissner, 1905), 5; E. M. Butler, *The Saint-Simonian Religion in Germany: A Study of the Young German Movement* (1926; rpt. New York: H. Fertig, 1968); and Dolf Sternberger, *Heinrich Heine und die Abschaffung der Sünde* (Hamburg: Claassen, 1972). For a discussion of Heine and philosophy limited to his explicit statements on philosophy see Wolfgang Wieland, "Heinrich Heine und die Philosophie," *Heinrich Heine,* ed. Helmut Koopmann (Darmstadt: Wissenschaftliche Buchgesellschaft, 1975), 133–55; Karl-Heinz Käfer, *Versöhnt ohne Opfer: Zum geschichtstheologischen Rahmen der Schriften Heinrich Heines 1824–1844* (Meisenheim am Glan: Anton Hain, 1978); and Heinz Pepperle, "Heinrich Heine als Philosoph," *Heinrich Heine: Ästhetisch-politische Profile,* ed. Gerhard Höhn (Frankfurt am Main: Suhrkamp, 1991), 155–75. For an incisive study on Heine's reading of Kant see Rudolf Malter, "Heine und Kant," *Heine-Jahrbuch* 18 (1979): 35–64. For a bibliography on Heine and Hegel see Jean-Pierre Lefebvre, *Der gute Trommler: Heines Beziehung zu Hegel,* trans. Peter Schöttler (Hamburg: Hoffmann und Campe, 1986), 207.

[3] Gerhard Höhn calls Heine with some right "le grand oublié de la littérature moderne" (*Heinrich Heine. Un intellectuel moderne* [Paris: Presses universitaires de France, 1994], 2). Cp. Norbert Altenhofer, "Chiffre, Hieroglyphe, Palimpsest," 104–53, and "Die exilierte Natur" 175, 289 n. 2, both in *Die verlorene Augensprache: Über Heinrich Heine* (Frankfurt am Main and Leipzig: Insel, 1993). For Nietzsche see Herwig Friedl, "Heinrich Heine und Friedrich Nietzsche," *Heinrich Heine im Spannungsfeld von Literatur und Wissenschaft*, ed. Wilhelm Gössmann and Manfred Windfuhr (Düsseldorf: Reimar Hobbing, 1990), 195–214, and Gerhard Höhn, "'Farceur' und 'Fanatiker des Ausdrucks.' Nietzsche, Heineaner *malgré lui*?" *Heinrich Heine: Neue Wege der Forschung*, ed. Christian Liedtke (Darmstadt: Wissenschaftliche Buchgesellschaft, 2000), 198–215. For Marx see Nigel Reeves, "Heine and the Young Marx," *Oxford German Studies* 7 (1972–1973): 44–97, and Renate Schlesier, "Homeric Laughter by the Rivers of Babylon: Heinrich Heine and Karl Marx," *The Jewish Reception of Heinrich Heine*, ed. Mark H. Gelber (Tübingen: Niemeyer, 1992), 21–43. For Freud see Hermann Levin Goldschmidt, "Heine und Freud," *"Der Rest bleibt": Aufsätze zum Judentum*, vol. 4 of *Werke* (Vienna: Passagen, 1997), 197–209, and Sander L. Gilman, "Freud Reads Heine Reads Freud," *The Jewish Reception of Heinrich Heine*, ed. Mark H. Gelber (Tübingen: Niemeyer, 1992), 77–94. For Benjamin, see Altenhofer ("Chiffre" and "Die exilierte Natur") and Betz, *Charme*.

[4] Heine alludes to himself as "ein Pantheist der heiteren Observanz" in *Ludwig Börne. Eine Denkschrift* (B 4: 18).

[5] For a detailed study see Stefan Bodo Würffel, *Der produktive Widerspruch: Heinrich Heines negative Dialektik* (Bern: Francke, 1986).

[6] See Altenhofer, "Chiffre." For a discussion of the Romantic discourse on hieroglyphs see Gideon Stiening, "Die Metaphysik des Hieroglyphischen," *Jahrbuch des Freien Deutschen Hochstifts* (1999): 121–62.

[7] Cp. Altenhofer's discussion ("Chiffre," 151).

[8] "Allegorie . . . ist nicht spielerische Bildertechnik, sondern Ausdruck, so wie Sprache Ausdruck ist, ja so wie Schrift" (Walter Benjamin, *Ursprung des deutschen Trauerspiels, Gesammelte Schriften,* vol. 1, ed. Rolf Tiedemann [Frankfurt am Main: Suhrkamp, 1978], 339); the translation is my own.

[9] "Mit einer sonderbaren Verschränkung von Natur und Geschichte tritt der allegorische Ausdruck selbst in die Welt" (Benjamin 344).

[10] For a good discussion of this passage see Würffel, *Der produktive Widerspruch,* 85.

[11] See Butler, *The Saint-Simonian Religion in Germany,* and the detailed discussion by Sternberger in his *Heinrich Heine und die Abschaffung der Sünde.* Sternberger provides useful material but his assessment is often philosophically inconclusive.

[12] I have discussed this in detail in my article "Heines Spinoza: Ent/Mythologisierung der Philosophie als Projekt der Entzauberung und Emanzipation," *Aufklärung und Skepsis: Internationale Heine-Kongreß 1997 zum 200. Geburtstag,* ed. Joseph A. Kruse, Bernd Witte, and Karin Füllner (Stuttgart and Weimar: Metzler, 1999), 571–85.

[13] See for example B 3: 536 and Altenhofer's commentary on this passage in "Chiffre" (141–42).

[14] For the context of Heine's pioneering role in Spinoza reception see my *Spinoza's Modernity: Mendelssohn, Lessing, Heine* (forthcoming).

[15] For Heine's early reference to Spinoza's equation of right with might see the early version of a passage in *Nordseereise:* "wenn man etwa nicht, *wie mein Unglaubensgenosse Spinoza* annehmen will, dass dasjenige, was sich nicht durch eigene Kraft erhalten kann, auch kein Recht hat, zu existieren" (DHA 6: 157, 736; emphasis given to phrase cut out of the published version. See also B 2: 232).

[16] DHA 8.1: 444. See also B 4: 215 where Heine recycled parts of the fragment in *Shakespeares Mädchen und Frauen.*

[17] For a detailed discussion of the time conceptions of Young Germany see Wulf Wülfing, "Schlagworte des Jungen Deutschland, B. 'Zeit,'" *Zeitschrift für deutsche Sprache* 22.3 (n.d.): 154–78.

[18] Cp. Heine's fragmentary piece *Ludwig Marcus Denkworte* (B 5: 177). This fragment dates from 1844. *Geschichtliche Grundbegriffe* (Kosselleck and Conze) and *Historisches Wörterbuch der Philosophie* both give only later sources for the term "Neuzeit." I thank Nils Roemer for having pointed out Heine's possible inauguration of this term.

[19] Albrecht Betz, *Der Charme des Ruhestörers,* Heine-Studien (Aachen: Rimbaud, 1997), 21–22; and also Betz, *Ästhetik und Politik: Heinrich Heines Prosa* (Munich: Hanser, 1971), 29. For Heine's concept of modernity see especially Altenhofer, "Die exilierte Natur," 186. For a discussion of Baudelaire on Heine see Gerhard R. Kaiser, "Baudelaire pro Heine contra Janin. Text — Kommentar — Analyse," *Heine-Jahrbuch* 22 (1983): 135–78.

[20] Part of this and the following paragraphs is based on my discussion in "Rhyming History: A Note on the 'Hebrew Melodies,'" *The Germanic Review* 74 (1999): 271–82.

[21] While critics have often maintained that Heine's choice of Jehuda Halevi as protagonist is arbitrary, Halevi's view that the Hebrew language is superior to other languages because the truth and accuracy of the transmission of meaning is sustained via its particular and unmatched system of accents may denote a decisive point crucial for Heine's use of Halevi as protagonist of his creative approach to re-imagining tradition. For a discussion of Halevi's theory of language see Raphael Jospe, "The Superiority of Oral Over Written Communication: Judah HaLevi's *Kuzari* and Modern Jewish Thought," *From Ancient Israel to Modern Judaism: Intellect in Quest of Understanding, Essays in Honor of Marvin Fox,* ed. Jacob Neusner, Ernest Frerichs, and Nahum Sarna, vol. 3 (Atlanta: Scholars Press, 1989), 127–56.

[22] See Mark H. Gelber on this matter in "Heinrich Heine und das Judentum: gestern und heute," *Heinrich Heine und das Judentum,* ed. Peter Grab (Augsburg: Presse-Druck, 1994), 8–13.

[23] While self-referentiality is certainly present in abundance, memory is more than merely a stage for self-representation, as Wolfgang Preisendanz would have it ("Memoria als Dimension lyrischer Selbstpräsentation in Heines Jehuda ben Ha-

levy," *Memoria: Vergessen und Erinnern,* ed. Anselm Haverkamp and Renate Lachmann, Poetik und Hermeneutik 15 [Munich: Wilhelm Fink, 1993], 348). On the contrary, Heine's self-referentiality becomes a site for rewriting history as counterhistorical critique.

[24] In the Masoretic notation of the Torah the sign for this cantillation is a zigzag line visualizing as it were the vocal triller's vibration. This sound image is also an appropriate illustration of Heine's conception of tradition and the dialectical movement between history and counterhistory.

[25] These are Reinhart Koselleck's categories ("'Erfahrungsraum' und 'Erwartungshorizont' — zwei historische Kategorien," *Vergangene Zukunft: Zur Semantik geschichtlicher Zeiten* [Suhrkamp: Frankfurt am Main, 1979)], 349–75).

[26] Cp. the earlier appearance of Queen Blanca in the poem "Spanische Atriden" in *Romanzero*'s middle part "Lamentationen" (B 6.1: 84–92).

[27] "denn nur als aesthetisches Phänomen ist das Dasein und die Welt ewig gerechtfertigt" (Nietzsche, *Sämtliche Werke. Kritische Studienausgabe,* ed. Giorgio Colli and Mazzino Montinari [Munich and New York: de Gruyter and Deutscher Taschenbuch Verlag, 1967–1977; 1980 (dtv)], vol. 1: 47).

[28] For the historical background of Pedro IV (1350–1369) and Blanca see Simon Dubnow, *Weltgeschichte des jüdischen Volkes,* vol. 5. (Berlin: Jüdischer Verlag, 1927), 238–40.

Works Cited

Altenhofer, Norbert. "Chiffre, Hieroglyphe, Palimpsest." *Die verlorene Augensprache: Über Heinrich Heine.* Frankfurt am Main and Leipzig: Insel, 1993. 104–53.

———. "Die exilierte Natur." *Die verlorene Augensprache: Über Heinrich Heine.* Frankfurt am Main and Leipzig: Insel, 1993. 174–206.

Benjamin, Walter. *Ursprung des deutschen Trauerspiels.* Vol. 1 of *Gesammelte Schriften.* Ed. Rolf Tiedemann. Frankfurt am Main: Suhrkamp, 1978. 13 vols. 1978–.

Betz, Albrecht. *Ästhetik und Politik: Heinrich Heines Prosa.* Munich: Hanser, 1971.

———. *Der Charme des Ruhestörers.* Heine-Studien. Aachen: Rimbaud, 1997.

Butler, E. M. *The Saint-Simonian Religion in Germany: A Study of the Young German Movement.* 1926. New York: H. Fertig, 1968.

Dubnow, Simon. *Weltgeschichte des jüdischen Volkes.* Vol. 5. Berlin: Jüdischer Verlag, 1927. 10 vols. 1925–1930.

Friedl, Herwig. "Heinrich Heine und Friedrich Nietzsche." *Heinrich Heine im Spannungsfeld von Literatur und Wissenschaft.* Ed. Wilhelm Gössmann and Manfred Windfuhr. Düsseldorf: Reimar Hobbing, 1990. 195–214.

Gelber, Mark H. "Heinrich Heine und das Judentum: gestern und heute." *Heinrich Heine und das Judentum*. Ed. Peter Grab. Augsburg: Presse-Druck, 1994. 8–13.

Gilman, Sander L. "Freud Reads Heine Reads Freud." *The Jewish Reception of Heinrich Heine*. Ed. Mark H. Gelber. Tübingen: Niemeyer, 1992. 77–94.

Goetschel, Willi. "Heines Spinoza: Ent/Mythologisierung der Philosophie als Projekt der Entzauberung und Emanzipation." *Aufklärung und Skepsis: Internationaler Heine-Kongreß 1997 zum 200. Geburtstag*. Ed. Joseph A. Kruse, Bernd Witte, and Karin Füllner. Stuttgart and Weimar: Metzler, 1999. 571–85.

———. "Rhyming History: A Note on the 'Hebrew Melodies.'" *The Germanic Review* 74 (1999): 271–82.

Goldschmidt, Hermann Levin. "Heine und Freud." *"Der Rest bleibt": Aufsätze zum Judentum*. Vol. 4 of *Werke*. Vienna: Passagen, 1997. 197–209.

Habermas, Jürgen. "Heinrich Heine and the Role of the Intellectual in Germany." *The New Conservatism: Cultural Criticism and the Historian's Debate*. Trans. Shierry Weber Nicholson. Cambridge, MA: MIT Press, 1989. 71–99.

Höhn, Gerhard. "'Farceur' und 'Fanatiker des Ausdrucks.' Nietzsche, Heineaner *malgré lui*?" *Heinrich Heine: Neue Wege der Forschung*. Ed. Christian Liedtke. Darmstadt: Wissenschaftliche Buchgesellschaft, 2000. 198–215.

———. *Heinrich Heine: Un intellectuel moderne*. Paris: Presses universitaires de France, 1994.

Hohendahl, Peter Uwe. "Heine's Critical Intervention: The Intellectual as Poet." *Heinrich Heine's Contested Identities: Politics, Religion, and Nationalism in Nineteenth-Century Germany*. Ed. Jost Hermand and Robert C. Holub. New York: Peter Lang, 1999. 175–99.

Jospe, Raphael. "The Superiority of Oral Over Written Communication: Judah Ha-Levi's *Kuzari* and Modern Jewish Thought." *From Ancient Israel to Modern Judaism: Intellect in Quest of Understanding, Essays in Honor of Marvin Fox*. Ed. Jacob Neusner, Ernest Frerichs, and Nahum Sarna. Vol. 3. Atlanta: Scholars Press, 1989. 127–56.

Käfer, Karl-Heinz. *Versöhnt ohne Opfer: Zum geschichtstheologischen Rahmen der Schriften Heinrich Heines 1824–1844*. Meisenheim am Glan: Anton Hain, 1978.

Kaiser, Gerhard R. "Baudelaire pro Heine contra Janin. Text — Kommentar — Analyse." *Heine-Jahrbuch* 22 (1983): 135–78.

Koselleck, Reinhart. "'Erfahrungsraum' und 'Erwartungshorizont' — zwei historische Kategorien." *Vergangene Zukunft: Zur Semantik geschichtlicher Zeiten*. Suhrkamp: Frankfurt am Main 1979. 349–75.

Lefebvre, Jean-Pierre. *Der gute Trommler: Heines Beziehung zu Hegel.* Trans. Peter Schöttler. Heine-Studien. Hamburg: Hoffmann und Campe, 1986.

Lichtenberger, Henri. *Heinrich Heine als Denker.* Dresden: C. Reissner, 1905.

Malter, Rudolf. "Heine und Kant." *Heine-Jahrbuch* 18 (1979): 35–64.

Nietzsche, Friedrich. *Sämtliche Werke: Kritische Studienausgabe.* Ed. Giorgio Colli and Mazzino Montinari. Munich and New York: de Gruyter and Deutscher Taschenbuch Verlag, 1967–1977; 1980 (dtv). 15 vols.

Pepperle, Heinz. "Heinrich Heine als Philosoph." *Heinrich Heine: Ästhetisch-politische Profile.* Ed. Gerhard Höhn. Frankfurt am Main: Suhrkamp, 1991. 155–75.

Preisendanz, Wolfgang. "Memoria als Dimension lyrischer Selbstpräsentation in Heines Jehuda ben Halevy." *Memoria: Vergessen und Erinnern.* Ed. Anselm Haverkamp and Renate Lachmann. Poetik und Hermeneutik 15. Munich: Wilhelm Fink, 1993. 338–48.

Reeves, Nigel. "Heine and the Young Marx." *Oxford German Studies* 7 (1972–1973). Oxford: Oxford UP, 1973. 44–97.

Schlesier, Renate. "Homeric Laughter by the Rivers of Babylon: Heinrich Heine and Karl Marx." *The Jewish Reception of Heinrich Heine.* Ed. Mark H. Gelber. Tübingen: Niemeyer, 1992. 21–43.

Sternberger, Dolf. *Heinrich Heine und die Abschaffung der Sünde.* Hamburg: Claassen, 1972.

Stiening, Gideon. "Die Metaphysik des Hieroglyphischen." *Jahrbuch des Freien Deutschen Hochstifts* (1999): 121–62.

Wieland, Wolfgang. "Heinrich Heine und die Philosophie." *Heinrich Heine.* Ed. Helmut Koopmann. Wege der Forschung 289. Darmstadt: Wissenschaftliche Buchgesellschaft, 1975. 133–55.

Wülfing, Wulf. "Schlagworte des Jungen Deutschland, B. 'Zeit.'" *Zeitschrift für deutsche Sprache* 22.3 (n.d.): 154–78.

Würffel, Stefan Bodo. *Der produktive Widerspruch. Heinrich Heines negative Dialektik.* Bern: Francke, 1986.

Eternal Return or Indiscernible Progress? Heine's Conception of History after 1848

Gerhard Höhn

> "Werden die Angelegenheiten dieser Welt wirklich gelenkt von einem vernünftigen Gedanken, von der denkenden Vernunft? Oder regiert sie nur ein lachender Gamin, der Gott-Zufall?"[1] (B 5: 214)

HEINE POSED THIS QUESTION in March of 1848 after witnessing a victorious revolution in Paris. For a good one and a half decades he had predicted that what had begun in 1789 and continued in 1830 would soon be brought to a close. All the more paradoxical then, that such a question should haunt one who had never tired of ascertaining the reasonable course of the "affairs of this world," of interpreting the omens of future progress for the German public, and of branding them into its consciousness. In fact, Heine had initially sought to accelerate the flow of events and, being for the most part furnished with a normative, Enlightenment conception of history spiced with the ideals of the French Revolution, was superbly equipped for such a mission.

The skeptical approach Heine took from 1848 onwards seems incongruous when one considers that he was a former student of Hegel and that his writings as a journalist and historian had paved the way toward a new understanding of French social as well as German intellectual history. Particularly his philosophical treatise of 1834, a brilliant elucidation and defense of the formidable dialectics of history proposed by his Berlin mentor, had successfully traced the development of the German mind from the Reformation to the present day as a revolutionary process in three phases that would necessarily lead from religious upheaval via philosophical revolt to culminate eventually in the "political revolution" that Heine was witnessing in his own time. In conjunction with Saint-Simonian aspirations toward an imminent reconciliation of these historical antagonisms, this vision harbored an almost solemn faith in scientific and technological progress and in a universal liberation of humanity that would even encompass human sensuality. But only fourteen years later confessions such as "ich glaube an den Fortschritt, ich glaube, die Menschheit ist zur Glückseligkeit bestimmt" (B 3: 519) were overshadowed by the impression that the "affairs of this world" inevitably veered toward unhappiness.

Observing the Revolution from the Margins

For Heine the year 1848 was as eminently symbolic as it was tragic. The long-awaited revolution failed and he himself was vanquished, as his body disintegrated.

In early February 1848 the already ailing poet found himself in a Parisian medical clinic from which he would not return home until three months later on May 7. The revolution broke out in Paris on February 22 and, to the amazement of all, the ensuing battles in the streets and at the barricades sealed the fate of the July Monarchy within a matter of hours. The victorious revolutionaries composed of radical opposition leaders, students, and the National Guard formed a provisional republican government, which was to stay in power until the beginning of May.

From the confines of his sanatorium Heine at first perceived the events only as a distant noise,[2] but once, on February 23, when his carriage was overturned on a return journey from his apartment to the clinic, he was able to witness the fighting on the barricades at close range. Surprisingly, however, Heine, as correspondent of the Augsburg *Allgemeine Zeitung,* reporting "live" from the battlefield, reacted like a passionate theatergoer attending a newly revised and successful performance of a "good play." He lent authenticity to his account in the following way: "Ich hatte einen guten Platz um der Vorstellung beizuwohnen, ich hatte gleichsam einen Sperrsitz" (B 5: 208). Looking upon the February events in France, which in March would spill over into Germany and Eastern Europe, one cannot help but notice a startling analogy. As the initially successful uprisings began to falter and fail, the "orchestra seat" mutated into a dismal "Matratzengruft" from which Heine was never again to rise. But even though illness and above all his bodily collapse in mid-May permanently prevented the poet from directly participating in an event which, alongside the July Revolution of 1830, featured as the most important of his life, he experienced it to the quick until in the end he came to physically identify with it.

From a garden pavilion in Passy, which the by now completely paralyzed poet occupied beginning on May 24, he witnessed the gruesome massacre of June 22 to 25, 1848.[3] Even as this initial armed conflict between the propertied classes and the poor raged on, Heine emphasized for the first time the connection between history and disease. Thus in a letter of June 25 he wrote: "Mes jambes n'ont pas survécu à la chute de la royauté et je suis à présent cul-de-jatte" (HSA 22: 284). In this manner, Heine concretely experienced his illness as a coinciding of history and biography. His physical torments come to represent the collapse of all revolutionary hopes in the years 1848–49, such that his personal fate effectively symbolizes that of the postrevolutionary age as a whole, while his own despair reflects the general woes of the era itself. This fusion of the individual and the collective is clearly evidenced in a letter dating from the end of January 1852. At a time when counterrevolution was in its ascendancy, the poet declared with a pinch of self-mockery: "In demselben Maße wie die Revolution Rückschritte macht, macht meine Krankheit die ernstlichsten Fortschritte" (HSA 23: 175).

If illness and counterrevolution are the only dynamic elements left, then follows the inevitable, grave question whether there is any point to history, that is to say, whether the progressive Hegelian conception of history has not perhaps proven futile. It is precisely this issue that Heine discussed at length, waxing very creative in places. In a letter of June 12, 1848, that is, even before the great massacre, he coined the metaphor "Weltrevoluzionsgepolter" (HSA 22: 282), and just a day after the "bloodbath" he told his mother of the "three terrible days," adding "Die Welt ist voll Unglück" (HSA 22: 285). On July 9, completely bewildered by the course of events, he wrote the following anti-Hegelian lines to Campe: "Über die Zeitereignisse sage ich nichts; das ist Universalanarchie, Weltkuddelmuddel, sichtbar gewordener Gotteswahnsinn!" (HSA 22: 287).

The onslaught of chaos and turmoil that followed necessarily plunged any teleological conception of history into a profound crisis. The ever-encroaching sense that a God of chance occurrence ("der Gott-Zufall") reigns supreme makes the faith in progress and in the perfection of mankind, which is so typical of French Enlightenment thought, appear obsolete. In Heine's view the famous thesis proposed by Hegel, "Die Weltgeschichte ist Fortschritt im Bewusstsein der Freiheit," had failed in 1848 to withstand the trials and tribulations of reality. The aftermath left this form of history in ruins, just as all other political ideals had been reduced to rubble. After Louis Napoleon's coup d'état in February 1852 Heine made a devastating confession to his friend Gustav Kolb: "Die schönen Ideale von politischer Sittlichkeit, Gesetzlichkeit, Bürgertugend, Freyheit und Gleichheit, die rosigen Morgenträume des achtzehnten Jahrhunderts . . ., da liegen sie nun zu unseren Füßen, zertrümmert, zerschlagen" (HSA 23: 181).

Here just a brief note to explain Heine's point of view at the time. As events progressed in France and across Europe, the poet soon realized that the revolution of February and March was not his revolution and that the revolutionaries involved were not his revolutionaries. His initial mixed feelings, which were later to develop into outright opposition, are easier to fathom when one considers that Heine had expected a *social* uprising, only to encounter a *political* one. The form of government had been altered, but the social question of equality remained unsolved.

The "Affairs of This World" on the Other "World Stage"

Exactly how novel in Heine's thinking would the alternative concepts of an all-guiding reason ("denkende Vernunft") versus the God of chance occurrence appear in 1848? Heine's immediate reaction from the vantage point of his "orchestra seat" appears to be symptomatic of his latest conception of history. On the one hand, it seems to renounce an idealist philosophy of history, particularly one in the Hegelian mode, while at the same time allowing him to reconsider substantial elements of his earlier worldview that had kept historical idealism in check. The fundamental doubts and deep-rooted skepticism that were now assuming such a pivotal role had in fact always been part of Heine's thinking on history. Only they had been relegated to the margins and had never been expressed as prominently as now. Thus, according to my main thesis, the elements that pushed their way into the limelight in 1848 actually represent the reverse side of a progressive conception of history that had never been one-sided, or entirely linear. Like no other comparable German poet of his time, Heine had believed in the overwhelming power of progress or the "force des choses," but this creed had never made him turn a blind eye to certain potentially negative consequences.

In fact, Heine's thinking on history was constantly informed by various sources, such that he could never come to a definite conclusion devoid of contradictions, or even to a homogenous doctrine, except, perhaps, for a very short phase.[4] Apparently his unsystematic method is not based on any one specific concept.[5]

Why, indeed, should one expect a poet who from a very early time had been wary of the totalitarian demands of an idealist philosophy of history to come up with a systematic and accomplished conception of history? In the *Reisebilder* does he not mock one of the key concepts of his mentor Hegel by having a logical discussion result in absurd categorization, ending with a man of the people exclaiming "eine Idee ist alles dumme Zeug" (B 2: 288)? In his poem "Im Hafen" is Heine not parodying his teacher when he conjures the "rote, betrunkene Nase, / Die Nase des Weltgeists," only to conclude with a jeering "Und um die rote Weltgeistnase / Dreht sich die ganze, betrunkene Welt" (B 1: 211)? Precisely this sense of contingency, which renders every systematic concept untenable — and which became dominant in Heine's thinking after 1848 — had always been part of his view of history. For instance, in a spirited celebration of life from his second *Reisebild,* he characterizes the world, much as he had in "Im Hafen," as a "Traum eines weinberauschten Gottes, der sich aus der zechenden Götterversammlung à la française fortgeschlichen." The god in question is none other than Dionysus, whose dream visions often appear "motley and mad, but at times also harmonious and reasonable" (B 2: 253). This caricature places the skepticism about reason that Heine expressed in 1848 in a familiar context. His early nods to skepticism clearly show that he had always believed that reason and divine providence alone do not determine the course of world history, but rather that irrational forces also play their part. This view surfaces in the *Reisebilder* whenever Heine ridicules the notion of world harmony, deferring rather to a sense of "divine" or "world irony" (B 2: 522). Similarly, in *Bäder von Lucca* the narrator puzzles over the likelihood of certain events happening simultaneously in two different locations and asks whether elsewhere there was "etwa eine ähnliche Szene und offenbarte sich darin die Ironie des großen Weltbühnendichters da droben" — suggesting that this "author of the world stage" might be playfully staging such schemes of self-caricature repeatedly (B 2: 424). This and nothing more is the idea that resurfaces twenty years later, namely the notion of a "world stage" of the absurd. Drawing on ancient mythology and the baroque metaphor of *theatrum mundi*, Heine had already presented in *Ideen* a poetic model — "die Verbindung des Pathetischen mit dem Komischen" (B 2: 282) — that would prove essential to his contrastive modern narrative technique and which in his opinion had already been employed by great world poets such as

Aristophanes, Goethe, and Shakespeare. This idea of a vast, chaotic global stage initially endowed his disillusioning humor with a quasi-objective or — to put it in philosophical terms — ontological quality. On the other hand, the aesthetic paradigm that informs the theater metaphor also encompasses a historical dimension. Heine continues:

> Sie [die großen Dichter] habens alle dem großen Urpoeten abgesehen, der in seiner tausendaktigen Welttragödie den Humor aufs höchste zu treiben weiß, wie wir es täglich sehen: — nach dem Abgang der Helden kommen die Clowns und Graziosos mit ihren Narrenkolben und Pritschen, nach den blutigen Revolutionsszenen und Kaiseraktionen kommen wieder herangewatschelt die dicken Bourbonen. (B 2: 282)

Heine's initial reactions to the events of 1848, when he reported that it was as if he had watched a "good play" and even had "a good seat from which to view the performance" (B 5: 208), reflect this same perspective. The prophecies of *Ideen* were later to fulfill themselves in a most unexpected and disappointing manner. Just as the Restoration period has come to be regarded as a comic intermezzo following the great tragedies of the Revolution and Napoleon, the aftermath of 1848 is considered an insignificant era. In *Ideen,* Heine proclaims further:

> auf dieser großen Weltbühne geht es auch außerdem ganz wie auf unseren Lumpenbrettern, auch auf ihr gibt es besoffene Helden, Könige, die ihre Rolle vergessen, Kulissen, die hängen geblieben, hervorschallende Souffleurstimmen, Tänzerinnen, die mit ihrer Lendenpoesie Effekt machen, Costümes, die als Hauptsache glänzen. (B 2: 283)

And on that "world stage" that Heine clapped together in his late poetry, events do indeed unfold "as upon rickety planks": "clowns und *graziosos*" take the stage triumphantly, while "drunken heroes" and demented monarchs romp about in grotesque settings.

Progressive Dialectics: The Flip Side

A glance at the complex notion of progress manifest in the *Reisebilder* and the Paris essays confirms what the experience of contingency has suggested. Despite the shifts in thinking precipitated by the events of 1848, Heine's spiritual and intellectual biography is characterized more by evolution and continuity than by rupture and discontinuity.[6] Following the line of my main thesis, one could say that those elements that had been latent now became manifest, while those that had been more prominent receded into the background. In many respects, Heine interprets history according to an either/or scheme, whereby his position can fluctuate at times from one side of the fence to the other. Optimism never succeeds in ousting skepticism, but, on the other hand, doubt always leaves ample room for hope.

Thus, even the most ardently worded declarations in favor of progress and emancipation never quite manage to quench the inner voice of opposition. This voice incessantly conjures up haunting suspicions and points out fundamental doubts that constantly stop the soldier-poet — who is otherwise ready and willing to fight and sacrifice — dead in his tracks with the paralyzing query whether his efforts are not in vain, or if the price of relentless progress may not be a trifle too high. Heine's conception of history raises so many complex questions *because* it reveals an aspect of historical reasoning so close to modern modes of thinking. His view clearly reflects the doubts and aspirations of our times at the turn of the new millenium. A voice consistent with his early recognition of historical contingency surfaces again in his writings after 1848, raising now a twofold objection against any overly enthusiastic embrace of progress, by first, assuming the perspective of those who were its inevitable victims, and second, highlighting the aesthetic loss that was considered a necessary sacrifice for the sake of progress.[7] (An alternative to the teleological concept will be discussed below.)

Even at the time of the *Reisebilder,* at the end of the 1820s, Heine had been aware of the consistently high cost of progress and of the sacrifices that liberation inevitably demands. These initial insights told him that such a tribute was payable in terms of individual sacrifice, even at the cost of human lives. Two examples will suffice: In *Nordsee III* (1827) Heine employs Hegelian dialectics on a grand scale for the first time — and promptly comes to the typical conclusion that for modern man emancipation comes at the price of alienation and inner strife. However, for the author and dialectic historian Heine a nostalgic return to the unproblematic immediacy of past existence was not possible. With the acute, disillusioned wit that is the trademark of a thoroughly modern intellectual, Heine immediately pinpoints the destructive aspects of progress, epitomized here in the irrevocable loss of traditional life among the Norderney islanders.[8]

An episode at an important historical venue during Heine's Italian journey provides a more paradigmatic example. As he takes in the scene, he begins to question the bloody toll that the War of Liberation has levied on humanity — a question that will remain with him. The setting is the battlefield of Marengo, where freedom danced on "Blutrosen"; where France, the groom of liberty who had invited "the whole world to its wedding" (B 2: 378), let the heads of the nobility roll on the eve of the wedding. Speaking in the first person, the narrator now poses the decisive question whether progress really justifies so high a price:

> Aber ach! jeder Zoll, den die Menschheit weiter rückt, kostet Ströme Blutes; und ist das nicht etwas zu teuer? Ist das Leben des Individuums nicht vielleicht eben so viel wert wie das des ganzen Geschlechts? Denn jeder einzelne Mensch ist schon eine Welt, die mit ihm geboren wird und mit ihm stirbt, unter jedem Grabstein liegt eine Weltgeschichte — Still davon, so würden die Toten sprechen, die hier gefallen sind, wir aber leben und wollen weiter kämpfen im heiligen Befreiungskriege der Menschheit. (B 2: 378)

The narrator refuses to distinguish between the individual and the human race as a whole, for he is convinced that the cost of liberty must include such "Blutrosen." At this point, he silences the dead and rallies his fighting spirit by proclaiming his determination for self-sacrifice.

In this *Reisebild*, Heine speaks in the manner of a faithful, if critical Hegelian. In his lectures on *Philosophie der Geschichte* Hegel had proposed his famous thesis, according to which the spirit's consciousness of its freedom would become the final purpose of existence. This ultimate purpose, Heine elaborates, is the thing "worauf in der Weltgeschichte hingearbeitet worden, dem alle Opfer auf dem weiten Altare der Erde und in dem Verlauf der langen Zeit gebracht worden" (62). A skeptical query about the victims follows:

> Aber auch indem wir die Geschichte als diese Schlachtbank betrachten, auf welcher das Glück der Völker, die Weisheit der Staaten und die Tugend der Individuen zum Opfer gebracht worden, so entsteht dem Gedanken notwendig auch die Frage, wem, welchem Endzwecke diese ungeheuersten Opfer gebracht worden sind. (64)

But Hegel concludes by shunning any hopes harbored by the Enlightenment: "*Die Weltgeschichte ist nicht der Boden des Glücks*" (70–71). Thus Hegel sanctions the means employed by the Spirit to achieve its final aim, employing even the very language echoed in Heine's Marengo musings, most notably in the "slaughtering block" metaphor. For Heine, the voices of the victims are always present in the background, above all when he reports on the casualties of the Napoleonic wars or on the greatness of the empire. Is it any wonder, then, that he should reveal their hidden truths with the aid of the very metaphor coined by Hegel? Similarly, in *Über die französische Bühne* he casts doubt on this period of the empire's glory, and dryly adds: "Die Äcker lagen brach und die Menschen wurden zur Schlachtbank geführt" (B 3: 309). The full extent of Heine's skepticism toward his intellectual mentor is best evidenced by the fact that in his own history of philosophy he demonstratively adheres to the eudaemonistic agenda propagated by the Enlightenment.

There is a second point of departure from Hegel that needs only brief mention. One may cull from Heine's oeuvre a type of general conception of history, according to which evolution appears as a progressive demystification of the world. Even as early as the *Reisebilder* the author experiences pangs of pain and sorrow when he comes to view the process of civilization as a steady waning of beauty and sensuality that is symptomatic of cultural leveling and homogenization. If one could somehow link this point of view to Max Weber's thesis on "demystification," then it could be argued that by means of his poetry Heine had fathomed the repercussions of formalist, occidental rationalization, as described in Weber's treatise on Protestantism. Weber, as we know, examines that "großen religionsgeschichtlichen Prozeß der *Entzauberung* der Welt, welcher mit der altjüdischen Prophetie einsetzte und, im Verein mit dem hellenischen wissenschaftlichen Denken, alle *magischen* Mittel der Heilssuche als Aberglaube und Frevel verwarf," claiming that it was to culminate in Protestant asceticism (94–95). During his pantheist phase Heine, who was a merciless critic of spiritualism and Christian asceticism, had roughly defined the history of the human race as being a history of demystification in three steps, concluding that emancipation constantly claims sacrifices in terms of artistic beauty and greatness.

The Eternal Return in *Romanzero*

On November 5, 1851 Heine wrote to his friend Georg Weerth informing him of his hopeless physical condition and divulging an issue which he had not dared to express in the "Nachwort" to *Romanzero*. He subsequently uttered the confession, "daß ich als Dichter sterbe, der weder Religion noch Philosophie braucht, und mit beiden nichts zu schaffen hat" (HSA 23: 147). This gives the impression of his wanting to distance himself — at least in part — from his return to monotheism,[9] which he had announced only five weeks earlier in the epilogue to his third anthology of poetry, provoking something of a scandal: "Ja, ich bin zurückgekehrt zu Gott, wie der verlorene Sohn, nachdem ich lange Zeit bei den Hegelianern die Schweine gehütet" (B 6.1: 182). My discussion of Heine's late, "post-philosophical" conception of history will address these matters in an attempt to determine to what extent the marginal aspects of his earlier thinking on history now, in the course of his alleged return to God, take center stage and relegate the teleological model to the margins.

The methodical starting point to be used here shall not rely on *explicit,* universal statements, but rather on the *implicit* development of his attitude in his late poetry; that is, his discursive turn against historical progress will be confronted with the poetry itself; a strategy that has been employed to great effect in the most recent research.[10]

The *Romanzero* poems tell of a world that has gone completely haywire, a world where dialectics have long been abandoned. These great narrative poems are not dominated by reason and common sense but by senselessness. Decline replaces evolution, while order surrenders to "universal anarchy" or "world fuddle-muddle."[11] In short, this global drama is not directed by a God of reason but by the "God of chance occurrence," or even a drunken deity. It is not happiness that is being invoked but suffering; the sufferings of countless victims as well as those of a handful of heroes, and those of the protagonist, who in this Lazarus cycle is the most miserable of all. No matter where the narrative chooses to venture, whether it be world history, biography, or the story of individual nations, it always comes down to the same basic pattern of ascent, decline, and ruin — that is, a pointless cycle that embraces the entirety of human greatness and beauty in its crushing hoop. Thus in part 1, entitled "Historien," the Valkyries make their appearance and announce the leitmotif of the whole oeuvre. Wodin's messengers are seen to hover above the battleground where men engage in the ceaseless struggle for power, and they mercilessly proclaim the triumph of evil over goodness:

> Und das Heldenblut zerrinnt
> Und der schlechtre Mann gewinnt. (B 6.1: 21)

The exact meaning of this is effectively demonstrated in the ensuing ballad. "Schlachtfeld bei Hastings" treats the undoing of King Harold in 1066 in these lines characteristic of the "Historien":

> Gefallen ist der beßre Mann,
> Es siegte der Bankert, der schlechte,
> Gewappnete Diebe verteilen das Land
> Und machen den Freiling zum Knechte. (B 6.1: 22)

Should a further confirmation of this central motif be required, it can come from a great poem from "Lamentationen," the second part of the anthology. "Im Oktober 1849" compares the heroic demise of the Hungarian revolution to the fall of the Nibelungen and then utters the bitter words:

> Es ist dasselbe Schicksal auch —
> Wie stolz und frei die Fahnen fliegen,
> Es muß der Held, nach altem Brauch,
> Den tierisch rohen Mächten unterliegen.
> (B 6.1: 117)[12]

The opening "Historien" read like an extract from a pessimistic world history. These poems cover many epochs, ranging from India and ancient Egypt to medieval Persia and feudal Europe. They talk of the end of the Aztec empire as well as modern Britain and France, until they eventually end up in contemporary Paris. Everywhere, though, one finds the same basic themes of violence, treason, revenge, crime, struggle, ruin, defeat, and death. The chain of violent acts constantly renews itself, and gloomy scenes of overthrown dynasties and *Götterdämmerungen* form an endless sequence. Kings of all continents and ages lie in their own blood or will one day be slain (like Charles I of England, who bore his future executioner on his lap). The arbitrary reign of despotic rulers goes unchecked, and they even go so far as to murder innocent children ("Spanische Atriden"), while yet others encourage murder ("König David") or turn out to be nothing more than impostors (like the Persian king in "Dichter Firdusi"). Even gods are allowed to go to the dogs, such as the title figure of "Der Apollogott," who must swindle his way through exile, or Vitzliputzli, the Mexican god of war who is honored with human sacrifices before witnessing his own downfall. Love is likewise doomed to failure. The Yemenite Asra, for instance, cannot love without losing his life; "Pfalzgräfin Jutta" must kill to experience love, and the Provençal couple Melisande and Rudèl may not embrace, except at the price of losing each other forever.

This progression of doom and vanquishment is programmatically pursued into part 2 of the anthology, where the first-person narrator reviews the shambles of his life as a blending of the illness shackling him to the "Matratzengruft" with universal suffering. The central section comprises the Lazarus cycle, in which the theme of suffering finds itself most radically and subjectively expressed. Together with Job, the diseased leper Lazarus comes to epitomize the apparent pointlessness of human misery.[13] In these personae the autobiographic element unpretentiously transcends the mask of fiction. Similarly, the proverb-like prologue "Weltlauf" recalls the poet's financial woes, that is, his bitter experiences with the power of money, by referring to the fundamental clash between wealth and poverty as portrayed in the Bible:

> Hat man viel, so wird man bald
> Noch viel mehr dazu bekommen.
> Wer nur wenig hat, dem wird
> Auch das wenige genommen.
>
> Wenn du aber gar nichts hast,
> Ach, so lasse dich begraben —
> Denn ein Recht zum Leben, Lump,
> Haben nur die etwas haben. (B 6.1: 105)

The theme of victimization and suffering eventually culminates in the fate of the Jewish people. Part 3 marks a transition from the exemplary individual martyr Lazarus to the exemplary martyr nation of history, telling the story of the suffering of the Jewish people. The "Hebräische Melodien" are not lullabies but rather songs of lament in which the victory of evil over goodness is portrayed as pointless pain in a world without cause. The pariah who appears in the poem "Prinzessin Sabbat" stands for a people who have been transformed into a dog and are therefore condemned to lead a dog's life. The beaten and the banished in "Jehuda ben Halevy" are none other than the great Spanish-Jewish poets who suffered death and degradation in exile — and with whom Heine identified.

Though Lazarus, the poet Firdusi, and Jehuda Halevi may be tragic figures, they are surrounded by a host of comic characters. Contemporary clowns come in the guises of treasure thieves, rogues, executioners, and impostors ("Historien"). They bear names such as Pomare, Apollo, Crapülinski, and Waschlapski ("Historien") or mysterious titles like "Der Ex-Lebendige" and "Der Ex-Nachtwächter" ("Lamentationen"). In some cases they make their appearance as bizarre duos such as Brother Jose and Rabbi Juda ("Hebräische Melodien"). This menagerie of curious figures in *Romanzero* is added to in the later poems by yet more grotesque individuals, as typified in the illustrious ruler and founding father of entire dynasties "Hans ohne Land," "Kobes I" (*Gedichte. 1853 und 1854*), "Simplizissimus I," and "König Langohr I" (unpublished works), not to mention the "Wahlesel" and the freakish bestiary with its wolves, cats, mice, dragonflies, sharks, and bugs. And also after *Romanzero,* a new brand of heroes, the fools of German politics, joins this parade of failure. The *Gedichte. 1853 und 1854* expose the political immaturity of the *Vormärz* poets and ridicule the naiveté of the 1848 Frankfurt delegates, who are held responsible for the snuffing out of the revolution. And they criticize German dependence on higher authority as a tendency that precludes revolution from the very outset and will continue to do so in the foreseeable future. Finally, the epic poem "Bimini" also tells of a great misadventure, namely the abortive expedition aboard a "magic ship" to the magical land of Bimini. Its goal of "imminent rejuvenation" is inverted into one of imminent death.

The Cyclical Conception of History and Circular Thinking

Given Heine's generally disillusioned view of the world and his pessimistic notion of history, it is hardly a coincidence that in the *Nachmärz* — itself the initial period of decline for modern history — the teleological concept should begin to fade, finding itself not merely challenged but actually eclipsed by the significant return of an alternative model. We should recall here that before as well as after 1830 Heine had employed the cyclical model alongside the teleological concept. Only the dialectic foundation of *Zur Geschichte der Religion und Philosophie in Deutschland* enabled him to overcome this ambivalence. As Jürgen Ferner has shown,[14] this conflict characterizes the years between 1822 until roughly 1834, but the question remains whether it does not perhaps also characterize Heine's oeuvre as a whole, albeit with varying degrees of intensity — that is, as my thesis to this point has claimed, this conflict surfaced as an *explicit* argument at first, only to be sustained *implicitly* in the poetry of the late period.

The notion of recurrence that makes its debut in *Ideen* becomes powerfully apparent toward the end of the already cited *Reise von München nach Genua,* where it forms an explicit antithesis to teleological thought. Here, influenced by the theory of metempsychosis, the narrator reflects on the cycle arising out of the transition from life to death and onwards to new life. He describes this cycle, which supports the preservation of the species rather than individual originality, as "a hopelessly eternal play of repetition" (B 2: 388). One fragment in particular emphasizes the materialistic attitude upon which this notion of historical return is founded. It suggests that because of the finiteness of things within an endless expanse of time all *material* phenomena will eventually recur (incarnation) according to the law of endless combinations that governs the "eternal play of repetition," with the result that all configurations that have already existed on earth will occur again (B 2: 616).[15]

In *Verschiedenartige Geschichtsauffassung,* a posthumously published fragment dating from 1833, Heine discusses the difference between the cyclical versus the evolutionary model explicitly, characterizing it in pointed fashion as the antithesis of the eternal return versus a linear historical dialectics. As representatives of the cyclical idea Heine mentions the historical school of jurisprudence (e.g., Friedrich Karl von Savigny), the poets of the Goethean "Kunstperiode," and the historian Leopold von Ranke — today, we think of Nietzsche and his notion of the eternal return, as evidenced in the eternal struggle for power that dominates human history.[16] The other side is represented by the "Humanitätsschule," that is, Enlightenment thinkers such as Lessing. The decisive matter, however, is that Heine then regarded the cyclical notion as purely negative, as "hopeless" and "fatalistic," his argument being that it led to a type of "elegiac indifference," and to political paralysis. The poet therefore defended the evolutionary model because it advocates the implementation of reason in everyday political practice. He did nevertheless limit his enthusiasm by adding the compelling reservation that, for all its superiority, this scheme sacrifices life in the present to a future form of existence. In other words, one is too caught up in the past, while the other looks too far ahead. Ultimately, he discarded both in favor of individualist existence in the present, the well-known formula being "das Leben ist weder Zweck noch Mittel; das Leben ist ein Recht" (B 3: 23).

What has not been given its full due until recently is the fact that in 1848 Heine began to reconsider the cyclical idea that he had previously rejected as anti-progressive. What he had considered an idea of the past began again to shape his view of history; and this metamorphosis can be deduced from his late lyrics and prose pieces.

Heine opened his *Allgemeine Zeitung* correspondence in March 1848 with a telling question which plagued him as he observed the February Revolution from his "orchestra seat," and in which the *theatrum mundi* metaphor becomes linked to the idea of eternal return: "Wiederholt sich der große Autor? Geht ihm die Schöpfungskraft aus?" Or to be specific, was February 1848 a repetition of July 1830? In *Französische Zustände* Heine had emphasized the continuity between 1789 and 1830, which then justified for him the bloodshed of the later uprising. "Die Revolution" he said "ist eine und dieselbe; . . . nicht für die Charte schlug man sich in der großen Woche, sondern für dieselben Revolutionsinteressen, denen man seit vierzig Jahren das beste Blut Frankreichs geopfert hatte" (B 3: 166). In his 1848 correspondence he writes in the same vein: "Hat er das Drama das er uns vorigen Februar zum Besten gab, nicht schon vor achtzehn Jahren ebenfalls zu Paris aufführen lassen unter dem Titel 'die Juliusrevolution'?" Then he briefly consoles himself with the assurance: "Aber ein gutes Stück kann man zweimal sehen" (B 5: 208).[17]

But where does the cyclical notion become evident in his poetry? In *Romanzero* it returns with full force in its negative configuration, as the poet accepts as uncontested, quasi-natural phenomena those maxims of the cyclical theorists which he had rejected in 1833.[18] It is expressed by Solomon the Preacher: "There is nothing new under the sun!" (1:9). A more concrete depiction of the fateful continuity of revenge appears in the romance "Spanische Atriden" with respect to a dynasty. Here, it leads to innocent royal children being caged like dogs.

The poem "König David" is much more impressive in this regard. It relates the ascent of a new ruler and paints an even more drastic picture of the bleak cycle of evil. With a knowing smile King David orders his son to have General Joab eliminated. The poems begins in the symptomatic fatalist vein:

> Lächelnd scheidet der Despot,
> Denn er weiß, nach seinem Tod
> Wechselt Willkür nur die Hände,
> Und die Knechtschaft hat kein Ende.
>   (B 6.1: 40)

Despotism is thus declared nothing less than a natural occurrence: evil has reigned for eons and will continue to do so forever.

The extent to which the cyclical model reinstates itself after 1848 is further highlighted by a poem from *Gedichte. 1853 und 1854*. The late poem "Pferd und Esel" quips directly at cyclical thought. A brief account of its content: In modern society with its revolutionary steam engines the equine species must brace itself for a bleak future, while the donkey apparently does not have to worry about what lies ahead — thus the donkey relishes its seeming superiority in a manner typical of Heine's late thinking on history:

> In diesem uralten Naturkreislauf
> Wird ewig die Welt sich drehen,
> Und ewig unwandelbar wie die Natur,
> Wird auch der Esel bestehen. (B 6.1: 295)

The poetry is complemented by a passage in his autobiographical prose that also resorts to those words of Solomon the Preacher quoted above. In *Geständnisse* (1854) the Lazarus-Heine alludes again to this biblical saying, now for the third time in the context of his thinking on history. As he invokes the cyclical view of history once again, he quotes Solomon almost literally: "es gibt nichts Neues unter der Sonne" (B 6.1: 501).

Ultimately the full scope of cyclical thought renascent in the *Nachmärz* lyrics is evidenced by the ubiquitous references to repetition. Initiated by a personal return ("ich bin zurückgekehrt zu Gott"), the final phase of Heine's work is dominated throughout by all forms of repetition, be they universal or individual in nature, of negative or positive import.

The predominance of the negative throughout history is one prominent aspect. Two longer poems in the third book of *Romanzero* elaborate on the ever-present, ceaselessly recurring fate of the Jewish people during the diaspora. The life of Jehuda Halevi serves as an example for the recurrence of suffering and the degradation of exiled poets in general. "Prinzessin Sabbat," cited above, tells how Prince Israel is changed back into a human being, but only for an evening because the curse placed on the Jewish people causes him to be turned back into a dog. The fate of the diaspora is likewise symbolized by a javelin, which is constantly hovering over "our heads" and "pierces the best hearts." It not only hits Jehuda Halevi but also Moses Ibn Esra and Salomon Gabirol. On another level, offenses or affronts suffered earlier return repeatedly. Such is the case for instance in the "garden of malediction" of the "Affrontenburg," which bears a veritable curse that the poem's narrator cannot seem to shake off (*Gedichte. 1853 und 1854*).

Events of contemporary history are often played out, but in comical fashion. The last four poems of *Gedichte. 1853 und 1854* as well as some unpublished *Zeitgedichte* repeatedly target ruling figures and representatives of the opposition in order to lampoon the permanence of German misery in the *Nachmärz*. For example, the black, red, and gold flag, referred to now as "old-Germanic rubbish," appears anew while Ernst Moritz Arndt and Turnvater Jahn, those "heroes from the days of old" rise once more from their graves (B 6.1: 271). "Im Oktober 1849" denounces the return of the Restoration era in the form of resurrected images of idyllic familial bliss. A part of the "Lamentationen," it is satire on Germany written in the wake of the ill-fated Hungarian revolution, which had signaled the end to the European uprisings of 1848. It opens with the mocking lines:

> Gelegt hat sich der starke Wind,
> Und wieder stille wirds daheime;
> Germania, das große Kind,
> Erfreut sich wieder seiner Weihnachtsbäume.
>
> (B 6.1: 116)

This hopeless state of affairs is also parodied in a series of animal satires from the final phase, in which the Germans' daftness and their addiction to authoritarianism is portrayed as a natural and thereby unchangeable phenomenon. "Schlosslegende" attacks the same issue. This poem directly unmasks the perverted ancestry of the Prussian royal family, whose supposed origins — which according to legend go back to horses — have marked all its monarchs with a stigma against which they are defenseless.

Certain fantasies repeat themselves as well. In the "Historien" the dead are resurrected and keep returning as ghosts: for example, "Pfalzgräfin Jutta" (with the seven dead souls), the "Himmelsbräute," or even the amorous "tender ghosts"[19] "Geoffroy Rudèl und Melisande von Tripoli." In the ghost drama "Maria Antoinette" the past returns in the form of an ancient and unchangeable courtly ritual. In "Kobes I" a certain portentous ghost by the name of "die Schaffnerin" makes its appearance whenever the Germans have committed a "grand act of folly" (*Gedichte. 1853 und 1854*). Also, mythological figures such as the Valkyries carry out their woeful duties as attendants of Odin. The Mexican god of war on the other hand comes to Europe and assumes a new career of devilry and vengeance as "the malicious enemy of enemies." Furthermore, questions of life philosophy churn in aporia-like circles, as is exemplified by the unsolvable conflict between beauty and truth treated in the great unpublished poem "Es träumte mir von einer Sommernacht" ("O, dieser Streit wird endgen nimmermehr, / Stets wird die Wahrheit hadern mit dem Schönen," [B 6.1: 349]). Similarly, the eternally futile religious disputation between the rabbi and the monk must remain unresolved because, in the end, "alle beide stinken."

The recurrent pattern also applies to formal elements. Motifs such as the presentation of the pearl case in "Jehuda ben Halevy" are expanded upon, and particular words are deliberately repeated several times within the text.[20] In *Gedichte. 1853 und 1854* entire stanzas find themselves repeated (e.g., in "Die Laune der Verliebten" [B 6.1: 218, 219, 220]), or whole verses (e.g., in "Die Libelle" [B 6.1: 209]; or in "Mimi" [B 6.1: 221]), or parts of verses (e.g., the phrase "die böse Welt" in "Schnapphahn und Schnapphenne" [B 6.1: 225]).

And finally, there is another, totally different genre of repetition or recurrence. A renewed veneration for poetry as such, which is central to "Jehuda ben Halevy," becomes even more pronounced in "Bimini," an epic that takes us back to the "age of faith in miracles" when the wondrous "blue flower" still blossomed freely. The "magical ship" being launched from the "slips of thought" is demonstratively flagged out in the "fabled colors of the Romantic" (B 6.1: 243, 247–48).

"eppure si muove" (Galileo): After all, history *does* move!

Contingency, recurrence, and cyclical thought are undoubtedly indicative of stagnation, but one must nevertheless ask whether things really do not move at all? Has reason, all "denkende Vernunft," really forsaken history altogether? The impression of a deep freeze in the dialectics of history categorically conveyed throughout the *Romanzero* and the late poetry revolves around one aspect in particular: Heine's rejection of Hegel.

His complex relations with Hegel after 1848 culminated in a public renunciation of his master. One should remember that at the beginning of the 1850s Heine announced a renewed faith in God and officially severed his links with Hegel, whom he now declared the initiator of certain fatal atheist tendencies in German philosophy, tendencies that had taken hold among the proletariat. It is, however, difficult to qualify Hegel as an atheist; and with this in mind, Heine's statements should be examined more closely. Having turned to religion, Heine now equates pantheism to atheism, declaring pantheists to be nothing other than "shameful atheists" (B 6.1: 183). But he is resolute in breaking away from the Left-Hegelians, for whom he now claims, in a well-known passage, he had once "herded swine" (B 6.1: 182); he now dismisses them as "godless self-gods" (B 3: 510). This renunciation of Ruge, Marx, Feuerbach, and Bruno Bauer is justified in this regard, because these thinkers actually did resort to atheist beliefs. In one instance, Heine even quotes Feuerbach expressly.

An unqualified break with Hegel or not? The answer to this question is so crucial because it also determines how one assesses the continuity of Heine's work.[21] Dolf Sternberger[22] and, more recently, Roger Cook[23] believe there was such a break, while Ortwin Lämke and Arnold Pistiak have recently joined Jean-Pierre Lefebvre in denying it. Without retracing this debate among Heine scholars in detail, this is the occasion to propose an alternative differentiation: when Heine *explicitly* severed his links with the "godless" Hegel, it remains open whether he actually cut himself loose intellectually and poetically from the Berlin philosopher, or whether in his writings an *implicit* adherence to Hegel's thought might still exist. Lefebvre, for example, who has analyzed the question in most detail, has been able to show to what extent *Romanzero's* triadic plot incorporates elements of Hegelian logic and dialectics, even if as parody. Similarly, he reads the "Historien" as a parody of Hegel's conception of world history. Moreover, Lefebvre, a scholar of both Heine and Hegel, is convinced that the line of argument in *Geständnisse,* written after Heine's rejection of Hegel, is still "definitely Hegelian" in essence. Not only the biblical Genesis-type story including the fall of man, but also a number of other text segments indicate a "relapse into Hegelianism."[24] On this level, one should also ask if *Lutezia,* with all its subsequent additions, adheres to a method other than the Hegelian, that is, whether one finds indications of more universally valid ideas in Heine's treatment of specific issues of his own times.[25] This idea has recently been explored by Lämke, who has analyzed a number of motifs and terms found in both *Französische Zustände* (1833) and in *Lutezia* (1854) — for example, money, Louis-Philippe, Napoleon, *Volk,* revolution, republic, and communism. In Lämke's conclusion, which sticks firmly to the thesis of continuity, he confirms that after 1848 Heine suppresses direct references to Hegel but that his dialectic notions of history nonetheless continue to evolve in another form (127–30, 136–39). Taking a different approach, Pistiak basically endorses this assumption. He believes that Heine's poetic practice in *Gedichte. 1853 und 1854* undermines his official statements about his return to God and his break with Hegel (182–96). Pistiak contends that the commonly held view that Heine gradually distances himself from Hegel cannot be supported by reference to either *Geständnisse* or to *Gedichte. 1853 und 1854* (192).

Heine's critique of Hegel is not the only available point of reference. His late oeuvre contains ample clear-cut indications of Heine's conviction that history is not eternally caught in a circle. Clearly, his prognoses for the future in *Lutezia* and *Geständnisse* suggest as much. In the German version of the preface to the French edition of *Lutezia,* for instance, he resolutely predicts that the future belongs to the communists. Without going into the specifics of this issue, I would offer this thought: despite his critical stance on proletarian egalitarianism and iconoclasm, for all his seemingly ambivalent statements concerning early communism, one cannot but conclude that Heine never questioned the historical legitimacy of communism. When one reads his declarations from the 1850s in the context of the immediate situation, as one must, they often turn out to be negative declarations that then deconstruct themselves through ironic or stylistic reversal.

Most prominently, Heine does not shy away from self-contradiction when he says that the future belongs to the communists *because* their leaders were schooled in Hegel. In *Geständnisse,* he even emphasizes in no uncertain terms the power that the German communists have garnered from the working classes: "diese Partei ist zu dieser Stunde unstreitig eine der mächtigsten jenseits des Rheines." He attributes this power to the party's uncompromising doctrine in which the "crassest atheism" plays a large part. The French version of this text furthermore stresses the superiority of German-style communists in comparison to the British Chartists and the Egalitarians from other countries, attributing it to the fact that their leaders are great logicians, "de grands logiciens" schooled in Hegel: "Ces docteurs en révolution et leurs disciples impitoyablement déterminés sont les seuls hommes en Allemagne qui aient vie, et c'est à eux qu'appartient l'avenir" (B 6.2: 186).

Heine believes the German communists capable of, first, solving the great social question of equality and justice, and, second, of dealing German nationalism a decisive blow. This harks back to the programmatic announcements he made in the 1830s. In the preface to *Lutezia* he again acknowledges the unquenchable inner voice of logic, which informs him "that all human beings have the right to eat." Although fearing the destruction of the "marble statues of his beloved world of art" and his "laurel forests," he nonetheless ends up praising even the greengrocer who uses the pages on which his poems are printed as paper cones, "worin er Kaffee und Schnupftabak schüttet für die armen alten Mütterchen, die in unsrer heutigen Welt der Ungerechtigkeit vielleicht eine solche Labung entbehren mußten — *fiat justitia, pereat mundus!*" (B 5: 233).

And then there is also the overwhelming voice of hatred. The Francophile Heine had always been aware of the fact that he and the communists were fighting a common enemy in Germany, and thus he had to concede: "Aus Haß gegen die Nationalisten könnte ich schier die Kommunisten lieben." Seen from this angle, the communists' faults (such as atheism) definitely appear to be the lesser of two evils, because their highest principles revere the same values Heine holds dear, namely "Kosmopolitismus, eine allgemeine Völkerliebe, ein Welt-bürgertum aller Menschen, welches ganz übereinstimmend ist mit dem Grunddogma des Christentums." Two years before his death Heine did not hesitate to make public his conviction that the communists were eventually going to crush the teutomaniacs "like a toad."

Ultimately, Heine's further thinking on the dialectic between theory and practice must be seen in connection with his prophecies about communism. As a symptom of his problematical relationship to Hegel, and thus to history itself, it also indicates to what extent he counters Hegel with his own ideas.[26] As we know, the author of *Zur Geschichte der Religion und Philosophie in Deutschland* adopted Hegel's idea about the close relation between thought and action, and chose to give it particular emphasis in his own treatise. However, he goes beyond Hegel in that he actually demands a transition from theory to practice. The notion of philosophy being no more than a temporary stage in the process of human liberation is incompatible with Hegel's system. Heine's groundbreaking motto, which paved the way for the young Hegelians, states, "Der Gedanke will Tat, das Wort will Fleisch werden" (B 3: 593).

Twenty years later Heine reassessed the length of time required for the idea of liberty to permeate all levels of society and to eventually become a reality. In reference to a development he terms "Volkwer-dung der Freiheit," he modifies his earlier maxim in this symptomatic way: "Das Wort wird Fleisch, und das Fleisch blutet" (B 5: 461). Hegel's dialectics and the theory of necessity thus receive a perceptible pruning and subsequently lose some momentum, but they are not entirely discarded, because the word is still to become deed. However, the metaphor of "bleeding flesh" again reminds one of the high cost of further progress, which demands sacrifice, pain, and renunciation. Still, in the end this blood metaphor, which appears both in the *Reise-bilder* and in his late work, signals the conviction that those "democratic principles" to which Heine had adamantly adhered throughout (B 6.1: 184) would eventually materialize in the long term, perhaps circuitously. As "Enfant perdu" will no doubt remind us, he was nevertheless aware of the fact that he would never live to see that day.

The Battle is Lost, But Not the War

However one views Heine's attitude toward Hegel and the communists, one thing is certain about it: the seemingly omnipotent God who plays dice with the world or the fateful recurrence of evil may well be able to postpone the goal of history, but they cannot totally avert progress. Reason has gone through a deep crisis, but it has not been eradicated, whether because the reign of folly is being challenged by reason, or because a crazed God has to be summoned before a tribunal[27] — and which other is there than that ruled by reason — or simply because the parody of the *Vormärz* poets and of those of 1848 would not be feasible without a blueprint for more inspired politics. Alternately put: Does the satire on the undone *Vormärz* poets and the failure of 1848 not provoke a desire for better politicians? Does a criticism of that which is wrong not point toward something better? Does the victim's perspective so overwhelmingly apparent in *Romanzero*[28] not carry with it the implication that the oppressed need not always remain trodden underfoot?

Even in death's antechamber, his mattress tomb, Heine still had not come to terms with postrevolutionary reality. Despite personal despair, his thinking and his poetry were neither resigned nor pessimistic. On the contrary, Heine kept producing critical lyrics[29] and maintained his fighting spirit without taking back any of his predictions about social revolution, a claim that, as mentioned previously, Lämke and Pistiak have now established convincingly.[30]

Though Heine's reputation as an intellectual who defended his ideals to the last has been reinstated, it is much harder to find corresponding positive strains in his poetic practice. But among recent critical studies, Cook has shown that the poet's renewed faith in the power of autonomous poetry represents an element of hope. This new poetic principle (as exemplified in *Romanzero*) returns to a particular romantic tradition, reviving by means of a modern poetic imagination its myths and legends, sagas and visions in the hope of freeing up potential forces that had been suppressed. Cook argues that the "new mythopoetic discourse" which Heine creates in the late work is "privileged in some way to express truths inaccessible to other discourses, including those of religion and philosophy."[31] However, this strategy, largely dependent on aesthetic tactics, strains the relationship between theory and practice. With his interpretation of *Gedichte. 1853 und 1854,* which focuses on socially critical aspects and attempts to demonstrate a political dimension, Pistiak, on the other hand, has demonstrated that the link between theory and practice *is* in fact carried through to the late poetry. Commenting, for instance, on the protagonists of history in this later collection, he maintains that the voice of the people ("das Volk") is only heard in the Lazarus poems (237). And what about the *Romanzero* which — with the exception of the two poets Firdusi and Jehuda Halevi — is positively crawling with false or, at the very least, comic heroes, while the real protagonists of history, although present, remain — according to Lefebvre — anonymous and obscure?[32]

Two famous and much-cited poems from *Romanzero,* among others, announce a positive countermovement against an evil universe by siding with the victims: "Im Oktober 1849" and "Enfant Perdu," both from the Lazarus cycle of "Lamentationen" (B 6.1: 116–18 and 120–21). Both poems acknowledge military defeat. The heroic battle of the Hungarians ends in the fall of "the last bastion of freedom," while the overpowered sentry has held out for 30 years in the "war for freedom" without a hope of victory and now lies wounded to death. In these poems either a "friend" or the narrator himself is stricken by a fatal bullet. Both glorify martyrdom, and the blood of heroes flows freely. The line in one, "Ungarn blutet sich zu Tode," finds its echo in the other: "Die Wunden klaffen — es verströmt mein Blut." The victors are qualified on the one hand as "beastly brutal forces," or, more precisely, as the "Ox" Austria, the Russian "Bear"; and on the other as "some suspicious fool" who fired the deadly bullet. But the narrators have not been left to fight alone. The first-person plural speaker of the Hungarian song knows a "friend who was shot" and declares his solidarity with the Magyars. The sentry likewise remembers his comrades as "a host of friends." Both retain the energy to console themselves and, more significantly, both speakers are convinced that they have not fought in vain. Thus the narrator of one poem calls out to his defeated hero "doch tröste dich, Magyar, / Wir andre haben schlimmre Schmach genossen," meaning, in contrast to you, we stray into "das Joch / Von Wölfen, Schweinen und gemeinen Hunden." After the changeover from "we" to "I" the speaker finally condemns the noisy victors by registering olfactory protest and then, in contrast, urging his poet self to resist in silence:

> Das heult und bellt und grunzt — ich kann
> Ertragen kaum den Duft der Sieger.
> Doch still, Poet, das greift dich an —
> Du bist so krank und schweigen wäre klüger.[33]

The epilogue to this cycle, where, as mentioned earlier, the poet's fate and the political destiny of his times coincide in exemplary fashion, takes up the theme of death in battle that he had addressed at the battlefield of Marengo, employing the "Blutrosen" of freedom metaphor. However, now his perspective on the matter is reversed. Although in *Romanzero* there is no more talk of the collective "we" who want to "live and . . . fight again" (B 2: 378), the "Verlorene Posten" nonetheless faces imminent death with the soothing hope that others will occupy his place and continue the fight. These closing words can be read as a legacy by means of which the dying, yet undefeated poet enters into the historical succession of generations, his consolation being rooted in the dynamics of a socio-genealogical continuity:

> Ein Posten ist vakant! — Die Wunden klaffen —
> Der eine fällt, die andern rücken nach —
> Doch fall ich unbesiegt, und meine Waffen
> Sind nicht gebrochen — Nur mein Herze brach.

The "Enfant Perdu" does not regard the lost battle as the end of the war, and associates the certainty of his own doom with the faith in the ongoing struggle for emancipation.

—Translated by Sebastian Stumpf

Notes

[1] This essay derives from a presentation in November 1998, which bore the same title and was given as part of a lecture series sponsored by the Düsseldorf Heinrich-Heine-Gesellschaft, entitled "150 Jahre Revolution 1848."

[2] B 5: 207: "Beständig Getrommel, Schießen und Marseillaise. Letztere, das unaufhörliche Lied, sprengte mir fast das Gehirn."

[3] On June 25 general Cavaignac, the minister of war, aided by the entire armed forces (national guard, mobile guard, and the army) as well as by canons, put down the people's rebellion. The revolutionaries suffered at least 3000 fatalities and there were 15,000 arrests, while the republican bourgeoisie lost about 1000 men.

[4] Heine scholars cannot agree as to whether he actually held a systematic view of history. In his monograph, Ferner regards the question of a "*geschlossene* diskursive Behandlung des Geschichtsproblems" or a "systemphilosophische Abrundung" to be irrelevant in the case of a poet like Heine (*Versöhnung und Progression: Zum geschichtsphilosophischen Denken Heinrich Heines* [Bielefeld: Aisthesis, 1994], 17). Ortwin Lämke on the other hand maintains that due to his understanding of He-

gel from the Berlin years up until 1848, Heine had advocated a systematic concept of history, which he then revised (*Heines Begriff der Geschichte: Der Journalist Heinrich Heine und die Julimonarchie*, Heine-Studien [Stuttgart and Weimar: Metzler, 1997], 142).

[5] In addition to the two aforementioned, authoritative monographs, Heine's conception of history has also been analyzed by the following authors: Karlheinz Fingerhut, *Standortbestimmungen. Vier Untersuchungen zu Heinrich Heine* (Heidenheim: Heidenheimer Verlagsanstalt, 1971), 53–91; Helmut Koopmann, "Heines Geschichtsauffassung," *Jahrbuch der Deutschen Schillergesellschaft* (1972): 453–76; Jost Hermand, "Gewinn im Verlust. Zu Heines Geschichtsphilosophie," *Text + Kritik* 18/19 (1982): 49–66; Antoon A. van den Braembussche, "Heines Geschichtsbild," *Rose und Kartoffel: Ein Heinrich Heine-Symposium*, ed. Antoon A. van den Braembussche and Philipp van Engeldorp Gastelaars (Amsterdam: Editions Rodopi, 1988), 85–101; Gerhard Höhn, "'Blutrosen' der Freiheit. Heinrich Heines Geschichtsdenken," *Heinrich Heine: Ästhetisch-politische Profile*, ed. Gerhard Höhn (Frankfurt am Main: Suhrkamp, 1991), 176–94; and Michael Werner, "Réflexion et révolution. Notes sur le travail de l'histoire dans l'oeuvre de Heine," *Revue Germanique Internationale* 9 (1998): 47–60. Those focusing on particular aspects of this concept include Bollacher ("Aufgeklärter Pantheismus," *Heinrich Heine: Artistik und Engagement*, ed. Wolfgang Kuttenkeuler [Stuttgart: Metzler, 1977], 144–86), Zantop ("Verschiedenartige Geschichtsauffassung: Heine und Ranke," *Heine-Jahrbuch* 23 [1984]: 42–68), Heinemann ("'Variazionen' — Heines Geschichtsauffassung nach 1848," *Rose und Kartoffel: Ein Heinrich Heine-Symposium*, ed. Antoon A. van den Braembussche and Philipp van Engeldorp Gastelaars [Amsterdam: Editions Rodopi, 1988], 69–84), Briegleb ("Abgesang auf die Geschichte? Heines jüdisch-poetische Hegelrezeption," *Heinrich Heine: Ästhetisch-politische Profile*, ed. Gerhard Höhn [Frankfurt am Main: Suhrkamp, 1991], 17–37), Briese ("'Schutzmittel *für* die Cholera.' — Geschichtsphilosophische und politische Cholera–Kompensation bei Heine und seinen Zeitgenossen," *Heine-Jahrbuch* 32 [1993]: 9–25), Höhn ("'La force des choses': Geschichtsauffassung und Geschichtsschreibung in Heines *Reisebildern*," *Lectures d'une oeuvre: Reisebilder. Heinrich Heine*, ed. René Anglade [Paris: Editions du temps, 1998], 84–102), and Erhart ("Heinrich Heine: Das Ende der Geschichte und 'verschiedenartige' Theorien zur Literatur," *Aufklärung und Skepsis: Internationaler Heine-Kongreß 1997 zum 200. Geburtstag*, ed. Joseph A. Kruse, Bernd Witte, and Karin Füllner [Stuttgart and Weimar: Metzler, 1999], 498–506).

[6] In contrast to earlier theses of a break, recent research has used various perspectives and methods to emphasize the continuity within Heine's oeuvre, both by retracing his intellectual development and by analyzing the way it translates into practice in his poetry. Concerning the problem of history, Ferner for instance speaks of a "revision" following 1848 (*Versöhnung und Progression* 292) but slots Heine's final phase into a rubric entitled "geschichtsphilosophische Variation." The abbreviated version of his work, "'O wer lesen könnte!'" also emphasizes the idea of continuity. Lämke distinguishes between reassessment, that is to say a "break" with the past in Heine's later conception of history, and the idea of continuity (*Heines Begriff der Geschichte* 141). Arnold Pistiak argues expressly that there was direct continuity (*"Ich will das rote Sefchen küssen": Nachdenken über*

Heines letzten Gedichtzyklus, Heine-Studien [Stuttgart and Weimar: Metzler 1999], 316).

[7] Both aspects, the dialectics of progress and the theory of demystification, are first introduced in Höhn, "'Blutrosen' der Freiheit."

[8] See Jost Hermand, "Gewinn im Verlust. Zu Heines Geschichtsphilosophie," *Text + Kritik* 18/19 (1982): 49–66.

[9] On Heine's religious turnabout, see Wilhelm Gössmann, "Die theologische Revision Heines in der Spätzeit" (320–35) and Hermann Lübbe, "Heinrich Heine und die Religion nach der Aufklärung" (205–18), both in *Der späte Heine, 1848–1856: Literatur — Politik — Religion,* ed. Wilhelm Gössmann and Joseph A. Kruse (Heine-Studien; Hamburg: Hoffmann und Campe, 1982). On the chronology of Heine's return to monotheism in 1848/1849, see Ludwig Rosenthal, *Heinrich Heine als Jude* (Frankfurt am Main: Ullstein, 1973), 281–83. On the crisis of 1848, see Roger F. Cook, *By the Rivers of Babylon: Heinrich Heine's Late Songs and Reflections* (Detroit: Wayne State UP, 1998), 51–89.

[10] On this approach, see more recent larger works concerning Heine's late writings (*Romanzero, Gedichte. 1853 and 1854,* and *Lutezia*) by Cook (*By the Rivers of Babylon*), Pistiak (*"Ich will das rote Sefchen küssen"*), and Lämke (*Heines Begriff der Geschichte*).

[11] "Weltkuddelmuddel"; in an unpublished poem, the alternative coinage "Erdenkuddelmuddel" also occurs (B 6.1: 311).

[12] Further verses home in on this key motif; for example poem 1 of "Zum Lazarus" — the just suffer, "Während glücklich als ein Sieger / Trabt auf hohem Roß der Schlechte" (B 6.1: 201). Also, the posthumously published "Ganz entsetzlich ungesund" (B 6.1: 330) and "Es kommt der Tod" (B 6.1: 341). See also the final paragraph of *Die Götter im Exil* (B 6.1: 423).

[13] See Joseph A. Kruse, "Heinrich Heine — Der Lazarus," *Heinrich Heine: Ästhetisch-politische Profile,* ed. Gerhard Höhn (Frankfurt am Main: Suhrkamp, 1991), 258–75.

[14] Ferner (*Versöhnung und Progression* 103–209) has meticulously analyzed the parallels from the *Reisebilder* era up as far as *Zur Geschichte der Religion und Philosophie in Deutschland* in 1834. His thesis is that Heine's wavering between the two alternative concepts ends with the Paris writings, the short text entitled "Verschiedenartige Geschichtsauffassung" (1833) marking the turning point. However, the cyclical model is also discussed in his essay on Shakespeare (1839; B 4: 214–17), and it makes a definite comeback in the late poetry. See also the important fragment on philosophy of history, B 6.1: 624.

[15] See Jan-Christoph Hauschild in the Düsseldorf Heine Edition (DHA 10: 795–801). And again in his "Différentes manières de considérer l'histoire. A propos des réflexions de Heine en matière de philosophie de l'histoire dans les années 1830," *Revue Germanique Internationale* 9 (1998): 61–72.

[16] For details on Nietzsche's relationship to Heine see Höhn, "'Farceur' und 'Fanatiker des Ausdrucks.' Nietzsche, ein verkappter Heineaner," *Heine-Jahrbuch* 36 (1997): 134–52.

[17] This "theater performance" returns in the poem "Sie erlischt" in the form of a death fantasy.

[18] Jean-Pierre Lefebvre also emphasizes the nature-like cyclical elements in *Romanzero* and adds the fitting remark that one finds nothing but dying phases, while the "joys of spring" are missing. (*Der gute Trommler: Heines Beziehungen zu Hegel*, Heine-Studien [Hamburg: Hoffmann und Campe, 1986], 134–35). See also Lefebvre, "Nachwort," Heinrich Heine, *Romanzero*, ed. Bernd Kortländer (Stuttgart: Reclam, 1997), 288–89.

[19] For a treatment of the "Gespenster" motif, see Isabelle Kalinowski, "L'histoire, les fantômes et la poésie dans le *Romancero*," *Revue Germanique Internationale* 9 (1998): 129–42, and Walter Erhart, "Heinrich Heine: Das Ende der Geschichte und 'verschiedenartige' Theorien zur Literatur."

[20] For an interpretation of the repetition in "Hitzig / Itzig" see Isabelle Kalinowski, "Trois Figures du *Romancero*: l'incongruité, la répétition, le paradoxe," in *La poésie de Heinrich Heine*, ed. Michel Espagne and Isabelle Kalinowski (Paris: CNRS Editions, 2000), 133–37.

[21] For a synthesis of the problematic relationships between Heine and Hegel and also Heine and the communists see Höhn, *Heine-Handbuch: Zeit, Person, Werk*, 2nd. ed. (Stuttgart and Weimar: Metzler, 1997), 354–57 and 476–78. See also Cook, *By the Rivers of Babylon*, 68–89, 91–94, 110–13, and 351–52.

[22] Sternberger: "Überhaupt spielt Hegel in Heines Werken bis zu den 'Geständnissen' eine vergleichsweise unbedeutende Rolle" (*Heinrich Heine und die Abschaffung der Sünde* [Hamburg: Claassen, 1972], 260). According to Sternberger's thesis, Hegel's thinking takes on a prominent role in 1854, as never before, but at this point Heine rejects it.

[23] In his introductory section to his *By the Rivers of Babylon*, entitled "The Renunciation of Modern Philosophy," Cook stresses Heine's "adamant opposition to Hegelian philosophy" (29), pointing to "Heine's castigation of Hegel after 1848" (31). For similar wording see also 57, 105, and 121.

[24] See Lefebvre, *Der gute Trommler*, 125–43, and also, "Nachwort," 284–88.

[25] Hauschild and Werner maintain that Heine's method of explanation in *Lutezia* remained Hegelian in essence (*Der Zweck des Lebens ist das Leben selbst. Heinrich Heine: Eine Biographie* [Cologne: Kiepenheuer & Witsch, 1997], 581).

[26] Lefebvre, *Der gute Trommler*, 29. It is Lefebvre who proposes the appropriate pun "hégélien défroqué."

[27] On July 9, 1848, Heine wrote to Campe about the "Gotteswahnsinn": "Der Alte muß eingesperrt werden, wenn das so fort geht" (HSA 22: 287).

[28] See Klaus Briegleb, who coined the concept "Poetik der Besiegten" (*Opfer Heine? Versuche über Schriftzüge der Revolution* [Frankfurt am Main: Suhrkamp, 1986], 127).

[29] B 6.1: 270–307. In this regard, the poem "Die Wanderratten" is worthy of mention, as it is the only piece announcing the need for a social revolution.

[30] See Lämke, *Heines Begriff der Geschichte,* 122–23; and Pistiak's chapter in his *"Ich will das rote Sefchen küssen"* entitled "Ansatzpunkte mündig-oppositioneller Haltungen im Spätwerk Heines" (225–41), and also 316.

[31] Cook, *By the Rivers of Babylon,* 44 and 48. His aim: to show "how Heine himself saw his last poems as the beginnings of a mythopoetic post-Enlightenment poetry that combines Romantic discontent with the world and critical inquiry" (364).

[32] Concerning the poems "Im Oktober 1849" and "Enfant perdu," Lefebvre writes that the agents of history "sind durch nichts anderes gekennzeichnet als durch diese Freundschaft, durch diese innere Beziehung zu Heine, ihr Heldenname wird nicht genannt" (*Der gute Trommler,* 136); cp. also "Nachwort," 290. Especially in reference to "Im Oktober 1849" and "Enfant perdu," see also Michael Werner, "Politische Lazarus-Rede: Heines Gedicht 'Im Oktober 1849,'" *Gedichte und Interpretationen,* vol. 4, ed. Günter Häntzschel (Stuttgart: Reclam, 1983), 288–99, and "Heines poetisch-politisches Vermächtnis," *Interpretationen: Gedichte von Heinrich Heine,* ed. Bernd Kortländer (Stuttgart: Reclam, 1995), 181–94.

[33] On the motif of silence and secrecy see Christian Liedtke, in particular: "dieses beredte Schweigen ist Heines Einspruch gegen den 'Raketenlärm' und die alles übertönenden dissonanten Tierlaute der Sieger" ("'Ich kann ertragen kaum den Duft der Sieger.' Zur politischen Dichtung Heinrich Heines nach 1848," *1848 und der deutsche Vormärz,* ed. Peter Stein, Florian Vaßen, and Detlev Kopp [Bielefeld: Aisthesis, 1998], 211).

Works Cited

Bollacher, Martin. "Aufgeklärter Pantheismus." *Heinrich Heine: Artistik und Engagement.* Ed. Wolfgang Kuttenkeuler. Stuttgart: Metzler, 1977. 144–86.

van den Braembussche, Antoon A. "Heines Geschichtsbild." *Rose und Kartoffel: Ein Heinrich Heine-Symposium.* Ed. Antoon A. van den Braembussche and Philipp van Engeldorp Gastelaars. Amsterdam: Editions Rodopi, 1988. 85–101.

Briegleb, Klaus. "Abgesang auf die Geschichte? Heines jüdisch-poetische Hegelrezeption." *Heinrich Heine: Ästhetisch-politische Profile.* Ed. Gerhard Höhn. Frankfurt am Main: Suhrkamp, 1991. 17–37.

———. *Opfer Heine? Versuche über Schriftzüge der Revolution.* Frankfurt am Main: Suhrkamp, 1986.

Briese, Olaf. "'Schutzmittel *für* die Cholera.' — Geschichtsphilosophische und politische Cholera–Kompensation bei Heine und seinen Zeitgenossen." *Heine-Jahrbuch* 32 (1993): 9–25.

Cook, Roger F. *By the Rivers of Babylon: Heinrich Heine's Late Songs and Reflections.* Detroit: Wayne State UP, 1998.

Erhart, Walter. "Heinrich Heine: Das Ende der Geschichte und 'verschieden-artige' Theorien zur Literatur." *Aufklärung und Skepsis: Internationaler Heine-Kongreß 1997 zum 200. Geburtstag*. Ed. Joseph A. Kruse, Bernd Witte, and Karin Füllner. Stuttgart and Weimar: Metzler, 1999. 489–506.

Ferner, Jürgen. "'O wer lesen könnte!' Heines geschichtsphilosophisches Denken im Kontext von Vor- und Nachmärz." *Vormärz — Nachmärz: Bruch oder Kontinuität?* Vormärz-Studien 5. Ed. Norbert Otto Eke and Renate Werner. Bielefeld: Aisthesis, 2000. 185–211.

———. *Versöhnung und Progression: Zum geschichtsphilosophischen Denken Heinrich Heines*. Bielefeld: Aisthesis, 1994.

Fingerhut, Karlheinz. *Standortbestimmungen: Vier Untersuchungen zu Heinrich Heine*. Heidenheim: Heidenheimer Verlagsanstalt, 1971.

Gössmann, Wilhelm. "Die theologische Revision Heines in der Spätzeit." *Der späte Heine, 1848–1856: Literatur — Politik — Religion*. Ed. Wilhelm Gössman and Joseph A. Kruse. Heine-Studien. Hamburg: Hoffmann und Campe, 1982. 320–35.

Hauschild, Jan-Christoph. "Différentes manières de considérer l'histoire. A propos des réflexions de Heine en matière de philosophie de l'histoire dans les années 1830." *Revue Germanique Internationale* 9 (1998): 61–72.

Hauschild, Jan-Christoph, and Michael Werner. *Der Zweck des Lebens ist das Leben selbst. Heinrich Heine: Eine Biographie*. Cologne: Kiepenheuer & Witsch, 1997.

Hegel, Georg Wilhelm Friedrich. *Philosophie der Geschichte*. Stuttgart: Reclam, 1961.

Heinemann, Gerd. "'Variazionen' — Heines Geschichtsauffassung nach 1848." *Rose und Kartoffel: Ein Heinrich Heine-Symposium*. Ed. Antoon A. van den Braembussche and Philipp van Engeldorp Gastelaars. Amsterdam: Editions Rodopi, 1988. 69–84.

Hermand, Jost. "Gewinn im Verlust. Zu Heines Geschichtsphilosophie." *Text + Kritik* 18/19 (1982): 49–66.

Höhn, Gerhard. "'Blutrosen' der Freiheit. Heinrich Heines Geschichtsden-ken." *Heinrich Heine: Ästhetisch-politische Profile*. Ed. Gerhard Höhn. Frankfurt am Main: Suhrkamp, 1991. 176–94.

———. "'Farceur' und 'Fanatiker des Ausdrucks.' Nietzsche, ein verkappter Heineaner." *Heine-Jahrbuch* 36 (1997): 134–52.

———. *Heine-Handbuch: Zeit, Person, Werk*. 2nd. ed. Stuttgart and Weimar: Metzler, 1997.

———. "'La force des choses.' Geschichtsauffassung und Geschichtsschrei-bung in Heines *Reisebildern*." *Lectures d'une oeuvre: Reisebilder. Heinrich Heine*. Ed. René Anglade. Paris: Editions du temps, 1998. 84–102.

Kalinowski, Isabelle. "L'histoire, les fantômes et la poésie dans le *Romancero*." *Revue Germanique Internationale* 9 (1998): 129–42.

———. "Trois Figures du *Romancero*: l'incongruité, la répétition, le paradox." *La poésie de Heinrich Heine*. Ed. Michel Espagne and Isabelle Kalinowski. Paris: CNRS Editions, 2000. 125–38.

Koopmann, Helmut. "Heines Geschichtsauffassung." *Jahrbuch der Deutschen Schillergesellschaft* (1972): 453–76.

Kruse, Joseph A. "Heinrich Heine — Der Lazarus." *Heinrich Heine: Ästhetisch-politische Profile*. Ed. Gerhard Höhn. Frankfurt am Main: Suhrkamp, 1991. 258–75.

Lämke, Ortwin. *Heines Begriff der Geschichte: Der Journalist Heinrich Heine und die Julimonarchie*. Heine-Studien. Stuttgart and Weimar: Metzler, 1997.

Lefebvre, Jean-Pierre. *Der gute Trommler: Heines Beziehungen zu Hegel*. Heine-Studien. Hamburg: Hoffmann und Campe, 1986.

———. "Nachwort." Heinrich Heine. *Romanzero*. Ed. Bernd Kortländer. Stuttgart: Reclam, 1997. 273–98.

Liedtke, Christian. "'Ich kann ertragen kaum den Duft der Sieger.' Zur politischen Dichtung Heinrich Heines nach 1848." *1848 und der deutsche Vormärz*. Ed. Peter Stein, Florian Vaßen and Detlev Kopp. Bielefeld: Aisthesis, 1998. 207–23.

Lübbe, Hermann. "Heinrich Heine und die Religion nach der Aufklärung." *Der späte Heine, 1848–1856: Literatur — Politik — Religion*. Ed. Wilhelm Gössmann and Joseph A. Kruse. Heine-Studien. Hamburg: Hoffmann und Campe, 1982. 205–18.

Pistiak, Arnold. *"Ich will das rote Sefchen küssen": Nachdenken über Heines letzten Gedichtzyklus*. Heine-Studien. Stuttgart and Weimar: Metzler, 1999.

Rosenthal, Ludwig. *Heinrich Heine als Jude*. Frankfurt am Main: Ullstein, 1973.

Sternberger, Dolf. *Heinrich Heine und die Abschaffung der Sünde*. Hamburg: Claassen, 1972.

Weber, Max. *Gesammelte Aufsätze zur Religionssoziologie*. Vol. 1. Tübingen: J. C. B. Mohr, 1988. 3 vols.

Werner, Michael. "Heines poetisch-politisches Vermächtnis." *Interpretationen: Gedichte von Heinrich Heine*. Ed. Bernd Kortländer. Stuttgart: Reclam, 1995. 181–94.

———. "Politische Lazarus-Rede: Heines Gedicht 'Im Oktober 1849.'" *Gedichte und Interpretationen*. Vol. 4. Ed. Günter Häntzschel. Stuttgart: Reclam, 1983. 288–99.

————. "Réflexion et révolution. Notes sur le travail de l'histoire dans l'oeuvre de Heine." *Revue Germanique Internationale* 9 (1998): 47–60.

Zantop, Susanne. "Verschiedenartige Geschichtsauffassung: Heine und Ranke." *Heine-Jahrbuch* 23 (1984): 42–68.

Heinrich Heine and the Discourse of Mythology

Paul Reitter

> Auch in der Mythologie ging es gut. Ich hatte meine liebe Freude an
> dem Göttergesindel, das so lustig nackt die Welt regierte. Ich glaube
> nicht, daß jemals ein Schulknabe im alten Rom die Hauptartikel sei-
> nes Katechismus, z.B. die Liebschaften der Venus, besser auswendig
> gelernt hat, als ich.
> — Heinrich Heine, *Ideen. Das Buch Le Grand* (DHA 6: 189)

> Es war im May 1848, an dem Tage, wo ich zum letzten Male aus-
> ging, als ich Abschied nahm von den holden Idolen, die ich ange-
> betet in den Zeiten meines Glücks. Nur mit Mühe schleppte ich
> mich bis zum Louvre, und ich brach fast zusammen, als ich in den
> erhabenen Saal trat, wo die hochgebenedeite Göttin der Schönheit,
> Unsere liebe Frau von Milo, auf ihrem Postamente steht. Zu ihren
> Füßen lag ich lange und ich weinte so heftig, daß sich dessen ein
> Stein erbarmen mußte. Auch schaute die Göttin mitleidig auf mich
> herab, doch zugleich so trostlos als wollte sie sagen: siehst du denn
> nicht, daß ich keine Arme habe und also nicht helfen kann?
> — "Nachwort" zu *Romanzero* (DHA 3.1: 181)

THUS HEINE REPRESENTS HIS renunciation of the Greek mythological figures that pervade his writings from the early poem "Die
Götter Griechenlands" through the expository works *Zur Geschichte
der Religion und Philosophie in Deutschland* and *Elementargeister* to
the ballet libretto *Die Göttin Diana,* which he wrote shortly before
the revolutionary tumult of 1848. The account is fictional, of course.
It is hard to image that Heine ever lay prostrate in the Louvre. And it
is even harder to imagine that Heine actually lay prostrate in the Louvre in front of a famous statue of Venus *the very last time* he went out
before an eight-year long confinement, the "Matratzengruft" period,
during which he in fact turned his attention away from Venus and the
other Greek gods. Of course, Heine did not abandon the gods completely. In an enigmatic late story, *Die Götter im Exil,* he appropriated
them as he had throughout his oeuvre: as ciphers for a "Hellenic" sen-

sualism forced underground by "Nazarene" spiritualism. The text is cryptic because, unlike *Elementargeister,* to cite just one example, it portrays the Greek gods not simply as exiled, but also as old, worn and, in some cases, complicit with the very spiritualist order that oppresses them. Furthermore, Venus, who had been Heine's preferred emblem of the salutary "mythic other" of spiritualism — he repeatedly calls Venus the "Erzteufelin" of Hellenic sensualism — is missing. Something drastic has happened to the sensuous mythological tradition. It has not only lost relevance because of Heine's physical degeneration and been supplanted by his renewed interest in Judaism; it has been deformed.

Heine's highly stylized sketch of his parting with the Greek gods gives us clues as to why. Drawing our attention to the year and the place, to the setting of his turn away from Greek mythology, Heine encourages us to understand this shift as intimately connected to its historical context. How did the Revolution of 1848 in Paris affect Heine's break with Venus? The question, or, rather, suggestion, is worth pursuing, as the few scholars who have acknowledged a substantive, post-1848 change in Heine's thinking about myth ascribe the change to the immediate biographical factors mentioned above: Heine's physical collapse and his late affinity with Judaism. While these developments might account for the diminished importance of the Greek gods for Heine, they do not explain the drastic resignification of mythological figures in *Die Götter im Exil.* And in the second part of this essay, 1 will try to add to scholarly discussions of Heine's mythological discourse by following up on Heine's hints. My claim is that *Die Götter im Exil* registers, and responds to, disruptions in the significance of mythological figures and the discourse of myth, disruptions largely caused, it would seem, by the Revolution of 1848 and its aftermath in a newly modernized Paris.

More specifically, I will argue that *Die Götter im Exil* is neither continuous with Heine's earlier representations of the exiled Greek gods, as some critics would have it, nor a simple function of his bad health and late philosemitism, but, rather, a very sophisticated reading of the post-1848 fate of what had been for him a potentially redemptive discourse prior to 1848. *Die Götter im Exil* is one of those places where Heine emerges as one of the first poets of modern life. For in giving critical expression to sensualism's second exile, that is, to post-1848 ruptures in the meaning and predicament of mythic sensualism, Heine suggests shifts that were very much part of the movement driving modernism. Indeed, according to several influential theorists of modernism, 1848 is the point at which "high art" tacitly renounced

explicit activism and turned inward, toward form.[1] The classic example
of this phenomenon, which culminated in the modernist obsession
with form at the beginning of the twentieth century, is Flaubert's *Sentimental Education,* whose affinities with the late Heine I will address
in the second part of my essay. The first part traces the trajectory of
Heine's "mythological writings," as the *Düsseldorfer Heine-Ausgabe*
rubricates them, from the very beginning of his career up until 1848.
Here, for the most part, I will be addressing Heine's work with classical mythological figures, since his engagement with the Judeo-
Christian tradition is examined elsewhere in this volume.

I

If, in his late representations of Greek mythological figures, Heine anticipated key aspects of modernist thinking about the function of critical art in advanced industrialized societies, he had earlier adumbrated,
as Markus Winkler points out, central features of Hans Blumenberg's
seminal work on myth, or, more specifically, on how working with
myth can redress some of the ills of modernity. In writings such as
*Religion und Philosophie in Deutschland, Die Romantische Schule, Ele-
mentargeister,* and *Die Göttin Diana,* Heine charts a course from neo-
Hegelianism to proto-western Marxism. He bemoans the reifying effects of conceptual abstraction, maintaining that the hostility of Enlightenment universalism to sensuous particularity could result in
ethical deficiencies and a dangerous loss of meaning, or indeed, in ni-
hilism. Yet, at the same time, Heine endorses the Enlightenment project, as, for him, it means emancipation from superstition and the
systematic injustices of arbitrary rule.

We should note here that Heine does not view mythic discourse as
coextensive with salubrious Hellenic sensualism. Sustaining myth often means perpetuating bad superstitions. Indeed, the persistence of
German "folk beliefs," that is, superstitious ideas about goblins and
forest demons, is what causes Greek mythological figures to be de-
monized as goblins in Germany, according to Heine. (However, as we
will see, such beliefs are, paradoxically, crucial to the survival of Hellenic sensualism, for they keep it alive in mythic discourse, even if they
do not treat the Greek gods so well.) An added complexity is that the
very Enlightenment rationalism that productively cuts through deleterious superstitions derives, at least in part, from Christianity, the very
mythological tradition that exiled the sensuous mythological tradition

Heine wants to rehabilitate. For Heine, Enlightenment reason may be hostile to Christianity, but Enlightenment abstraction nonetheless stands in the tradition of Christian spiritualism and thus perpetuates Christianity's resistance to the healthier mythological tradition of Hellenism. And the irrational mythological energy from which Enlightenment reason flows forth occasionally makes itself felt, for example, in the excessive destructiveness of certain manifestations of the Enlightenment. This is how Heine understands Kant. On the one hand, he is a liberator. He forcefully promotes the rule of reason, and thereby emancipates everyone who had suffered under arbitrary power. But Kant cuts through the superstitious old order with a ruthless, primordial blood lust that makes him more terrifying — more dangerous — than Robespierre. Where the Enlightenment wants to stamp out myth completely, it is, paradoxically, at its most mythological. And this kind of "mythological thinking" is, for Heine, clearly harmful.

Let me offer some examples. In *Religion und Philosophie in Deutschland* Heine writes: "Man sagt, die Nachtgeister erschrecken, wenn sie das Schwert eines Scharfrichters erblicken — Wie müssen sie erst erschrecken, wenn man ihnen Kants *Kritik der reinen Vernunft* entgegenhält! Dieses Buch ist das Schwert, womit der Deismus hingerichtet worden in Deutschland" (DHA 8.1: 80–81). The motif of prerational mythic creatures fleeing in terror before a hostile spiritualism, be it Christianity or philosophy, is the principle of construction behind Heine's representations of mythological figures. Accordingly, I will examine it in detail shortly. First, however, it is important to note again that Heine does not simply work with a nondialectical spiritualism versus sensualism, or abstraction versus mythology dichotomy. Mythology can be a kind of spiritualism, it would seem, for the mythological figures that Kant threatens are insistently called "Nachtgeister." Moreover, Kant is not just a forceful purveyor of rationalizing progress. Not only does he deal in terror, but he also bears affinities with an executioner — Heine makes the executioner's sword into the analogue of Kant's philosophy — and the executioner is one of the darkest emblems of an old tyrannical order that drew support from the very superstitions Kant supposedly puts an end to. Indeed, Kant turns out to be something of an "elemental spirit" himself. For there is an elemental aspect to his "Zerstörungswut." Compared with him, Robespierre is "zahm und moderant." And Heine goes on to write: "Man erzeigt wirklich dem Maximilien Robespierre zu viel Ehre wenn man ihn mit dem Immanuel Kant vergleicht" (DHA 8.1: 81). Robespierre committed crimes of passion; Kant was eerily systematic in his destructiveness, and this, for Heine, makes him all the more terrifying. Another important issue is Kant's relation to art. Heine writes:

> Diese große Geisterbewegung hat Kant nicht sowohl durch den Inhalt seiner Schriften hervorgebracht, als vielmehr durch den kritischen Geist der darin waltete, und der sich jetzt in alle Wissenschaften eindrängte. Alle Disciplinen wurden davon ergriffen. Ja, sogar die Poesie blieb nicht verschont von ihrem Einfluß. Schiller z.B. war ein gewaltsamer Kantianer, und seine Kunstansichten sind geschwängert von dem Geist der kanteschen Philosophie. Der schönen Literatur und den schönen Künsten wurde diese kantesche Philosophie, wegen ihrer abstrakten Trockenheit, sehr schädlich. Zum Glück mischte sie sich nicht in die Kochkunst. (DHA 8.1: 90–91)

Here again, Heine plays with the semantic density of the word *Geist* to evoke improbable associations between Kant and the world of mythological superstitions and spirits or *Geister* that his devastatingly critical mind, or *Geist*, was supposed to explode. In the passage cited above, the connection was a product of Kant's elemental, Germanic violence, of his affinities with the world of vicious German superstitions that he destroys. Here, the link becomes thicker. For there seems to be something ghostly or *geisterhaft* about Kant's philosophy. Its abstractness stands in opposition to, is even a natural enemy of, the healthy material beauty, the life-promoting, nourishing sensuousness of art. This abstractness could even compromise the way we nourish ourselves on the most basic level: with food.

What revitalizes culture and also serves as a buffer against the nihilistic, eviscerating abstraction is a mythological tradition, a discourse of myth, very different from the superstitious folk beliefs that Kantian philosophy seems alternately to be opposed to and allied with. This is the salutary tradition of Greek sensualism. The problem is that this tradition cannot be appropriated as an immediate cultural resource. Powerful spiritualisms, for instance, Christianity, have actively suppressed it, and this led to strange convolutions in its significance. Greek sensualism has been embedded in spiritualist folk beliefs that are so foreign to it. Indeed, Heine repeatedly represented the Greek gods as being mistaken for wood spirits and goblins by German peasants. In doing so, he was not just adding poignancy to his preferred figure of the Greek gods in exile. As Heine knew from reading Jakob Grimm, this actually happened: the Greek gods did find their way into German traditions of folk mythology (from there they occasionally migrated even farther — into the kabbala), where they were treated as sylvan spirits.

Heine's thinking here was radically historical in another sense as well. He was not interested, as Robert Holub has shown, in any kind of pure historical reconstruction of Greek mythology. He realized that historical appropriations of the discourse of myth — many of them quite recent — had become part of its significance, and that in order to appropriate the discourse of myth effectively himself, he would have to work through the history of its reconstructions. He began by taking on the "Grecophilia" of the very artist he singled out as a victim of Kantian abstraction: Friedrich Schiller.

Indeed, Heine's first substantial poetic reckoning with the motif of Greek mythology in exile immediately evokes Schiller's poem of the same name: "Die Götter Griechenlands." Holub has perceptively catalogued the incongruities between Heine's poem and Schiller's. He notes that Heine reflects from a "semi-conscious, dreamlike state," and that this forms "a sharp contrast to Schiller's philosophical clarity" (57). Here, then, Heine *performs* the critique of Schiller that he developed explicitly in *Religion und Philosophie in Deutschland*. For if poetry in general, and, we can presume, poetic representations of the Greek gods in particular, have become too philosophical under Kant's influence, one way to redress this problem would be to bring forth more poetic portrayals of the fate of Greek mythology. And this is just what Heine is doing. However, we cannot assume that Greek mythology is somehow more immediate for Heine than it was for Schiller simply because Heine's style seems to be directly inspired by the mythological objects of his reflection. As Holub remarks, "That the gods appear from cloud formations [in Heine's poem] is significant; for it emphasizes both the ephemeral quality of these mythological figures and the aimless wandering of their exile" (57). Whereas Schiller can access the gods with "clarity," they remain murky for Heine; they are shadowy apparitions enveloped in the mists of their difficult history. Yet they have drifted through history, if also in contorted and distorted form, and have a kind of real presence in the *present*, which they lack in Schiller's elegiac poems named "Die Götter Griechenlands" and "Der Spaziergang." For in these poems the Greek mythological figures are represented as shining and heroic, but also as irretrievably lost, as belonging, very clearly, to the *past*. For Schiller, Greek mythology can serve as an inspiring example of cultural achievement, but it is thoroughly antiquated as a way of relating to the world.

Heine's poem resists Schiller's classicist grecophilia on the levels of both form and content. In Heine's poem, we cannot see the gods as they were, but, rather, only as they are. And, floating immediately before us in the present, they would seem to be in a position to influence us more profoundly than they might as historical matter, as they appear in Schiller's poems. The problem, of course, is that the gods have lost their power. How can they function as a productive influence when they are in such a ghostly state? Hence the melancholic tone of Heine's early poetic ruminations on Greek mythology.

> Das sind sie selber, die Götter von Hellas,
> Die einst so freudig die Welt beherrschten,
> Doch jetzt, verdrängt und verstorben,
> Als ungeheure Gespenster dahinziehn
> Am mitternächtlichen Himmel. (DHA 1.1: 412)

It should be evident that Heine is not yet holding out sensualist Greek mythology as a way of counteracting the excesses of spiritualism. The mythological figures appear, in fact, as spirits, "ungeheure Gespenster." This evocation of the uncanny, it is worth noting, produces a haunting effect that is foreign to Schiller's oddly optimistic elegies, which seem to mourn the past in order to announce an even greater cultural future. Indeed, the politics of Heine's grecophilia differ dramatically from that of Schiller's. Holub makes this point when he writes, "The most significant change in Heine's 'Götter Griechenlands,' however, is that the entire conception of the gods and religion is built around political struggle" (57). For, as Russell Berman has argued, in celebrating not the "joyous" sensualism of the Greek gods, but rather the unity, discipline and personal sacrifice that allegedly enabled Greek culture to thrive, Schiller put forth in his poems admonitions to order (148). Heine, on the other hand, is bringing to light a suppressed conflict and exposing the costs of the sacrifices spiritualist culture demands: joyous sensualism has been "repressed," and it is all but "extinct." And yet the gods are not completely drained of their force. Even their barely recognizable shadows can inspire us to new poetic forms: Heine's "Die Götter Griechenlands" is, again, one of the dreamiest, one might even say, most mythic of his early poems. The implication is that reflection on Greek mythology can lead to what Winkler calls "mythic thinking," a discourse in the present that takes on elements of repressed, mythic, sensuously particular, non-conceptual, non-instrumental ways of relating to the world.

In "Die Götter Griechenlands" Heine's poet-narrator pledges to fight for the battered pagan "old gods" and against the "new gods," who — and here Heine anticipates Nietzsche rather strikingly — exult in their power even as they present themselves as "meek." But the gods vanish, leaving the poet uncertain. Moreover, the poet claims that he was always repulsed by the Greek gods, and that he can be mobilized into action on their behalf because he, ostensibly a champion of justice, chafes at their mistreatment. He admires what they were, and what they stood for, only tentatively. By the time he wrote *Elementargeister* (1837), Heine's use of the discourse of myth had changed appreciably. This transformation is worth emphasizing for several reasons. First, it has been largely overlooked by two of the most astute commentators on Heine's work with myth: A. I. Sandor and Winkler. Secondly, by pursuing it, we arrive at insights into Heine's relation to his context, to his ability to pick up on, and critically respond to, developments and ruptures in the discourses with which he engaged. I am indebted to both scholars; to Sandor for pointing out the general importance of the exile motif in Heine's "mythological writings," and to Winkler for showing how the form of Heine's writing corresponds to his call for the rehabilitation of mythological discourse as a key component of ethical life. But, in what follows, I will extend this line of analysis, at least in a certain, very specific direction, and examine areas they have left unexamined.

We might start with the question of Jakob Grimm's influence on Heine. For even though Heine himself hints at Grimm's importance for his, Heine's, attitude toward Greek mythology, very little has been written on the topic. Heine, in fact, begins *Elementargeister* by praising Grimm's work on Germanic folk tales, and claiming that he will occasionally rely on it in recounting samples of Germanic folk mythology for his French readers. (Like *Religion und Philosophie in Deutschland* and *Die Romantische Schule*, *Elementargeister* is set up as an attempt to introduce constitutive, but not-so-accessible features of German culture to the French.) What soon becomes clear is that Grimm's new (1836) book *Deutsche Mythologie* transformed not only Heine's understanding of German mythology, but also his understanding of *Greek* mythology. For here Heine learned that, as mentioned above, the motif of the Greek gods in exile, the image of the gods wandering desperately far away from their hallowed home, was not simply a literary trope. Greek mythological figures really did immigrate into other mythological traditions, where they were in fact treated as fugitives. Their modern history is not simply one of cruel displacement, as seems to be the case in "Die Götter Griechenlands." It also holds out the promise of reintegration. And, accordingly, in *Elementargeister*, Heine's tone is considerably more optimistic, even as it is often ironic. Heine even changed his terms to mark this shift. Whereas in earlier works he had spoken of the dichotomy of "spiritualism" and "sensualism," in *Elementargeister*, he employs the terms "Nazarenism" and "Hellenism."

Before I address what Heine found in Grimm and how he appropriated it, I want to note that there were other factors at work here, that is, there were other factors behind Heine's move to a less dolorous, more energetic representation of the gods in exile. The mid-1830s seems to have been a high point for such a sanguine sensualism among the Left-Hegelian writers grouped around the Young Germany movement. Witness Theodor Mundt's *Die nackte Madonna* and Karl Gutzkow's controversial *Wally, die Zweiflerin*. Furthermore, and perhaps paradoxically, the ban of 1835 might also have contributed to Heine's increased investment in Greek mythological figures. For they could function as political allegories with which to express obliquely the repressiveness of the current order. In other words, the gods were handy ciphers in a time of intense censorship. There were biographical considerations as well. Jeffrey Sammons points out that in *Elementargeister* Heine used the Venus and Tannhäuser myth to give mock epic status to his own difficulties with Mathilde, whom he regarded, somewhat ironically, as the Venus figure in his own life. Heine playfully transposed the dynamic between himself and Mathilde — whose attraction for him he could neither understand nor resist — onto Venus and Tannhäuser (217).

All this, however, does nothing to diminish the significance of the historical facticity of the Greek gods in mythological exile. For, whatever else Heine uses the motif of the gods to say, here the message is that the Greek gods can live on — and have indeed lived on in certain exalted places in Germanic folk mythology — even though in a Christian age all religious faith in them is dead. Heine criticizes the neo-Platonists who tried to defend paganism on theological grounds for failing to recognize that Hellenic sensualism, "Hellenism," is, in a Christian age, an alternative way of living, an ethics or a politics rather than a religion. "Es galt nemlich nicht, die tiefere Bedeutung der Mythologie durch neoplatonische Spitzfündigkeiten zu beweisen, . . . es galt vielmehr den Hellenismus selbst, griechische Gefühls- und Denkweise, zu vertheidigen. . . . Die Frage war: ob der trübsinnige, magere, sinnenfeindliche, übergeistige Judäismus der Nazarener, oder ob hellenische Heiterkeit, Schönheitsliebe und blühende Lebenslust in der Welt herrschen solle?" (DHA 9: 47). This is a political-ethical-aesthetic struggle, and theological arguments are irrelevant.

Of course, the gods have become weak as a political power. And Heine reiterates the jeremiad he delivered in "Die Götter Griechenlands." He writes: "All diese Lust, all dieses frohe Gelächter ist längst verschollen, und in den Ruinen der alten Tempel wohnen, nach der Meinung des Volkes, noch immer die altgriechischen Gottheiten, aber sie haben durch den Sieg Christi all ihre Macht verloren" (DHA 9: 47). Yet there has also been a key shift in perspective. The poet is no longer relating *his own doleful visions* of the vanquished Greek gods. Here the gods have lost their power, "*according to the folk belief.*" What soon becomes clear is that, for Heine, the gods' very existence within the popular imagination, as well as the effect that they seem to have had there, suggest that Hellenism still has considerable power, perhaps enough to function as a productive complement, not to the Christian religion, but rather to the Nazarene way of life. To be sure, Heine pokes fun at the simple-mindedness of such folk beliefs and their puerile dichotomies. For example, he ascribes to the folk mind the following polarity: the "guileful gods" come out of their hiding places at night to seduce "guileless wanderers." But he also claims that the sagas about these beliefs are the most beautiful that Christian poets have produced, the sanguine implication being that exposure to Hellenism can in fact inspire Christians to lead a more Hellenic way of life, that is, to produce beautiful, sensuous poetry. Heine writes, "Auf diesen Volksglauben beziehen sich nun die wunderbarsten Sagen, und neuere Poeten schöpften hier die Motive ihrer schönsten Dichtungen" (DHA 9: 47). Heine's superlatives are strong. The "most wonderful sagas" and "most beautiful poems" derive directly from contact with Hellenism. That Hellenism, even in its exiled and beleaguered state, can revivify Nazarene culture is much more than a utopian speculation. What the sagas and poems in question show is that remnants of Hellenism have already done precisely this, even if these same sagas often portray the gods as lacking such redemptive might. Poems inspired by Hellenism that depict Hellenism as weak commit, on some level, a major performative contradiction.

But Heine also takes pains to show that the gods are not always depicted as effete exiles. It turns out that there is folk belief in their power to revitalize, which, suggestively enough, means that a folk-belief basis is in place that could support the Hellenism that Heine champions. Offering a synopsis of a story in which such a belief is expressed, Heine writes,

> Aber plötzlich steht er [der deutsche Ritter] vor einer marmornen
> Bildsäule, bey deren Anblick er fast betroffen stehen bleibt. Es ist
> vielleicht die Göttinn der Schönheit, und er steht ihr Angesicht zu
> Angesicht gegenüber, und das Herz des jungen Barbaren wird
> heimlich ergriffen von dem alten Zauber. Was ist das? So schlanke
> Glieder hat er noch nie gesehen, und in diesem Marmor ahndet er
> ein lebendigeres Leben, als er jemals in den rothen Wangen und
> Lippen, in der ganzen Fleischlichkeit seiner Landsmänninnen gefun-
> den hat. (DHA 9: 47–48)

Now it is important to note that Heine does not see in this story the
antecedent to the Romantic obsession with grotesque encounters
between humans and inanimate anthropomorphic objects, such as statues and puppets. The knight's fascination with the Venus statue, his
divining in her more life than there is in the living, signifies his perspi-
cacity, not his incipient madness. For she does indeed come alive. And
the figure who intervenes and puts an end to their romance, the priest
Palumnus, is portrayed by Heine as a misanthrope rather than as the
knight's rescuer. That a cruel spiritualism prevails here is a disappointment. But, again, the fact that the merits of Hellenism gain some
recognition — even in its exilic state its life is livelier than that of living spiritual — is promising. And Heine makes sure to mention that
the story has exercised a salubrious influence on his own immediate
literary context, by noting that it provided the material for an important contemporary novelist's (that is, Wilibald Alexis's) "best work"
(DHA 9: 51).

Heine's appropriation of the Venus and Tannhäuser story is
somewhat more complicated, since, as noted, he inserts his own relationship into the story. But what Heine says about the story and his
sense of its general trajectory is telling. He speaks of its "elementally
powerful words," calling it a song "das zu den merkwürdigsten
Sprachdenkmalen gehört, die sich im Munde des deutschen Volkes
erhalten" (DHA 9: 52). The lingering force of Hellenism is again evidenced by its ability to inspire such works. But the power of Hellenism within the story is ambiguous, and Heine makes a number of
interesting dialectical turns here. Tannhäuser and Venus are able to
overcome the spiritualist resistance of the knight Eckhart and cohabit in
the Venusberg. But this life proves to be unsatisfying to Tannhäuser.
For, as Heine puts it, "der Mensch ist nicht immer aufgelegt zum Lachen." Tannhäuser has a spiritualist past, and cutting himself off from
spiritualism, which he has to do in order to be with an exiled god,
entails a crushing loss of soul, ". . . die Vergangenheit ist die eigentli-

che Heimath seiner Seele, und es erfaßt ihn [Tannhäuser] ein Heim-
weh nach den Gefühlen" (DHA 9: 52). The message, it seems, is that
there is no going back to pure Hellenism. Nazarenism is part of our
psychic constitution now. Moreover, the Enlightenment, which is a
great achievement according to Heine, is also for him a form of spiritualism. A happy mixture of spiritualist and sensualist ways of relating
to the world is what we should strive for.

A decade later, Heine expressed similar sentiments in the ballet libretto *Die Göttin Diana,* whose plot structure is the same as the one
that governs the Venus and Tannhäuser story. Here, however, the
possibility of a reconciliation between spiritualism and sensualism
seems to have become more tenuous. For the knight-seeker in *Die
Göttin Diana* is actually killed by Eckhart, and he must be magically
brought back to life by Dionysus before he can experience the discontent of sensualist isolation. Heine's work with the discourse of
myth was about to undergo a major change.

II

Where is Venus in *Die Götter im Exil?* This question might well sound
ingenuous. To be sure, in 1848 Venus does disappear peremptorily
from the core cast of exiled Greek and Roman gods who, as we have
seen, make their way through Heine's works, from the early poem
"Die Götter Griechenlands" to the "short story" *Die Götter im Exil,*
which, published in 1854, is the last of Heine's mythological writings.[2] But what entitles us to expect rigid consistency from an appropriation of classical mythological figures as unsystematic as Heine's?[3]
Heine, after all, moves fluidly between travesty and jeremiad in depicting the gods' exile. And yet, once we have reflected on the meaning and function of Venus in Heine's early engagement with the discourse of myth, we will find ourselves hard pressed not to find meaning in the blank space of Venus's absence from *Die Götter im Exil.*

To recapitulate, all its countervailing tendencies notwithstanding,
up until 1848 Heine's appropriation of Greek mythological figures
does exhibit a programmatic aspect. In the 1830s and 1840s, in writings such as *Elementargeister* and *Die Göttin Diana,* Heine employed
the motif of Greek and Roman gods in exile not simply to lament the
fate of "Hellenic" sensualism under the tyranny of "Nazarene" spiritualism. Rather, these writings also gesture at the possibility of a reconciliation with spiritualism. Again, spiritualism is, in Heine's mythic

narrative, the tradition that has dominated Western civilization since spiritualist Christian iconoclasts stormed the pagan temples of classical antiquity and drove the sensualism that dwelled there into exile. Banished by Nazarenism to the margins of society, Hellenism, sensualist ethics and sensualist art, lives on in other mythic discourses such as the Germanic folktale, and helps give life to mythic otherness in the modern world.

With the advent of the French Revolution and idealist philosophy, spiritualism enters a new age. Here spiritualism turns against its progenitor, Christianity. As we have seen, Heine reads the Enlightenment, and especially Kantian rationalism, as a kind of spiritualist violence against spiritualism. In debunking religion, idealist philosophy does not liberate the sensualist gods from their exile, for, like Christianity, it is a sort of spiritualism and, as such, stands in tension with the sensualist tradition. At the same time, however, the spiritualism of idealist philosophy is more progressive than the spiritualism of Christianity. Philosophy's spiritualist abstraction is emancipatory — with their claims to universal validity, Enlightenment ideals are necessarily abstract. But this abstraction is also destructive. It is reifying and nihilistic, hostile to the sensuous particularity that the gods symbolize. In the age of the French Revolution the gods' exile endures, and the need for a balance of spiritualism and sensualism remains as urgent as ever. What has changed is the tenability of such a balance. According to Heine, Kant is both a freedom fighter and a terrorist; Heine claims that Kant's violent tendencies are of even greater magnitude than Robespierre's. Still, where Christianity demonizes the gods, philosophy simply denies their existence. Philosophy is relatively indifferent to the gods, and its advance entails a slackening of the campaign against them. As Heine puts it in *Die Götter im Exil*:

> Letztere [die Kirche] erklärte die alten Götter keineswegs, wie es die Philosophen gethan, für Chimären, für Ausgeburten des Lugs und des Irrthums, sondern sie hielt sie vielmehr für böse Geister, welche durch den Sieg Christi vom Lichtgipfel ihrer Macht gestürzt, jetzt auf Erden, im Dunkel alter Tempeltrümmer oder Zauberwälder, ihr Wesen trieben und die schwachen Christenmenschen, die sich hierhin verirrt, durch ihre verführerischen Teufelskünste, durch Wollust und Schönheit, besonders durch Tänze und Gesang, zum Abfall verlockten. (DHA 9: 125)

Heine's representations of the gods in exile in the 1830s and early 1840s are animated by a sense of possibility. They call, at times ironically, yet often ardently, for the gods' rehabilitation. The celebration of sensuous particularity would function as a corrective to philosophy's emancipatory, but, again, nihilistic and even violent abstraction.

As the classical symbol of classical sensualism, and as a cipher of fecundity, of imminent progress, Venus figures centrally in these exhortatory writings. Of all the gods, Venus seems to have had the most success at negotiating life as a refugee, coming tantalizingly close, in German traditions of folk mythology, to forming a union with the medieval knight Tannhäuser, and thus to effecting a moment of *Aufhebung* in the dialectic of spiritualism and sensualism. For Heine, therefore, Venus was a kind of historical precedent and "local" foundation for the cultural synthesis he was after. And, in fact, it is precisely Heine's invocations of the story of Venus and Tannhäuser that give his appropriation of classical mythology in the 1830s and early 1840s its programmatic ring.

Accordingly, when Heine later hedges on his programmatic sensualism, he uses Venus as a metonymy for it. I refer here to the epilogue to *Romanzero,* where Heine ceremoniously takes leave of his Hellenism of the 1830s and 1840s after his physical breakdown of 1848. And, in the passage cited at the beginning of this essay, Heine stages his collapse before the statue of Venus di Milo in the Louvre. In having Venus stand for the sensualism he had propagated until his collapse in 1848, Heine, however ironically, frames Venus as the paradigmatic figure of this sensualism.

There is, then, considerable intertextual motivation for reading Venus's absence from *Die Götter im Exil* as a positive sign. To the best of my knowledge, the text is Heine's only account of the gods' exile that makes no mention of Venus. And so we might well ask at this point: If Venus can function as a metonymy for the gods' exile during the 1830s and 1840s, might not her absence from the later texts signal a substantive shift in the nature of their exile? My contention is that, far from being arbitrary, Venus's absence is emblematic of sensualism's post-1848 condition. Venus has been exiled from exile, and the remaining gods are subjected to a new exile in *Die Götter im Exil.*

If we understand the gods' exile as a kind of symbolic representation of repressed modes of sensualist otherness in spiritualist modernity, then it would seem that in *Die Götter im Exil,* in addition to being forced underground, sensualism has been disrupted. As mentioned above, Heine's early mythological writings depict the gods' exilic existence as more or less homogenous. Venus, to be sure, fares somewhat better than the rest. But the gods all huddle anxiously in the sylvan seclusion of medieval German forests, fearful of being mistaken for demons or goblins by superstitious German Christians. Though persecuted, the gods, and thus sensualism, exist in a unified state.

In *Die Götter im Exil* the gods have been dislodged from this relative security. Catapulted peremptorily into a more modern setting, their lifestyles are radically diverse, their exile radically disjointed. Dionysus has managed to install himself as a monk in Tirol and enjoys institutional prestige and power (DHA 9: 130). And, disguised as a Dutch merchant, Mercury turns a nifty profit by selling his services as a psychopompos (DHA 9: 133). Conversely, Apollo and Jupiter are subjected to severe ignominies. After working briefly as a shepherd in lower Austria, Apollo is identified by a suspicious monk and is executed, albeit less than successfully: for when his superstitious executioners attempt to disinter him, they find his grave empty (DHA 9: 127). Finally, old, haggard, and bitter, Jupiter leads an isolated and difficult life, trading rabbit skins on a desolate arctic island. For the first time, Heine has one of his exiled gods bear signs of age (DHA 9: 143).

This splintering of sensualism is perhaps most powerfully expressed through the figures of Dionysus and Jupiter. Dionysus is excessively sensual; though he himself is attractively androgynous, one of the two false monks who accompany him to an annual bacchanal outside Tirol turns out to be a satyr-like creature, who, the narrator remarks, has not only "ein widerwärtig lüsternes, ja unzüchtiges Gesicht," but also "eine lächerlich übertriebene Geschlechtlichkeit, eine höchst anstößige Hyperbel" (DHA 9: 129). Furthermore, in having Dionysus thrive as a Franciscan monk and "learned exorcist" by employing his sensualist "virtues," that is, skills at leading ecstatic ceremonies, Heine reveals that even primordial Dionysian sensualism can cohere with its apparent opposite: ascetic cruelty (DHA 9: 131).

Heine has other gods exploit their original characteristics to achieve modern success in a spiritualist system, and this implies that sensualism or mythic otherness has effectively sold out. Mercury, for example, succeeds as a capitalist because he has an inveterate inclination to trading and stealing. Here sensualism is complicit with superstitious Christian spiritualism as well as with the bourgeois mentality against which Heine had inveighed in earlier writings precisely on account of its denigration of sensualism. In other words, in *Die Götter im Exil* sensualism is not simply counterposed to a deleterious tradition of spiritualism. No longer foregrounded as a prospective solution to the ills of Christianity and modernity, sensualism is also part of the problem. For with his ruddy cheeks and rapacious good health, Mer-

cury's sensualism, far from offering a joyous and necessary complement to the repressive bourgeois order, evokes the greedy bourgeois
vitality of Thomas Mann's Herr Klöterjahn.

If the gods choose disguises that, paradoxically, reveal something
about their basic characteristics, then Dionysus's decision to seek refuge in a monastery cannot be seen as arbitrary. Dionysus's brand of
sensualism possesses a dark, destructive side, which enables him to rise
as an arbiter of repression. In addition, commenting on his ballet libretto *Der Doktor Faust,* Heine notes that according to certain folk
myths, the devil masks himself as a monk. Dionysus's "disguise" carries with it suggestions of the demonic as *Die Götter im Exil* inverts
Heine's long-standing strategy of opposing and exposing the demoni-
zation of the gods.

The phallic "hyperbole," to use the narrator's phrase, that sur-
rounds Dionysus contrasts sharply with Jupiter's barren situation.
Stripped of his lightning bolts and worn down by the experience of
exile, Jupiter is desensualized to the point of emasculation. The story
of Jupiter is in fact pervaded by symbols of impotence. A frame narrative, it is told by a friend of the narrator, Niels Andersen, an old
whaler who has, suggestively enough, lost a leg. In introducing his
friend Andersen, the narrator offers a brief account of his own whaling
adventures, which reveals his symbolic potency has also been com-
promised: apparently, the narrator is no longer able to throw har-
poons (DHA 9: 139–41). Jupiter's story is thus literally framed by
figures of disrupted or even mutilated sensualism, and, again, this setting of impotence is radically different from the "laughably exaggerated male member" that stands next to Dionysus. Marred by
desiccation, excess, complicity with capitalism, and internal oppositions, sensualism in *Die Götter im Exil* seems to have been largely
emptied of the progressive possibility it had carried in the 1830s and
1840s.

Although Heine's turn away from Hellenism in 1848 has been
widely acknowledged, *Die Götter im Exil,* curiously enough, has generally been regarded as continuous with Heine's earlier representations
of the gods' exile. One prominent Heine scholar has even suggested
that it was written around 1846, that is, before Heine's break with his
programmatic sensualism (Sammons 212). To be sure, the text almost
seems to encourage such readings. Not only does it announce itself as
a straightforward extension of the gods' story, but Heine, in taking
Christian moralism to task for its rigid opposition to the salutary
pleasures of Dionysian dancing, also has recourse to his standard in-

vectives against spiritualism.[4] But all exiles are not alike. Exile, as we have seen and will see, is far from a monolithic trope in Heine's works, as so many critics would have it, particularly those who lionize exilic writing as somehow epistemologically honest because it attacks from a place of absence or dislocation the myth of presence.[5] Pursuing Venus's conspicuous absence as a kind of intertextual marker, we become alert to the differences between the gods' early exile and their exile in *Die Götter im Exil*. And once we begin to read their status in *Die Götter im Exil* as a disrupted exile, the text's erratic invocations of continuity become further emblems of the confusion that is constitutive of this new exile. Accordingly, readings of the text that impute to it the same progressive orientation we find in *Elementargeister* seem forced.

In the only full-length monograph on the motif of mythological sensualism in exile in Heine's writings, Sandor simply notes the most obvious changes that occur in *Die Götter im Exil* (for example, its new setting). He makes no attempt to interpret these changes, and ultimately winds up claiming that this later work represents a straightforward extension of the gods' earlier exile. While Sandor does acknowledge that the tone of the text is appreciably more melancholy than was the case in, say, *Elementargeister* or the Börne *Denkschrift,* he skips over such jagged edges as Dionysus's new violent tendencies and Jupiter's exile from his earlier exile. Sandor's study is, in general, quite useful for anyone interested in the motif of mythology in exile in Heine's works. But like most critics, he ascribes little importance to the late and fragmentary *Die Götter im Exil,* ultimately treating it rather tersely.

Winkler's recent and erudite study *Mythisches Denken zwischen Romantik und Realismus* exhibits a different problem in offering a similar reading of *Die Götter im Exil*. Picking up on suggestive remarks by Manfred Frank as to Heine's role in the large project of mediating myth in modernity, of activating myth as a resource of meaning without regressing into irrationalism, Winkler argues that Heine finds in "mythic thinking" a kind of creative, meaning-bearing alternative to the modern understanding of reality, one that has been suppressed, but has not disappeared. Winkler writes:

> The suppression or reduction of myth, the critique of myth and attempts to mythologize or remythologize reality prove to be, in the preceding chapters, opposed traditions of thought which form the horizon of Heine's treatment of myth and mythology. Heine comes to the question that his own "mythic" thinking answers by critically engaging with these traditions. He asks whether they provide appro-

priate answers to problems which are rooted in the fact that myth has become foreign, yet remains alive and even promises compensation for the deficiencies of the modern understanding of reality. (266)

I am, as I emphasized above, both sympathetic and indebted to Winkler's general orientation and to his interpretation of Heine's early "mythic thinking." Like Winkler, I stress the "compensatory moment" that Heine divined in the discourse of myth, and which he tried to develop in his writings of the 1830s and 1840s. I have, moreover, borrowed directly from Winkler's analysis of Heine's sensitivity to the bad remythologization to which the crusade against old myths leads: the reinscribing of the Greek tradition as demonic. But Winkler and I part ways at *Die Götter im Exil.* For in his reading of this text, he seems to project his own views on myth onto Heine. In other words, while his investment in mythic thinking gives his book pathos and critical energy, it leads to exegetical excesses. Winkler wants Heine to valorize repressed mythic thinking and to foreground the possibility of reintegrating it, even in his late writings, because he clearly believes that mythology and mythic thinking should be treated in just this way. And so Winkler tries to locate in *Die Götter im Exil* a sense of the positive possibility of myth that, along with Venus, is patently missing from the text.

Without considering the intensified suffering and the corruption or complicity that marks the gods' new exile in modern society, Winkler reads the change in setting as a major step toward their deliverance.

> There the gods, whom the narrator characterizes as gods in exile, have no subterranean hiding place, and, in contrast to the nymphs who are discussed at the end of *Ludwig Börne,* these gods are not (as dream-images) exiled into the interior of the poet. They now share the space of the Christians, instead of being repressed into the past by the Christians. . . . As some of the gods disguise themselves as members of the *res publica,* they survive in the middle of a culture that is foreign to them. (268)

In *Die Götter im Exil,* Heine's optimistic, progressive sensualism reaches, for Winkler, its apogee. The gods have become integrated into the rationalistic culture that is foreign to them. No longer repressed, they are now members of a spiritualist society in which they can be accessed as a crucial alternative, or as "mythically other" resources of meaning. But the text simply does not support this reading. Its tone is saturnine and bitingly ironic rather than hopeful. As mentioned, Mercury and Dionysus have become complicit with the very order they are supposed to resist. And Jupiter, the leader of the gods, has not been inte-

grated at all. If *Die Götter im Exil* is so optimistic about the reconciliation of sensualist myth and modern society, why has the god who,
for Heine, best embodies sensualism been banished from this society?
And how can Jupiter possibly bring forth a potent contribution to society when his powers have dwindled so painfully, when he has been
emasculated? The text describes Jupiter's situation as follows:

> Als die Schiffer hineintraten, erblickten sie einen uralten Greis, der
> kümmerlich bekleidet mit zusammengeflickten Kaninchenfellen, auf
> einem Steinstuhl vor dem Heerde saß, und an dem flackernden Rei-
> sig seine magern Hände und schlotternden Kniee wärmte. Neben
> ihm zur Rechten stand ein ungeheuer großer Vogel, der ein Adler zu
> seyn schien, den aber die Zeit so unwirsch gemausert hatte, daß er
> nur noch die langen struppigen Federkiele seiner Flügel behalten,
> was dem nackten Thiere ein höchst närrisches und zugleich grausen-
> haft häßliches Aussehen verlieh. Zur linken Seite des Alten kauerte
> am Boden eine außerordentlich große haarlose Ziege, die sehr alt zu
> seyn schien, obgleich noch volle Milcheutern mit rosig frischen Zit-
> zen an ihrem Bauche hingen. (DHA 9: 141–42)

The lone, improbable moment of fecundity here is the old goat,
which still produces milk, apparently quite abundantly. But while this
image may serve to complicate the barren larger picture, it also works
as a foil that throws this very barrenness into relief. The white spot of
life-giving milk shows us just how dark the scene is. It is more a reminder of what sensualism was than an emblem of its present possibilities. For here sensualism has become profoundly desensualized. It
is everything traditional sensualism is not: old, emaciated, impoverished, shivering, depressed. Sensualism is no longer persecuted. But
persecution is not necessary because real sensualism has been rendered
impotent, subjected to a new, harsher exile. Here Heine almost seems
to be anticipating Adorno's melancholic theory of modern art, according to which the price of aesthetic freedom is powerlessness, and
"integrated" art is commodified art. Again, a number of eminent theorists of modernism place the beginning of this process, high art's
turning inward, its obsession with form, right around 1850, that is, at
just about the time Heine wrote *Die Götter im Exil*.[6] My claim is that
it is possible to read Heine's late gods in exile as a perspicacious early
representation of just this process.

Certainly the formal change in the gods, their *deformation,* is suggestive. Sensualism no longer waits formally unscathed and unchanged
for a moment of possibility. It has been marked, scarred by modernity.
It may still be fertile, but that fertility is harder to find, necessarily far

away or hermetically sealed off from the culture it stands to help. For without the distance, it, like Mercury, would be co-opted. That last repository of mythic otherness, to speak with Winkler, ceases to be other and loses its progressive force. And, again, the otherness of myth has already been transformed. The gods are no longer so cheerful, which is what, in the writings of the 1830s and 1840s, distinguished them most palpably from the grim spiritualism of modernity. Now, as with modernist art for Adorno, the most basic expression of an ethical mythic otherness appears to be a shudder: Jupiter cries copiously in *Die Götter im Exil*. One of Adorno's "definitions" of modernist art is "mimetic adaptation to what is hardened and alienated" (39), and this, rather than an exiled, but otherwise unsullied, ingenuous sensualism, appears to be the real ethical alternative to an oppressive spiritualist order. I certainly would not want to overemphasize the proto-Adornian resonances in Heine. Heine seems to be portraying the exile of the poet figure rather than the alienation of modern art as an institution. However, his proximity to Adorno here is striking. And mentioning it underscores the point that the partial integration of the gods into modern society, their sudden immediacy to the present in *Die Götter im Exil,* is a problematic shift. It is not, as Winkler maintains, sensualism's productive return. This is a failed integration in the case of Jupiter, and a bad integration, a co-optation, where it is successful. It represents, in fact, the disruption of sensualism rather than its fulfillment.

But why has the gods' exile been disrupted? What, to use one of Heine's preferred formulations, is the "social significance," of the shift in his account of the gods' exile? Heine's break with his programmatic Hellenist sensualism has generally been discussed in terms of three developments: his physical breakdown, his paradoxical return to a Judaism to which he had never belonged, and his late disillusionment with Hegelianism. These factors may help us make sense of the general drop in Heine's enthusiasm for Hellenism after 1848. They cannot, however, account for the strangely dichotomous, largely opportunistic sensualism portrayed in *Die Götter im Exil*.

And this, in fact, is precisely what makes *Die Götter im Exil* so interesting and deserving of more attention than it has received. Its resistance to the standard interpretations of the late changes in Heine's appropriation of Greek mythology compels us to broaden our understanding of the relation of these changes to the context in which they took place. When we look closely at this context, we see that around 1848 in France and Germany something like a rupture developed in what we might call the discourse of sensualism and its symbols. To be sure, there was no such thing as a unified discourse of sensualism prior to 1848. For example, vaudeville travesties of Greek mythology — harbingers of Offenbach — were apparently a popular form of entertainment in Paris in the 1830s and 1840s.[7] But what matters here is that there was still a strong tradition of a relatively "untroubled" progressive, neo-classicist discourse of sensualism. The trajectory of Venus's career in French and German culture between 1835 and 1870 provides graphic evidence of the disruption and resignification of the discourse of sensualism. *Die Götter im Exil* is, in large part, about this process. Indeed, the fragmented and problematic sensualism of *Die Götter im Exil* registers, and responds to, the development of modern problems in the discourse of sensualism, preserving, as we have seen, a certain negative moment of progressive possibility for mythic otherness: the shudder.

Venus's absence from *Die Götter im Exil* is more than an intertextual marker, a sign that prompts us to recognize the text's break with earlier representations of the gods' exile; Venus's absence reflects the sudden departure of the progressively sensuous Venus from the cultural scene. In support of this claim, the contrast between the sanguine Venus in Theodor Mundt's *Die nackte Madonna* of 1835 and the sanguinary Venus in Leopold Sacher-Masoch's *Venus im Pelz,* which was published in 1869, can be cited,[8] as can the disparity between Jean-Auguste-Dominique Ingres's classic *Vénus Anadyomène* (1848) and Manet's *Olympia* (1865), which, according to the art historian T. J. Clark, represents Venus as a modern prostitute. For Clark, in fact, Ingres's Venus is the last great "unproblematic" nude (126–42). After 1848, the discourse of classical or progressive sensualism breaks apart under the pressure of modern urban "sexual" problems, like prostitution, that arose in modern forms in post-1848 Paris, which in certain respects became a modern city structurally, that is, a city with wide boulevards, as a direct result of the Revolution. Clark's elaborate observations about the nude might help us make sense of a parallel change in the closely related discourse of mythic sensualism. He writes:

> No critic worth his salt would have wished to deny that Ingres's Venus was sexually enticing, and intended to be. . . . What is left behind is a body, addressed to the viewer directly and candidly, but grandly generalized in form, arranged in a complex and visible rhyming, purged of particulars, offered as a free but respectful version of the right models, the ones that articulate nature best.

> The painting of the nude in the 1860s could be characterized by its inability to do the things Ingres does here. In the pictures I have presented already, sexual force and nakedness are most often not disentangled. When they are, and the active proponents of desire are included, there seems to be a massive uncertainty about how much reality to grant them: satyrs, fauns, and cupids, regularly take on too much the look of goats, male models, and three year-old children. The naked body itself, as the critics in the 1860s never tired of saying, is curiously left hybrid, marked by modernity in an incoherent way. If it is chaste, and sometimes it is, it is rigid and inanimate with its own decorum; and if it engages with sexuality, it does so in ways which verge on violence or burlesque. Something is wrong here: a genre is disintegrating. (126–27)

Clark's claim is that there is a direct, causal relation between revolutionary violence and the end of the nude as an unproblematic discourse. The classical nude is riven by structural shifts in the city, its emergence as a modern city with modern sexual problems. I am suggesting that Heine's discourse of mythic sensualism became caught up in these processes in much the same way, and that *Die Götter im Exil* is both a registering of, and a response to, this shift. Clark's example of Ingres is compelling because it offers a (literally) graphic example of the movement from a progressive, healthy Venus to a deformed one. Once alerted to this change, we find that examples of it abound.

Shifts in the discourse of sensualism do not only occur in the long aftermath of 1848. A kind of immediate disruption seems to have taken place. Heine, it will be recalled, suggestively sets his break with Hellenism against the backdrop of revolution; as the sick poet lies before Venus, the revolution rages outside. The revolution, Heine thereby implies, represents the context that has made Venus powerless. J. M. Bernstein's reading of what he calls "the time of 1848" is worth mentioning in this context. According to Bernstein, the vacuous time of the failed Revolution conditions the infertile, non-productive, hopelessly unsatisfying relationship Frédéric maintains with Madame Arnoux in Flaubert's *Sentimental Education*. Bernstein writes:

> But *Sentimental Education* is not written from the perspective of the period of the constitutional republic; it is written from the perspective of the empty time following the republic when even the rhetoric of action dissolved. We might put it this way: for Flaubert 1848 was never a time of revolution; properly speaking, it was, at best, a period mimicking revolutionary history (1849–1850), whose truth was a period in which action, change, history were impossible (post-1851). What an examination of the temporal structure of *Sentimental Education* shows

us is a world in which, through the repression of death and history, action, significant, transforming action has become impossible. (140)

In addition to being attenuated in the violent torpor of 1848, the discourse of sensualism seems to have become associated with revolutionary violence. Marx speaks of Dionysus as Louis Napoleon's "Schutzgott" (83). And in his short essay on the February Revolution, Heine draws an analogy between Dionysus and Robespierre. This move is telling, for as we have seen, Heine formerly viewed Kant, an avatar of spiritualism, as Robespierre's analogue. Now it is Dionysus, a sensualist symbol, who somehow connotes political terrorism.

The revolutions also pushed sensualist discourse in the opposite direction, and this further contributed to its rupturing. While some thinkers and artists began to represent sensualism as inextricably intertwined with the ejaculatory force and carnival character of the revolutions, others attempted to purge sensualism of such associations. In the contemporaneously published novels *Nachsommer* and *Der grüne Heinrich* (1855), the elusive figure of Nausikaa emerges as the central trope in a manically conservative appropriation of sensualism. In Stifter and, to a lesser degree, in Keller, sensualism has been turned on its head; it has been recuperated as a discourse of restraint. Sensualism is no longer a productive complement to the constraints of *Bildung;* it is made to conform exactly to the strictures of *Bildung,* to an ethos of discipline and endlessly deferred pleasure.

Die Götter im Exil represents, and is thus representative of, this disruption of sensualism. Dionysus goes the one way, becoming prurient and sadistic; Jupiter the other; again, he is relegated to a cold island, where, suddenly marked by age and deprived of his thunderbolts, he exists in a state of depotentiation. Within this new context, an unproblematically progressive Venus would have been sorely out of place. Hence her double exile, her absence from *Die Götter im Exil.*

I claimed that *Die Götter im Exil* not only registers and represents a fissuring of the discourse of sensualism, but that, even with its melancholic tone, it also negotiates, or critically responds to, this break. I have in mind here the figure of Jupiter. First, Jupiter is richly syncretic: part Greek god, part Old Testament prophet, he is animated by the same ambiguous pathos that makes Heine's late representations of Moses and the medieval Jewish poet Jehuda Halevi so poignant. Although the Jupiter scene in *Die Götter im Exil* is certainly not free of irony, Jupiter's lamentations do indeed resonate evocatively with Jehuda Halevi's jeremiads in Heine's "Hebräische Melodien," as both figures are left mourning the destruction of the sacred sites from which they have been exiled. Jupiter begins sobbing when he learns from Greek sailors that his temple lies in ruins. Hellenism, the seat of poetry, has become compatible with the spiritual imagination of the Hebrew tradition. We might say, then, that *Die Götter im Exil* and, more generally, Heine's late poetry manage an unlikely, productive reconciliation between sensualism and a certain form of spiritualism.

Of course, this is not the kind of reconciliation Heine envisioned in the 1830s and 1840s. It is, rather, a melancholic reconciliation, compensatory as opposed to emancipatory, as its basis is sensualism's second exile or depotentiation. And yet, the term "compensatory" does not quite do justice to Heine's late vision of sensualism or sensualist art in exile. For in figuring art as wounded or abject as opposed to simply exiled (again, Jupiter is physically marked with the trauma of exile for the first time in *Die Götter im Exil*), Heine confronts us with an image of mythic otherness that defiantly continues to exist. Heine's accomplishment is to find a way for ethical mythic otherness to continue to exist under more difficult, particularly modern circumstances. For the brute fact of its existence holds out the possibility of a different, non-spiritualist, non-instrumental way of relating to the world; Jupiter's goat is still full of milk, after all, even if Venus has vanished. Moreover, and perhaps even more important, the new difficulties of mythic discourse lead to a new kind of expressive force. Indeed, Heine's gaunt and shuddering, yet somehow still formidable Jupiter may just be, from an aesthetic standpoint, the most interesting of his gods.

Notes

[1] See Jochen Schulte-Sasse, Foreword, *Theory of the Avante-Garde,* by Peter Bürger, trans. Michael Shaw (Minneapolis: U of Minnesota P, 1984), xii–xiii; see also Peter Bürger, *Prosa der Moderne* (Frankfurt am Main: Suhrkamp, 1988), 275–300.

[2] It is hard to assign a genre designation to *Die Götter im Exil*. The same can be said of *Elementargeister*. And this, in all probability, is significant. For while some works by Heine that have nothing to do with the discourse of myth are equally difficult to categorize, this formal ambiguity can almost always be tied to particular historical circumstances; for example, Heine often had to lengthen his works to escape censorship rules that were set up to hinder the publication of pamphlets. *Elementargeister* was in fact made longer for just this reason. But there is also the sense that Heine set up the form, a sometimes slippery mixture of expository writing and fiction, as an attempt at the synthesis of spiritualism (conceptual dis-

course) and mythic sensualism (literary language) he calls for in the work. Here Heine arrives at what Winkler calls a "mythic thinking."

[3] Again, for an overview of Heine's work with the discourse of Greek mythology, see Robert Holub, *Heinrich Heine's Reception of German Grecophilia: The Function and Application of the Hellenic Tradition in the First Half of the Nineteenth Century,* Reihe Siegen Beiträge zur Literatur- und Sprachwissenschaft 27 (Heidelberg: Carl Winter, 1981).

[4] The first line of *Die Götter im Exil* can in fact be easily mistaken for an invocation of continuity. The text begins, "Schon in meinen frühesten Schriften besprach ich die Idee, welcher die nachfolgenden Mittheilungen entsprossen" (DHA 9: 125).

[5] See Jennifer Kapczynski, et al., "The Polish Question and The Question of Heine's Exilic Identity," *Heinrich Heine's Contested Identities: Politics, Religion, and Nationalism in Nineteenth-Century Germany,* ed. Jost Hermand and Robert C. Holub (New York: Peter Lang, 1998), 135–36.

[6] Cp. Schulte-Sasse, xii.

[7] See Siegfried Kracauer, *Jacques Offenbach und das Paris seiner Zeit* (Amsterdam: Albert De Lange, 1937), 232–35.

[8] It is interesting to note that Sacher-Masoch's dark views on female sexuality were apparently formed during the revolutions of 1848. As a child he witnessed Polish women in revolt commit acts of violence, and this image, as he himself emphasized, loomed large in his consciousness for the rest of his life.

Works Cited

Adorno, Theodor. *Ästhetische Theorie.* Frankfurt am Main: Suhrkamp, 1970.

Berman, Russell. *Cultural Studies of Modern Germany: History, Representation and Nationhood.* Madison: U of Wisconsin P, 1993.

Bernstein, J. M. *The Philosophy of the Novel: Lukács, Marxism, and the Dialectics of Form.* Minneapolis: U of Minnesota P, 1984.

Blumenberg, Hans. *Arbeit am Mythos.* Frankfurt am Main: Suhrkamp, 1979.

Bürger, Peter. *Prosa der Moderne.* Frankfurt am Main: Suhrkamp, 1988.

Clark, T. J. *The Painting of Modern Life: Paris in the Art of Manet and His Followers.* Princeton: Princeton UP, 1989.

Holub, Robert. *Heinrich Heine's Reception of German Grecophilia: The Function and Application of the Hellenic Tradition in the First Half of the Nineteenth Century.* Reihe Siegen Beiträge zur Literatur- und Sprachwissenschaft 27. Heidelberg: Carl Winter, 1981.

Kapczynski, Jennifer, et al. "The Polish Question and The Question of Heine's Exilic Identity." *Heinrich Heine's Contested Identities: Politics, Religion, and Nationalism in Nineteenth-Century Germany.* Ed. Jost Hermand and Robert C. Holub. New York: Peter Lang, 1998.

Kracauer, Siegfried. *Jacques Offenbach und das Paris seiner Zeit.* Amsterdam: Albert De Lange, 1937.

Marx, Karl. *Der achtzehnte Brumaire des Louis Napoleon.* Berlin: Dietz Verlag, 1988.

Sammons, Jeffrey. *Heinrich Heine: A Modern Biography.* Princeton: Princeton UP, 1979.

Sandor, A. I. *The Exile of Gods: Interpretation of a Theme, a Theory and a Technique in the Work of Heinrich Heine.* The Hague: Mouton, 1967.

Schulte-Sasse, Jochen. Foreword. *Theory of the Avante-Garde.* By Peter Bürger. Trans. Michael Shaw. Minneapolis: U of Minnesota P, 1984.

Winkler, Markus, *Mythisches Denken zwischen Romantik und Realismus: Zur Erfahrung kultureller Fremdheit im Werk Heinrich Heines.* Tübingen: Niemeyer, 1995.

Religion, Assimilation,
and Jewish Culture

Troubled Apostate:
Heine's Conversion and Its Consequences

Robert C. Holub

I

H EINE OFTEN WROTE ABOUT himself, but the status of these self-references should not always be considered autobiographical. Heine's first-person comments have a variety of different functions in his writings: some do indeed impart information relating to Heine and his life, but many others are included to create an effect. If we want to be less charitable to Heine, then we could simply state that Heine sometimes lies about himself, but we would want to note that his falsehoods are hardly ever without a purpose. When Heine calls himself the first man of the century, for example, he does not literally mean that he was born on January 1, 1800, and although his birthday and his remarks about it are still the source of some confusion, we understand that in this case his comment is meant to convey the coincidence of his approximate date of birth and his claim of preeminence in the nineteenth century. Similarly, when in *Ideen. Das Buch le Grand* he has Napoleon appear in his native Düsseldorf in the middle of a beautiful summer day, when we know that the French leader in fact visited Düsseldorf in 1811 "Im traurigen Monat November" — as it is called in his famous mock epic, *Deutschland. Ein Wintermärchen* — we recognize that Heine rearranges the calendar slightly to celebrate the emancipatory aspects of the French occupation. I could enumerate further, since the inaccuracies and exaggerations in Heine's works are sufficiently abundant, but I think my point is already rather obvious. Heine is an unreliable reporter about Heine. And because Heine's statements about himself in his writings are so often hyperbolic, fictionalized, or simply contrary to fact, it is difficult to gather accurate biographical information from him simply by taking him at his word.

Heine is even more unreliable about himself when he is dealing with matters that were very close to him personally and about which he had conflicting emotions. In these cases he seems less in control of his writing; instead a kind of psychic pressure relating to an uncomfortable biographical fact or event seems to exert a distorting influence on his writing, resulting in displacements, false attributions, and related confusions. One of the issues that caused him the most psychic distress was his Judaism in general and specifically his conversion from Judaism to the Protestant faith. This conversion occurred, as we know, in June of 1825, shortly before Heine completed his doctoral degree in jurisprudence at the University of Göttingen, and although Heine later characterized it in a famous *bon mot* as his "Entréebillett zur europäischen Kultur" (B 6.1: 622), we must suspect that its impact on him was far more serious than a mere joke. Conversion, of course, was not so unusual for German Jews in precisely the early years of the Restoration, and we often hear the undoubtedly correct observation that many assimilated Jews, having already become integrated into German society, converted to Protestantism in order to facilitate professional life.[1] The Napoleonic Code, which had brought some degree of emancipation to the Jews of Germany, especially in those areas under the direct jurisdiction of the French, had been annulled by Restoration authorities, and Jews who had ambitions to enter the German civil service, which encompassed, of course, a large number of professional positions from university professor to doctors at hospitals, found themselves faced with a choice of professional proscription or conversion. In light of this alternative, many of Germany's intellectually enlightened Jews — I cite the names of Eduard Gans, Ludwig Börne, and Heinrich Marx (the father of Karl Marx) by way of example — opted for a formal conversion to a belief to which they adhered in name only. Although there were some cases in which the converted Jew genuinely embraced his new religion, Heine's conversion of the 1820s, in contrast to his conversion of his later years, was certainly of the insincere variety: we have no record of him attending church, and no evidence whatsoever that he believed in a Christian God. In *Geständnisse* he writes that he embraced Protestantism because it did not embarrass him (B 6.1: 482), which is hardly an enthusiastic endorsement of the evangelical faith. If he subscribed to anything in Protestantism, it was, as he suggests, the protest that he later associated with Luther's defiance of the Catholic hierarchy. Heine informs us that he remains "nach wie vor, ein protestierender Protestant," who now protests against the damage done to his good name by the false rumors and accusations concerning his religious convictions (B 6.1: 491).

Despite his own witty remarks about his baptism, we should not believe that he took his conversion lightly. Psychologically the conversion was an action that took a heavy toll. Perhaps most importantly it signaled for Heine the end of the German-Jewish synthesis that he had tried to perpetuate during the early 1820s. Heine experienced the impossibility of this synthesis clearly and painfully in the third decade of his life, which was also the first decade of his career as a writer.[2] Indeed, this period, and in particular his stay in Berlin from March of 1821 until July of 1823, is decisive for an understanding of the role the Jewish heritage played in Heine's life and works, since it includes important events and experiences for the young Jewish man who wished to become a celebrated German writer. The most important of these is probably Heine's acquaintance with other young Jewish intellectuals in the *Verein für Cultur und Wissenschaft der Juden,* an organization Heine joined in August of 1822. Until his association with members of the *Verein* we have scant evidence about Heine's own feelings toward his co-religionists and about his knowledge of the traditions, practices, and history of Judaism.[3] Most of what we do possess, including his personal correspondence, does not indicate that the young Heine had an avid interest in Jewish affairs. At Bonn and Göttingen he evidently did not seek out Jewish friends or organizations; he appears instead to have led a rather typical German student existence, although it is quite possible that his expulsion from a nationalist student club (*Burschenschaft*) in Göttingen at the end of December in 1820 was related to his religious heritage: Heine preferred to claim that he violated the chastity oath, but this sort of statement probably reflects less the real course of events than the locker-room braggadocio of the nineteenth century and Heine's endeavor to conceal a mortifying reality about religious discrimination among his peers. In any case, during his stays in Bonn and Göttingen, he does not appear to have hidden his religious affiliation, but he also does not seem to have emphasized his Jewishness in his dealings with friends and acquaintances. Indeed, his main interests before he arrived in Berlin in March of 1821 were related to romantic poetry, to the theoretical and poetic insights of his teacher at Bonn, August Wilhelm Schlegel, and to a progressive strand of German nationalism, which was commonplace for the liberal young men of his era.

It appears that before his arrival in Berlin the tension inherent in the existence of a German poet with a Jewish heritage was either not felt or not particularly urgent for Heine. In Berlin, however, Heine could not avoid a confrontation any longer, even though one could argue that his initial experiences in Berlin actually affirmed the compatibility of Germanness and Jewishness under enlightened, modern Prussian conditions. The two most important circles he frequented could be viewed as illustrations of the harmonious coexistence of Jewish and German life. In the salon of Rahel von Varnhagen, a former Jewess married to the retired Prussian diplomat Varnhagen von Ense, Heine encountered not only a successful German-Jewish symbiosis embodied in the host and hostess, but also a social forum for important intellectuals who were both Jewish and Gentile. Even more decisive for Heine's development was his association with the *Verein*. Heine had gained entrance to Rahel's salon a few months after he arrived in the Prussian capital, and approximately a year later he first made the acquaintance of Eduard Gans, who had presided over the *Verein* since March of 1821. Heine himself became a member on August 4. Although he left for Poland shortly thereafter, upon his return he was a fairly regular participant at the meetings of the *Verein* and its affiliated scholarly institute until he left Berlin the following May. From the letters Heine wrote to Moses Moser, his closest friend in the *Verein*, after his departure from the Prussian capital, it is apparent that he retained an interest in it until its dissolution in 1824. Significant about the *Verein* was that it did not emphasize a separatist Jewish identity outside of Germanness, but that it sought to bring Judaism into the framework of modern European thought. The *Verein* was an openly assimilationist organization; the guiding spirit behind it believed in and propagated the compatibility of Judaism in contemporary Germany. If there still existed tensions between Jews and Germans — at least on an intellectual level — then the problem was just as likely to result from Jewish backwardness as German intolerance. And as predominantly enlightened Hegelians, the members of the *Verein* appeared to envision a future in which cultural differences might be further sublated and an even more harmonious state of affairs might be attained.

Although Heine's stay in Berlin obviously introduced him to many examples of an apparently successful Jewish-German synthesis, it simultaneously exposed him to several situations in which he could have easily doubted the ultimate efficacy of remaining Jewish in a predominantly Christian social order. It is not apparent whether Heine considered relinquishing his connections to his Jewish heritage before he arrived in Berlin, but certainly one of the results of his experiences in the Prussian capital was the recognition of conversion as a potential, practical, and acceptable means of integration. Indeed, conversion was an option that was being preached to Jews from a number of angles. Christian Friedrich Rühs, for example, a professor of history in Berlin who died shortly before Heine's arrival, decried the Enlightenment tendency toward tolerance for the Jews, insisting that if Jews wanted to be full members of a Christian state, they would have to convert to the Christian religion. Rühs' views were not unchallenged, but his opinions were sufficiently popular and representative that they attracted much support as well.[4] While Heine could ignore or oppose reactionary positions such as Rühs', it was more difficult for him to avoid the support that conversion received inside the Jewish community itself. Although earlier estimates of mass conversion have been revised somewhat in recent years, it still appears that a significant number of Jews converted to Protestantism, especially in the 1820s and 1830s, and in particular in urban centers like Berlin.[5] We may not be dealing with the phenomenon of "mass baptisms," which Heinrich Graetz thought he could deduce from the statistics,[6] but Deborah Hertz has recently asserted with confidence that we can speak of a "conversion wave" in Berlin of the third and fourth decades of the nineteenth century.[7] What made this wave particularly important for Heine was that it encompassed many prominent members of the Jewish community.[8] Four of the six children of Moses Mendelssohn eventually left the religion of their illustrious father, and Leah Salomon, the granddaughter of Daniel Itzig, and Abraham Mendelssohn had their own children baptized, among them the seven-year-old Felix, in 1816, six years before their own conversion (Hertz, "Why Did," 91–95). Heine was undoubtedly familiar with these conversions, as well as the baptisms that had taken place or were contemplated within his closest circle of friends. Rahel Levin, after all, along with her brothers, had abandoned their orthodox Jewish roots before Heine made their acquaintance, and Eduard Gans, well before his baptism in 1825, had been in a struggle with the Prussian state focusing on conversion and the possibility of obtaining an academic position. The irony, therefore, of Heine's intensive introduction to the German-Jewish synthesis was that it simultaneously legitimated conversion as the next logical step toward full integration into Christian society.

It is thus not surprising that at the same time that Heine was becoming acquainted with paradigms of German-Jewish integration, he also appears to have suffered his most severe crisis of identity with regard to his status as a German poet of Jewish heritage. Reacting to the climate created by the anti-Jewish writings of Rühs and Jakob Friedrich Fries, who both insisted on the incompatibility of Jews for German intellectual life, and possibly also to the defections from the Jewish community around him, Heine went through a period during which he emphasizes the utter incongruity of the German-Jewish synthesis. Writing to Christian Sethe in April of 1822 he expresses his disgust for everything associated with Germany: "Alles was deutsch ist, ist mir zuwider; und Du bist leider ein Deutscher. Alles Deutsche wirkt auf mich wie ein Brechpulver. Die deutsche Sprache zerreißt meine Ohre. Die eignen Gedichte ekeln mich zuweilen an, wenn ich sehe, daß sie auf deutsch geschrieben sind" (HSA 20: 50). This attitude represents a decisive change from his previous identification of himself not only as a German writer, but as a writer in the German national tradition; from this point in time onward, we have to consider Heine cured of his youthful flirtation with Germanness, at least of the nationalist variety. A letter from the following February, written to Moritz Embden, indicates certainly that his allegiances to the nationalist cause were severely damaged, and that he must now differentiate between progressive and nationalist sentiments. Although he believes from an English perspective he belongs to the radicals according to the English and from the Italian viewpoint to the Carbonari according to the Italians, in Germany he cannot identify himself with the "demagogues" (the group he feels corresponds to these foreign radicals) since a victory of this revolutionary group would mean that the necks of a few thousand Jews would be severed (HSA 20: 70). For a time he appears to have accepted his own disenfranchisement from a German identity. Writing to Moser in May of 1823, he calls himself "ein jüdischer Dichter" and states that he prefers speaking with him "in unseren Nazionalbildern," by which he means, of course, the images of the Jewish nation (HSA 20: 87). In two other letters he cites anti-Jewish writings as ironic confirmation that he is not a German. As is so often the case, the irony reveals two levels: on one Heine is obviously pointing to the absurdity of such Judeophobic nonsense. But on another level Heine is wounded, alienated from the nationalist feelings he had previously embraced. In March of 1824 he writes in a similarly ironic tone to Rudolf Christiani, prefiguring caput 11 of *Deutschland. Ein Wintermärchen*. He speaks first about the misfortune of Arminius's victory, which has caused him to learn Latin as a foreign language, and he continues:

> Ich will nicht weiter schreiben, ein alt-Deutscher könnte mich überraschen, und mir den Dolch ins undeutsche Herz stoßen mit einem pathetischen: Stirb verfehmter Zwingherrnknecht und Vaterlandsverächter! Aber ich ergreife dann das neben mir liegende Nibelun-

genlied und halte es als Schild dem jenäischen Donquixote entgegen, und der Dolch entfält ihm, und er faltet betend die Hände: O sancta Chrimhilda, Brunhilde et Uhta ora pro nobis!

But in this letter he also reveals how difficult it will be for him to discard his Germanness:

Ich weiß daß ich eine der deutschesten Bestien bin, ich weiß nur zu gut daß mir das Deutsche das ist, was dem Fische das Wasser ist, daß ich aus diesem Lebenselement nicht heraus kann . . . Ich liebe sogar im Grunde das Deutsche mehr als alles auf der Welt, ich habe meine Lust und Freude dran, und meine Brust ist ein Archiv deutschen Gefühls, wie meine zwey Bücher ein Archiv deutschen Gesanges sind. (HSA 20: 148)

Clearly Heine was going through an identity crisis forced on him by a bifurcation in an existence he had previously considered relatively unproblematic. With some degree of certainty we can maintain that during the early 1820s Heine came to recognize that one could not be simply a German-Jewish writer; the conflict between the problematic halves of this artificial synthesis would have to be resolved, and when it was, there would inevitably be a loss.

His writings from this period are a reflection of this dichotomous existence. In his public persona Heine remained primarily a German romantic poet during the first half of the 1820s. Despite his membership in the *Verein* and his increasing familiarity with Jewish culture and tradition — to a degree that probably exceeded anything he had experienced in his early years — this knowledge of and identification with Judaism remained largely confined to a private sphere. Although he had touched on the topic of religious discrimination in his play *Almansor,* which he began at Bonn and finished during his first stay in Göttingen, it is not insignificant that he does not thematize directly the fate of the Jews in Spain, but rather uses the Moslems, who were persecuted at the same time as the Jews, as a cipher for the plight of the Jews in modern Europe.[9] Indeed, mention of Jews and the Jewish question in Germany is fairly infrequent in his published works. In the second of his *Briefe aus Berlin,* dated March 22, 1822, Heine reports on the new, refurbished project of Jewish conversion, but he claims he does not want to describe it in detail because "die Juden ein gar zu trauriger Gegenstand sind" (B 2: 36). By the time he composed his report *Über Polen,* he had already been involved in the *Verein,* and it is not surprising to find a preoccupation with his co-religionists. In Heine's analysis of Polish society, the Jews occupy a separate class between the nobility and the peasants, a sort of "third estate," to which he devotes a great deal of attention. He shows sympathy with the Jewish plight and concern with their future; and it is interesting and consistent with the remarks cited from his correspondence that at one point he contrasts Polish Jewry favorably with the more assimilated German Jews with whom he has obviously had more contact and affinities. But in the poetic production of his early years we find very few traces of Jews and Judaism.[10] For the reading public, Heine, even after his baptism, remained H. Heine, the witty German romantic poet of unrequited love. If the plight of the Heine as a Jew is thematized, then it is indirect:

> Ich bin ein deutscher Dichter,
> Bekannt im deutschen Land;
> Nennt man die besten Namen,
> So wird auch der meine genannt.
>
> Und was mir fehlt, du Kleine,
> Fehlt manchem im deutschen Land;
> Nennt man die schlimmsten Schmerzen
> So wird auch der meine genannt. (B 1: 115)

The "great sorrows" the poet persona experiences could be the result of many disorders; we certainly cannot conclude that they are solely the consequence of his Judaism, despite our knowledge that Heine was preoccupied with the German Jewish question. At the same time that these words appeared in print, Heine was privately disavowing his Germanness and proclaiming his identity as a Jewish writer. Eventually Heine defiantly reasserted his Germanness even in his correspondence. In June of 1824 he includes the following irony-laden sentence in a letter to Moser: "O wie haben wir Deutsche uns vervollkommt!" (HSA 20: 168). And similarly he writes to Friederike Robert almost a year later that there are people in India who have suffered and endured even more than "wir Deutschen" (HSA 20: 198). But his only real Jewish work of these years of his identity crisis, *Der Rabbi von Bacherach,* remained fragmentary, and would be published only a decade and a half later during the Damascus crisis of 1840.

The identity Heine eventually embraced was therefore filled with contradictions that should not be glossed over in the easy formula "German-Jewish writer." After 1825 Heine became a Protestant, and although he was never an adherent to the Protestant religion in anything more than name, it would be inaccurate to call him simply a German Jew: his disavowal of Judaism was forced upon him to a certain degree, but there were also reasons for his conversion that had to do with a commonly held notion that Protestantism was the most progressive religion of the time. In any case, we should exercise caution in applying the label German-Jewish to Heine (or to any writer who has converted), lest we fall into the same camp with a certain breed of racist who contends that Jewishness is located in the blood or some other unalterable part of a person's being or upbringing. With regard to Heine and his identity, we can probably state the following with some degree of certainty: he identified with Germany and evidenced German pride, but he abhorred narrow German nationalism and unreflective patriotism. And he remained a former Jew, whose uneasiness with his own conversion and concern with his quondam co-religionists never found resolution in his writings — or in his own thoughts. When during the course of the nineteenth century Heine's identity crisis, which marked of course simultaneously a number of social crises in German life, became resolved in an *ex post facto* German-Jewish synthesis, he became known primarily as the composer of a Romantic poetry in which there are few overt traces of his actual personal conflicts or ethnic heritage. The *Buch der Lieder* became one of the most popular lyric collections in the world, and the poems in it were set to music by major and minor composers of all religious backgrounds. Significantly, the single transparently "Jewish" poem in the style of his early verse is included in no public collection of verse by H. Heine, but instead appears in one of the letters written to Moser and is conceived as a private, future dedication to his friend in connection with the *Rabbi* project:

> Brich aus in lauten Klagen,
> Du düstres Martyrerlied,
> Das ich so lang getragen
> Im flammenstillen Gemüt!
>
> Es dringt in alle Ohren,
> Und durch die Ohren ins Herz;
> Ich habe gewaltig beschworen
> Den tausendjährigen Schmerz.
>
> Es weinen die Großen und Kleinen,
> Sogar die kalten Herrn,
> Die Frauen und Blumen weinen,
> Es weinen am Himmel die Stern!

Und alle die Tränen fließen
Nach Süden, im stillen Verein,
Sie fließen und ergießen
Sich all in den Jordan hinein. (B 1: 271)

Immediately after writing these poignant lyrics, Heine reminded his friend "daß die Verse welche ich jetzt schreibe wenig werth sind und bloß zu meinem eignen Vergnügen gemacht werden" (HSA 20: 178). We may want to dispute this self-deprecating evaluation or consider it a rare moment of "Jewish" modesty in contrast to the versified "German" boasting cited above. It is nonetheless clear that the poem evidences formal continuities as well as content-related ruptures with his early verse. The rhyme scheme, strophic form, and even some of the figurative language are similar to those we find in the *Buch der Lieder*. But the narrative persona for this poem is not a longing German lover obsessed with a woman who has spurned his advances, leaving him pining away for her, but a suffering Jew, identifying with a persecuted people. Here the "I" is not looking inward at his sorrow, bewailing his personal fate as part of the German Fatherland, but reflecting on a tradition of anguish and pain that a Jewish collective has experienced. It is not Heine's individual tears alone that will flow into the River Jordan, but the tears of the entire Jewish community on earth. What is significant about this poem, therefore, is that, exceptionally, the speaker is not H. Heine, German poet, and certainly not the baptized German-Jewish writer Heinrich Heine, but most definitely Harry Heine, the German poet of Jewish origins.

II

Considering his identity crisis in the early 1820s, we should not be surprised to find Heine's conversion a source of psychic disruption. One sign of Heine's difficulties in coping with his conversion was his reluctance to write or speak about it. In his correspondence from June 1825 onward we note that Heine is hesitant to report his baptism openly, even to his closest friends. A little over a month after he had become a Protestant, he wrote to his sister Charlotte Embden, telling her to communicate to her husband that he "sey nicht nur Dr. Juris, sondern auch" — leaving what he has "also" become intentionally unnamed. He continues by stating "es hat gestern geregnet, so wie auch vor 6 Wochen" (HSA 20: 208). Heine had mentioned his impending conversion to Moritz Embden prior to the event (HSA 20: 196; letter dated May 11, 1825), and in this letter he is obviously letting his sister know that it has occurred: the mention of rain is an indirect reference to the baptismal water. But in letters to his best friend Moses Moser written directly after the baptism, Heine says absolutely nothing about his abandonment of Judaism. Three months after his conversion, at the beginning of October, he drops a hint that he has become a Protestant. In the same letter he speaks about Eduard Gans's conversion (HSA 20: 215–16). Since Gans was the acknowledged leader of the *Verein,* his conversion had a devastating impact on the association of Jewish scholars, and, indeed, when Heine composed this letter on October 8, the *Verein* had already dissolved because of the lack of leadership. But Heine does not speak directly of his own baptism until almost six months after it had occurred. On December 14, 1825 he wrote to Moser that he would not have had himself baptized if the theft of silver spoons had been allowed (HSA 20: 227). A month later he expresses his regrets that he converted, since he is now accepted by neither Christians nor Jews and has suffered only misfortune since then (HSA 20: 234). But Heine is generally silent about conversion in his letters after January of 1826, preferring to include his reflections on this topic in somewhat distorted, and often humorous or satirical form in his literary works.

The way in which conversion appears in these texts is anything but a simple reflection of the actual event or its genuine place in Heine's psychic economy. Instead, Jewish apostasy is depicted in a series of distortions, displacements, and refractions. An especially important technique Heine employs is projection; self-accusations and thoughts that may have occurred to him about conversion are projected onto others. This form of projection is complicated by the fact that Heine did not simply take his own thoughts and feelings and impute them to other people or to the quasi-fictional characters in his works. Rather projection functions, I believe, in ways of which Heine himself may not have been totally aware. The most famous example of this technique is probably Heine's poem "Einem Abtrünnigen," which scholars presume was written about Eduard Gans, although there are many features of the poem that suggest Heine had more on his mind than the former leader of the *Verein.* Heine's poem castigates his unnamed apostate for betraying his own youthful ardor, selling out to social pressures, and hypocritically embracing a faith that he had recently despised. It closes with a strophe that blames erudition, or at least the exposure to conservative thought, for the renegade's actions:

O des heilgen Jugendmutes!
O, wie schnell bist du gebändigt!
Und du hast dich, kühlern Blutes,
Mit den lieben Herrn verständigt.

Und du bist zu Kreuz gekrochen,
Zu dem Kreuz, das du verachtest,
Das du noch vor wenig Wochen
In den Staub zu treten dachtest!

O, das tut das viele Lesen
Jener Schlegel, Haller, Burke —
Gestern noch ein Held gewesen,
Ist man heute schon ein Schurke. (B 1: 266)

Unusual about the list of reactionaries is that Heine did not otherwise associate them with Gans. Obviously Friedrich Schlegel and Karl Ludwig von Haller may have been included because of their own conversions; both men left the Protestant faith for Catholicism, Schlegel in 1808, Haller — with much fanfare — in 1820. Edmund Burke is oddly out of place in this group, having undergone no religious conversion; he belongs with Schlegel and Haller only as a fellow conservative thinker, a feature that Gans does not share. In any case, the grouping is odd because of their dissimilarity with Gans on political issues, and may reflect Heine's momentary anger with his friend more than any true political affinities. But more germane for our concerns is the obvious and frequently remarked displacement of self-accusation and self-betrayal onto a third party. Gans had done the same thing in October of 1825 that Heine had done several months earlier: he had abandoned the religious tradition of his youth, and, like Heine, we presume he had done so without any real religious conviction and for precisely the same practical reasons that are usually attributed to Heine. Heine may be chastising his friend in this poem, but it could hardly have escaped his notice that his own actions were just as worthy of castigation.[11]

If we examine closely Heine's literary works from the years immediately following his conversion, we notice several instances of his uneasy conscience with regard to his own baptism. The most obvious of these examples comes from *Die Bäder von Lucca,* where the main character, the former banker Christian Gumpelino, has abandoned not only his Hamburg name, Lazarus Gumpel, and his class — he has been ennobled with the title Marquis — but also his religion. The irony here, of course, is that Heine, not Gumpel, was a religious apostate who left Hamburg to travel in Italy. Here conversion is ridiculed and viewed as an artificial contrivance of the *nouveaux riches* trying to abandon their roots and assimilate, in this case into a Roman Catholic society. Heine's selection of Gumpelino provides him with humorous material, but here again we have to wonder about the psychic mechanism that caused the author to mock a former co-religionist and to reverse the roles of apostate and faithful Jew. Gumpelino comes to represent almost everything Heine despises: he is Roman Catholic with exaggerated Romantic longings and a superficial knowledge of art and literature; his wealth has brought him his title and his connections to higher society, but he is without merit in matters of the heart and the world of refined culture. In selecting a former Jew as the butt of his ridicule, however, Heine included conversion among the outstanding characteristics that he disdained. Gumpelino, like the anonymous apostate of his poem, would therefore appear to be a product of guilt, self-reprobation, and embarrassment, an easily decipherable reflection on himself and the act of conversion, which, during the 1820s at least, remained unmentioned in published works.

In the aftermath of his conversion the topic also injected itself into Heine's writings in more surreptitious ways. In chapter 15 of *Ideen. Das Buch le Grand,* written at about the time that Heine became a Protestant, the narrator relates a different and humorous sort of conversion, from the party of the fools to the party of the reasonable ones. The text is obviously not an allegory in which Jews and Christians line up precisely with fools and reasonable ones; Heine's displacement in this case, and in most cases, does not operate with one-to-one correspondences. Rather this passage repeats themes and sentiments that are bound up in Heine's religious conversion and refracts them in various ways. At the outset the reasonable ones are said to have been at war with the fools for 5588 years, a clear reference to the date according to Jewish calculations. At another point, Heine relates the hatred of the fools for him:

> Mich Armen hassen sie aber ganz besonders, indem sie behaupten: ich sei von Haus aus einer der Ihrigen, ich sei ein Abtrünniger, ein Überläufer, der die heiligsten Bande zerrissen, ich sei jetzt sogar ein Spion, der heimlich auskundschafte, was sie, die Narren, zusammen treiben, um sie nachher dem Gelächter seiner neuen Genossen Preis zu geben; und ich sei so dumm, nicht mal einzusehen, daß diese zu gleicher Zeit über mich selbst lachen und mich nimmermehr für ihres Gleichen halten — Und da haben die Narren vollkommen Recht. (B 2: 298)

Here Heine repeats the reproaches or imagined reproaches a converted Jew would have suffered from his old co-religionists, as well as the suspicions Heine himself harbored about many of his new co-religionists. The resentment toward a traitor, which Heine himself expressed in his poem about Gans, the inability to become a Christian despite one's profession of a change in faith, the furtive ridicule a convert experiences from those who do not truly accept him — all of these motifs, which are sentiments expressed privately in Heine's correspondence, are contained in the passage from *Ideen* in distorted and displaced form. At this point in his life Heine was unable to speak about his conversion openly; indeed, as we have seen, he referred to it infrequently even in his correspondence with his most intimate friends. But in a displaced fashion his status as an apostate finds its way nonetheless into his published writings.[12]

III

Heine's preoccupation with his conversion appears to have diminished noticeably in the 1830s, perhaps because in Paris he was no longer confronted with the ambiguous identity of a German Jew. Initially in France he seems to have identified himself and to have been identified simply as a German writer, and it was not until 1840 and the Damascus crisis that we find Heine again taking up Jewish concerns with any intensity. In this context conversion again became a theme. It is noticeable in the *Ludwig Marcus Denkworte*, where Heine, like Marx in "On the Jewish Question," argues against conversion, insisting instead that the Jews must emancipate themselves and in this way integrate into German Christian society. But conversion is also a topic in *Ludwig Börne. Eine Denkschrift*, in a typically Heinesque manner. In the heavily fictionalized meeting between Heine and Börne in book one, Heine places the following sentiments into Börne's mouth:

> Die Taufe ist jetzt bei den reichen Juden an der Tagesordnung, und das Evangelium, das den Armen Judäas vergebens gepredigt worden, ist jetzt in Floribus bei den Reichen. Aber da die Annahme desselben nur Selbstbetrug, wo nicht gar Lüge ist, und das angeheuchelte Christentum mit dem alten Adam bisweilen recht grell kontrastiert, so geben diese Leute dem Witze und dem Spotte die bedenklichsten Blößen. Oder glauben Sie, daß durch die Taufe die innere Natur ganz verändert worden? Glauben Sie, daß man Läuse in Flöhe verwandeln kann, wenn man sie mit Wasser begießt? (B 4: 31)

This passage was written long after both Börne and Heine had chosen to discard their putatively "parasitic" nature by leaving the religion of their birth. It is quite possible, of course, that Börne may have uttered something like this to Heine at some point. But one must suspect, again, that Heine was projecting his own feelings onto the person purportedly accompanying him through the Frankfurt ghetto. A half year after his conversion Heine recognized that baptism was a futile concession to the Christian world. "Ich bin jetzt bey Christ und Jude verhaßt," Heine reported to Moser six months after his conversion. "Ich bereue sehr daß ich mich getauft hab; ich seh noch gar nicht ein daß es mir seitdem besser gegangen sey, im Gegentheil, ich habe seitdem nichts als Unglück" (HSA 20: 234).[13] And approximately a year after his baptism he writes of "die Qual persönlicher Verhältnisse (z.B. der nie abzuwaschende Jude)" (HSA 20: 265). The difference between his private comments in 1826 and his public remarks in the Börne *Denkschrift* are considerable, however. In the 1820s Heine is bitter; his conversion has not brought him the opportunities that he desired. He has abandoned his heritage without apparent gain. In 1840 he is less concerned with his own status as an apostate; secure in his adherence to no positive religion, he appears neither to regret his baptism, nor accept its religious consequences. As he makes clear in the *Denkschrift*, he belongs to the heathens, to the Hellenes, not to any species of Judeo-Christians or Nazarenes.

That Heine had difficulties in the psychological processing of his conversion is further evidenced by a conversation reported by Alexandre Weill. Responding to the question of why he converted, Heine evidently answered in a rather strange manner. He spoke of his return from visits to Italy and England, and that he felt no strong sentiments for his religious heritage. He then brought up his appointment to edit a German journal and stated that as a Jew he could not possibly assume that position. He then cited Börne as a similar example since Börne likewise could not have edited *Die Wage* without having himself baptized.[14] The reason Heine gives for his conversion is thus one of employment, but the time line he has established is well off the mark. Heine's sojourn in London occurred from April until June of 1827; his short-lived editorship of the *Neue Allgemeine Politische Annalen*, the only journal to which he could have possibly referred in his conversation with Weill, began in January of 1828 (and lasted less than a year); he traveled to Italy only in August of the same year. If Weill's report is at all accurate, then Heine's recollection is faulty here, as it so often was in connection with this important and traumatic event. His conversion in June of 1825 happened before his European trips and well before he could have conceived of becoming the editor of a political journal.

A meaningful public discussion of his conversion did not occur until the appearance of *Geständnisse* in 1854. As many commentators have noticed, Heine's entire attitude toward Judaism underwent a rather substantial revision during the final decade of his life. Although, as I noted earlier, Heine had occasionally shown sympathy for the Jewish cause in the 1820s, his early work, in particular his poetry, exhibits almost no hints of his heritage. In the *Reisebilder* there are numerous references to Jews and Jewish themes, many of them quite deprecatory to converted Jews, but Heine most often distanced himself from his religious and cultural origins, writing of the Jews as if he did not belong to them — which, strictly speaking, after June 28, 1825, he did not. In the 1830s we find an even greater endeavor to dissociate himself from Judaism. In response to a description of him as an "israélite" he claims that he is not a member of the Israelite religion, and adds that he has never set foot in a synagogue, while reaffirming in no uncertain terms his Lutheran affiliation (B 5: 19). Only in the 1840s, perhaps as a result of the Damascus crisis, did Heine again allow the public to glimpse his Jewish origins, for example, in the sincere homage to Ludwig Markus, and in the dubious tribute to Ludwig Börne. In the "Matratzengruft" he is more candid still. A published remark in the Augsburg *Allgemeine Zeitung* contains the following statement:

> Unterdessen, ich will es freimütig gestehen, ist eine große Umwandlung mit mir vorgegangen: ich bin kein göttlicher Bipede mehr; ich bin nicht mehr der "freieste Deutsche nach Goethe," wie mich Ruge in gesündern Tagen genannt hat; ich bin nicht mehr der große Heide Nr. 2 den man mit dem weinlaubumkränzten Dionysus verglich, während man meinem Kollegen Nr. 1 den Titel eines großherzoglich weimarschen Jupiters erteilte; ich bin kein lebensfreudiger, etwas wohlbeleibter Hellene mehr, der auf trübsinnige Nazarener herablächelte — ich bin jetzt nur ein armer todkranker Jude, ein abgezehrtes Bild des Jammers, ein unglücklicher Mensch! (B 5: 109)

Here we find an openness toward his former Judaism that goes well beyond anything he had written publicly during the previous three decades. In most remarks from his last years Heine, of course, still refrained from identifying himself as a Jew — or he was at least ambiguous — and in this passage his admission is almost surely done for its dramatic effect. But it is evident in nearly all of his late writings that he had altered fundamentally his perspective toward Jews and Judaism, now finding them a past that he no longer wished to deny, a fate from which he no longer felt it necessary to flee.

In this context Heine was able to write in a more forthright fashion about his conversion in 1825. Answering questions putatively posed about his current religious beliefs, Heine asserts in his *Geständnisse* that with regard to Lutheranism, his status remains unchanged. He characterizes his own conversion as one undertaken in a lukewarm, official fashion, and maintains that "wenn ich überhaupt dem evangelischen Glauben angehörig bleibe, so geschieht es weil er mich auch jetzt durchaus nicht geniert, wie er mich früher nie allzusehr genierte" (B 6.1: 482). He continues by claiming that during his stay in Berlin he would have declared himself independent of any organized religion, as some of his friends had done, if the absence of an identifiable confession had not been a reason for which one could be denied residence in Prussia and its capital. This explanation is odd. His conversion, as we know, did not occur while he was in Berlin, but during his second stay in Göttingen, shortly before the completion of his law degree and several years removed from his sojourn in the Prussian capital. And certainly we have no evidence that any of his acquaintances abandoned religion entirely and officially, which, according to Jacob Toury, was a practical impossibility before 1848.[15] He continues in the *Geständnisse* to write about his conversion by posing, and then circumventing, the question of whether he has become a believing Protestant. He claims that in former years he appreciated Protestantism because of its association with freedom of thought and German philosophy, which begins with the Reformation. Now, however, he reveres Protestantism for rediscovering and disseminating the Bible. But after praising the Reformation for the rediscovery of the Hebrew texts and for translating the Old Testament from its original language into a modern idiom, he turns to an extended discussion of the Jews as prototypical democrats, and eventually builds his tribute to a climax in a veritable *laudatio* to Moses as a socialist revolutionary. In other words, he addresses the question of his Protestantism by writing about Judaism.[16]

What is going on in this unusual passage? Why do we again have mysterious remarks concerning Heine's conversion? Why does Heine appear to be avoiding the issue once again? My hunch is that Heine's discussion of religion and religious conversion in the *Geständnisse* has something to do with a displacement involving his more recent and less official conversion. The fact that Heine so easily slips from his conversion in 1825 to his later change of beliefs indicates that they were closely associated in his mind. But what is unusual about his later conversion is the way it is repeatedly characterized in his writings both public and private. More than anything else Heine depicts his religious transformation in the "Matratzengruft" as a rejection of Hegel and a renewal of former beliefs. The insistence on a renewal has led some commentators to believe Heine embraced something akin to Judaism, although Heine insists that his God is a personal one. By renewal it seems obvious that Heine simply means that he again harbors a conviction that God, as a Supreme Being, exists. The rejection of Hegel, however, is more difficult to explain. It is true of course that Heine writes about Hegel in his earlier works with considerable respect and admiration, as well as occasionally with some humor. We know that Friedrich Engels later considered Heine's *Zur Geschichte der Religion und Philosophie in Deutschland* to be the first work of a Left-Hegelian. And Heine tells us after the fact that he himself composed a two-volume book on Hegel that he consigned to the fires after he rejected Hegelian philosophy. But there is no strong indication of an avid adherence to Hegel, or even a deep understanding of Hegel, at any place in Heine's writings from the 1820s to the 1840s. Hegel is conspicuous by his marginality in *Religion und Philosophie in Deutschland,* where he is called "der größte Philosoph, den Deutschland seit Leibniz erzeugt hat" (B 3: 633), but also cited for his support of the Prussian state and the Protestant church. And the famous line in the poem "Doktrin" that equates Hegelian philosophy with drumming people out of an inactive lethargy and kissing young salesgirls is more easily conceived as a vast and ironic oversimplification than as a validation of one of the most eminent minds of the nineteenth century.

The association of Hegel with Heine's late renewal of faith makes sense — at least psychic sense — if we view it again in terms of displacement. We know, for example, that the real Hegelian convert among the members of the *Verein* was Eduard Gans, and certainly his embracing of Protestantism can be conceived more easily as a rejection of Judaism for Hegelianism than Heine's. That Hegel is not on the list of authors the apostate read in Heine's poem covers up the one genuine ideological influence Heine could have associated with his friend, and perhaps the one intellectual influence that really mattered in his conversion. But there is another Hegelian convert who could have affected Heine's anti-Hegelian crusade and his depiction of conversion in *Geständnisse.* The most obvious candidate is Karl Marx, another former Jew whose Hegelianism led him precisely to the type of atheism that Heine, in his later writings, decries so vociferously. It was the Left-Hegelian socialists and communists, after all, who relinquished all religious belief, and who were banned from Germany because of their political and religious views. In his late reflection on his conversion in 1825, where he recalls friends who abandoned all religion and were banned from Prussia, Heine may have been projecting forward into the 1840s. And in citing the heritage of Judaism in such a pronounced fashion when he should have been discussing Lutheranism, Heine may have been identifying with the religious roots he shared with the more apparent Hegelian converts Eduard Gans and Karl Marx.

This explanation for the discrepancies in Heine's text is of course highly speculative; there is no way to offer a secure proof since we are dealing with Heine's psychic economy, which was neither precise nor consistent. I could mount more evidence for the associations I have found, but no textual evidence would be definitive. Indeed, my more general contention is that the autobiographical oddities in Heine's works, especially the strange claims and bizarre statements he sometimes makes, can often be accounted for by the ways in which particularly sensitive issues in his personal life played themselves out in his writings. Conversion was obviously one issue that Heine had trouble confronting or processing mentally. The transition from a German poet of Jewish origins to a converted Lutheran poet with oppositional and pantheistic convictions was a difficult one. In the 1820s we therefore find Heine avoiding the topic of his own baptism, while simultaneously heaping ridicule or scorn on others who had done exactly what he did not want to promulgate in public. Only in his deathbed writings, when another conversion had taken place, was he able to speak about his 1825 conversion a bit more openly. But even then he apparently confused his own conversion with that of others, confounding his beliefs with theirs, displacing his own views with those that were not quite his own. The confusion and displacement of Heine's autobiographical writings makes them of dubious value for facts and actual occurrences, but it makes them invaluable if we hope to understand the complex workings of Heine's mind.

Notes

[1] Jacob Katz notes that there were three main reasons for conversion: religious conviction, material gain, and ideological belief (*Jewish Emancipation and Self-Emancipation* [Philadelphia: Jewish Publication Society, 1986], 37–38). Guido Kisch tends to agree with this evaluation and points out that few converts embraced Christianity out of religious conviction.

[2] For an analysis of the role of Judaism in Heine's early years, see Jürgen Voigt, *O Deutschland, meine ferne Liebe . . .: Der junge Heinrich Heine zwischen Nationalromantik und Judentum.* (Bonn: Pahl-Rugenstein, 1993).

[3] Some writers, for example Israel Tabak, have placed a great deal of emphasis on what they assume Heine must have experienced as a child and young man of Jewish heritage (*Judaic Lore in Heine: The Heritage of a Poet* [Baltimore: Johns Hopkins UP, 1948]). But the evidence of a thoroughgoing preoccupation with Judaism is simply missing or indirect at best. Ruth Jacobi is probably more accurate when she claims that Heine had only a superficial knowledge of Hebrew and Jewish customs from his parents' home (*Heinrich Heines jüdisches Erbe* [Bonn: Bouvier, 1978], 55).

[4] For a brief review of the debates around emancipation in the early nineteenth century, see David Sorkin, *The Transformation of German Jewry 1780–1840* (New York: Oxford UP, 1987), 13–40.

[5] See Jacob Toury, *Sociale und Politische Geschichte der Juden in Deutschland 1847–1871: Zwischen Revolution, Reaktion und Emanzipation* (Düsseldorf: Droste, 1977), esp. 51–68.

[6] For a statistical analysis of conversions in Berlin see Peter Honigmann, "Jewish Conversions — A Measure of Assimilation? A Discussion of the Berlin Secession Statistics of 1770–1941," *Leo Baeck Institute Yearbook* 34 (1989): 3–39.

[7] Hertz, "Why Did the Christian Gentleman Assault the Jüdischer Elegant?: Four Conversion Stories from Berlin, 1816–1825," *Leo Baeck Institute Yearbook* (1995): 85–106.

[8] Hertz points to the significant number of "elites" who converted ("Seductive Conversions in Berlin, 1770–1809," *Jewish Apostasy in the Modern World*, ed. Todd M. Endelman [New York: Holmes & Meier, 1987], 59–62). It is also interesting to note that the number of women who converted outnumbered men in the eighteenth century, but that during the time of Heine's conversion, more men than women were baptized from the Jewish community.

[9] Similar to Michael Beer, who selected an Indian setting for his *Paria.* See Jacob Katz, "Rezeption jüdischer Autoren durch deutsche Kritik und deutsches Publikum," *Bulletin des Leo Baeck Instituts* 75 (1986): 41–53.

[10] The most obvious exception is the poem "Donna Clara," in which the knight with whom Donna Clara falls in love turns out to be the son of a rabbi.

[11] In a letter to Moser from December 19, 1825, Heine indicates the similarity between his conversion and Gans's when he refers to the stealing of silver spoons

(HSA 20: 227). Two factors that Heine may have believed distinguished his conversion from Gans's are mentioned by Heine occasionally. Heine claims that Gans actively sought to persuade other Jews to convert, and Gans had more responsibility to remain Jewish because of his leadership role in the *Verein*.

[12] For a discussion of other works relating to his conversion, as well as of the baptism itself, see Ludwig Rosenthal, *Heinrich Heine als Jude* (Frankfurt am Main: Ullstein, 1973), 218–53.

[13] Other Jews obviously felt the same way. See Voigt, *O Deutschland, meine ferne Liebe . . .,* 10–11.

[14] Cited in Rosenthal, *Heinrich Heine als Jude,* 234. The passage Rosenthal cites is not quoted in its entirety in *Begegnungen mit Heine.*

[15] "Praktisch bestand bis 1848 in keinem deutschen Lande die Möglichkeit, aus der jüdischen Gemeinde auszuscheiden, ohne gleichzeitig einer anderen konfessionellen Gemeinschaft beizutreten" (Toury, *Sociale und Politische Geschichte der Juden in Deutschland 1847–1871* 61).

[16] The most extensive treatment of Heine's Judaism, S. S. Prawer's *Heine's Jewish Comedy,* does not focus on the strange way in which Heine's conversion was thematized in *Geständnisse.*

Works Cited

Hertz, Deborah. "Seductive Conversions in Berlin, 1770–1809." *Jewish Apostasy in the Modern World.* Ed. Todd M. Endelman. New York: Holmes & Meier, 1987. 48–82.

———. "Why Did the Christian Gentleman Assault the Jüdischer Elegant?: Four Conversion Stories from Berlin, 1816–1825." *Leo Baeck Institute Yearbook* (1995): 85–106.

Honigmann, Peter. "Jewish Conversions — A Measure of Assimilation? A Discussion of the Berlin Secession Statistics of 1770–1941." *Leo Baeck Institute Yearbook* 34 (1989): 3–39.

Jacobi, Ruth L. *Heinrich Heines jüdisches Erbe.* Bonn: Bouvier, 1978.

Katz, Jacob. *Jewish Emancipation and Self-Emancipation.* Philadelphia: Jewish Publication Society, 1986.

———. "Rezeption jüdischer Autoren durch deutsche Kritik und deutsches Publikum." *Bulletin des Leo Baeck Instituts* 75 (1986): 41–53.

Kisch, Guido. *Judentaufen.* Berlin: Colloquium Verlag, 1973.

Prawer, S. S. *Heine's Jewish Comedy: A Study of his Portraits of Jews and Judaism.* Oxford: Clarendon, 1983.

Rosenthal, Ludwig. *Heinrich Heine als Jude.* Frankfurt am Main: Ullstein, 1973.

Sorkin, David. *The Transformation of German Jewry 1780–1840.* New York: Oxford UP, 1987.

Tabak, Israel. *Judaic Lore in Heine: The Heritage of a Poet.* Baltimore: Johns Hopkins UP, 1948.

Toury, Jacob. *Sociale und Politische Geschichte der Juden in Deutschland 1847–1871: Zwischen Revolution, Reaktion und Emanzipation.* Düsseldorf: Droste, 1977.

Voigt, Jürgen. *O Deutschland, meine ferne Liebe . . .: Der junge Heinrich Heine zwischen Nationalromantik und Judentum.* Bonn: Pahl-Rugenstein, 1993.

Heine and Jewish Culture:
The Poetics of Appropriation*

Jeffrey Grossman

I

HEINE RESEARCH IS FAMOUS for the debates it provokes, and perhaps no question is less settled than that of Heine's response to Jewish culture, a question also bound up with that of Heine's place in German culture. Critics have sought in various ways to resolve this question, which Oskar Walzel, writing a century ago, asserted to be "the most important problem in the field of Heine research." This article seeks to intervene in the discourse on the question of Heine, Jewish culture, and Jewish identity, and, it is hoped, to offer an alternative approach to those questions. It argues first that any attempt to find the *key* to or *essence* of Heine's work in his Jewishness is misguided. It also questions the view that Heine's response to Jewish culture was inauthentic or somehow detrimental to Jewish life. And it further questions the claims, most notoriously made by German nationalists, that Heine's Jewishness made his writings less authentically German. For all their differences, these claims display a problematic structure that lends them a disturbing resemblance to one another. That structure rests on a prescriptive view of group identity — a view (of Jewishness or Germanness) that, in each case, excludes from German life or Jewish life expressions of that life that fail to conform to its norms.[1] Yet, Heine's work does relate in important and complex ways to Jewish culture and the place of Jews in Germany. Indeed, the complexity of this relationship invests it with greater, rather than less, importance, since it also raises more general theoretical questions about the ways that literary works relate to problems of identity, the social world, ideology, poetics, and the culture(s) — dominant or nondominant — that impinge upon and are shaped by those works.

In exploring these problems, I wish in this article to focus especially on two distinct but related questions, the first regarding the status of the poetic or fictional utterance and its relationship to the historical figure of the writer, and the second related to the position of the writer in society, both of which were issues that Heine himself responded to at various times.[2] In an 1823 letter to Immermann, for instance, Heine questioned the value of historical approaches to poetic works:

> Nur etwas kann mich aufs schmerzlichste verletzen, wenn man den Geist meiner Dichtungen aus der Geschichte . . . des Verfassers erklären will. . . . Wie leicht auch die Geschichte eines Dichters Aufschluß geben könnte über sein Gedicht, wie leicht sich wirklich nachweisen ließe daß oft politische Stellung, Religion, Privathaß, Vorurtheil und Rücksichten auf sein Gedicht eingewirkt, so muß man dieses dennoch nie erwähnen, besonders nicht bey Lebzeiten des Dichters. Man entjungfert gleichsam das Gedicht, man zerreist den geheimnißvollen Schleyer desselben, wenn jener Einfluß der Geschichte den man nachweist wirklich vorhanden ist; man verunstaltet das Gedicht wenn man ihn fälschlich hineingegrübelt hat. Und wie wenig ist oft das äußere Gerüste unserer Geschichte mit unserer wirklichen, inneren Geschichte zusammenpassend! Bey mir wenigstens paste es *nie*. (HSA 20: 92–93)

It exceeds the scope of this essay to explore in detail Heine's important and much discussed point about aesthetic experience, or to explore his sense of wonder before the "mysterious veil" of the poetic work and his rejection of any attempt to "deflower" the poem. More to the point here, Heine's letter questions both the accuracy and the value of naively positivistic or "identitarian" readings of poems as unrefracting mirrors of a poet's life, history, or political views, though Heine himself later contradicted the wholly anti-historicist thrust of this letter. In *Die Romantische Schule* (1833), for instance, he attributes Uhland's cessation of writing to that poet's awareness of the political conditions and functions of his work (B 3: 487). And his views of poetry underwent further revisions throughout his life, especially, it seems, after the onset of his debilitating illness in 1848 (Cook 20–21). Heine's letter does raise the question of how one can relate poetic works to the historical world beyond the poem without violating the value of the poem itself, a violation that would place in question the value of reading or writing poetic works at all.

In response to Heine's point, I wish to rephrase the question so as to focus *not* on the problem of relating the poetic utterance to an unmediated view of the poet's history or the historical context. I explore rather how such utterances relate to the various discourses and institutions that help to enable or constrain them — institutions and discourses of literature and culture, religion, politics, and so forth, that shape and circulate in the social field. To pose the question in this way is to raise as well the question of the writer's position in the social field, and hence the possible functions of his or her utterances. That position is one that Pierre Bourdieu explores in depth in *Distinction,* his vast study of culture and the social field, and which he describes succinctly in his essay, "Field of Power, Literary Field and Habitus." Writers and artists, Bourdieu suggests, "occupy a dominated position in the dominant class, they are owners of a dominated form of power at the interior of the sphere of power" (164). While Bourdieu's formulation suggests that works aspiring to the status of literature will inevitably be controlled or dominated, Heine, in those works that evoke or focus on Jewish figures, developed writing strategies that point to the problematic interaction of culture and power, and to the contradictory role that writing and culture risk playing in determining the position of both Jews and writers in society.[3]

Responding to this contradictory situation, Heine seeks, in works ranging from *Deutschland. Ein Wintermärchen* to the reportage *Über Polen,* the "travel picture" *Die Bäder von Lucca,* the fictional fragment *Der Rabbi von Bacherach,* and the late poem "Jehuda ben Halevy," to transform the symbolic function of Jews in the German cultural sphere. To that end, he appropriates cultural elements, symbols, texts, and figures that have one function in the dominant discourse and incorporates them in his texts to produce an alternative discourse and alternative cultural space within Germany. The term *appropriation,* as used here, draws from the work of the cultural historian Roger Chartier, who defines it in terms opposed to the meaning given by Michel Foucault when Foucault speaks of the "social appropriation of discourse" as, in Chartier's words, "one of the primary procedures for gaining control of discourses and putting them beyond the reach of those who were denied access to them" (89; Foucault 229). Chartier also departs from the hermeneutic notion of appropriation as interpretation. He proposes alternatively a view that emphasizes "differentiated practices and contrasted uses of the same texts, codes, or models," within and across cultural boundaries, in this case across the boundary from elite or high culture to popular audiences (89). While Chartier elaborates a new approach to the study of popular culture, he defines appropriation in ways that suggest how one might grasp a writer's struggle to negotiate the conditions of writing that Bourdieu describes. It may in particular help to illuminate the strategies Heine develops as he responds to the constraints imposed on Jews and Jewish culture, while seeking to transform their symbolic function in the German sphere.[4]

II

Heine's narrative poem, *Deutschland. Ein Wintermärchen,* may seem an odd starting point for a discussion of Heine and Jewish culture. *Deutschland* refers primarily to politically charged symbols of German culture and national identity, which Heine appropriates for the sake of satire directed primarily at nationalist ideologies. References to Jewish culture, political rights, and social position lead, as Susanne Zantop notes, only a "submerged life" in *Deutschland,* surfacing mainly in the margins of the poem (183). Yet Heine injects these references precisely in ways that challenge the nationalist narrative of German history and culture. A digression into the famous eleventh chapter will serve to show Heine's overriding strategy for exposing how that narrative constructs a nationalist view of history. That chapter subjects the Romantic nationalist appropriations of the German past to satire; it does so by evoking the image of Hermann leading the German nation to victory over the Romans in the Teutoberg forest. It continues by citing a series of images envisioning the fate of German culture, had Hermann been defeated and Germany Romanized: the mediocre poet Freiligrath transformed into Flaccus Horatius, the "loutish beggar" Vater Jahn a "Lautianus," and the philosopher Schelling as Seneca dying in civil strife, only to conclude with an ironic expression of gratitude to Hermann for saving the German nation, an act to commemorate with a monument (B 4: 600–602).

This section exploits for humorous ends the matching of Roman with German figures, foregrounding differences that produce a deflationary effect, as in the case of Horace and Freiligrath. But beyond the humor, the construction of a Romanized Germany also presents an alternative or counterfactual history. Counterfactual histories, as one student of the subject notes, expose the problems of deterministic views of history by exploring other possible worlds and histories, other possible responses to and results from a given set of conditions and events (Ferguson 2, 88). Heine's counterfactual history undermines the teleology of nineteenth-century nationalist-historicist accounts that viewed German history as a predestined organic unfolding of the German spirit seeking its fulfillment in nationhood. Opposing that view, Heine suggests that the present moment in Germany depends on a series of contingencies — on the specific conditions, cultural forces, events, choices, and outcomes that went into producing the present moment. Heine thus invokes the monument erected to the Cheruskan Hermann, much under discussion at that time, which sought to *commemorate* the originary moment organically lodged in German history. By satirizing both Hermann and the act of monument-building, Heine exposes this ostensible act of commemoration as an attempt rather to invent the moment of German national origins, fixing in stone, as it were, the flux of national identity and its memory. Thus, as shown more recently by George Mosse and Simon Schama, it was not some elusive national spirit but the very acts of designing and financing the monument — by soliciting German *Gymnasium* students for funds and hence galvanizing them throughout the German states — that nationalized the German population (Mosse, *Nationalization* 60; Schama 109–11).

Deutschland also reveals how Heine's mix of styles, his shift in tones and registers, and his juxtaposing of discordant events and images work to evoke and satirize cultural norms and ideologies. When, for instance, Heine evokes Hermann, he refers to him as "der edle Recke" only to recontextualize his and the German nation's conquest in the Teutoberg forest by claiming: "Die siegte in diesem Drecke," a phrase that deflates the conquest semantically, supplanting "Drecke" for the majestic forest, and phonologically, by rhyming "Drecke" with "Recke" (B 4: 601). Beyond the obvious political satire, Heine's inscription of the Hermann figure in a new context that proposes alternative histories and exploits the more subversive functions of language presents a poetics that opposes such monumentalizing gestures as the *Hermannsdenkmal* or, for that matter, the dramas seeking to create national myths, such as Kleist's and Grabbe's versions of *Die Hermannsschlacht*.

Where Jewish figures appear in *Deutschland,* they similarly serve to deflate nationalist discourse and the icons it creates. When, for instance, in chapter 16, the twelfth-century emperor Friedrich Barbarossa enters the poem, Heine exploits the symbolic capital invested in this icon to undermine the pejorative image of Jews often promoted by German nationalists. The medieval German emperor asks about his subject Moses Mendelssohn, whose adherence to Jewish religious tradition and to German Enlightenment culture defied the nationalist impulse that sought a homogenous German culture and denied the possibility of felicitous coexistence between Germans and Jews. By having Barbarossa ask about Mendelssohn, Heine reappropriates a national icon to expose the problem of appropriation, showing how in this case German nationalists manipulate past figures and events, a point made clear once one recalls Friedrich Barbarossa's relatively positive treatment of Jews under his own jurisdiction (Prawer 455).

When Barbarossa asks about Mendelssohn, the poet-narrator responds by noting that he, along with his children, "ist längst gestorben, . . . gestorben, verdorben" but that his grandson, Felix Mendelssohn-Bartholdy, "brachte es weit in Christentum / Ist schon Kapellmeister" (B 4: 613). By citing both the renowned Mendelssohns and injecting between their names the rhyme "gestorben, verdorben," Heine evokes the hopes for an emancipation that had first been implemented, and the failure of those hopes, since emancipatory legislation in Prussia had been largely retracted. The reference to Mendelssohn-Bartholdy further suggests Heine's own rather different encounter with conversion, an act that, unlike that of the composer, failed, years earlier, to help him ensure the civil service position he sought.

The later part of the poem again shows how Heine appropriates conventions and strategies — social, political, or Romantic — to undermine the nationalist values attaching to them. The poem's trajectory, expressed by the poet-narrator's arrival in Hamburg in the last chapters, suggests again its inversion of the symbolic value attaching to the Prussian state, the *Machtstaat* seeking to define Germany's national future — so that the view into that future, the unspoken image of Hammonia's putrid chamber pot, remains famously (or infamously) bleak. Yet, its refusal to describe that image draws, in turn, on a Romantic convention — the principle that to name the moment of fulfillment ironically destroys it — only to subvert the convention's more traditional uses. By not specifically naming or describing the bleak image of Germany's future, Heine invests that image with intense evocative power, but only with the power of a possible *negative* rather than *positive* fulfillment. At the same time, the city-state Hamburg stands opposed to Prussia, functioning as a place where cultural hierarchies are leveled. An independent space located outside the Prussian sphere of domination, Hamburg is shaped not by the Junker and militarism, but by its harbors and commerce that open it internationally, and by the leveling image of its libidinous red-light district. This leveling space also serves as the place where Jews and Christians can coexist (B 4: 627). Yet, the narrator goes further, invoking the conflict that divides the old-style, traditional or orthodox Jews from the new reform-minded Jews when he declares:

> Die Juden teilen sich wieder ein
> In zwei verschiedne Parteien;
> Die Alten gehn in die Synagog,
> Und in den Tempel die Neuen.
>
> . . .
>
> Ich liebe die Alten, ich liebe die Neun —
> Doch schwör ich, beim ewigen Gotte,
> Ich liebe gewisse Fischchen noch mehr,
> Man heißt sie geräucherte Sprotte. (B 4: 627–28)

The invoking of the Hamburg Jewish population performs two functions in the narrative poem. It first criticizes the nationalist chauvinism associated with Prussia, whose representative *Adler* the poet-narrator wants to strip of claws and feathers and display for a shooting contest. It then provides an occasion for Heine the Saint-Simonian to criticize organized religion, emphasizing his preference for a gratification of the senses in the form of smoked fish (Butler 141–44, 153–54). Heine's poetic appropriation of the Hamburg Jews thus enables a double movement of ideological positioning, a critique of nationalism and anti-Jewish sentiment, on the one hand, and a critique of religion, on the other. This same poetic act gestures further toward a third position, the production of a cultural space open to Jewish existence but removed from its institutionalized forms, traditional or otherwise. By incorporating such references into his poem, by seeking to raise the status of the concrete quotidian expressions of Jewish life, related to the senses and their gratification, and by writing them into a long, narrative poem with a middle-brow or high cultural appeal, Heine deflates the norms of German and Jewish culture alike. Subverting the elevated cultural sphere, Heine simultaneously satirizes political and religious institutions at points where culture comes to symbolize social dominance and the dominance of the senses.

III

While *Deutschland* enlists Jewish figures to expose the emerging German nation as a modern invention and to subvert the cultural hierarchies that support it, Heine's earlier and perhaps more subtly political reportage of 1823, *Über Polen*, seeks to subvert the cultural hierarchies emerging at that time between German and Polish Jews. Heine focuses on the Jewish problem, in that essay, as part of a more general critique of Prussian imperialist politics, a critique implicating as well the Austrian and Russian policies toward Poland. The title itself, by naming Poland as a place in existence, already points to this critique of the imperial powers' attempt to erase Poland from existence (Hermand 44–45). Describing three groups in Poland, the Jews, the peasants, and the aristocracy, Heine presents Polish Jews as a surrogate "bourgeoisie" or third estate, who in that capacity serve as a potential source of political transformation. The essay describes the Yiddish language and the physical appearance of Polish Jews as abhorrent, descriptions that have prompted critics to read it either as an expression of self-hatred or as an early contribution to the stereotype of the *Ostjude,* one that mixes nostalgia and antipathy.[5]

For all the physically pejorative descriptions, *Über Polen* retains a multivalence that becomes more apparent if it is read as a response to David Friedländer's polemical essay of 1819, *Ueber die Verbesserung der Israeliten im Königreich Pohlen,* and the cultural hierarchies it adhered to. Heine cites Friedländer's essay in his reportage, recommending it to readers who seek details about Polish Jews more specific than those he intends to provide (B 2: 74). A close, though ultimately more reform-minded follower of Moses Mendelssohn and the Jewish Enlightenment in Germany, Friedländer presented Polish Jews as suffering from a self-imposed ghetto, culturally stagnant and educationally deprived. Friedländer sought to report on Polish Jews, but his essay also enlisted them as an anti-type to the cultural ideal of *Bildung* pursued by German Jews seeking to transform themselves and integrate in Germany.[6] Yiddish was, in Friedländer's terms, a combination of "rabbinism, Aramaic, and Chaldean, mixed with Arabic and Greek words, elaborate idioms that cannot be forced into any grammatical rules" (22). Its vocabulary and lack of grammatical form manifested in its composition the backwardness or *Unbildung* of a rabbinically dominated Polish Jewish culture, and he prescribed for Polish Jews a form of improvement modeled, as his title implies, on Christian von Dohm's 1780 treatise *Ueber die bürgerliche Verbesserung der Juden in Deutschland.* Dohm had argued that there was a need to reform Jewish cultural and economic practices, but that such reform would follow from the granting of civil rights and institutional integration of Jews (1: 27–36, 88–96, 120). Friedländer thus adopted toward Polish Jews virtually the same position that Dohm adopted toward Jews in Germany, who, in Friedländer's view, had however already embarked upon the necessary transformation (Friedländer 22).

Despite the ostensibly positive reference to Friedländer, Heine actually seeks to revise Friedländer's image of Polish Jews. In particular, Heine appropriates the ideal of *Bildung* in order to expose from within its problematic ideology. Heine seeks to show that as an ideal of cultural change, the ideology of *Bildung* misreads the problem of Jewish existence by conflating aesthetic and ethical categories, while ignoring institutional and material constraints. Heine thus begins by reiterating certain aspects of Friedländer's Enlightenment critique of Polish Jews. The ideal of *Bildung*, central to that critique, promoted the cultivation of the inner man (or woman), but its emphasis on form and cultivation also suggests the aesthetic dimension of this ideal, since the image of the cultured man or cultured Jew was supposed to point to a refined inner character. After evoking Friedländer's critique, Heine, who does accept aspects of Friedländer's view, nonetheless proceeds to show how in advocating change on the level of aesthetic culture this view fails to account for the power of social and political institutions in effecting change. Those institutions, though affected by changes in German culture, operated as powerful constraints on Jews and Jewish culture, constraints that persisted even after German Jews embarked upon their attempt to transform themselves according to the norms of *Bildung*.

Heine's approach to Polish Jews differs from Friedländer's position and effects its critique of that position by presenting Polish Jews in their language and culture as unaesthetic. Polish Jews appear, for instance, as "zerlumpte Schmutzgestalten"; the Yiddish language as "ein mit Hebräisch durchwirktes, und mit Polnisch façonniertes Deutsch," an idiom that tortures the ears (B 2: 76). But Heine at the same time seeks to recontextualize the abhorrent physical image of Polish Jews, presenting their appearance not as a sign, let alone a product of, their inner condition, but as a function of their material condition. Abhorrence thus gives way to sympathy when Heine remarks that "die schweinestallartigen Löcher . . ., worin sie wohnen, mauscheln, beten, schachern und — elend sind" (B 2: 76). Further, Heine also subtly challenges the norms attaching to the *Bildungsideal*. Heine initially accepts, for instance, the teleology of Friedländer's approach to Polish Jewish culture and *Bildung* when he writes that Polish Jews failed to progress along with European culture. But he then dismantles the social hierarchies implied by this view when he notes the Jewish contribution to Polish culture and society. Heine evokes the cultural ideal when he mentions the German Jew, "der seinen Bolivar auf dem Kopf und seinen Jean Paul im Kopfe trägt," but he undermines it by embedding this reference within a sentence expressing preference for the Polish Jew "mit seinem schmutzigen Pelze, mit seinem bevölkerten Barte und Knoblauchgeruch und Gemauschel" (B 2: 76–77). And he challenges as well the symbolic value attaching to modern forms of social organization, the "staatspapiernen Herrlichkeit" of German Jews, forms of social organization that upheld the ideal of *Bildung,* but transformed it into the means for shoring up the power of the Prussian state. Beyond its role as cultural ideal, *Bildung* became for German Jews a necessary condition, imposed by the state, but in the 1820s it was not sufficient to gain for them anything more than a theoretical promise of emancipation accompanied by a flawed and faltering emancipatory practice. Whatever else it did for German Jews, *Bildung* thus also trapped them in a series of contradictions. Thus, Heine compares the physically present, if unattractive, Polish Jew to the cultivated German Jew, claiming: "Der innere Mensch wurde kein quodlibetartiges Kompositum heterogener Gefühle und verkümmerte nicht durch die Einzwängung Frankfurter Judengaßmauern, hochweiser Stadtverordnungen und liebreicher Gesetzbeschränkungen" (B 2: 77).

Heine presents here a fantasy of the wholly integrated, culturally stable Polish Jew, a fantasy that both evokes and criticizes the Romantic discourse on the *Volk* and the Enlightenment discourse on tolerance, while making overt his critique of political conditions in Germany, which is in any case where his target audience resides (letter to Christian Sethe on January 21, 1823; HSA 20: 69). According to Heine's critique, German Jews have moved historically only within a restricted sphere, from state-imposed ghetto walls to dissolution deriving from state-imposed assimilation. In their pursuit of acceptance and their uncritical adoption of German cultural norms, Heine suggests, German Jews pay with their integrity: they adhere to an aesthetic-cultural ideal, based in liberal values, but fail to gain the civil emancipation they sought. Pointing to the debilitating effects of this contradiction on German Jews, Heine suggests that the aestheticizing imagery of *Bildung* obscures these institutional constraints, rather than helping Jews to escape them. Heine himself appropriates the imagery of the *gebildeten* versus the *ungebildeten,* even to the point of affirming the pejorative image of the Polish Jew, but, in the process, he exposes the problem of conflating changes in aesthetic and cultural models with institutional change. Moving beyond current institutional constraints will, Heine suggests further, ultimately depend on finding new terms and images for configuring Jewish and European selves, while exposing the conditions that determine those limits.

Heine revisits the question of Jews and *Bildung* in one of his later "travel pictures," *Die Bäder von Lucca* (1830), a story that discloses two opposed strategies by which Jews can appropriate the dominant cultural ideals, one that subordinates itself to the force of those ideals and one, more subtly present in the narrative, that seeks to draw from the more positive aspects of those ideals while staving off their debilitating effects. More elaborately than *Über Polen, Die Bäder von Lucca* also discloses the dislocation and contradictory structuring of feeling that accompany attempts by German Jews to transform their position, to enlist culture to improve their social status in Germany. Ostensibly, *Die Bäder von Lucca* tells satirically of the narrator's encounter in Italy with two acculturated German Jews, the Marchese Gumpelino, formerly Gumpel, a convert to Catholicism, and his Reform Jewish servant Hirsch Hyazinth. At its core, though, Heine's travel narrative reappropriates a whole series of social and cultural conventions promoted from without and within the sphere of German Jews. It seeks thereby to show that the German-Jewish pursuit of a certain cultural disposition and the cultural capital it promises leads to dislocation and bitter disappointments. In the process, the narrative shows how linguistic and bodily expressions reveal this dislocation and undermine the newly acquired disposition.

The Marchese Gumpelino links overtly the pursuits of *Bildung* to the pursuit of a form of capital when he declares: "Geld ist rund und rollt weg, aber Bildung bleibt" (B 2: 404). He also denotes, if unconsciously, the limits of cultural and symbolic capital when he refers to Rothschild in the same context, limits marked further by the continuance of institutional constraints, and by the refusal of others to recognize the ostensibly positive transformative effects that *Bildung* has on Jews. Name changes in the story similarly point to this pursuit of *Bildung*. The awkward "Gumpel" becomes a noble romantic "Gumpelino," the Jewishly rustic "Hirsch" a Greek mythical "Hyazinth."

Yet, Gumpelino and Hirsch Hyazinth unconsciously subvert their own efforts to appear as cultivated. Asserting the social power of names, Hirsch Hyazinth notes that "in this world, it depends on how you are called," but the unnamed narrator-protagonist exposes the limits of this power. He reveals the vulnerability of such maneuvers by repeatedly referring to Hyazinth and Gumpelino as *Hirsch* Hyazinth and *Gumpel* — a vulnerability more recently explored by the linguist Dietz Bering in *Der Name als Stigma,* a study of German-Jewish name

changes (B 2: 429; Bering 246–49, 297–316). Further, Hirsch Hyazinth signals his own flawed commitment to the transformative value
of names when, upon meeting the familiar Hamburg figure of the narrator-protagonist, he is quick to reveal their former identities as well as
the purpose of assuming new names. When Hyazinth explains his following of Gumpelino to Italy — "ich tu es der Ehre wegen, und der
Bildung wegen, und wirklich, man hat Ehre bei Ihnen, und bildet
sich" — his gesture betrays him: "Bei diesem Worte putzte er sich die
Nase mit einem sehr weißen Taschentuch" (B 2: 403). Gumpelino, on
the other hand, subverts his own quest to fulfill his libidinal longings.
Absorbed in the theater of his pursuit of Lady Maxfield, Gumpelino
misses his chance to win her over (Robertson 88). More stereotypi-
cally, the narrator repeatedly focuses on how Gumpelino's nose betrays his origins.

The uncultured Jewish persona also intrudes into Hirsch Hyazinth's language, who, longing for the life left behind in Hamburg,
remembers the zoo with its tigers, bears, and "Papagoyim" (B 2: 402).
A hybrid neologism, *Papagoyim* attests to Hirsch Hyazinth's flawed,
Yiddishized German, but also puns on "parroting the goyim." It thus
points to the strategies of "becoming cultivated" he and Gumpelino
have adopted, while suggesting the dislocation such strategies produce.
Responding to that dislocation, Hirsch Hyazinth longs not for an originary, or traditional, pre-emancipatory Jewish culture but for the intimacy of Hamburg society, with its father-Gentiles and parroted
Gentiles. That longing marks the story as one not seeking to recover
an old lost order, but rather a place in the present world from which
to act, as a story that evokes disorientation and loss, but resists and
mocks the sentimental nostalgia of Romantic longings for the *Volk* and
its world. Spoken from the perspective of a first-person narrative, the
entire episode expresses many views Heine articulated elsewhere, but it
also suggests self-parody. It resembles, for instance, the poem Heine
wrote, but did not publish, in which he bitterly castigates Eduard Gans,
the brilliant Hegelian legal theorist and former leader of the *Culturverein,* for his conversion. That poem itself suggests how Heine's irony
also voiced dislocation — overtly targeting one subject, but more clan-
destinely pointing to another — something revealed only when one notes
that Gans converted several months after Heine himself (B 1: 266).

Heine was not the only writer to satirize Jews for their pursuit of
Bildung. Jews similarly became targets of satire by anti-Semites like
the actor Albert Wurm and the playwrights Karl A. B. Sessa and Julius
von Voss, who, with their popular farces, *Unser Verkehr* (1813) and

Der travestirte Nathan der Weise (1804), savagely lampooned their cultural aspirations (Neubauer 322–27, Erspamer 137). Heine's satire nonetheless differs from that of anti-Semites. Where their works sought to stigmatize and isolate, Heine seeks to point to the conflicts, contradictions, and compromises of German Jews. Heine's text also suggests the closeness of its own position to that of its satirized characters. The longings, unsophisticated behavior, and melancholic expressions voiced by Hirsch Hyazinth point to a sense of dislocation found elsewhere in Heine's writing. When Hyazinth, for instance, expresses envy for the inner happiness felt by the traditional bearded Jew Moses Lump, he echoes aspects of *Über Polen*. And *Die Bäder von Lucca* itself is a text marked by longing and melancholy from the outset (B 2: 430). Early in the story, the narrator describes Mathilde by reference to the invisible fracture in a bell made of fine metal. Though invisible, the fracture announces itself, reverberating subtly and sonorously within the sounding of the bell, a quality the narrator likens to the sadness in Mathilde's voice when, no longer young, she seeks confirmation of her beauty (B 2: 395–96). The description at the outset of the travel picture frames and marks it. The German Jews' response to *Bildung*, their striving for acceptance and improved status in Germany, resonates in *Die Bäder von Lucca* with fractures of sorrow concealed within. Heine thus reappropriates the ideal of *Bildung* to uncover the hollowness of its promise; ostensibly qualifying Jews with the disposition to succeed in German society, *Bildung* betrays itself, concealing in the image of the cultured Jew the dislocation and loss undergone by German Jews; *Bildung* conceals further the fact that it gains currency as part of the *quid pro quo* of emancipatory legislation, and thus, having emerged under these conditions, contains the terms and conditions for its own satirical treatment.

In a letter to Moses Moser, written in 1823, Heine voiced a similar sense of dislocation. Recounting to Moser a dream, Heine mocks the efforts by members of the *Verein für Cultur und Wissenschaft der Juden* to recast Jewish life and culture in terms of Hegelian philosophy:

> Du öffnetest mir Deine Freundes Arme, und sprachest mir Trost ein, und sagtest mir ich solle mir nichts zu Gemüthe führen, denn ich sey ja nur eine Idee, und um mir zu beweisen daß ich nur eine Idee sey, griffest Du hastig nach Hegels Logik und zeigtest mir eine konfuse Stelle darinn, und Gans klopfte ans Fenster, — ich aber sprang wüthend im Zimmer herum und schrie: ich bin keine Idee und weiß nichts von einer Idee und hab mein Lebtag keine Idee gehabt —
> (HSA 20: 86)

Taking up the subject again several weeks later, Heine declares to Moser his plan to write an essay on "den großen Judenschmerz" and adds:

> Um des Himmels willen, sag nicht noch einmahl daß ich bloß eine Idee sey! Ich ärgere mich toll darüber. Meinethalben könnt Ihr alle zu Ideen werden; nur laßt mich ungeschoren. Weil Du und der alte Friedländer und Gans zu Ideen geworden seyd, wollt Ihr mich jetzt auch verführen und zu einer Idee machen. (HSA 20: 97)

Such Hegelian approaches do nothing for Heine — despite his Hegelian affiliations — but rationalize the disappearance of lived Jewish culture, by asserting its preservation — or sublation — as idea within the World Spirit marching forward in history. Such approaches cannot resolve for Jews the conflict between the loss of a stable cultural location that had hitherto contributed to the survival of the Jewish people and the gains and attractions for individual Jews, not least for Heine himself, of entering European culture, especially not in a time of continued social and political disabilities and anti-Semitic outbreaks.

Like *Über Polen, Die Bäder von Lucca* does not resolve the conflicts it points to. But if *Über Polen* suggests the need to go beyond the limited and conflicting ways of conceptualizing Jewish existence in Europe, Heine's use of linguistic hybrid forms like "Hirsch Hyazinth" and "Papagoyim" now suggests an alternative approach to these conflicts and limits. By exposing the way that "low" or cast-off forms of Jewish culture and life intrude into the lives of the *gebildeten* German Jews, Heine's hybrid forms satirize Jewish adaptive strategies. They attest at the same time to the actual German-Jewish transformation underway and provide new images by which to conceptualize and express that process.

IV

With other works, like the play *Almansor* (1821), the novel fragment *Der Rabbi von Bacherach* (1824/40), and the late narrative poem "Jehuda ben Halevy" (1851), Heine again appropriates materials from Jewish and non-Jewish culture to challenge the constraints imposed in Germany on Jewish culture. At the same time, Heine sought to challenge the traditional forms of Judaism as an institutionalized religion, while modeling literary strategies for transgressing the boundaries dividing Jewish from German and, more generally, European culture.

The play *Almansor,* for instance, begins with the Moslem Almansor recounting his family's flight after the Christian siege of Granada. Almansor describes his father's preparations for departure in terms that evoke Jews going into exile, especially when, describing the Koran, he speaks of the "scroll of the law of Mohammed" (B 1: 285). While this line in the play names the Koran, its language encodes a different reference as well. The Koran is known mainly as a bound book, not a scroll, and is not considered to encode the *law* of Mohammed. The historical name that the expression "the scroll of the law" anticipates is Moses, and the book it implies is the Torah. Also known as the Mosaic law or the "five books of Moses," the Torah played a central role in the survival of Jews as a distinct people in the diaspora. Heine thus condenses in one sentence a double reference to both Islam and Judaism, evoking images of violence and expulsion that, one year after the Hep-Hep riots against Jews in Germany, suggest both Moslem attempts to survive the Christian conquest of Spain *and* the practices and forms of literacy by which Jews survived in exile. Later, in his novel fragment *Der Rabbi von Bacherach,* Heine focuses overtly on the place of Jews in Europe. Yet, in turning to Jewish materials, *Der Rabbi von Bacherach* departs from traditional Jewish culture even as it attempts to appropriate Jewish elements for German literature. Heine began *Der Rabbi von Bacherach* in the period following his involvement with the *Culturverein,* but left it unfinished. He began to work on it again after the Damascus blood libel of 1840, in which Jews were blamed for the murder of a Franciscan monk.

If *Almansor* intervenes in European literature by producing a hybrid form drawing from Islamic and Jewish culture, *Der Rabbi von Bacherach* draws elements from Jewish culture but rewrites those cultural elements by incorporating forms from European literature, and especially from the historical romances of Sir Walter Scott (Skolnik, "History" 65–72). Thus, while *Der Rabbi von Bacherach* deals with anti-Semitic events and Jewish suffering, it responds to those events and to the present conditions of Jews in Europe not by polemicizing against anti-Semitism, but rather by modeling cultural forms that defy and exceed German cultural norms. It seeks thereby to transform the symbolic function of Jewish images in European culture, but also to transform Jewish culture by enlisting European literary forms.

Der Rabbi von Bacherach enlists a series of strategies to pursue this change. It plays, for instance, with narrative focus in ways that first evoke, then challenge the image of Jewish culture as exotic. At the outset of the first and second chapters, the narrative focuses broadly on European town- and cityscapes, then shifts to Jewish actors in those contexts. The first chapter begins by giving a broad view of the town of Bacherach, seeking briefly to convey the present fallen condition of the town while pointing to its once vibrant past. That past presents imagery drawn from historical romances, but it appears, additionally, to precede the blood libel against the Jews of Bacherach, a persecution arising in the wake of the crusades and, though never stated directly, perhaps reducing Bacherach to its current state of darkness and decay. The second chapter similarly opens by focusing broadly on the great medieval city of Frankfurt am Main, viewed by Abraham and his wife Sara as they approach the city by boat along the Main. They land, oddly in high spirits, wondering at the city's splendor and plunging into the midst of its bustling docks and markets (B 1: 474–76). Heine evokes this image of urban excitement only to explode any suggestion that it expresses a unitary, unconflicted world. The narrative soon refocuses on the darker images of Jewish conditions embedded within the city. The imperial capital, for instance, confines its Jews to a ghetto, demanding payment for their residential privileges in the form of five thousand rats' tails each year (B 1: 475, 479). Heine's lighthearted treatment of these conditions and his presenting Abraham in high spirits, although the rabbi has just abandoned his community to almost certain death, has provoked criticism of the story's lack of plausibility (e.g. Sammons, *Elusive Poet* 308–9; Prawer 95, 400). Yet these images point nonetheless to a darker side of the story, its awareness of the way deep-rooted assumptions about culture limit the possibilities for Jews in Germany. Whatever its failings — and Heine did ultimately abandon the novel fragment — the second chapter's lightheartedness thus makes more sense if one considers Heine's struggle to transgress literary and cultural boundaries. As the story defies the boundary between Jewish and German culture, it also defies the conventional distinction between tragedy and comedy, striving to produce a narrative form in which one plays off the other. The lighthearted atmosphere helps, for instance, to set the context for the shock at the chapter's end, when Sara, upon hearing the names of her murdered friends and relatives read out at the synagogue, collapses (B 1: 493–94).

The second chapter's shift in focus points to yet another way in which Heine seeks to interweave elements drawn from Jewish and mainstream European culture. In shifting from the initial broad view of the city to the contained world of the ghetto and further to the synagogue, and, still further, to the personal lives of the characters, the narrative zeroes in on the intimate sphere of Jewish life, but contrasts it with the initial exoticizing view of the Jewish world. That movement into the intimate sphere of the Jewish world corresponds further to the story's movement in the scene depicting the seder, an event constructed in terms that exoticize it, but that also undermine the aura of the exotic by shifting to an intimate view of an environment ultimately made familiar. The narrator produces this image of the seder as something exotic and romantic by describing it as an ancient and wondrous event, occupying a space adorned with silk cloth and gold fringes, radiant tableware and goblets — an event that is invested with meaning by the symbolic foods and wine to be consumed by black-cloaked men in yarmulkes and women adorned in splendorous glitter (B 1: 465–66). Heine gives this event a mood, "[w]ehmütig heiter, ernsthaft spielend und märchenhaft geheimnisvoll," and transforms the central text of the event, the Passover Haggada, into a romantic adventure, "eine seltsame Mischung ... von Sagen der Vorfahren, Wundergeschichten aus Ägypten, kuriosen Erzählungen, [rabbinischen] Streitfragen, Gebeten und Festliedern" (B 1: 465).

At the same time, the narrator invests the seder with the aura of intimacy: the "Hausfrau" lighting the candles, the gathering of relatives, friends, and the rabbi's students, and the rabbi's reading of the Haggada to this familiar audience. The story also limits the use of Hebrew terms, relying on German expressions to translate the rituals, symbols, and Haggadic tales. In these ways, it seeks to make the exotic familiar, a familiarizing that nonetheless depends on the aura of the exotic conveyed initially. The same strategy determines the description of the seder as an "Abendfeier" and "Abendmahlzeit," terms stemming from the Christian tradition. In this way, Heine retains the notion of Jewish difference, but subverts both the negative value attaching to that difference and the notion of its absolute foreignness.

In rewriting the seder further, Heine's story also draws from its ritual practice to reflect on the role of reading and writing in cultural change and survival. It presents reading as a practice, embedded in a specific culture and focused on a specific text, that invents and reinvents the past, investing the present moment with the status and power of a transformative event. Reading from the Haggada to an audience of family and friends, the Rabbi appears in a scripted role as ritual reader and "Hausvater." Responding in chorus, collectively repeating the reader's words, the audience produces a tone "so schauervoll innig, so mütterlich einlullend, und zugleich so hastig aufweckend" that it transforms and penetrates even to the emotional core of apostates (B 1: 465). The rabbi and his congregants give the seder a power and immediacy that exceed the present moment, linking the present event to the past and the future. That event derives its force by reference to the past, even as it marks its distance from that past, marking as well its dependence on the act of reading itself.

This image of reading stands in relation to Heine's rewriting of the Haggada. That rewriting refuses to view Jewish history as an act of submission to God or any other authority. It focuses instead on those events linked to rebellion, beginning with Abraham's revolt against his father's idols — the foundational event in Jewish history — proceeding to the canonical story of exodus from Egyptian bondage, and concluding with arrival in the promised land. It all the while de-emphasizes the accounts in the Haggada of the plagues imposed on Egypt, their multiplication by rabbinical authorities, and the appeal to God in his omnipotence to pour out his wrath on non-Jews. Heine thus emplots Jewish history as a series of revolts against authority, rather than as appeals to authority, and as attempts to re-define human relations rather than to merely invert hierarchies of power. The Rabbi of Bacherach himself, named for the patriarch Abraham, stands within this tradition, having broken out from the constraints of his small German town to study in Spain, where he acquired great learning, but also, according to rumor, a free spirit. Heine deviates from the Haggadic text not because he lacked profound knowledge of Jewish texts and tradition, which he did,[7] but because that rewriting allows him to model two possible responses to Jewish history: submitting oneself to tradition and its oppressive tendencies, as do Bacherach's "graybeards" spreading their rumors, or appropriating that history to continue a practice of revolt and self-assertion, as does Rabbi Abraham. Revolt does not preclude commitment, for instance, to the group reading practice or to the text that is read, a commitment also symbolically conveyed by the story of the binding of Isaac, which marks the beginning of God's covenant with the Jewish people, and which, deviating again from standard Jewish practice, is read in Heine's story at synagogue the day after the seder.[8] Revolt does, though, amount here to appropriating a model, rewriting it in response to present conditions and one's sense of what the present demands.

More to the point, the story traces its license to rewrite the Haggada and Jewish ritual back to the form of the Haggada itself, if not necessarily to its contents. By presenting the Haggada as an accumulated mix of genres, prayers, commentaries, and so forth, Heine rejects any notion of the Haggada as a monologic text, viewing it instead as a multivalent work that rewrites and interweaves past events and the discursive responses they evoked. Heine's own act of rewriting, of deviating from the model and producing a hybrid text, appears at the same time as a sign of commitment to the discursive practice of the Haggada. Even more, by describing the Haggada in the terms of German and European poetics, but also presenting Jewish readers engaged in the group reading practice of the seder, *Der Rabbi von Bacherach* seeks to elevate the status of the Haggada and of Jewish practices in German and European culture. And in elevating the status of the Haggada and of a ritualized Jewish reading practice, Heine seeks to transform the symbolic function of Jewish culture in Germany, giving it new value while striving to retain an image of its difference.

V

Where *Der Rabbi von Bacherach* enlists a European narrative form to transform the symbolic function in German culture of a Jewish religious text and Jewish practices, Heine's long, narrative poem "Jehuda ben Halevy" raises questions about how poetic works, in general, and Sephardic or Spanish Jewish poetry in particular, are transmitted, exploring directly the role of power in that transmission process.

In the third part of "Jehuda ben Halevy," the speaker of the poem digresses from his story, which focuses mainly on the Sephardic poet Jehuda Halevi, but also on the poets Salomon Gabirol and Ibn Esra. The speaker begins to recount the history of the transmission of a string of pearls that Alexander of Macedonia appropriated after the Battle of Arabella (B 6.1: 142–44). The pearls had once been presented as a gift to the Queen Atossia; Alexander now gives them to a beautiful Corinthian dancer who wears them in her hair, thereby incorporating them in a fiery Bacchanalian dance that lights up the victory celebration. After the dancer's death sometime later, the pearls are auctioned off, whereupon they pass continuously from the hands of one figure of power in one culture to those of another, eventually traveling halfway around the world and landing, not without some irony, around the neck of the Baroness Rothschild. At each station, the pearls' owner invests them with a new function or wears them decoratively at the site of one abuse of power or another, generating a series of images that presage Walter Benjamin's oft only partially quoted remark: "There is no work of art which is not at the same time a document of barbarism. And just as such a document is not free of barbarism, barbarism taints also the manner in which it was transmitted from one owner to another," where the reference to the work's transmission is generally omitted.[9]

The images in the pearls' history include, among other things, Cleopatra making a fool of Anthony, and Abderam the Third fatally stabbing an opponent in a sports competition. But perhaps the most powerful image is that of the Catholic Queens of Spain during the Inquisition who don the pearls for various festivities, not least the autos-da-fé,

> Wo sie, auf Balkonen sitzend,
> Sich erquickten am Geruche
> Von gebratnen alten Juden. (B 6.1: 144)

— whence the irony of the pearls' ultimate arrival in the possession of the Baroness Rothschild. The poem symbolically links the pearls with poetry when it shows Alexander removing them from a container and replacing them with "die Lieder / Des ambrosischen Homeros." The narrator of the poem wishes, in addition, to use the same container to house the poems of Jehuda Halevi, which he refers to as "teardrop pearls" a reference taken from a contemporary of Jehuda Halevi's named Al Charisi. Al Charisi is cited in a study known to Heine, where he describes Jehuda Halevi's works as "a string of pearls" that hangs as an ornament around the head of the community (B 6.1: 147, 151; Sachs 287).

By focusing on the uses and abuses made of the pearls and on Alexander's own attempt to appropriate, isolate, and literally contain Homeric verse, Heine's poem points to appropriation as the rule governing the way works of art are transmitted, but it also seeks to show how poetry can exceed the constraints imposed upon it.[10] It does so by re-appropriating the earlier images of Jehuda Halevi Heine encountered and removing them from a theologically centered discourse. As in *Der Rabbi von Bacherach,* Heine seeks in this late poem to transform elements of Jewish culture. He seeks to integrate them into a poetic practice that, despite growing bitterness in the "Matratzengruft," the departure from his earlier more overtly political writing, and the religious elements of his later poetry, nonetheless opposes a withdrawal inward away from the secular world and the world of politics.

The principal, though not sole, source for Heine's knowledge of Jehuda Halevi's life was Michael Sachs's 1845 study *Die religiöse Poesie der Juden in Spanien,* which provided historical accounts of the various Sephardic poets; this book was also the principal source for Heine's knowledge of Jehuda Halevi's poetry, since it contains in anthology form the first translations into German of that poetry, and Heine's knowledge of Hebrew was insufficient to read it in the original. Heine derived his knowledge of Jehuda Halevi from Sachs's presentation, but his response to that presentation is significant perhaps less for what he takes from Sachs, the point on which criticism tends to focus, than for the ways he rewrites the image of the Sephardic poet for purposes other than those of the translator-historian Sachs (Tabak 52–53).

By providing a literary history in German of the medieval Hebrew poets of Spain and by appending 140 pages of their religious poetry in German translation, Sachs sought to intervene in the mid-nineteenth-century discourse on Jews, Jewish religion, and German culture. He also broke new ground in the newly invented fields of "Jewish litera-ture" and the academic study of Judaism or *Wissenschaft des Juden-tums.* The question presents itself: how did Sachs seek to intervene in this discourse and what image of Jehuda Halevi did he construct? — this question is central as well to understanding the function of Heine's own poetic intervention.

Although little is known about the life of Jehuda Halevi, Sachs constructed a life of the poet consisting of a series of events marked by a search for closeness to God. It is not surprising when Sachs notes that Jehuda Halevi embarks on his journey to Jerusalem because he seeks, like the ancient prophets before him, to be "close to God," since that was generally the only reason that Jews went to Jerusalem in the Middle Ages. Yet, by inscribing Jehuda Halevi in the context of the prophets, Sachs also seeks to invest his poetry with a visionary quality reminiscent of those who, like Jeremiah, foresaw the tragic fate of the ancient Hebrews (293). More problematically, Sachs implies that all of Jehuda Halevi's poetry was written in "ardor for the di-vine," and consists primarily of praising God and fulfilling his com-mandments (304, 306). For his translation, Sachs selects 11 poems, all devotional, from the entire corpus that was available to him. The ini-tial lines of the poems inscribe these works repeatedly within a relig-ious framework that confirms Sachs's assertion: "O herrliche, ein Strahl aus Gottes Licht" or "O Gott! Wo find' ich dich?" and "O wär' ich / Ein Knecht, dem Herrn gehörig!" (poems 2, 3, and 7, 92, 93, 99). The reader of Sachs's book would never know that religious poetry represents only about a quarter of Jehuda Halevi's entire known cor-pus or that Sachs's historical account of the poet, who is known today not least for his secular poetry, provides only a fragmentary image of Jehuda Halevi's intellectual and spiritual development (Scheindlin 43, 118–27). That Jehuda Halevi also wrote poetry expressing his passion for wine, not the divinity, would not occur to the German reader of the poet, until a later translator eventually introduced this excluded

Other into the German language with, for instance, the following lines:

> Begeisterung quilt mir aus dem Kruge
> Hebt mich empor auf Liedes Schwingen
> O Süße Lust bei jedem Zuge!
> Die Lippe schlürft, der Mund muß singen.
>
> (*Diwan* 143)

Sachs focused on the religious Jehuda Halevi, because he perceived the newest and strongest threat to Jewish life not in the malicious manipulations of certain antagonistic Christian scholars, but in the far worse "boasters and slanderers of the teachings of their faith" among the Jews themselves, among whom he counts "the heroes of the word and the pen" (xix), a reference that suggests figures like Heinrich Heine and Ludwig Börne, among others.

Heine's poetic appropriation of Jehuda Halevi departs radically from the theological focus given by Sachs. "God" makes only a few appearances, primarily as the force whose grace instills the poet with genius in a literary figure that appears to place Heine's conception of God closer to that of Feuerbach's in *Das Wesen des Christentums* than to those found in any organized Western religion.[11] Heine departs from Sachs in another, perhaps obvious but no less significant way. Unlike Sachs, Heine constructs a narrative poem that ostentatiously collapses the distinction between poetry and history, a distinction *ostensibly* maintained, but *actually* blurred in Sachs's own partial rewriting of Jehuda Halevi, Sachs's claims to the contrary notwithstanding.

Unlike Sachs, Heine thus self-consciously appropriates historical facts for a fictional narrative poem. He cites for instance the fact that Jehuda Halevi embarked on a journey to Jerusalem, but invents the story of his religious education in Talmud and Torah, a quite plausible event, but into which Heine injects a more speculative innovation about the poet's interests. In this connection, Heine further appropriates a distinction between Halacha and Aggada made by the German-Jewish scholar Leopold Zunz, an act that allows Heine to reflect the centrality of narrative invention for his own poetic practice.[12] One might note in passing that Zunz also devoted much time to uncovering Sephardic poetry, showing that it constituted much of the synagogue liturgy, and presenting it in terms that would show Jewish religious tradition to have a poetry corresponding to the poetic norms of contemporary European literature, although Zunz's major works on the subject only appeared after Heine's poem.[13] More relevant here, the narrator ascribes to Jehuda Halevi a disinclination toward Halacha, the strict legalistic interpretation of scripture, and an inclination toward Aggada, the fictional stories that provide a more imaginative engagement with scripture.[14] By introducing these terms, Heine further develops in German poetry a repertoire of Jewish cultural allusions that he simultaneously synthesizes with aspects of Romantic poetics that appealed to him, the focus on irony and poetic power, as expressed, for instance, in his remarks on Goethe and Tieck in *Die Romantische Schule* (B 3: 421–30). Unlike certain Romantics, though, Heine does not enlist poetic irony to uphold an idealistic conception of poetry as a world solipsistically enclosed within the confines of its own impermeable boundaries, but includes various images of violence that lead beyond the text of "Jehuda ben Halevy" and into the world.

Violence marks the poem, afflicting both Jews and poets. Poets are linked, moreover, to the Yiddish word "Schlemihl," for which the speaker concocts a fictional etymology by appropriating the biblical story of Phinehas, the first in the line of the ancient priests. Phinehas saved Israel by slaying the man who provoked God's wrath by bringing a Midianite woman into Israel's house (Numbers 25: 7–8, 12–13). In Heine's rewriting, Phinehas's spear misses the man and kills an innocent bystander named Schlemihl, from whom all poets are descended, an account that introduces an element of black humor into the poem. Where Heine failed in *Der Rabbi von Bacherach* to successfully mix darker and comic images, he succeeds here, perhaps because this tale, transgressing the boundaries between comic and tragic discourse, does not negate either one or the other, but places them each in tension with one another. But by constructing a fictional referential framework that consists of a fabricated biblical story and invented etymology, each communicated by popular oral transmission, this section does more than disturb such generic boundaries. The poem models how a fictional work can in its transmission produce real effects insofar as the audience-narrators who hear and retell the story invest it with truth value, or derive new truths of their own from its telling and retelling. While the story appears to allegorize ahistorically the incarnation of fanatical violence, suggesting its descent from biblical times and turning poets into the eternal innocent bystander-victims, its focus on the role of a story's audience and transmitters points to the fact that forces, violent and otherwise, beyond the poet's control structure and constrain poetic activity.

Elsewhere, the poem links more specifically the vulnerable position of poets to that of Jews in exile, even to the point of collapsing the distinction between poet and Jew. The poet Ibn Esra is enslaved by Tartars; Jehuda Halevi is murdered by a Saracen while standing in the ruins of Jerusalem; and Salomon Gabirol is murdered by a Moor envious of his poetic talent. These images point to the referential aspect of the poem, the concern with the history of anti-Semitism, most immediately, the Damascus affair of 1840 noted earlier. Similarly, the reference to Phinehas points to the violence perpetrated by those who punish the transgressors of national or religious boundaries, or even the traditional order, thus evoking however indirectly the suppression of the 1848 uprisings.

Yet, "Jehuda ben Halevy" also suggests that what is contained can reassert itself, that poems and literary figures can exceed the constraints imposed upon them, transgressing the boundaries imposed by cultures, conventions (poetic and otherwise), powerful authorities, and others who seek to control their circulation. The pearls circulating among figures of power ultimately outlive each of their possessors. Jehuda Halevi's poetry survives the passing of the Sephardic Middle Ages and the expulsion from Spain, providing material from which future poets can draw to produce new images by which they seek to grasp and engage with the world.

In citing Psalm 137, Heine seeks to exceed traditional boundaries, to inscribe within his own text an earlier text, but make it in turn responsive to present conditions. When quoted at the outset of the second section, Psalm 137 signifies the sorrow of exile stemming from biblical times and recurring into the present:

> Bei den Wassern Babels saßen
> Wir und weinten, unsre Harfen
> Lehnten an den Trauerweiden —
> Kennst du noch das alte Lied?
>
> Kennst du noch die alte Weise,
> Die im Anfang so elegisch
> Greint und sumset, wie ein Kessel,
> Welcher auf dem Herde kocht?
>
> Lange schon, jahrtausendlange
> Kochts in mir. Ein dunkles Wehe!
> Und die Zeit leckt meine Wunde,
> Wie der Hund die Schwären Hiobs.
> (B 6.1: 135)

The speaker's intruding voice in the last line of the first stanza juxtaposes the colloquial "Kennst Du noch das alte Lied?" with the biblical passage, mixing biblical and colloquial registers, something the poem does again when it describes the salving effects of time on the poet's wounds in terms of the dog licking the wounds of Job. If the citing of the psalm first suggests an archetypal and transhistorical view of exile, the colloquial utterance makes the passage urgent and immediate. It suggests Heine's own pain at the failed attempts to transform European culture and society, no less than the pain from wounds inflicted by disease on his ravished body. But as a poetic act, this mixing of registers and reference also suggests how poetry can transgress traditional boundaries to respond to pain, loss, and the rule of arbitrary power and violence. Various images late in the poem echo this response. The fig tree that Salomon Gabirol's death gives rise to betrays his murderer; the mournful song Ibn Esra sings persuades his captors to liberate him; and — in an even more fantastic vein — Jehuda Halevi's murderer, says "an ancient legend," turns out to be an angel sent to call the poet to heaven.

While such images may suggest a search for compensation in poetry, they suggest more powerfully Heine's search for a poetry that marks moments of loss, but that in the act of marking also models possible responses to loss. This search and the writing strategies Heine develops suggest further his awareness of Bourdieu's suggestion, cited earlier, that writers are "owners of a dominated form of power at the interior of the sphere of power." With this awareness, Heine pursued a practice of writing that denotes the kinds of constraints imposed on writers and poetic invention. At the same time, he appropriates and transforms elements from different cultural spheres, modeling ways to exceed those constraints. What distinguishes Heine's work on Jewish figures is his pursuit of a writing strategy that responds both to the position of writers in the social field and to the position of Jews in German culture. In seeking to transform the symbolic functions of Jews and Jewish culture in German literature, he thus also responds to problems of writing, literary conventions and the cultured or *gebildeten* reader; and in seeking to invest his own writing with new social and cultural functions, he also seeks to transform the socially symbolic value of Jewish texts and reading practices. In this way, Heine appropriates elements from the Jewish sphere to generate within German literature a repertoire of Jewish cultural allusions and a new Jewish cultural space, a space occurring beyond the sphere of traditional Jewish culture, but at the interior of the sphere of German culture. While partaking of German culture, Heine's transformed image of Jewish culture challenges from within the way German culture associates with power, hence the role of Jewish figures in *Deutschland* and, on a more general level, the metapoetic moments of "Jehuda ben Halevy." Such moments point toward the conditions in which poetic works must contend and the powers that shape their transmission. But in seeking to dismantle the cultural hierarchies dominant in Germany, this challenge also seeks to link Jews and writing in Germany, suggesting the mutual dependence of finding a new place for Jews and new roles for writers within German culture.

Notes

* I wish to thank Ralph Cohen and Katherine Arens for their comments on earlier versions of this article.

[1] To note this structural affinity is not to dispute the fact the two groups, Jews and non-Jewish Germans, have historically occupied different positions vis-à-vis structures of power in Germany. With regard to Heine and Jewish identity, one might also note here the cautious formulation by one prominent historian writing in what is meant to be the current standard history of German Jewry: noting Heine's distance from organized religion, Michael Meyer nonetheless claims his writings as "the most important contribution to German literary culture [until Kafka] made by anyone who was born a Jew" ("Becoming German, Remaining Jewish," *German-Jewish History in Modern Times,* vol. 2, ed. Michael A. Meyer and Michael Brenner [New York: Columbia UP, 1996], 208). Robert Holub similarly describes Heine as a "German poet of Jewish origin," while problematizing more simplistic attempts to grasp Heine's complex self-understanding (*Deutscher Dichter jüdischer Herkunft,* 44–50).

[2] The feminist critic Susan Gubar, a critic whose reputation rests not least on her relating texts to relations of power, recently addressed the problem of identity and fictional texts: "in the case of fiction . . . writers *are* free to select a racial identity at odds with the one they were assigned at birth" as attested, for instance, by the fact that "the best-selling Native-American classic *Education of Little Tree* was actually composed by the KKK author of Governor George Wallace's 'Segregation now . . . Segregation tomorrow . . . Segregation forever' speech" ("Women Artists and Contemporary Race Changes," *Critical Condition: Feminism at the Turn of the Century.* [New York: Columbia UP, 2000], 30).

[3] Heine employed such strategies in other works as well, and they perhaps explain somewhat why Heine's works defy explanations that seek to ground themselves in one essential or univocal authorial position. Indeed, the view that Heine produced a range of complex and, at times, contradictory responses to questions of society, politics, and poetics has quite a few adherents, who often otherwise advocate quite diverse and even opposed approaches to Heine's work. For a small sample, see E. M. Butler, *The Saint-Simonian Religion in Germany: A Study of the Young German Movement* (1926; rpt. New York: Fertig, 1968), 129; Jeffrey Sammons,

"Who Did Heine Think He Was?" *Heinrich Heine's Contested Identities: Politics, Religion, and Nationalism in Nineteenth-Century Germany,* ed. Jost Hermand and Robert Holub, German Life and Civilization 26 (New York: Lang, 1999), 17–18, and elsewhere; Sander L. Gilman, *Jewish Self-Hatred: Anti-Semitism and the Hidden Language of the Jews* (Baltimore and London: Johns Hopkins UP, 1986), 182–83, 187; and Peter Uwe Hohendahl, "Heine's Critical Intervention: The Intellectual as Poet," *Heinrich Heine's Contested Identities,* ed. Jost Hermand and Robert C. Holub, 8. On the subject of Heine's identity, my own view differs from that presented by Hans Mayer and critically explored by Sammons. For Mayer, it suggests the image of Kaspar Hauser, devoid of a past and having to invent himself, which Heine accordingly does by appropriating different traditions at will, without being determined by one specific past or tradition that shapes the self (*Von Lessing bis Thomas Mann: Wandlungen der bürgerlichen Literatur in Deutschland* [Württemberg: Neske, 1959], 275–76). Sammons views Heine's attempt to construct himself as a source of strength at times, but as ultimately narcissistic, and as accounting for Heine's repeated frustrations in his dealings with people (17–18). One might, however, revise the question to focus not on *whether* one invents oneself, but rather on how one negotiates the resistance to such attempts at invention. Heine's failure to acknowledge those resistances may indeed be narcissistic, but it does not necessarily follow from the attempt to invent oneself by appropriating different traditions, but rather from the failure to recognize others and develop refined mechanisms for assessing what is possible and what not; Heine succeeded at this more in his poetry and prose, despite some foolish exceptions (most notably, the attacks on Platen and Börne) than in other aspects of his life.

[4] To a certain degree, I view appropriation in terms similar to those by which Robert Holub understands reception in his 1981 study, *Heinrich Heine's Reception of German Grecophilia: The Function and Application of the Hellenic Tradition in the First Half of the Nineteenth Century,* Reihe Siegen Beiträge zur Literatur- und Sprachwissenschaft 27 (Heidelberg: Carl Winter, 1981), especially his focus on "what [Heine] . . . did with the knowledge which he had obtained, how he utilized this most important heritage [of classical Greece] to propagate his goals and opinions" (15). I wish, however, to stress an added sociocultural dimension. Heine, in this case, appropriates not what was viewed as an important part of German heritage, but cultural forms and traditions that, in early nineteenth-century Germany, possessed little of what Bourdieu calls "symbolic capital" — social recognition or accumulated prestige — and "cultural capital," the skills, dispositions, practices, habits, etc., whose mastery helps one to determine what makes something socially and culturally acceptable and to gain, for oneself or one's group, social acceptance and distinction. Bourdieu stresses the important role played by artistic appropriation in the pursuit of cultural capital. On symbolic capital see Bourdieu, *Language and Symbolic Power,* ed. and intro. John B. Thompson, trans. Gino Raymond and Matthew Adamson (Cambridge: Harvard UP, 1991), 14, 106; on cultural capital, see Bourdieu, *Distinction: A Social Critique of the Judgement of Taste,* trans. Richard Nice (Cambridge: Harvard UP, 1984), here, especially 92–96; 281–83.

[5] Gilman, *Jewish Self-Hatred* 173–74; Steven Aschheim argues subtly that Heine's essay represents a conflicted pejorative description together with a longing for wholeness of the lost world represented by Polish Jews (*Brothers and Strangers: The East European Jew in German and German Jewish Consciousness, 1800–1923* [Madison: U of Wisconsin P, 1982], 185, 187). Tracing trends in artistic and literary production, and the collection of artefacts, Richard I. Cohen finds in such works a nostalgia for the ghetto, but, drawing on Prawer, locates this turn only in the late Heine of the *Geständnisse* ("Nostalgia and 'return to the ghetto': A Cultural Phenomenon in Western and Central Europe," *Assimilation and Community: The Jews in Nineteenth-Century Europe*, ed. Jonathan Frankel and Steven J. Zipperstein [Cambridge: Cambridge UP, 1992], 159).

[6] S. S. Prawer, *Heine's Jewish Comedy: A Study of his Portraits of Jews and Judaism* (Oxford: Clarendon, 1983), 64–66; George L. Mosse and David Sorkin both stress the importance of *Bildung* for German Jews, arguing its centrality to the constitution of a German-Jewish subculture (Mosse, *German Jews Beyond Judaism* [Bloomington: Indiana UP, and Cincinnati: Hebrew Union College P, 1985], 7–10; David Sorkin, *The Transformation of German Jewry, 1780–1840* [New York: Oxford UP, 1987], 5, 21–33, 84–99, 172–77).

[7] This lack of knowledge did not prevent Heine from having his friend Moses Moser translate the *Haggada* for him; nor did it prevent him from reading extensively to write the story (Ludwig Rosenthal, *Heinrich Heine als Jude* [Frankfurt am Main: Ullstein, 1973], 168–69).

[8] The Torah portion dealing with the binding of Isaac is traditionally read in the synagogue at Rosh Hashana, not Passover. The story, recounted in Genesis 22: 1–19, attests to the covenant between the Patriarch Abraham, willing to sacrifice his only son at God's command, and God, sending the angel to stay Abraham's hand at the last moment.

[9] Walter Benjamin, "Theses on the Philosophy of History," *Illuminations*, ed. Hannah Arendt, trans. Harry Zohn (1968; rpt. Schocken: New York, 1985), 256. The suggestion by Karlheinz Fingerhut that the pearls become transformed into bourgeois commodity seems to me less credible (Fingerhut, "Spanische Spiegel: Heinrich Heines Verwendung spanischer Geschichte und Literatur zur Selbstreflexion des Juden und des Dichters," *Heine-Jahrbuch* 31 [1992]: 128); their transmission occurs by many routes, and their treatment as commodities to be bought and sold is hardly mentioned; additionally, the pearls are repeatedly found in the possession of various powerful figures, not only of the bourgeoisie.

[10] Compare Roger Cook's comments on Heine's situating his own poetic persona in what Cook calls the "expanded tradition of the great Sephardic poets." Cook draws from the work of Kristeva to suggest that Heine finds in that tradition a potential for opposing the "constraining, legislative, and socializing elements" of the unitary subject (*By the Rivers of Babylon: Heinrich Heine's Late Songs and Reflections* [Detroit: Wayne State UP, 1998], 333). I focus here more on the constraints imposed by social and cultural institutions and conventions, but seek similarly to show that Heine finds in this tradition potential for opposition to those constraints.

[11] The last of the three poems that constitute the "Hebräische Melodien," "Disputation," points to this rejection of institutionalized religion, a rejection acerbically suggested by the concluding word that comments on rabbi and monk alike: "sie alle beide stinken" (B 6.1: 172).

[12] See Leopold Zunz's groundbreaking study of Midrash and Aggada, *Die gottesdienstlichen Vorträge der Juden,* published in 1832 (44, 61).

[13] See Leopold Zunz's *Die synagogale Poesie des Mittelalters* (1855: 231–37), *Literaturgeschichte der Synagogalen Poesie* (1865: 203–7), and "Israels Gottesdienstliche Poesie" (1870: 130–32).

[14] Heine follows the older tradition of transliterating Aggada as "Haggada." To prevent confusion with the specific case of the Passover Haggada, I am following here the current standard practice of transliterating the term as "Aggada."

Works Cited

Adorno, Theodor W. "Die Wunde Heine." *Noten zur Literatur.* Vol. 11 of *Gesammelte Schriften.* Ed. Rolf Tiedemann. Frankfurt am Main: Suhrkamp, 1974. 95–100. 20 vols. 1970–1986.

Aschheim, Steven. *Brothers and Strangers: The East European Jew in German and German Jewish Consciousness, 1800–1923.* Madison: U of Wisconsin P, 1982.

Benjamin, Walter. "Theses on the Philosophy of History." *Illuminations.* Ed. Hannah Arendt. Trans. Harry Zohn. 1968. Schocken: New York, 1985.

Bourdieu, Pierre. *Distinction: A Social Critique of the Judgement of Taste.* Trans. Richard Nice. Cambridge: Harvard UP, 1984.

———. "Field of Power, Literary Field and Habitus." *The Field of Cultural Production.* Ed. Randal Johnson. Trans. Richard Nice, Claud du Verlie et al. 1993. 161–75.

———. *Language and Symbolic Power.* Ed. and intro. John B. Thompson. Trans. Gino Raymond and Matthew Adamson. Cambridge: Harvard UP, 1991.

Butler, E. M. *The Saint-Simonian Religion in Germany: A Study of the Young German Movement.* 1926. New York: Fertig, 1968.

Chartier, Roger. *Forms and Meanings: Texts, Performances, and Audiences from Codex to Computer.* New Cultural Studies. Philadelphia: U of Pennsylvania P, 1995.

Cohen, Richard I. "Nostalgia and 'return to the ghetto': A Cultural Phenomenon in Western and Central Europe." *Assimilation and Community: The Jews in Nineteenth-Century Europe.* Ed. Jonathan Frankel and Steven J. Zipperstein. Cambridge: Cambridge UP, 1992. 130–55.

Cook, Roger F. *By the Rivers of Babylon: Heinrich Heine's Late Songs and Reflections.* Detroit: Wayne State UP, 1998.

von Dohm, Christian Konrad Wilhelm. *Über die bürgerliche Verbesserung der Juden.* Hildesheim and New York: Georg Olms, 1973. Reprint in one volume of the two parts published in Berlin and Stettin, 1781–1783.

Ferguson, Niall. Introduction. *Virtual History: Alternatives and Counterfactuals.* Ed. Niall Ferguson. 1997. Cambridge: Papermae, 1998. 1–90.

Fingerhut, Karlheinz. "Spanische Spiegel: Heinrich Heines Verwendung spanischer Geschichte und Literatur zur Selbsreflexion des Juden und des Dichters." *Heine-Jahrbuch* 31 (1992): 106–36.

Foucault, Michel. "The Discourse on Language." *The Archaeology of Knowledge.* Trans. A. M. Sheridan Smith. New York: Pantheon, 1972.

Friedländer, David. *Ueber die Verbesserung der Israeliten im Königreich Pohlen.* Berlin: Nicolaischen Buchhandlung, 1819.

Geiger, Ludwig. *Die Juden und die deutsche Literatur.* Berlin: Georg Reimer, 1910.

Gilman, Sander L. *Jewish Self-Hatred: Anti-Semitism and the Hidden Language of the Jews.* Baltimore and London: Johns Hopkins UP, 1986.

Gilman, Sander L., and Peter Hohendahl. Introduction. *Heinrich Heine and the Occident: Multiple Identities, Multiple Receptions.* Ed. Peter Uwe Hohendahl and Sander L. Gilman. Lincoln: U of Nebraska P, 1991. 1–18.

Goldstein, Bluma. "Heine's 'Hebrew Melodies': A Politics and Poetics of Diaspora." *Heinrich Heine's Contested Identities: Politics, Religion, and Nationalism in Nineteenth-Century Germany.* Ed. Jost Hermand and Robert Holub. German Life and Civilization 26. New York: Peter Lang, 1999. 49–68.

Greenberg, Martin. "Heinrich Heine: Flight and Return. The Fallacy of Being Only a Human Being." *Commentary* 7 (1949): 225–31.

Gubar, Susan. "Women Artists and Contemporary Race Changes." *Critical Condition: Feminism at the Turn of the Century.* New York: Columbia UP, 2000. 21–44.

Hermand, Jost. *Der frühe Heine: Ein Kommentar zu den Reisebildern.* Munich: Winkler, 1976.

Holub, Robert C. "Deutscher Dichter jüdischer Herkunft." *Ich Narr des Glücks: Heinrich Heine 1797–1856. Bilder einer Ausstellung.* Ed. Joseph A. Kruse. Stuttgart and Weimar: Metzler, 1997.

———. *Heinrich Heine's Reception of German Grecophilia: The Function and Application of the Hellenic Tradition in the First Half of the Nineteenth Century.* Reihe Siegen Beiträge zur Literatur- und Sprachwissenschaft 27. Heidelberg: Carl Winter, 1981.

Jehuda Halevi. *Diwan des Jehuda Halevi: Eine Auswahl in deutschen Ueber-tragungen.* Trans. Abraham Geiger, Moritz Steinschneider, et al. Berlin: Schildberger, 1893.

Katz, Jacob. *Out of the Ghetto: The Social Background of Jewish Emancipation, 1770–1870.* Cambridge: Harvard UP, 1973.

Koopmann, Helmut. "Nachtgedanken zu Heinrich Heines Gedicht 'Denk' ich an Deutschland in der Nacht.'" *Von Dichtung und Musik: "Heinrich Heine." Ein Lesebuch.* Internationale Hugo-Wolf-Akademie für Gesang Dichtung Liedkunst. Tutzing: Schneider, 1995. 39–61.

Lutz, Edith. *Der "Verein für Cultur und Wissenschaft der Juden" und sein Mitglied Heinrich Heine.* Heine-Studien. Stuttgart and Weimar: Metzler, 1997.

Mayer, Hans. *Von Lessing bis Thomas Mann: Wandlungen der bürgerlichen Literatur in Deutschland.* Württemberg: Neske, 1959.

Meyer, Michael A. "Becoming German, Remaining Jewish," *German-Jewish History in Modern Times.* Ed. Michael A. Meyer and Michael Brenner. Vol. 2. New York: Columbia UP, 1996. 199–250. 2 vols.

Mosse, George L. *German Jews Beyond Judaism.* Bloomington: Indiana UP, and Cincinnati: Hebrew Union College P, 1985.

———. *The Nationalization of the Masses: Political Symbolism and Mass Movements in Germany from the Napoleonic Wars through the Third Reich.* Ithaca and London: Cornell UP, 1975, 1991.

Neubauer, Hans-Joachim. "Auf Begehr: *Unser Verkehr.*" *Antisemitismus und Jüdische Geschichte: Studien zu Ehren von Herbert A. Strauss.* Ed. Rainer Erb and Michael Schmidt. Berlin: Wissenschaftlicher Autorenverlag, 1987. 313–27.

Pazi, Margarita. "Die biblischen und jüdischen Einflüsse in Heines 'Nordsee-Gedichten.'" *Heine-Jahrbuch* 13 (1973): 3–19.

Prawer, S. S. *Heine's Jewish Comedy: A Study of his Portraits of Jews and Judaism.* Oxford: Clarendon, 1983.

Robertson, Ritchie. *The "Jewish Question" in German Literature, 1749–1939: Emancipation and its Discontents.* Oxford: Oxford UP, 1999.

Rosenthal, Ludwig. *Heinrich Heine als Jude.* Frankfurt am Main: Ullstein, 1973.

Rürup, Reinhard. "The Tortuous and Thorny Path to Legal Equality: 'Jew Laws' and Emancipatory Legislation in Germany from the Late Eighteenth Century." *Leo Baeck Institute Yearbook* 31 (1986): 3–33.

Sachs, Michael. *Die religiöse Poesie der Juden in Spanien.* 1845. Berlin: Poppelauer, 1901.

Sammons, Jeffrey. *Heinrich Heine: The Elusive Poet.* New Haven: Yale UP, 1969.

————. "Who Did Heine Think He Was?" *Heinrich Heine's Contested Identities: Politics, Religion, and Nationalism in Nineteenth-Century Germany.* Ed. Jost Hermand and Robert Holub. German Life and Civilization 26. New York: Lang, 1999. 1–24.

Schama, Simon. *Landscape and Memory.* New York: Knopf, 1995.

Scheindlin, Raymond P. *Wine, Women, and Death: Medieval Hebrew Poems on the Good Life.* Philadelphia: The Jewish Publication Society, 1986.

Schorsch, Ismar. *From Text to Context: The Turn to History in Modern Judaism.* Hanover and London: Brandeis UP and UP of New England, 1994.

Skolnik, Jonathan. "Die seltsame Karriere der Familie Abarbanel." *Aufklärung und Skepsis. Internationaler Heine-Kongreß 1997 zum 200. Geburtstag.* Ed. Joseph A. Kruse, Bernd Witte, and Karin Füllner. Stuttgart and Weimar: Metzler, 1998. 322–33.

————. "'Who Learns History from Heine?' The German-Jewish Historical Novel as Cultural Memory and Minority Culture, 1824–1953." Diss. Columbia U., 1999.

Sorkin, David. *The Transformation of German Jewry, 1780–1840.* New York: Oxford UP, 1987.

Tabak, Israel. *Judaic Lore in Heine: The Heritage of a Poet.* New York: Arno P, 1979. Reprint of: Baltimore: Johns Hopkins UP, 1948.

Treitschke, Heinrich von. *Deutsche Geschichte im Neunzehnten Jahrhundert.* Vol. 3. Leipzig: Hirzel, 1889. 5 vols. 1880–1920.

Veit, Philipp F. "Heine: The Marrano Pose." *Monatshefte* 66.2 (1974): 145–56.

Zantop, Susanne. "1844: After a Self-imposed Exile in Paris, Heinrich Heine Writes *Deutschland: Ein Wintermärchen.*" *Yale Companion to Jewish Writing and Thought in German Culture, 1096–1996.* Ed. Sander L. Gilman and Jack Zipes. New Haven: Yale UP, 1997. 178–85.

Zunz, Leopold. *Die Gottesdienstlichen Vorträge der Juden historisch entwickelt.* Berlin: Asher, 1932.

————. "Israels Gottesdienstliche Poesie." *Gesammelte Schriften.* Ed. Curatorium der "Zunzstiftung." 3 vols. in 1. Berlin: Gerschel 1875–1876. Reprint: Hildesheim, New York: Georg Olms, 1976. 1: 123–33.

————. "Juden und jüdische Literatur." *Gesammelte Schriften.* Ed. Curatorium der "Zunzstiftung." 3 vols. in 1. Berlin: Gerschel 1875–1876. Reprint: Hildesheim, New York: Georg Olms, 1976. 1: 86–114.

————. *Die synagogale Poesie des Mittelalters.* 1855. Frankfurt am Main: 1920. Reprint: Hildesheim, New York: Georg Olms, 1967.

Modernity:
Views from the Poet's Crypt

Mathilde's Interruption: Archetypes of Modernity in Heine's Later Poetry

Anthony Phelan

I. Heine in the Passagen

IN HIS CENTENARY LECTURE in 1956 Adorno tried to fix Heine's historical position by way of a comparison with Baudelaire. In this view, by being subjected to the processes of reproduction in the literary sphere, Heine was brought into direct contact with the most modern currents of the nineteenth century — "Damit ragt Heine in die Moderne des neunzehnten Jahrhunderts hinein gleich Baudelaire,"[1] but while Baudelaire heroically extracts his imagery from the increasingly corrosive experience of modernity, transfiguring the loss of all images into itself an image, Heine apparently, in his own historical moment, was unable to develop sufficient resistance to the onward march of capitalism. He applies techniques of industrial reproduction to an inherited repertoire of Romantic archetypes, but the other modernity — the modernity of the city — is reserved for Baudelaire. Even though Baudelaire was six in the year *Buch der Lieder* appeared, Heine's claim to have inaugurated modern poetry was made only three years before the publication of *Les fleurs du mal*,[2] and many of the earlier poems in Baudelaire's cycles date from the 1840s or even earlier. Since Heine had been in Paris with only brief interruptions from 1831, his experience of Paris life and of the social formations of the July Monarchy, the Second Republic, and the Second Empire was not radically different from that of the younger poet.

Adorno's notion of modern archetypes almost certainly derives from his knowledge of Benjamin's *Passagen* project, although neither critic knew much of Heine's work beyond *Buch der Lieder*. Indeed Benjamin began to consider Heine only because of Baudelaire's sympathetic interest in him.[3] In a 1935 letter, Adorno suggested to Benjamin that Heine might be expected to provide further evidence of the process of commodification (Adorno and Benjamin 145–46); and he made one further suggestion by sending two stanzas from the *Romanzero* poem "Jehuda ben Halevy" because they allude to a number of issues important to Benjamin:[4]

> Der Jehuda ben Halevy,
> Meinte sie, der sei hinlänglich
> Ehrenvoll bewahrt in einem
> Schönen Futteral von Pappe
>
> Mit chinesisch eleganten
> Arabesken, wie die hübschen
> Bonbonnieren von Marquis
> Im Passage Panorama. (B 6.1: 149)

Benjamin's reply is both excited and aggrieved. Adorno would never have *found* these lines, he suggests, had he not been guided by Benjamin's work on the Paris arcades and by the themes of his 1935 sketch (Adorno and Benjamin 135). For it is not only Heine's familiarity with the *Passage des panoramas* that is important here, but also the sweet-box from Marquis's shop in the arcade that might appropriately hold Halevi's poems. In the poem Heine's wife, Mathilde, complains that the jewel box that had contained the gems and pearls of King Darius and which, when it passed into his possession, Alexander had used to hold manuscripts of Homer, should be sold for cash if it ever came into Heine's possession. An ornate cardboard box, like Marquis's, would be good enough for Halevi's works. These lines take on a peculiar resonance in the light of Benjamin's remarks on "Louis-Philippe or the Interior" (Benjamin 5.2: 1243–44). As will become clear, the reduction of art to the status of a modern commodity in the course of its historical reception is among the central concerns of Heine's late verse. The *chinoiserie* of Marquis's sweetbox traces out the lineaments of Halevi's poetry seen, through Mathilde's modern eyes, as no more than oriental exoticism.

II. Tradition and Modernity

Heine's later poetry has been widely recognized as innovatory and incommensurable (Hofrichter 136; Robertson 95; Preisendanz 115). *Romanzero* is divided into three unequal parts: "Historien," "Lamentationen," and "Hebräische Melodien." "Jehuda ben Halevy" is the middle poem of the three making up the last part. Heine's letter to

Campe of August 28, 1851 suggests that he had misgivings about the poem reminiscent of those surrounding the composition of *Atta Troll* (Bark 260–61):

> Nur eine kurze Vorrede werde ich geben, obgleich ich doch so manches im Interesse des Autors zu sagen hätte. Das Gedicht, welches 'Disputazion' überschrieben, machte ich nach Ihrer Abreise in großer Eile; das vorhergehende ist eigentlich nur ein Fragment — es fehlte mir die Muße zu Feile und Ergänzung — . . . Die Mängel, welche einem Buche durch solche Eilfertigkeit anhaften, bemerkt nicht die große Menge, aber sie sind darum nicht minder vorhanden und quälen manchmal das Gewissen des Autors. (B 6.2: 15–16)

Given that the "Hebräische Melodien" were the last poems in the collection to be completed, his complaint that he was short of time is probably no less than the truth, but the similarity of Heine's excuses here, and of his remarks about the insensitivity of the audience, to what he says in his correspondence about *Atta Troll* suggests a common motivation. What is at stake is the unity of the poem and the plausibility of Heine's intention to complete it.

Along with "Der Apollogott" and "Der Dichter Firdusi," "Jehuda ben Halevy" deals with the fate of poets and poetry. At the end of its first part Heine makes the scant regard he shows for his audience the privilege of true genius:

> Solchen Dichter von der Gnade
> Gottes nennen wir Genie:
> Unverantwortlicher König
> Des Gedankenreiches ist er.
>
> Nur dem Gotte steht er Rede,
> Nicht dem Volke — In der Kunst,
> Wie im Leben, kann das Volk
> Töten uns, doch niemals richten. —
> (B 6.1: 135)

This conclusion is reached at the end of a meditation on the early life of the great Jewish poet, prompted by a reminiscence of the opening of Psalm 137. Among the shadowy figures conjured by the lament for Jerusalem is Halevi. He thus becomes visible within a certain tradition, both religious and poetic, whose voices are heard "Psalmodierend, Männerstimmen" (B 6.1: 130), 750 years after Halevi's birth. The first part of the poem then tells how, touched by the primal language of the Torah and Talmud, Halevi's poetry became a pillar of fire to the diaspora. The second part of the poem returns to Psalm 137. Heine's narrator identifies himself with this old song that moans and hums like a kettle:

> Lange schon, jahrtausendlange
> Kochts in mir. Ein dunkles Wehe!
> Und die Zeit leckt meine Wunde,
> Wie der Hund die Schwären Hiobs.

> Dank dir, Hund, für deinen Speichel —
> Doch das kann nur kühlend lindern —
> Heilen kann mich nur der Tod,
> Aber, ach, ich bin unsterblich! (B 6.1: 135–36)

An important and difficult temporal dislocation is involved in this positioning of Heine's narrator. He speaks within the tradition of dereliction that includes Job and the Babylonian exiles of the psalm, and yet unmistakably defines himself in relation to Heine's own mortal sickness and to history as a repetition of suffering. Both timeless and subject to time, the substance of this tradition is grasped by the modern poet in his own time as a "spleen," which is also a revolutionary animus cited from the end of Psalm 137:

> Tolle Sud! Der Deckel springt —
> Heil dem Manne, dessen Hand
> Deine junge Brut ergreifet
> Und zerschmettert an der Felswand.

> Gott sei Dank! die Sud verdampfet
> In dem Kessel, der allmählich
> Ganz verstummt. Es weicht mein Spleen,
> Mein westöstlich dunkler Spleen — (B 6.1: 136)

Time licking his wounds identifies the narrator with the long history of human suffering, in a trajectory that leads to revenge with its implication of a postrevolutionary happiness (Briegleb 98–99, 255–56). Yet the poem will not project this utopian possibility. Its preoccupations are with the European literary tradition in which Halevi and his modern avatar Heinrich Heine are situated.

The twelfth-century Spanish poet is placed in the company of the troubadours of Provence and of Petrarch, but for Jehuda the distant beloved becomes Jerusalem and its ruins. In its turn, this nostalgia is compared to Geoffroy Rudèl's inexplicable desire for Melisande of Tripoli. Throughout, the movement of the second section is accomplished via a number of digressions: the elegy of the psalm leads to Heine's "westöstlich dunkler Spleen" and thence to Jehuda, whose desire for Jerusalem is set against the traditions of courtly love.[5] Its essential relation to that tradition is confirmed by the similarity of Halevi's death at the feet of his beloved Jerusalem to the death of Geoffroy at the feet of Melisande.

At the same time the poem exquisitely recalls the opening of the Book of Lamentations: ". . . Jerusalem! // Sie, die volkreich heilge Stadt / Ist zur Wüstenei geworden" (B: 6.1: 139) renders Luther's "Wie liegt die Stadt so wüste, die voll Volks war?" of Lamentations 1:1. The subsequent references to jackals, snakes, and birds of the night have an Old Testament resonance: the jackal in Lamentations 5:18 and the derelict owl of Psalms 102:6. The overall effect of this is to place Halevi *and Heine* in a tradition of lament — to which the immediately previous book of *Romanzero* has borne witness. The literary allusions open a temporal perspective that the remaining parts of the poem will extend in an extreme way to establish an encounter with the demands of modern civilization. In the third section a digression bridges the time of Halevi and Heine's own age, the one leading the "caravan of pain" of Israel's exile, the other "Krüppelelend" as his Jewish successor in modern Paris.

The link between them is, to say the least, implausible: Heine describes a highly ornate casket looted by Alexander from Darius at the battle of Arabella.

> Dieses Kästchen, selbst ein Kleinod
> Unschätzbaren Wertes, diente
> Zur Bewahrung von Kleinodien,
> Des Monarchen Leibjuwelen. (B 6.1: 142)

The poem recounts that Alexander had subsequently used this jewel case to hold the manuscripts of "ambrosian Homer" (B 6.1: 144), and placed it by his bed so that memories of Homeric heroes might fill his dreams. Heine has an alternative proposal. Were he in possession of the casket, he would place in it "all the poems of our rabbi,"

> Des Jehuda ben Halevy
> Festgesänge, Klagelieder,
> Die Ghaselen, Reisebilder
> Seiner Wallfahrt — alles ließ' ich

> Von dem Besten Zophar schreiben
> Auf der reinsten Pergamenthaut,
> Und ich legte diese Handschrift
> In das kleine goldne Kästchen. (B 6.1: 145)

By means of an unmistakable self-reference, the author of the *Reise-bilder* imagines here a time in which he is the beneficiary of the tradition of Halevi, enshrined in Darius's jewel-box and maintained in Heine's own "pilgrimage" (the stress on "*Seiner* Wallfahrt" is unmistakable). Heine's preference for Halevi articulates a change of traditions. The casket had contained the works of Homer, representing the sensual world of Greek antiquity and Heine's own Hellenic principle; and he imagines himself in Dionysian terms, crowned with vine-leaves and drawn by panthers. Darius's casket comes therefore to represent, figuratively and imaginatively, the *vehicle* of these traditions; but they have to be sustained by the transcription that writes them again for the present, just as the practiced scribe (Hebrew *sofer*) must transcribe the holy texts. The box, which has contained the relics of the great traditions of Greek and Hebrew poetry, hence comes to figure as Heine's own writing, which also "holds" this tradition.

However, literary tradition and its continuities do not provide the main instance of cultural transmission in "Jehuda ben Halevy." In part 3 Heine pursues the extremely digressive history of the artifacts contained in Darius's casket. Among these, the poem concentrates on the pearls that pass — by gift, sale, or inheritance — from Thais of Corinth via Cleopatra and the Catholic Kings of Spain to the wife of Baron Salomon Rothschild in Paris. These pearls are poor stuff, the poem tells us, when compared to the pearls of Halevi's lament for Jerusalem:

> Perlentränen, die verbunden
> Durch des Reimes goldnen Faden,
> Aus der Dichtkunst güldnen Schmiede
> Als ein Lied hervorgegangen. (B 6.1: 147)

This identification of the pearls that the casket had contained with the poetry of Jehuda, which, according to the narrator's conjecture, it *might* contain, provides the highly attenuated logic that holds together the ostensible theme of the poem and the elaborate digression of part 3. Part 4 begins by appearing to raise this very anxiety:

> Meine Frau ist nicht zufrieden
> Mit dem vorigen Kapitel, (B 6.1: 149)

In fact, Heine's wife has other things on her mind, but the digressions that have supervened in part 3 will be the first point of reference for most puzzled readers. This section of the poem successfully completes the *vita* of the poet-saint by describing his death in Jerusalem at the hands of a Saracen and his reception into heaven to the strains of "Lecho Daudi Likras Kalle," which Heine believes is Jehuda's own Sabbath hymn. But the digressions of the narrative threaten to frustrate the telling of his story. In an important sense, the interruptions to the poet's biography as told in the poem *parallel* the provenance of Baroness Rothschild's pearls. The metaphor presenting Jehuda Halevi's writing as "Perlentränen" insists that the central issue is the process of transmission in the reception and renewal of his work.

However, the intervention from "my wife" at the opening of part 4 is guided by a different consideration. She is alarmed by the idea that her husband might *not* immediately sell the casket for cash in order to buy her a cashmere shawl. This repeats the earlier reference to Heine's financial worries (B 6.1: 145), but more importantly stresses a factor already apparent in the dispersal of Darius's state jewels. Increasingly, the process that begins with Alexander's gifts (to his army, his mother, and even to his old "Weltarschpauker" Aristotle) comes to be dominated by the cash-nexus. The same power is also evident in the encounter with tradition worked out at the end of *Romanzero*.

Mathilde's query and the fact that she has never heard of Halevi sets off a recapitulation of the question of tradition traced out in the poem — but its narrative continues to be subverted by digressions. Heine first attributes his wife's ignorance to the inadequacy of Parisian girls' schools, and sketches a history of Jewish poetry in Spain. His assessment of Gabirol and Ibn Esra alongside Halevi is derived from "Alcharisi":

> Alcharisi — der, ich wette,
> Dir nicht minder unbekannt ist,
> Ob er gleich, französ'scher Witzbold,
> Den Hariri überwitzelt
>
> Im Gebiete der Makame,
> Und ein Voltairianer war (B 6.1: 151).

Once again, Heine is himself implied by this citation. The Arabic form of the "Makame," developed by the poet al-Hariri, deploys parody and allusion for critical effect; and al-Charisi had written a verse history of his antecedents in this form, just as Heine's narrative now repeats the action of retrospection in the witty form of his Spanish trochees. Yet in the very moment of re-establishing the continuity of the tradition and the supremacy of Jehuda Halevi, Heine interrupts his poem again with a digressive and fantastical account of Ibn Esra's travels.[6]

In the uncertainties and disappointments of Ibn Esra's life Heine recognizes the fate of all poets. Even Apollo, the father of all poets, suffered such ill fortune when he lost Daphne to her laurel bush and so became "der göttliche Schlemihl." The Jewish nickname for those dogged by bad luck starts a further digression on the etymology of the word made famous by Chamisso's tale, *Peter Schlemihl*. Chamisso and his book's Jewish dedicatee are dragged into the poem as expert witnesses. A retelling of the tale of zealous Phinehas follows. In Numbers 25 he kills a man who had brought a Midianite woman into the Israelite camp. In Heine's version Phinehas killed the wrong man, and "Schlemihl ben Zuri Schadday" died instead of the guilty Zimri.[7] Acknowledging this universal fate of poets, the poem ends with the story of the third of the Jewish poets of Spain, Gabirol. He is murdered by an envious moor whose guilt is revealed by the sweetness of the figs borne on the tree under which he buried the poet's body. Under torture, the moor confesses his crime: but at this point the work breaks off, and it is not at all clear how such a fragment could have been completed (Kaufmann 143). "[M]it Pomp bestattet" (B 6.1: 158), the poet's funeral extends the celebration of his fame in life — a fame to which the poem itself now significantly contributes. As has been noted, an element of self-reference is apparent in this fantasy of posthumous glory also: envious neighbors get their comeuppance, like Heine's treacherous cousins. The digressive pattern of the poem has made it more or less impossible to return to the eponymous hero; but in the end all paths will lead back to the author, the modern instance of a line descended variously from Apollo, Psalm 137, and Schlemihl ben Zuri Schadday.

Heine's poem has by now offered an alternative tradition. The transmission of the substance of tradition enacted earlier in the poem is now shadowed by the inheritance of the Schlemihl. Heine marks the parallel by a characteristic repetition. In part 1, Halevi's life in the tradition of Psalm 137 opens with "Jahre kommen und verfließen"; in part 4 the Schlemihl digression too ends with this phrase:

> Jahre kommen und vergehen —
> Drei Jahrtausende verflossen,
> Seit gestorben unser Ahnherr,
> Herr Schlemihl ben Zuri Schadday.

Längst ist auch der Pinhas tot —
Doch sein Speer hat sich erhalten,
Und wir hören ihn beständig
Über unsre Häupter schwirren.

(B 6.1: 156)

Phinehas and his spear come to represent here all those, like Ludwig Börne, whose zeal and Puritanism set out to destroy the happy and the sensual, the witty and the frivolous — the poet's privilege. The constant disturbances of tradition and cultural transmission are hence bridged by the other history of authoritarian repression. The exile of the Jewish poet Heine, in Paris and in his protracted final illness, becomes the ultimate figure of a tradition of dereliction *and* heroic survival.

The tradition, displayed through Apollo, the Schlemihl, Jeremiah and the Babylonian exile, ekes out a threadbare existence in modern Paris. The verses that caught Adorno's attention present a different kind of threat or attenuation, however. Mathilde suggests that Darius's casket should be sold — since a cardboard box will suffice for Halevi's poems; but the status of the work handed on and worthy of preservation changes radically. The chinoiserie of the Marquis's *bonbonnière* (B 6.1: 149) reveals it as the decorative and merely functional substitute for the original casket which might have *treasured* the auratic texts of the past. We have seen that Heine's poem struggles to recall an almost forgotten tradition (that of the Jewish poets of twelfth-century Spain) in its proper context of courtly love, and then relates the *modern* poem's own lament to the tradition of dereliction in which Halevi stands. In modernity the tradition is worn out. Its continuities have been disrupted by the failures of pedagogy and the enervation of narrative. Heine's tumbling anecdotes can remember what the memory of tradition was like, but they can only realize anamnesis as exhaustion.

The vehicle for this is the mimed form of the Spanish romance. In the context of *Romanzero*, however, this form becomes more significant. Heine's "Nachwort" says he chose the title because the tone of the romance dominates in the poems (B 6.1: 180), but it is nevertheless clear that the proposal for the title came from his publisher. Campe promoted the new collection with enormous energy. Even the illustrated dust-jacket in which the book was issued was a major innovation in the history of the book-trade (Sammons 126; Ziegler 202–3); the title too played a significant role in this commercial promotion because the romance as a genre (and even the title itself) had been in vogue right across Europe ever since the mid 1840s (Bark 237). In this context, Mathilde's suggestion about Marquis's *bonbonnières* seems to recognize the commercial appropriation of the poetic tradition.

Among the "Historien," "Der Dichter Firdusi" illustrates another encroachment of cash values into the sphere of the artist of tradition. Firdusi wrote a history of the ancient kings of Persia, and cherished the memory of Iran's ancient Parsee religion. But the Shah, instead of paying him for his labors in gold coin, as he seemed to have promised, sends silver. The Shah's promise is conceived less as a "unit price" — a thoman per line — than as an appropriate but not expressly calculated reward for the poet's skill. Firdusi needs the money — but instead of honoring Firdusi's genius in a way commensurate with the Shah's promise, the Shah's calculation makes of it a negotiable price. That is the point of Firdusi's reaction: he divides the silver between the three men who have served him most recently: the Shah's messengers and the bath attendant. This restores the money to the status it should originally have had, in an act of gratitude and generosity. Firdusi's greatest scorn is reserved for the Shah's unworthy exploitation of an ambiguity based on the fact there is only one name for the coin, whether of silver or gold. In the face of this false equivalence, the poet withdraws; and the generous gifts of the repentant Shah do not reach him before his impoverished death. Firdusi's practice of memory and tradition cannot survive in an age when the uniqueness of genius is subject to money's law of equivalencies.

The relevance of Firdusi's fate to Heine's own circumstances is apparent. The relationship between poet and patron stands for the breakdown in his relationship with his publisher, Campe, between 1848 and 1851, and also for the financial anxieties caused by the death of his uncle. Heine himself was profoundly affected by the process in which lyrical greatness is measured by monetary values. However, the structure of "Der Dichter Firdusi," as well as the tenor of its narrative, repeats the lesson of exhaustion that is apparent when "Jehuda ben Halevy" peters out. Firdusi's epic emerges in a moment when the history of Persia's ancient kings has run aground on the reign of a Shah who has substituted trickery for generosity. When the poet takes up his "Wanderstab" and sets off into exile, it is poetry itself that has departed. The ancient unity of poet and king cannot be recovered, no matter how generous any subsequent act of restitution may be — and there is every reason to think that the Shah would like to restore the poet:

Firdusi? — rief der Fürst betreten —
Wo ist er? Wie geht es dem großen Poeten?
(B 6.1: 52)

Yet the Shah's reawakened generosity fails to reach the poet. The tale unfolds in a relentless linearity: as the caravan of unimaginable wealth reaches Firdusi's place of exile, the poet's body is carried out for burial.

In another sense, however, the unrelenting declension of the poem is played off against its variety. Each of its three parts is cast in a different form: the opening section deals with Firdusi's *Book of the Kings* ("Schach Nameh") in unrhymed trochaic four-line stanzas, which adopt an appropriate range of images for the Persian subject. Against this grand orientalizing manner, the second section establishes a conversational tone in which Firdusi speaks in his own interest ("'Hätt er menschlich ordinär / Nicht gehalten was versprochen,'" [B 6.1: 51]) and in *abba* rhymed four-liners. Finally, the third part completes the narrative in iambic couplets demonstrating, from time to time, Heine's notorious wit as a rhymster: "Zins" rhymes with "Provinz," "Kamele" variously with "erwähle," "Befehle," and "Kehle"; and "Karawane" with "Führerfahne." Only the four-beat rhythm remains consistent amid this burgeoning variety, but it has moved from the oriental mimicry of the first section to a verse narrative form close to *Knittelvers* in the third. Such formal variations demonstrate a virtuoso control of form and tone, and measure Heine's credentials as a poet. His retelling of an old tale, presented as oriental pastiche, as travesty, in the demotic speech attributed to Firdusi, reveals the modern gaze turned on the remote past. Heine the modern is apparent in the irony, which knows that the Shah's meanness and Firdusi's fate are all too familiar. The sheer variety of ironic forms, however, threatens to slip into an infinite series.[8] Only a random interruption — the end of this particular narrative — avoids the implied principle of proliferation.

Mathilde's intervention in part 4 of "Jehuda ben Halevy" puts an end to these apparently endless variations by distracting the narrative with its own real-time context in Paris. Her interruption is significant in two ways: in offering to substitute run-of-the-mill packaging for an ancient artifact she demonstrates that the principle of "the exchange of equivalent values" is incompatible with tradition.[9] More generally, her utterance draws attention to the discrepancy between the heroic world of the figures of tradition and the disenchanted truth of the everyday.

III. The Modern City

The progress of the secular, charted in the decline of Firdusi and the desacralization of art in "Jehuda ben Halevy," is seen most clearly in "Der Apollogott." The god is first glimpsed in the context of a Romantic ballad: a young nun observes his passage down the Rhine in the company of the Muses. Far from being the *Apollon Mmousagetes* of classical myth, this exiled divinity is no more than the secularized figure of a popular street song. The young nun pursues her idol, only to be told that Phoebus is now identified as the cantor of the German synagogue in Amsterdam, Rabbi Faibisch. A *Jewish* Apollo most fully expresses the reality of the exile experience: the exiled god is Heine's contemporary — indeed, he has become identical with Heine, Jewish poet of and in exile (von Wiese 126). In this way, "Der Apollogott" parallels the structure of "Jehuda ben Halevy" in settling the exhausted legacy of the great tradition on its own author: the encounter of modernity with its predecessors in antiquity and history — Apollo and the muses, Jehuda, Firdusi — is articulated as the constant meeting of the mythical with the personal and historical in the figure of Heine himself.

The provisional end of a classical tradition is twice marked as *urban*. In the second poem of "Der Apollogott," ancient Greece and modern Paris are elided:

> Ich bin der Gott der Musika,
> Verehrt in allen Landen;
> Mein Tempel hat in Gräcia,
> Auf Mont-Parnaß gestanden.
>
> Auf Mont-Parnaß in Gräcia,
> Da hab ich oft gesessen
> Am holden Quell Kastalia,
> Im Schatten der Zypressen. (B 6.1: 32–33)

The insistent "-a" rhymes of this text, sustained over eight stanzas, indicate parody and travesty (Bark 300). Yet "Mont-Parnaß in Gräcia" is neither Mount Parnassus (*pace* Draper) nor, quite, Montparnasse: it indicates a point at which it is possible to see where the tradition of Parnassian Apollo and the Muses has now come to rest — in the theaters and bars of modern Paris; similarly, the discovery that "Faibisch" Apollo gathered his muses from the popular stage in an Amsterdam "Spielhuis" makes the moment of the advent of modernity specific as the nineteenth-century city.

If "Der Apollogott" and "Jehuda ben Halevy," in their different ways, argue that the final resting place of an exhausted tradition is the modern city, the poem preceding "Der Apollogott" provides the historical data of this emerging secular modernity. "Pomare" takes the most significant place possible in the "Historien" (Tales). All the preceding poems have recalled the defeat and discomfiture of aristocrats and monarchs. (This is even true of the satire on Gautier's Parnassian celebration of Countess Marie Kalergis, "Der weiße Elephant.") "Pomare" interrupts and redefines this theme by presenting a vaudeville dancer who has named herself after the queen of Tahiti. The poems appearing under her name mark the point at which modern Paris, and therefore a modern polity, emerges in the historical series that has just concluded with poems on Charles I and Marie Antoinette, both of them victims of revolutionary execution.

"Karl I" presents an extremely sophisticated use of the traditional historical ballad. Its reference to the ballad tradition makes possible a contemporary political critique of great subtlety. While appearing to *rehearse* the popular form, with the reminiscences of a feudal-aristocratic society appropriate to its genre, Heine's poem opens up the generic text to contemporary reference.[10] "Karl I" requires a double reading: in the terms given by its first publication, in 1847, it meditates on a moment before the decisive act of regicide. The ballad projects both the anxieties of a feudal order, aware of the growth of forces that will ultimately overthrow it, and the ideological lullaby that is designed to prevent those forces from recognizing their own strength. *After* 1848, however, the ballad evokes not so much aristocratic fears of proletarian overthrow as the acknowledgment that democratic aspirations have come to nothing. The simple chronological parallel between 1649 and 1847/48/49 provides the groundwork for a complex argument about literature (the ballad as a popular form), ideology (the maintenance of feudal order in Germany), and revolutionary change. The twin impulses that provide the poem's energy are prerevolutionary aspiration coupled with the anxiety and, ultimately, the pessimism of radical politics about the prospects for change. This is a pessimism of the intellect without much optimism of the will, and it finally resolves into postrevolutionary disappointment. The argument of the poem hence remains historical; it can at most take the measure of a *deferred* modernity. This is what modern readers sense as the element of pastiche in "Karl I," miming a form that it has shown is fossilized while acknowledging that its own ironies may be self-defeating.

"Marie Antoinette," with its recollection of antecedents in the *Gespensterballade* (Hinck 57), functions in a similar way. The ghosts of the dead queen and her courtiers are literally the spirits of the *ancien régime* haunting the scenes of their former splendor. In an act of archeological interpretation, Heine points out the political meanings attached to the Tuileries. However, the poem does more than warn against the political dangers implicit in Bourbon aspirations. Its grotesque heroine, daughter of Maria Theresia and granddaughter of German Kaisers ("deutscher Cäsaren"), can do no more than haunt the present:

> Sie muß jetzt spuken ohne Frisur
> Und ohne Kopf, im Kreise
> Von unfrisierten Edelfraun,
> Die kopflos gleicherweise. (B 6.1: 27)

The rules of the royal *levée* are now fundamentally ludicrous. Heine's sense of the ridiculous perhaps even overextends his description of the court ceremonial, "Ein leeres Gespreize, ganz wie sonst." Ultimately the scene of royal pretension is finished off rhetorically by the sheer vulgarity of the modern world:

> Die Oberhofmeisterin steht dabei,
> Sie fächert die Brust, die weiße,
> Und in Ermangelung eines Kopfs
> Lächelt sie mit dem Steiße. (B 6.1: 28)

What is coarse here successfully confronts the gallicisms and archaisms of Heine's parody of ceremony. This ritual of the past may haunt the present, but it cannot survive the secularizing movement of history.

"Karl I" and "Marie Antoinette" provide the decisive context for "Pomare" in relation to the aristocratic theme of the earlier parts of the "Historien" and its political secularization. The images of a monarchy deposed are now realized in the strictly metaphorical sense of Pomare's claims to be a queen. Her travesty of royalty provides an index of secular modernity, in the very moment at which Paris fully appears in *Romanzero*. The dense meanings of the two preceding poems invite a similar vigilant reading of "Pomare," of course: if she reveals kingship as at best metaphorical, in the second poem of the series her dance recalls a beheading. Salome's dance, which Pomare evokes, refers, in the context of Parisian politics after the July Revolution, to the Saint-Simonian triumph of the flesh over the Baptist's asceticism, as well as recalling the guillotining of "Marie Antoinette." However, there is a wider pattern in the poem's handling of an antiquated monarchical institution. The modern gaze turned on the past can only cite it as myth. Poems on King David and the golden calf later in the "Historien" repeat this movement of secularization: the dance around the golden calf of Exodus is only intelligible as the glorification of capital in modern Paris, just as the patriarchal King David can only be quoted as evidence of the cynicism of autocracy.

Pomare's revolutionary cancan establishes the political meanings of her popularity, but the remaining poems of the sequence present a different destiny. In the first instance, Pomare is lured by her new-found wealth to behave with the disdain of the *ancien régime;* however, her success as a latter-day Salome is overwhelmed, in poem 3, by her career as a courtesan, by her death and, in the last poem, by her funeral. The poems had previously appeared separately, and in one sense Heine's montage simply and realistically reconstructs the Parisian milieu in which a dancer might well accept the role of mistress, only to become a common prostitute dying in penury. The circumstances of her burial —

> Keinen Pfaffen hört' man singen,
> Keine Glocke klagte schwer;
> Hinter deiner Bahre gingen
> Nur dein Hund und dein Friseur. (B 6.1: 31)

— both marvelously anticipate Heine's own "Gedächtnisfeier" in his last collection, and indicate the desacralization of life and death by the everyday, figured here by the dog and hairdresser. In "Pomare," therefore, Heine could be said to fulfill one of Adorno's fundamental requirements by way of the archetypes of modernity; for he presents the extent to which human beings are transformed into mere commodities.[11]

In the classical case of such reification, Baudelaire's "Une charogne," the dead prostitute is presented as entirely physical, a being reduced merely to its constituent parts:

> Le soleil rayonnait sur cette pourriture,
> Comme afin de la cuire à point,
> Et de rendre au centuple à la grande Nature
> Tout ce qu'ensemble elle avait joint.

> [The sun on this rottenness focused its rays /
> To cook the cadaver till done, / And render to
> Nature a hundredfold gift / Of all she'd united
> in one. (60–61)]

Comparison with Heine's procedure is instructive. He too presents the dead body of the dancer-prostitute as a merely physical object; but instead of allowing the cadaver to return to nature, Pomare becomes the necessary commodity of the anatomy class: which is not to say that the medical school is ultimately any different from the knackers.

> Und der Carabin mit schmierig
> Plumper Hand und lernbegierig
> Deinen schönen Leib zerfetzt,
> Anatomisch ihn zersetzt —
> Deine Rosse trifft nicht minder
> Einst zu Montfaucon der Schinder.
>
> (B 6.1: 30)

In the whole movement of "Pomare," Heine constantly provides a social context for his critique of the commodity as it is given institutional status in theater or vaudeville, prostitution and anatomical dissection. But the form of this third poem should not escape attention. The contexts of the commodity appear, here, in trochaic couplets. Pomare's fate emerges in a vernacular form reminiscent, again, of *Knittelvers,* and hence appears as the most everyday event. Perhaps these lines should recall popular *Bänkelsang,* in a devalued and disenchanted moral judgement of the way of all flesh. The knackers of Montfaucon, as the pseudocomic rhyme on "nicht minder" and "Schinder" indicates, put a stop to the proliferating couplets of the third poem, but they cannot provide a closure that is not ironic.

There is another important way in which "Pomare" provides a key to the forms in which Heine derives archetypes for the Parisian modernity that dominates in this poem. In the last section, he scans the traditional sources of consolation — a good death and Christian burial. But this funeral is bare and impoverished, conducted without benefit of clergy and theologically hollow:

> Arme Königin des Spottes,
> Mit dem Diadem von Kot,
> Bist gerettet jetzt durch Gottes
> Ewge Güte, du bist tot.
>
> Wie die Mutter, so der Vater
> Hat Barmherzigkeit geübt,
> Und ich glaube, dieses tat er,
> Weil auch du so viel geliebt. (B 6.1: 31)

The fluency of Heine's verse contains huge complexity. Pomare is not rich but rather the *poor* queen of scorn, and it is unclear whether she is "queen of scorn" because she dispenses contempt or because she is the object of social contempt. Nothing remains of her previous ability to command respect and admiration. Ultimately the queen of derision is defined by her laughable pretensions, on the stage where she began. The rhyme of "Spottes" with the enjambement on "durch Gottes / Ewge Güte" indicates a comic turn, but only in preparation for the theological bathos of "du bist tot." Salvation is reduced here, finally, to death itself, which is at least preferable to the ministrations of the medical students. Finally, even this is capped by the last stanza's blasphemous paraphrase of Luke 7:47: "Ihr sind viele Sünden vergeben, denn sie hat viel geliebt." Pomare's death comes about because she has "loved" so much, with the implication that its cause was venereal disease. Such is the mercy of God the Father.

When Pomare dies in her poor old mother's garret the resources of sentiment are demonstrably exhausted. This old woman looks back to the poverty of "Das is ein schlechtes Wetter," "Heimkehr" 19 in *Buch der Lieder;* the parallel between God the Father and Pomare's mother in the final stanza ("Wie die Mutter, so der Vater") remains uneasy because the pastoral effects of the contrast between divine love and maternal human care that it sketches are undone by the context of theatrical sleaze, betrayal, and poverty. In Heine's modernity, the residual *memento mori* that concludes Baudelaire's "Une charogne" ("— Et pourtant vous serez semblable à cette ordure" ["And you in turn will be rotten like this"]) is not possible. Modern Paris sours the very material of moral consolation.

IV. Everyday Life

The city appears in "Pomare" in its most public forms: the vaudeville theaters, the public streets and parks, and finally the cemetery. This Paris leaves an intermittent trace through Heine's later poetry from the "Verschiedene" sequences of *Neue Gedichte* and the Jardin des plantes in *Atta Troll* to *Gedichte. 1853 und 1854.* Just as Apollo acknowledges the imperative of the quotidian, so too Heine's lyrics of Parisian life accede to the dominance of the everyday. One of Heine's best known poems, "Gedächtnisfeier" in the Lazarus cycle of the second book of *Romanzero,* rejects even the formalities of funeral ceremonial and liturgical commemoration in favor of an everyday mourning.

His wife Mathilde visits the cemetery in Montmartre, and however moved she may be, the poem ends with a wonderful note of realism:

> Keine Messe wird man singen,
> Keinen Kadosch wird man sagen,
> Nichts gesagt und nichts gesungen
> Wird an meinen Sterbetagen.
>
> Doch vielleicht an solchem Tage,
> Wenn das Wetter schön und milde,
> Geht spazieren auf Monmartre
> Mit Paulinen Frau Mathilde.
>
> Mit dem Kranz von Immortellen
> Kommt sie mir das Grab zu schmücken,
> Und sie seufzet: Pauvre homme!
> Feuchte Wehmut in den Blicken.
>
> Leider wohn ich viel zu hoch,
> Und ich habe meiner Süßen
> Keinen Stuhl hier anzubieten;
> Ach! sie schwankt mit müden Füßen.
>
> Süßes, dickes Kind, du darfst
> Nicht zu Fuß nach Hause gehen;
> An dem Barrieregitter
> Siehst du die Fiaker stehen. (B 6.1: 113)

The cabs wait at the city boundary marked by Louis-Philippe's fortifications: Heine's poem moves from the secular impulse of its opening to ready acquiescence in the ordinary realities of Paris at its close.

"Gedächtnisfeier" works its way toward this unemphatic last line via a careful management of the resources of irony. The familiar trochaic tetrameters of the first stanza in fact present a much grander rhythmic movement, focused on the words "Messe," "Kadosch," and the repetition of "nichts"; this gains a strong sense of cadence from the enjambement of "gesungen / Wird" leading to the rhyme. The "Doch" of stanza two, introducing the unceremonious celebration of the anniversaries of Heine's death, therefore, also introduces a tripping counterrhythm which echoes the good spirits of his wife and her friend Pauline Rogue as they set out for Montmartre on a fine day. The third stanza distances itself from the emotion of the occasion by including a French phrase, so that the less-than-silent final /e/ of "homme" becomes comically overstressed by its position in the metrical scheme. The emergence of the poem into French at this point has been prepared by the earlier appearance of Montmartre and of the "immortelles" of Mathilde's wreath. French is also the language of the everyday, set in contrast to the ritual Hebrew of the Kaddish and the implied Latin of the Requiem. The stanza wryly acknowledges the limits of Mathilde's sentimental "Feuchte Wehmut," but it does not undermine its sincerity; and the final stanzas continue to hold this hint of irony in check. The notorious rhyme and assonance on "meiner Süßen" / "mit müden Füßen" does not step beyond the bounds of realism. Mathilde, overweight, must take a cab; and with a final French word the poem comes to rest, apparently as reconciled to its urban setting as T. S. Eliot's "lonely cab-horse" in the "Preludes."

Yet this recognition of the day-to-day plainness of city life, formally echoing the rejection of ceremony announced at the start, excludes any satisfactory tone of closure just as much as it does any emotional afflatus. Such an uneasy balance is characteristic.[12] Heroic gestures, for instance, are demonstrably inappropriate. In "Zwei Ritter" they are unmasked as the bad faith of self-deluded Polish patriots. Crapülinski and Waschlapski are down-at-the-heel survivors who, like Herwegh in "Der Ex-Lebendige" and Dingelstedt in "Der Ex-Nachtwächter," must come to an accommodation with the slackening of energy and resolve in everyday life. Conversely, in Heine's domestic poems in which he worries about his wife, such as "An die Engel" in the *Romanzero* Lazarus cycle or "Ich war, o Lamm, als Hirt bestellt" from the *Nachlese*, the high style and high feeling of religious rhetoric is ironically undone by the particularity of the case: in "An die Engel" the mythological grandeur of "Das ist der böse Thanatos," with its associated language of "Schattenreich" and the classicizing syntax of the line "Wird Witwe sie und Waise sein" is challenged by the rhymes on Mathilde ("eurem Ebenbilde," "Huld und Milde") which conclude the last two stanzas. It would be inappropriate to describe this effect as bathos. There is real sentiment in the way the poem names Mathilde, but her ordinariness, rather than the older language of myth or of a prayer to the guardian angels, is the focus of attention.

The interruption of tradition and of narrative that Mathilde's intervention brings about in "Jehuda ben Halevy" is recapitulated whenever banal daily life takes over from poetic imagery and diction. Within the severe constraints of Heine's sickroom and "Matratzengruft," it is often sound alone that comes to signify the dystopia of the everyday. "Frau Sorge" focuses on the squeaking lid of the snuffbox used by the nurse who sits with Heine, and, in the final stanza, on the noise of her blowing her nose, which interrupts his reverie.

> An meinem Bett in der Winternacht
> Als Wärterin die Sorge wacht.
> Sie trägt eine weiße Unterjack,
> Ein schwarzes Mützchen, und schnupft Tabak.
> Die Dose knarrt so gräßlich,
> Die Alte nickt so häßlich. (B 6.1: 115)

This poem takes up themes and diction from the motto poem of the "Lamentationen" and from "Rückschau," the second of the Lazarus poems. Its central figure, "Frau Sorge," is named in such a way as to recall the last and most persistent of the four gray women in Goethe's *Faust, II. Teil,* and there may even be a more extensive Faustian subtext. Goethe's Sorge is an appropriate sickroom attendant for Heine: she is sister to death and heralds his coming; indeed, the sound associated with Frau Sorge's snuffbox announces her arrival in *Faust:* "Die Pforte *knarrt,* und niemand kommt herein" (344). She puts in an appearance elsewhere in Heine's work. In "Rückschau" the poet had been "bedrängt von schwarzen Sorgen" (B 6.1: 106), so that when "die schwarze Frau . . . küßte mir blind die Augen" (B 6.1: 202), in the second of the "Zum Lazarus" poems from *Gedichte. 1853 und 1854,* there is a reminiscence of the moment when Sorge blinds Faust in Goethe's drama. This blinding goes hand-in-hand, for Faust, with his disenchantment and the foreswearing of magical powers that must precede his full imaginative recognition of a human world and its incessant and heroic activity. But in poem after poem Heine shows the failure of this utopia. Modernity for him is an experience of standstill.

V. Modernity and Continuity

Everyday life is indicated by images of banality and articulated by strategies of nonclosure, often working against the emotional or rhetorical force of poetic diction. The subject himself, in poems of extraordinary finality, is presented in antiheroic terms of exhaustion and emptiness. "Sie erlischt," poem 18 in the *Romanzero* Lazarus cycle, and "Der Scheidende" define Heine's sickness and prospective death as the exhaustion of the poetic. Here modernity, understood as the supervention of the everyday, is presented as an empty theater:

Der Vorhang fällt, das Stück ist aus,
Und Herrn und Damen gehn nach Haus.
Ob ihnen auch das Stück gefallen?
Ich glaub, ich hörte Beifall schallen.
Ein hochverehrtes Publikum
Beklatschte dankbar seinen Dichter.
Jetzt aber ist das Haus so stumm,
Und sind verschwunden Lust und Lichter.

Doch horch! ein schollernd schnöder Klang
Ertönt unfern der öden Bühne; —
Vielleicht daß eine Saite sprang
An einer alten Violine.
Verdrießlich rascheln im Parterr
Etwelche Ratten hin und her,
Und alles riecht nach ranzgem Öle.
Die letzte Lampe ächzt und zischt
Verzweiflungsvoll und sie erlischt.
Das arme Licht war meine Seele. (B 6.1: 119)

The image of the final curtain was sufficiently powerful for Heine to repeat the opening line of this poem within the different poetic development of "Der Scheidende" (B 6.1: 349–50).[13] There the departing audience provides a prospect of domestic pleasures preferable even to heroic death. In "Sie erlischt," what dominates is the emptiness of the theater. The sensitivity to sound that was apparent in the squeaking of Frau Sorge's snuffbox produces the Chekhovian effect of the snapping violin string; but that noise, both uncanny and vulgar ("schnöd"), is succeeded by the "groaning" and "hissing" oil-lamp of the soul (Bark 388).

These noises suggest a later archetype: the irritated solitude of the domestic interior in Baudelaire's *Spleen* poem "Pluviôse irrité contre la ville entière" in *Les fleurs du mal*.

L'âme d'un vieux poète erre dans la gouttière
Avec la triste voix d'un fantôme frileux.

Le bourdon se lamente, et la bûche enfumée
Accompagne en fausset la pendule enrhumée. (144)

Baudelaire's interior is dominated by the sight of his mangy cat and by reminiscences of malicious gossip and old love affairs. Heine, on the other hand, is constantly accompanied by his anxieties about Mathilde's future and by his own inescapable illness. In the empty auditorium, the extinction of the soul leaves an uncanny and anxious space, populated by scurrying rats. Survival, in this group of poems, can only be unheroic, and the shade of Achilles is right. Yet vestiges of a moralizing interpretation of the fact of death remain: even in this darkened theater, the utterance "Das arme Licht war meine Seele" retains the pathos of individuality, prepared in the fine extension of "ächzt und zischt" by their adverb "Verzweiflungsvoll" at the beginning of the previous line. Ultimately even this pathos can be withdrawn.

In Heine's later poetry his astonishing craftsmanship manipulates versification in the direction of prose. In poem 8 of the "Zum Lazarus" cycle in *Gedichte. 1853 und 1854,* for example, in which Heine (probably) meditates on the letter of sympathy written by his cousin Therese after her belated visit to Paris in 1853, prose rhythm renders the line-end inoperative:

> Er [dein Brief] zeigte blendend hell, wie tief
> Mein Unglück ist, wie tief entsetzlich. (B 6.1: 206)

Alternatively, excessive rhyme withdraws the legitimacy of the poetic, as in poem 6 from the same group of amatory reminiscences in "Zum Lazarus":

> Du warst ein blondes Jungfräulein, so artig,
> So niedlich und so kühl — vergebens harrt ich
> Der Stunde, wo dein Herz sich erschlösse
> Und sich daraus Begeisterung ergösse —
>
> Begeisterung für jene hohen Dinge,
> Die zwar Verstand und Prosa achten gringe,
> Für die jedoch die Edlen, Schönen, Guten
> Auf dieser Erde schwärmen, leiden, bluten.
> (B 6.1: 204–5)

The excessive rhymes ("artig" / "harrt ich," "Dinge" / "gringe"), the rhyming subjunctives of the first stanza, the parallel lists at the end of the second, together with the explicit contrast with prosaic understanding and the consistent dominance of prose syntax (in stanza 1) mean that, cumulatively, the opening of this poem does more than challenge the inauthenticity of poetic diction. In what follows, of course, cliché is the main target, until the poem climaxes in sarcasm:

Als wie ein Mädchenbild gemalt von Netscher;
Ein Herzchen im Korsett wie'n kleiner Gletscher.
                                    (B 6.1: 205)

Even here the additive structure of the couplets weakens the sense of closure proffered by the extreme rhyme on a proper name.

In such poems verse technique is deployed to dramatize nonclosure. The everyday presents itself as the "normal" continuity of the mattress-grave, as the unexceptional pleasures of an "homme moyen sensuel," as the ordinary demands of domesticity. In two important cases, the possibility of closure is disturbed in a different way: "Disputation," the poem that concludes "Hebräische Melodien" in *Romanzero,* and "Für die Mouche," the poem generally regarded as Heine's last. In each case, the poem abandons an exhausted "irony" in which dialectical tension has been reduced to a banal repetition of blank contradictions — between Jew and Christian, between Hellenic pleasure and Mosaic asceticism. To awake from an endless series of contradictions returns the dissatisfied visionary to the everyday — of the grimly empty theater and the domesticity of "Der kleinste lebendige Philister / Zu Stukkert am Neckar" (B 6.1: 350). The boredom of unresolved controversy or the ennui of bourgeois daily life are experiences of temporal continuity in which even death itself fails to constitute an event.

VI. Modernity at a Standstill

In the "Nachwort" to *Romanzero,* Heine offers a final image of the empty continuity of modernity as he sets out to bid a tearful farewell to his readers. To avoid such sentimentality he reminds them of the prospect of renewed acquaintance in the afterlife, where, he is convinced, he will continue to write and his audience to read. His guarantor for this conviction is Swedenborg. The point of this reference to Swedenborg has been taken to be Heine's return to belief in a personal God; yet there are also signs that the context is at least lighthearted and even antitheological.

Heine's attention appears to have been drawn to Swedenborg by Eduard von Fichte, who understood his appearance in the "Nachwort" as evidence of Heine's determination to rid himself of philosophical arguments for the survival of the soul. Heine's own letter to I. H. Fichte about the "Nachwort" gives the same impression.[14] This appropriation of Swedenborg suggests opportunism, and Heine's account of his revised religious understanding is presented as a negotiation of social and political debates. His need for a divinity with the intentional and even physical attributes of a personal God is dated to 1848. According to the "Nachwort," the failure of Heine's health (and wealth) occasioning the revision happened in May, while in his autobiography, the *Geständnisse* (B 6.1: 475), the date is February. The promise of an afterlife, that is, emerges in the historical moment of a workers' revolt, the ludicrous hesitations of the Provisional Government of 1848;[15] and the "after" of this afterlife clearly points toward the failure of the June Days and the suppression of revolt by a bourgeois republican regime. Against this "atheist" bourgeois republic (itself shortly to become Louis Bonaparte's Second Empire), Heine reasserted his democratic credentials, his belief in a personal God, and his continued devotion to the pagan gods of his earlier work.

All this needs to be borne in mind if Heine's use of Swedenborg is to be understood. The failure of the ancient gods, figured as the amputations of the Venus de Milo, bonds them to Heine's own physical debility: though he must bid Venus farewell, he has foresworn nothing; and, as we have seen, the secularization and even judaization of Apollo in his exile from Greece makes his condition coincide with Heine's. The experience of present reality is suffused with the transmission of the past, and in an imaginative leap, tradition is enlivened at the very moment of its destruction. This had been the fundamental structure of *Romanzero*. Heine's most immediate personal reality is his own interminable dying: "ich sterbe so langsam, daß solches nachgerade langweilig wird für mich," he remarks (B 6.1: 180); and his moribund continuance figures in the poems as a domestic status quo.

The "Zum Lazarus" cycle of the *Gedichte. 1853 und 1854* twice presents Heine's condition as an immobilized continuity. Poem 3 of "Zum Lazarus" very precisely sets out two temporal frames. The first is the time of the present as stasis:

> Wie langsam kriechet sie dahin,
> Die Zeit, die schauderhafte Schnecke!
> Ich aber, ganz bewegungslos
> Bleib ich hier auf demselben Flecke. (B 6.1: 202)

The poem goes on to describe the author's condition as a kind of death ("Vielleicht bin ich gestorben längst") haunted in his dreams by the phantoms of pagan divinities. The only place in which these two temporalities — of contemporary stasis and historical haunting — can be brought together is in the action of the poem itself:

Die schaurig süßen Orgia,
Das nächtlich tolle Geistertreiben,
Sucht des Poeten Leichenhand
Manchmal am Morgen aufzuschreiben. (B 6.1: 203)

This double time, held in the structure of the poem, is the mark of the great poems of *Romanzero* as well as the *Gedichte. 1853 und 1854;* and it looks back to *Atta Troll* and its "wilde Jagd," forward to "Für die Mouche." Heine finds no scope for heroic gestures in dreaming and registering what has been lost. In the Lazarus poem the poet's corpse-like hand only *attempts* to record his dreams. The alternative is provided by poem 11 of "Zum Lazarus," in which, like the Greenlanders at the end of the *Romanzero* "Nachwort" who reject a Christian heaven that has no place for their seals, Heine renounces the joys of the afterlife for the continuity of bourgeois domesticity: "Bei meiner Frau in statu quo!" (B 6.1: 208).

Heine's "Nachwort" to *Romanzero* reveals that his paralysis also coincides with the condition of modernity. But while his immobilization can be projected as the continuity of domestic bliss, the afterlife cited from Swedenborg defines its own paralysis ("fossile Erstarrung" [B 6.1: 185]) as an endless repetition of the same: in Heaven the majority of history's famous personalities "blieben unverändert und beschäftigten sich mit denselben Dingen, mit denen sie sich auch vormals beschäftigt; sie blieben stationär" (B 6.1: 185). On the rare occasions when some of the great and good have changed, this can only serve to confirm the unchallenged way of the world. In Swedenborg's afterlife nothing changes, and even the corruption of saints (Anthony and Susanna) or the moral conversion of the sexually perverse (Lot's daughters) simply reflect the sheer pointlessness of life after 1848. Beyond the walls of his sickroom, outside the "Matratzengruft," Heine senses with growing anxiety the rapacious modernity that has been unleashed in Paris, not merely, as Benjamin's Baudelaire book has it, the capital of the nineteenth century, but "die leuchtende Hauptstadt der Welt" ("Babylonische Sorgen" [B 6.1: 194]).

VII

Heine's sensitivity to Mathilde's interruption sounds a familiar note of warning in relation to the modernizing and secularizing forces that the "Historien" record. Mathilde interrupts an already disjointed and meandering narrative to insist that, like anything else, the casket of

Darius — and the process of tradition that it represents — has its price. A parallel anxiety is evident in *Lutezia,* when Heine contemplates the somber iconoclasts of the communist movement who will use pages from *Buch der Lieder* for a bag of coffee or a twist of snuff (B 5: 224, 232). In the late poetry Heine recognizes all too clearly the consequences for poetry, and for the articulation of experience, of social forms dominated by the commodity. Unlike Benjamin, Heine derives the baleful condition of modernity from the political failure of 1848 rather than from economic and sociopsychological factors structuring the experience of time (Osborne 81–85). Against the homogeneity of this political afterlife, projected as Swedenborg's vision of Heaven in the *Romanzero* "Nachwort," Heine pits all the resources of tradition, classical and above all Jewish, renewed and revitalized in the work of the poems themselves and in his own activity as poet. It is an unequal struggle. In engaging these resources with cultural and political history focused prismatically in his own experience of exile, Heine can register the condition — and claims — of modernity after 1848, even if the position is hopeless, a "verlorner Posten in dem Freiheitskriege" (B 6.1: 120).

This famous phrase opens the last of the Lazarus poems in *Romanzero,* a poem that Heine originally intended to call "Verlorene Schildwacht"; its final French title, "Enfant perdu," is largely unexplained. It has been suggested that Heine was already thinking of a French translation of his original title as "sentinelle perdue,"[16] but the retrospective character of the poem suggests the child we should think of is the one who wanted to have been born on New Year's Eve 1799, and thus to be biographically in the vanguard of nineteenth-century modernity. Heine's emancipatory project "in dem Freiheitskriege" was overtaken by another modernity, after 1830 in the July Monarchy and again after 1848. As it scans the fate of tradition, his late poetry engages with the claims of this modernity so that, in the great poems, through the paralysis of his own experience, and in imaginative self-identification with poets of the past, a whole history becomes legible. Walter Benjamin could hardly have asked for more.[17]

Notes

[1] Theodor W. Adorno, "Die Wunde Heine," *Noten zur Literatur,* vol. 11 of *Gesammelte Schriften,* ed. Rolf Tiedemann (Frankfurt am Main: Suhrkamp, 1974), 97: my translation. The standard translation has "looms large" ("Heine the Wound," *Notes on Literature,* trans. Shierry Weber Nicholson [New York: Columbia UP, 1991], 82).

[2] ". . . die neue Schule, die moderne deutsche Lyrik, [ward] von mir eröffnet" (1854), *Geständnisse* (B 6.1: 447).

[3] See *Das Passagen-Werk,* in Walter Benjamin, *Gesammelte Schriften,* ed. Rolf Tiedemann and Hermann Schweppenhäuser (Frankfurt am Main: Suhrkamp, 1982), vol. 5.1: J8a, 2; J38a, 5.

[4] Cp. *Passagen-Werk,* A7a, 1; Adorno's letter has not been preserved.

[5] Roger Cook stresses the contrast in *By the Rivers of Babylon: Heinrich Heine's Late Songs and Reflections* (Detroit: Wayne State UP, 1998), 325–26.

[6] See Joachim Bark, citing Fränkel's commentary from Walzel's edition ("Die Muse als Krankenwärterin," *Romanzero,* by Heinrich Heine [Munich: Goldmann, 1988], 412).

[7] For a different and fuller reading see Cook, *By the Rivers of Babylon,* 330–39.

[8] See Luciano Zagari "'Das ausgesprochene Wort ist ohne Scham.' Der späte Heine und die Auflösung der dichterischen Sprache," *Zu Heinrich Heine,* ed. L. Zagari and P. Chiarini, Literaturwissenschaft — Gesellschaftswissenschaft 51 (Stuttgart: Klett, 1981), 124–40; and "La *Pomare* di Heine e la crisi del linguaggio 'lirico,'" *Studi germanici* 3 (1965): 9–10.

[9] These terms are derived from Adorno's later essay, "Über Tradition" (*Gesammelte Schriften,* vol. 10, ed. Rolf Tiedemann [Frankfurt am Main: Suhrkamp, 1974], 310–11).

[10] My discussion of "Karl I" is indebted to Hans-Peter Bayerdörfer, "Politische Ballade. Zu den 'Historien' in Heines *Romanzero,*" *Deutsche Vierteljahresschrift* 46 (1972): 435–68, in particular 440–68. For a more skeptical view see Alberto Destro's commentary (DHA 3.2: 600–602).

[11] Cp. "Das Sklavenschiff" in *Gedichte. 1853 und 1854.* For Benjamin, the prostitute is the key figure of this process of commodification; however, he also neglects the historical precedent of the slave trade. See also Walter Klaar on "Das Sklavenschiff" at B 6.2: 71.

[12] Klaus Briegleb identifies the post-1848 sense of balance with the term "satirisch-resignative Nachmärzgedichte"; see B 6.2: 57 on "Im Oktober 1849."

[13] Destro identifies a sudden change of direction in "Der Scheidende" (DHA 3.2: 1503); it is equally plausible to see the departure of the audience for domestic pleasures as the unheroic alternative to the dying poet's lot.

[14] The Fichtes' visit is described in Michael Werner, ed., *Begegnungen mit Heine: Berichte der Zeitgenossen, in Fortführung von H. H. Houbens "Gespräche mit Hei-*

ne" (Hamburg: Hoffmann und Campe, 1973), vol. 2: 276–79, cited in DHA 3.2: 979, and — to different effect — in B 6.2: 63.

[15] See the "Waterloo-Fragment" (B 6.1: 505).

[16] See Michael Werner in Bernd Kortländer, ed. *Interpretationen von Heines Gedichten* (Stuttgart: Reclam, 1995), 188.

[17] See Peter Osborne, "Small-scale Victories, Large-scale Defeats," *Walter Benjamin's Philosophy*, ed. Andrew Benjamin and Peter Osborne (London: Routledge, 1994), 68, on *Passagen-Werk* N 11, 3.

Works Cited

Adorno, Theodor W. "Heine the Wound." *Notes on Literature.* Trans. Shierry Weber Nicholson. New York: Columbia UP, 1991.

———. "Über Tradition." *Gesammelte Schriften.* Vol. 10. Ed. Rolf Tiedemann. Frankfurt am Main: Suhrkamp, 1974. 310–25. 20 vols. 1970–1986.

———. "Die Wunde Heine." *Noten zur Literatur.* Vol. 11 of *Gesammelte Schriften.* Ed. Rolf Tiedemann. Frankfurt am Main: Suhrkamp, 1974. 95–100. 20 vols. 1970–1986.

Adorno, Theodor W., and Walter Benjamin. *Briefwechsel.* Ed. Henri Lonitz. Frankfurt am Main: Suhrkamp, 1994.

Bark, Joachim. "Die Muse als Krankenwärterin." *Romanzero.* By Heinrich Heine. Munich: Goldmann, 1988.

Baudelaire, Charles. *The Flowers of Evil.* Trans. James McGowan. Oxford: Oxford UP, 1993.

Bayerdörfer, Hans-Peter. "Politische Ballade. Zu den 'Historien' in Heines *Romanzero*." *Deutsche Vierteljahresschrift* 46 (1972): 435–68.

Benjamin, Walter. *Das Passagen-Werk.* Vol. 5 of *Gesammelte Schriften.* Ed. Rolf Tiedemann. Frankfurt am Main: Suhrkamp, 1998. 13 vols. 1978–.

Briegleb, Klaus. *Opfer Heine.* Frankfurt am Main: Suhrkamp, 1986.

Cook, Roger. *By the Rivers of Babylon: Heinrich Heine's Late Songs and Reflections.* Detroit: Wayne State UP, 1998.

Goethe, Johann Wolfgang von. *Dramen I.* Vol. 3 of *Werke. Hamburger Ausgabe.* Ed. Erich Trunz. Munich: C. H. Beck, 1976.

Hinck, Walter. *Die deutsche Ballade von Bürger bis Brecht.* Göttingen: Vandenhoeck, 1968.

Hofrichter, Laura. *Heinrich Heine: Biographie seiner Dichtung.* Göttingen: Vandenhoeck, 1966.

Kaufmann, Hans. "Heinrich Heine. Poesie, Vaterland und Menschheit." Vol. 10 of *Werke und Briefe*. By Heinrich Heine. Berlin and Weimar: Aufbau, 1980. 5–166. 10 vols.

Kortländer, Bernd, ed. *Interpretationen von Heines Gedichten*. Stuttgart: Reclam, 1995.

Osborne, Peter. "Small-scale Victories, Large-scale Defeats." *Walter Benjamin's Philosophy*. Ed. Andrew Benjamin and Peter Osborne. London: Routledge, 1994. 59–109.

Preisendanz, Wolfgang. *Heinrich Heine: Werkstrukturen und Epochenbezüge*. Munich: Wilhelm Fink [UTB], 1983.

Robertson, Ritchie. *Heine*. London: Weidenfeld & Nicholson, 1988.

Sammons, Jeffrey L. *Heinrich Heine*. Stuttgart: Metzler, 1991.

Werner, Michael, ed. *Begegnungen mit Heine: Berichte der Zeitgenossen, in Fortführung von H. H. Houbens "Gespräche mit Heine."* Hamburg: Hoffmann und Campe, 1973. 2 vols.

von Wiese, Benno. "Mythos und Historie in Heines später Lyrik." *Referate und Diskussionen. Internationaler Heine-Kongreß Düsseldorf, 1972*. Ed. Manfred Windfuhr. Hamburg: Hoffmann und Campe, 1973. 121–46.

Zagari, Luciano. "'Das ausgesprochene Wort ist ohne Scham.' Der späte Heine und die Auflösung der dichterischen Sprache." *Zu Heinrich Heine*. Ed. L. Zagari, P. Chiarini. Literaturwissenschaft — Gesellschaftswissenschaft 51. Stuttgart: Klett, 1981. 124–40.

———. "La *Pomare* di Heine e la crisi del linguaggio 'lirico.'" *Studi germanici* 3 (1965): 5–38.

Ziegler, Edda. *Heinrich Heine: Leben — Werk — Wirkung*. Zurich: Artemis & Winkler, 1993.

Late Thoughts: Reconsiderations from the "Matratzengruft"

Joseph A. Kruse

I. Prelude to a Taboo Subject

WHENEVER THE SUBJECT OF Heinrich Heine's final years crops up, his biographers and commentators tend to display a degree of diffidence. This is excusable since the depiction of mortality and death as a tangible reality stripped of fictionalization has never been a popular topic among the living. Though there are a number of other topics and motifs to keep it company, necessity nonetheless compelled the author to devote the end of his days to this abysmal theme, which to him became literally a life-and-death struggle. However, he handled it with such a sense of ease and liberty that his readers were left bewildered and helpless (and to some extent this is still true of his current readership), even while his visitors, according to reports by contemporaries, were frequently irritated by his manner.[1] Still, Heine's oeuvre does not present a picture of consistency followed seamlessly by silence. His preparations for the hour of death are reminiscent of the Baroque tradition,[2] but they are transposed into secular realms, without, however, omitting questions about the final order of things.

To this day Heine's late poetry and prose cause the kind of discomfort we experience at our own inability to aid others with incurable infirmities, who nonetheless are able to talk with us about their frailties in detail. Thus the late writing is sometimes seen as a foreign corpus whose free form and self-perpetuating autonomy are each fascinating in their own right. Indeed, Heine could not possibly be more direct in addressing his audience — he never leaves the certainty of physical decay to conjecture and, yet, he would not dream of appealing to public commiseration. Polite euphemisms are not tolerated, except in the final letters to his mother in Hamburg.[3] Elsewhere the prevailing tone is one of unblinking honesty, as he puts his conscience through the subtlest introspections, probing both his physical reactions and those of his soul. On September 12, 1848 he wrote his physician brother Maximilian this shockingly crude observation: "Dieser lebendige Tod, dieses Unleben, ist nicht zu ertragen, wenn sich noch Schmerzen dazu gesellen. . . . meine Lippen sind gelähmt wie meine Füße, auch die Eßwerkzeuge sind gelähmt ebensosehr wie die Absonderungskanäle. Ich kann weder kauen noch kacken, werde wie ein Vogel gefüttert. Dieses Unleben ist nicht zu ertragen" (HSA 22: 294). The rapid reiteration of the word "Unleben," epitomizing the sheer horror of his illness serves to underline the hopeless extent of the poet's perdition. In a letter of February 7, 1850 to Heinrich Laube he describes his condition as "Verzweiflung des Leibes" and then makes allusions to a so-called religious conversion, which naturally enough contains a bold hint of negative inversion, where "fear" of the Lord actually assumes blasphemous connotations. In fact, the text as a whole playfully explores the alleys of colloquial speech and its religious substructure: "Gottlob, daß ich jetzt wieder einen Gott habe, da kann ich mir doch im Uebermaße des Schmerzes einige fluchende Gotteslästerungen erlauben; dem Atheisten ist eine solche Labung nicht vergönnt" (HSA 23: 26–27). Such strong language suggests intimacy with his God rather than denoting a metaphysical conversion. An unpublished poem entitled "Unbequemer neuer Glauben" has a similar ring to it, surmising that the notion of the lord God should be retained,

> Nicht zum Lieben, nein, zum Hassen,
>
> . . .
>
> Weil man sonst nicht fluchen könnt' —
> Himmel — Herrgott — Sakrament! (DHA 3.1: 400)

As Heine's case shows, such a disrespectfully direct and intimate treatment of one's own death was considered, especially in former times, taboo, for it exposed the private realm in an indecent and embarrassing manner. Of course, within the scope of our predictable quotidian existence literature serves to expand our consciousness and provide alternative perspectives on life. Still, we do not like to be involuntarily dragged into the discussion of certain topics that are preferably kept at arm's length, especially those of human mortality and all its complexities. Should such themes appear in literature, it is imperative that they be shrouded in poetry and artifice. Heine, however, has an antidote for the psychological precautions that anticipate contact with such unwelcome themes. Equipped as it is with all the tricks of the trade, such as allegory and masquerade, Heine's ultimate remedy nevertheless consists of boldly looking doom straight in the eye. Employing literary form, rhythm, and rhyme, he conjures up the hidden dilemmas of his own predicament and sounds the abysmal depths of his despair.

But is it not perhaps a bit much to expect the public to put up with the notions and fantasies of a moribund poet, who, having once been a self-assured advocate of liberty and life, now surprisingly displays even more confident resolve in heralding the lamentable torments of a slow and painful demise? Is it not also impractical to allow one's hectic daily life to be disrupted by what the author himself refers to as unburied corpses, or by the way in which he guides his readers to the edge of that grave where he hopes soon to find rest from a morphine-soothed limbo he finds so hard to accept as "life"? In *Gedichte. 1853 und 1854* the second and third poems of the Lazarus cycle talk of this transient state. Although they give the appearance of internal monologue, they were obviously committed to paper with an audience in mind:

> Mein Leib ist jetzt ein Leichnam, worin
> Der Geist ist eingekerkert —
> Manchmal wird ihm unwirsch zu Sinn,
> Er tobt und rast und berserkert. (DHA 3.1: 199)

In many cultures and epochs the body has been seen as a vessel that houses the mind and soul, or even as a dungeon that imprisons them until the ultimate religious deliverance of death. Here, however, an anachronistic experience of temporal warping comes into play, upsetting the very balance of time itself. While the body and its designated mind had once been granted a harmonious, reconciled existence, the spirit now finds itself rebelling against a lifeless shell. From a poem whose exploration into "Zeit, die schauderhafte Schnecke" blurs the borders between objective perception, fantasy, and death, the lines

> Vielleicht bin ich gestorben längst;
> Es sind vielleicht nur Spukgestalten
> Die Phantasieen, die des Nachts
> Im Hirn den bunten Umzug halten.
> (DHA 3.1: 199)

display a similar understanding of the neuropathological processes underlying poetic creation. These dispatches emanating from the "Schädel eines todten Dichters," which apparently is playing host to a motley band of ghosts claiming (in the ensuing verse) to be descended

from "Altheidnisch göttlichen Gelichters," are indeed hard to accept.
They reveal a despair-induced relapse into paganism that easily sur-
passes even the most horrific coffins, yawning graves, and eerie
churchyards of that black Romanticism that had characterized the
early poetry of the young Heine from his "Traumbilder" to "Lyrisches
Intermezzo."

In those early realms of black Romanticism, construed from flights
of fancy and elaborately playful language, the youthful poet invented
phantasmagoria in which eroticism and death motifs are inextricably
interwoven. A scene where he and his lover decide to ignore the clar-
ion of the Last Judgment is but one example among many. Back then,
however, he had been in full control of what was, for him, a literary
game. The overwrought imagery was a largely artificial product of the
intellect; his fantasies a mannerist variant of amorous language.

> Mein süßes Lieb, wenn du im Grab,
> Im dunkeln Grab wirst liegen,
> Dann will ich steigen zu dir hinab,
> Und will mich an dich schmiegen,
>
> Ich küsse, umschlinge und presse dich wild,
> Du Stille, du Kalte, du Bleiche!
> Ich jauchze, ich zitt're, ich weine mild,
> Ich werde selber zur Leiche.
>
> Die Todten stehn auf, die Mitternacht ruft,
> Sie tanzen im luftigen Schwarme;
> Wir beide bleiben in der Gruft,
> Ich liege in deinem Arme.
>
> Die Todten stehen auf, der Tag des Gerichts
> Ruft sie zu Qual und Vergnügen;
> Wir beide bekümmern uns um nichts,
> Und bleiben umschlungen liegen. (DHA 1.1: 163–65)

The late Heine, on the other hand, does not toy with death wishes
and erotic dreams. The days of facade and lyric escapism are over. The
description of his protracted yet very real encounters with a death that
was as lingeringly imminent as it was inevitable became serious business, as did the final revision of his earlier French and German writings, which were to be his gift to posterity. Though his assuming the
guise of Lazarus the beggar (a biblical name featured not only in a
parable, but also where Christ raises an eponymous friend from the
dead) as a means of gaining deeper insights[4] and of providing his read-

ership with a universally comprehensible metaphor is clearly borrowed from the time-honored literary tradition of role-playing, his premature aging, the more than taxing experience of pain and agony, of waning life and stagnant death somehow enriched or, to be more precise, lent gravity to his poetic vision. Without wishing to canonize his own image and thereby to resort to yet another method of overcoming anxieties concerning the subject, Heine seemed to know how to make the most even of this dismal development.

During his final years he no longer looked upon love and death as useful literary correlations, but, defying physical handicaps, came to regard them as mutually dependent prerequisites of life itself. This new view is evidenced in some late poems to his wife Mathilde, as well as in those dedicated to his young friend Elise Krinitz, whom he called his "Mouche,"[5] and also in the late prose, notably the posthumously published fragment of his memoirs.

These observations concerning Heine's final years are intended to clarify and explain the various degrees of ironic gravity and witty melancholia the author chose to employ. Heine's final years are extensively documented, as his illness and death were made into issues of public concern. The prospect of inevitable doom coupled with bouts of intense pain frequently drove him to the brink of despair, and his stoic courage in overcoming any suicidal thoughts underlines his determination to explore the limits of his staying power and not to disappoint the high hopes of his doting mother, his wife, and his sister. Although this study focuses on his last years, the various stages of Heine's life may be regarded as a chain of unified extremes and of extreme unions (see part 2 below). His final years were conditioned by agony and ailment, forcing the author to analyze his physio-psychological situation, which in turn revived some religious thoughts (part 3). This resurrection resulted in an amazing variety of fresh insights and new perspectives (part 4), where death and related ultimate topics stood out as the principal driving force (part 5).

II. The Stations of Heine's Life:
Unified Extremes and Extreme Unifications

Many biographies of artists and writers have come to epitomize the tragedy that can ensue from fortune's fickle nature. But fate is not the only thing apt to turn sour: the lives of those involved in art and literature often seem to affirm the widely held opinion that certain talents and achievements inevitably come at the price of personal sacrifice. Genius and madness, poetry and poverty, lifelong failure and limitless posthumous fame are considered to be closely linked even to this day. The life and works of Heinrich Heine are a striking example of this existential conundrum. Notably his gradual decline in the "Matratzengruft" — as he dubbed his confinement to bed by terminal illness in the "Nachwort" to *Romanzero* — serves to confirm the grim aspects of his successful but also controversial existence in the limelight.

In his *Geständnisse*, written in the winter of 1854, two years before his death, Heine surmised "Ich habe es, wie die Leute sagen, auf dieser schönen Erde zu nichts gebracht. Es ist nichts aus mir geworden, nichts als ein Dichter." This pursuit is, he acknowledges, a far cry from the dazzling career as a Catholic cleric that his mother and teachers had allegedly mapped out for him and which was eventually, according to his fanciful conjecture, to have culminated in Rome with his extending the world a papal blessing. He does, however, buffer his resignation by professing his esteem for the poetic profession: "Man ist viel, wenn man ein Dichter ist, und gar wenn man ein großer lyrischer Dichter ist in Deutschland, unter dem Volke, das in zwey Dingen, in der Philosophie und im Liede, alle andern Nazionen überflügelt hat" (DHA 15: 55). This ambivalent attitude toward his accomplishments is also evidenced in his correspondence, where his self-assessments often veer in the direction of bitterness, as can be seen in a December 3, 1853 letter to his mother: "Ich bin sehr ruhig, lasse fünf eine grade Zahl sein. Es ist mir nichts geglückt in dieser Welt, aber es hätte mir doch noch schlimmer gehen können. So trösten sich halbgeprügelte Hunde" (HSA 23: 302).

On the whole, Heine provides us with an unwavering account of his feelings, experiences, and beliefs, his doubts, fears, and insights as death draws near. The audience is assigned the role of an intellectual sparring partner who must absorb and evaluate his thoughts. In his "Nachwort" to *Romanzero* he quips "Der Autor gewöhnt sich am Ende an sein Publikum, als wäre es ein vernünftiges Wesen" (DHA 3.1: 181). And his contemporaries did indeed listen with a kind of inquisitive sympathy as he proclaimed his woes. Until many years after his death this reluctant reception process and its after-effects caused Heine's life and oeuvre to become the subject of intense controversy and violent clashes, especially when it came to the naming of institutions, streets, etc. and of monuments and memorials[6] — this was even more problematic in Germany than abroad, where his unconventional ambivalences actually heightened his appeal. Depending on the audience in question, the reasons for such controversy may stem from his choice of subject matter and his unconventionally liberal handling of it, from his dissonant style, which was forever oscillating between irony and sentimentality, from his unorthodox poetic form, from his Jewish background,[7] from the many years spent outside his homeland in France, or from his public life as a journalistic writer. The moribund poet, who had once gone so far as to affirm the contemporary assumption that his eight-year ordeal was caused by a venereal disease, namely syphilis, was considered by many to be a public scandal, and he himself was held solely responsible for the reckless lifestyle upon which his ailment was blamed. This added yet another blemish to a reputation already tarnished by his Jewish identity.[8]

It is therefore not surprising that Heine's last statements were not received with the kind of enthusiasm that such strikingly genuine accounts from the frontiers of the netherworld might have merited,[9] though it should be added that the most recent research has finally taken steps to boost their standing. This disregard is clearly evidenced by many thousands of musical compositions written for Heine's poems, the vast majority of which are based on *Buch der Lieder* (1827) and the stylistically similar "Neuer Frühling" cycle in *Neue Gedichte* (1844), and whose tone is one of sentimental romanticism.[10] Only gradually did his later, more political works catch the attention of composers, which is remarkable, given their even more strongly musical language. On the other hand, this bias among musicians reflects how musical tastes in particular tend to mirror prevailing fashions. Nor should it come as much of a shock that despite a sporadic fascination with Heine's political writings, research interests have followed this trend in giving preference to his early and mid-period works. But, as already mentioned, there are numerous recent studies of various origins and variable quality that signal a shift in emphasis to the late period. They home in on the ailing Heine of the final years, who epitomizes the modern poet, and, in his sovereign sense of despair, gives expression to the most diverse and intimate facets of his life as writer.[11]

One could claim, in fact, that Heine's final years and his last works, created in defiance of all odds, mark the culmination of an early nineteenth-century existence distinguished by its own unique brand of diversity. One should also bear in mind that his was, in a sense, a pan-European achievement. He became a prominent literary figure in both Germany and France at the same time, even as his works were gaining recognition in the neighboring countries; and his fame continued to spread internationally during his lifetime. One could describe his life, which was as quintessentially European then as it would be today, as a sequence of linear threads disjoined by occasional breaks. While this schematic characterization may be useful for the many biographies, in the end it proves not as well-suited to Heine's actual life story as one would have it. For those breaks in the linear narratives result from extremes that can only be reassembled into a convincing whole by force. Thus extremes and even contradictions find themselves reconciled into a seemingly harmonious whole, and yet, almost paradoxically, these reconciliations can only be maintained through extreme exertion. This is true, for instance, of Heine's circumstantially motivated transition from a business career to that of a legal student and his subsequent relocation. It applies as well to the Düsseldorf business failure that forced the family to forfeit their belongings and set up shop in — of all places — the north German town of Lüneburg, in order to be close to their millionaire relative Salomon Heine. Similarly, it informs his ambivalently successful attempt to establish himself as a German Romantic poet, and also plays a role in his involvement with the *Verein für Cultur und Wissenschaft der Juden*. It also features in his clandestine conversion to Protestantism, without which his aspirations toward a position in the civil service would have been futile. Furthermore, it accounts for the versatility of those writings designed to subvert censorship; for his mediator status between France and Germany, and for his precarious position as a German poet living in Paris on a stipend issued by the French government, who nevertheless enjoyed the liberties of a journalist writing between two fronts. It also shows in his ambiguous assessment of political trends, such as emergent communism, and, finally, in his variable religious attitude toward the end of his life. One could no doubt draw out this litany even further, but the aim here is to impress upon the reader the diversity of Heine's life and to highlight the most significant elements comprising this colorful mosaic. Not yet mentioned are Heine's numerous journeys within Germany and into neighboring countries and his travels throughout France after his immigration in 1831, which help complete Heine's image as an author who ventured beyond the ivory tower to experience the world at first hand. Only his eventual confinement to one spot necessitated a recourse to his innermost perception, and this served to deepen his understanding of the world, as is often reflected in his writings, albeit in the form of irony. Even this last phase does not have the feel of an ivory tower but rather that of some monkish cell far removed from time and space, where one must suffer the martyrdom of bare survival for the sake of its accurate description. Thus the term "stylite," which in today's usage generally carries sardonic connotations, could be applied in its original sense with respect to Heine's plight, though his was not a self-imposed condition, but rather an inevitable ordeal sublimated through liberal artistic expression.

It is precisely this ability to blend into one the most diverse elements and to find compositional solutions for combining even the most blatant contradictions encountered along the many stations of his life that, to this day, sets Heine apart. Therein lies the magic of his humanitarian and poetic accomplishments. In conjunction with his publisher Julius Campe, Heine's objective was to craft his whole existence into a modern piece of art, one that would transcend Classicism and Romanticism. It internalized the ideals of *Junges Deutschland* and those of the *Vormärz* to eventually end up breaking new ground in the form of a phantasmal symbolist realism. This is evidenced both in the way his work is programmatically organized into cycles ranging from small to large, and in his own day-to-day lifestyle (as opposed to those chunks of biography strategically intended for the press). He fashioned himself as a writer so as to epitomize the intricate social, political and cultural fabric of life during his era. Heine consciously rode on the back of tradition only to vary and ultimately overcome it, and in order to ensure a more humane future.

The sequence of events shaping this process may be traced according to a number of criteria. First and foremost, however, there is the obvious chronological categorization on the basis of biographical events: the initial phase of literary preparation, up to 1819; early writings as a student, from 1819 to 1825; first literary successes with *Reisebilder* and *Buch der Lieder*, from 1826 to 1831; the first French phase, from 1831 until the prohibition of the Young German movement in December 1835; the second French phase until his *Denkschrift* on Ludwig Börne, from 1836 to 1840; the culmination of his political influence marked by two trips to Germany (1843/44), from 1841 to 1844; the years preceding the outbreak of his illness, from 1845 to 1848; and his final years in the "Matratzengruft." Other types of categorization could follow the literary cycles during his French years. The titles of books and individual pieces alone suffice to demonstrate Heine's uncanny capacity for pinpointing the trends and peculiarities of his epoch.

Decades of debate on the subject of Heine — employing methods ranging from enthusiastic data delving to psychoanalysis, from hermeneutics to structuralist evaluations — have undoubtedly lead to great discoveries, but none have managed to dispel in full the mysteries surrounding his life, especially those of his final years. These secrets have always been treated with due respect, but efforts to solve them have so far remained tentative and essentially incomplete, a situation that will not change in the near future. In other words, no matter what new evidence comes to light, be it Heine's definitive or at least near-exact date of birth, or even an authoritative coroner's report establishing the true cause of his death, it will not adequately explain why he became a poet in the first place nor why he remained one to the end. For it is the bizarre discrepancy between innate predispositions and the choices he made that brings his work to life. The difficulties scholars have had establishing the facts of Heine's life has come to be seen as paradigmatic for his inner life, which consistently eludes the beholder. As is particularly evident from Heine's remarks during the later period, his internal world had a dynamic of its own. It would pay to heed his voice from the "Matratzengruft" more closely. It would yield not only a better understanding of the European historical context of the time, but would even contribute greatly to the work of those Heine scholars who clearly favor the young, contentious lyrical poet over the older, more problematical Heine. This is not to insinuate that his late observations and unpublished pieces have been actively suppressed, but certainly their significance has been played down. It has been as though they did not fit the received image and needed thus to be hidden behind a veil of respect for his privacy, perhaps out of fear that they might contain unexpected contradictions or even recantations.

A recalibrated view of Heine and his work would not only show that each season of his life had its own particular emphasis, but that he was also able to adapt his message and his discourse to the changing seasons of his reading public Thus, his attention to the shifts in his reading public mirrors his comment about the impact of *Don Quixote* on its readers, which varies dramatically, he claims, according to the particular phase the reader happens to be experiencing. In his introduction to Cervantes's novel, Heine ponders on the respect he bore for *Don Quixote* in his youth in contrast to his current view, and then applies this relational perspective to the many major and minor discords manifest in his own biography:

> Ist mein Herz die ganze Zeit über stabil geblieben, oder ist es, nach einem wunderbaren Kreislauf, zu den Gefühlen der Kindheit zurückgekehrt? Das letztere mag wohl der Fall seyn: denn ich erinnere mich, daß ich in jedem Lustrum meines Lebens den Don Quixote mit abwechselnd verschiedenartigen Empfindungen gelesen habe. Als

ich ins Jünglingsalter emporblühte . . .: da war mir der Don Quixote
ein sehr unerquickliches Buch . . ., Späterhin, als ich zum Manne
heranreifte, versöhnte ich mich schon einigermaßen mit Dulcineas
unglücklichem Kämpen, und ich fing schon an über ihn zu lachen.
Der Kerl ist ein Narr, sagte ich. Doch sonderbarerweise, auf allen
meinen Lebensfahrten verfolgten mich die Schattenbilder des dürren
Ritters und seines fetten Knappen, namentlich wenn ich an einen
bedenklichen Scheideweg gelangte. (DHA 10: 250–51)

This self-interrogation concerning Heine's ever-changing attitude toward one and the same book, which seems to make a new impression
on him every five years, also applies indirectly to the assessment of his
late oeuvre.

III. The Determinate Factors of the Late Period

There is a huge difference between those writings of Heine that are
based upon direct encounters with life on the streets of Paris and
those that are based on fleeting impressions caught from the window
of his sick chamber. While articles described as "Berichte über Politik,
Kunst und Volksleben" (this being the subtitle of *Lutezia,* the 1854
collection of articles he had published in the Augsburg *Allgemeine
Zeitung*) are written with all the gusto of a hawkeyed reporter on the
beat, his later musings have a much more introspective feel. They rely
heavily on second-hand sources, that is, anecdotes, books, and maga-
zines, and it is not without cause that Heine got into the eccentric
habit of having others read to him books he had borrowed from the
public libraries of Hamburg rather than Paris. This further widened
the gulf between an imaginary world perceived in German and the
purely French exchange with his wife and domestic help. Heine, who
prided himself upon having mediated some intra-European conflicts,
now was confined to his rooms, as his illness reinforced the psychic
rifts that had always been part of his multipolar cultural world. This
may well be the reason behind sudden pangs of homesickness and the
desire to rejoin his relatives in Hamburg, sentiments that he had dis-
pensed with earlier, for example, in the famous lines of "Nachtgedanken," the final poem in the "Zeitgedichte" group of *Neue Gedichte.*
Though his twelve-year absence from home induced him to profess a
deep affection for his mother, he eventually decided to abandon the
political mire of his "deutschen Sorgen" in favor of his merry wife and
"französisch heit'res Tageslicht" (DHA 2: 129–30).

His forced withdrawal from Parisian life and his being at the mercy of doctors, nurses, secretarial assistants, and the whims of his wife are obviously reflected in his work. Having last seen him in Hamburg in 1844, even his publisher Julius Campe could not imagine the extent of Heine's physical decay and could not, therefore, pardon him for his tantrums and insinuations, until he was shocked into pity and forgiveness upon witnessing for himself the sheer horror of Heine's condition. Then he realized that all Heine's injurious remarks were indeed the product of despair and solitude. As is clear from a letter Campe wrote from Paris to his wife in Hamburg on April 20, 1855, he was deeply pessimistic about the ailing poet's ability to write, due in no small part to his opinion of the whimsical Mrs. Heine. She had apparently been unable to receive Campe in the mornings, "Und doch hatte diese dicke wabblige Person, fast im Hemde nur mit einem dünnen Ueberwurf, einem Sacke gleich, halbe Tage lang, ab- und zugehend, sich neben mir bewegt." And thus he had to negotiate with a family friend by the name of Mlle. Pauline. When he "unrolled" three copies of Heine's portrait, which he had brought along, "kamen noch drei weiblich dienstbare Geister dazu — es begann ein langes Geschnattere, Vergleich, wie er vor 3 Jahre [en] ausgesehen und wie *ietzt*!" This is followed by a detailed description of Heine: "Sein *Geist* und *Lebensmuth* ist derselbe. Aber die *Person,* die hat zum Erschrecken abgenommen! So wie er da liegt, geht es nicht lange mehr weiter —" (Werner 2: 369). One should therefore imagine Heine's last poetic projects not as having been conceived in a sort of bedridden idyll, but rather in a living hell.

To make matters worse, the treatment Heine received was no less agonizing than the persistent pains he had to endure. Although written in symbolic and metaphorical language, the poems "Wenn sich die Blutegel vollgesogen" or "Laß mich mit glühnden Zangen kneipen" reflect the harsh reality of Heine's experiences of medical treatment. It is not surprising that such torments should cause the heart to falter. In fact, the impact of Heine's health on his work was already a subject of academic discussion while he was still alive. Even when he was still the young poet who loved to strike a pose, Heine had not been in the best of health. In his *Die Romantische Schule* of 1836, he comments on the degenerate quality of poems by E. T. A Hoffmann and Novalis, voicing suspicions that poetry as such may well be "eine Krankheit des Menschen . . . wie die Perle eigentlich nur der Krankheitsstoff ist, woran das arme Austerthier leidet." However, he promptly professes his solidarity with these men: "Aber haben wir ein Recht zu solchen

Bemerkungen, wir, die wir nicht allzu sehr mit Gesundheit gesegnet sind? Und gar jetzt, wo die Literatur wie ein großes Lazareth aussieht?" (DHA 8.1: 193). But all those headaches, migraines, and hypochondrias for which the author sought relief at spas during his earlier years in Germany and France were a mere joke compared to the incurable torments of his slow demise. Those very real pains were infinitely worse than any prior imaginary ailment, and they therefore required a whole new mode of expression.

Despite Heine's forced confinement after 1848, his late work remains loosely tied to the relatively active life he had previously enjoyed. The aforementioned *Lutezia* is a prime example of this. But even the slightly older *Romanzero* does not entirely reflect that sense of banishment and exile asserted in its "Nachwort." Heine began drafting his testament concerning the distribution of his literary and material estate as early as March 1843, and this was followed by other versions in September 1846, February 1847, yet another version in June 1848, and eventually the legally binding document of 1851. This would seem to indicate that his last thoughts were not solely the product of physical imprisonment in a sick chamber, but that they had actually begun to take shape well before then. His *Vermischte Schriften* as well as his autobiographic *Geständnisse* already reflect the doom of fatal illness and death. As is the case with his last will and parts of his *Memoiren,* it has to be remembered that some of his final poems and musings were not submitted to any publisher and should therefore be classified as private documents. Of course this does not necessarily mean that they were not intended for publication, but it did result in their not becoming available to a broader audience until much later. It is not without reason that Adolf Strodtmann calls his epilogue to the first critical edition of Heine's complete works "Letzte Gedichte und Gedanken" (1869), as these do indeed call from the grave in a very different manner than those last poems and proclamations purposefully (and strategically) dispatched to the printers by the author himself. Even modern readers can still detect in the late unpublished works a certain amount of camouflage, even as Heine mercilessly dissects and avows his darkest memories, bringing to light the deepest afflictions of his soul. Whether it be his strained, dysfunctional relationship with his Hamburg clan, his difficult rapport with his much younger and socially inferior wife Mathilde, or his "Gesundheitsliebe" (DHA 3.1: 396) for his last woman friend Elise Krinitz, affectionately known as "Mouche," all these profoundly worrying interpersonal problems are not successfully dealt with, except in his unpublished works. The very fact that these were not submitted to the press may in itself indicate that they are much closer to the core than his "public" work. This is especially true of those verses dedicated to Mouche, but it also applies to the epic "Bimini" and to his great poems "Beine hat uns zwey gegeben," "Citronia," and "Am Himmel Sonne Mond und Stern."

Whether he died of syphilis, tubercular meningitis, or myatrophic lateral sclerosis does not really make a difference, as their effects and symptoms are all equally gruesome. All we need to keep in mind is that his sufferings were atrocious, that the treatment methods were barbaric, and that he was completely dependent on others for support. The ultimate cause of death could in fact have been an overdose of painkillers, that is, morphine abuse. At any rate, disputes about Heine's illness and how he might have contracted it do not serve any purpose, and speculations concerning a venereal disease in particular are nothing more than questionable moralizing. However, for Heine himself they triggered his renewed interest in *Minnespiel* and *Minneleid* and his return to those themes in *Buch der Lieder,* at the beginning of the "Heimkehr" cycle, and in his reworking of the "Tannhäuser" legend in both *Neue Gedichte* and *Elementargeister* — with the result that ultimately he held the Loreley and Frau Venus responsible for his demise. From a chronological perspective, this is precisely the guiding train of thought behind that scene in the Louvre in which he bids farewell to the Venus de Milo in May 1848 (as described in his "Nachwort" to *Romanzero*). On that occasion the marble deity counsels him to seek out a "personal" god equipped with arms and the all-important ability to help in times of need. Simultaneously his own affliction was thought to parallel the 1848 Revolution, which he saw in a very negative light. This is typical of Heine who had always regarded individual biography as being inextricably linked with world history; he believed that the February Revolution did not benefit the public in that it went over the heads of individuals, especially his own in his capacity as a poetic mediator representing the entire populace. From that moment forth there remained nothing but the "schwarze Frau," whom he alternately refers to as "Frau Sorge" or "Frau Unglück," who presses him to her bosom, sucks the marrow from his spine, and eventually administers the kiss of death. Heine saw in his (alleged) venereal disease a kind of secret message, as is evident from the four stanzas of his second "Zum Lazarus" poem (*Gedichte. 1853 und 1854*):

> Es hatte mein Haupt die schwarze Frau
> Zärtlich ans Herz geschlossen;
> Ach! meine Haare wurden grau,
> Wo ihre Thränen geflossen.
>
> Sie küßte mich lahm, sie küßte mich krank,
> Sie küßte mir blind die Augen;
> Das Mark aus meinem Rückgrat trank
> Ihr Mund mit wildem Saugen.
>
> Mein Leib ist jetzt ein Leichnam, worin
> Der Geist ist eingekerkert —
> Manchmal wird ihm unwirsch zu Sinn,
> Er tobt und rast und berserkert.
>
> Ohnmächtige Flüche! Dein schlimmster Fluch
> Wird keine Fliege tödten.
> Ertrage die Schickung, und versuch
> Gelinde zu flennen, zu beten. (DHA 3.1: 198–99)

The author is thus entirely at the mercy of this vampirism of love and pity.

Blindness and a degenerative spine had depleted Heine's life, and the only thing he could do at this stage was to battle his worsening condition by means of poetic configuration, thereby enhancing his self-awareness. Besides the Lazarus role, he also assumed the persona of such figures as Merlin and Juan Ponce de Leon. The medieval wizard-poet taken from old English lore is not dissimilar to Lazarus in that his character combines various strands of history. While his lovelorn solitude and proximity to both the devil and the Holy Grail appealed to Heine's late mysticism. Ponce de Leon is an early Renaissance conquistador who sets out to the New World in quest of the magical island Bimini. These are both rather presumptuous choices. Then again, someone who could envisage himself as pope may well choose his colleagues and fellow sufferers from among biblical characters, from mystical literature and lore, and from the annals of that exciting age when El Dorado was discovered. Without implicating any doctrinal beliefs, Heine employs in his own unique fashion certain religious ideas that stem both from beliefs and traditions associated with his Jewish origins and from the Christian culture of the occidental environment he adopted. However, he embeds them in his narratives in a most remarkable manner: more as simple citations than as religious proclamations.

In this regard, the idea of a religious return or conversion appears more than questionable. These examples serve rather to validate the notion that his would-be conversion may merely have been a "final theological reconsideration,"[12] albeit one with strong religious overtones. For despite all his scholarly analysis and critique of religion, Heine exhibits a certain mystical leaning toward negative theology, which enabled him to engage the God of his forefathers in a contentious dialogue. Psychologically speaking, this process no doubt helped Heine reconfigure his relationship to his father, while his bond with his Uncle Salomon appeared to be irreversibly damaged. And while both were long dead and buried, a pronounced cult of the dead and efforts at remembrance, which could already be observed when the author was still in his prime, now became an integral part of his admirable endeavor to describe and thereby overcome even his most existential problems.

IV. Multiple Insights and Amazing Observations

What was true of earlier phases of Heine's life also applies to his situation and insights during the final phase. The starting point of his career was characterized by an unusual degree of liberty, both from a material and from an educational point of view. Relative financial independence allowed Heine to steer clear of or move freely among those religions that dictated life choices so thoroughly at the time. Despite his occasionally humiliating status as a Jewish outsider, he was nonetheless able to survive as a writer without having to cast around for other sources of income. Paradoxical though it may sound, his socialization was thus more cosmopolitan than that of his Christian peers. Repeated claims that he had to endure a life of poverty are valid only when contrasted with the legendary wealth of his Hamburg kinsmen as well as that of his Parisian friends. It is equally true, however, that his earnings were not sufficient to support medical treatment that was as expensive as it was protracted. As early as November 16, 1849 Heine wrote the following lines to his publisher: "Meine Krankheit ist halsstarriger, als ich erwartete, und ich leide außerordentlich viel. Sie haben außerdem keine Idee davon, wie kostspielig meine Schmerzen. Daß ich mich unter diesen Umständen auch noch anstrengen muß, die Mittel zu diesen Ausgaben herbeyzutrommeln, ist entsetzlich" (HSA 22: 321).

As far as Heine's thinking in general was concerned, his ailment enabled him to expand on former themes and to broaden his horizon.

He did not spurn his prior convictions and experiences, but rather he adjusted his interests and insights in a shift that he himself referred to, in somewhat inflated terms, as a "renunciation." This term is accurate insofar as it attests to the extreme polarity of his thought, while at the same time allowing the extremes to be unified into that consistent whole that characterizes his life and work, despite the most jarring contradictions. Interestingly, his religious return is less evident in his literary texts than in a German draft of his legally binding will, which was completed in French on November 13, 1851. Designed to secure the material future of his wife and the regulation of his literary estate, the two versions of his will are of strategic importance. Most of the clauses contained in them refer to the property of his late Uncle Salomon and the ensuing inheritance quarrel with his cousin Carl, which took many years to resolve. Heine humbly entreats Carl to support Mathilde after his death. Not only the events of February 1848 but also the exertions of the inheritance struggle over his Hamburg uncle's estate had taken their toll on Heine's health; his share of the fortune had been much smaller than certain promises had led him to expect. The testament is written in a personal tone and contains confessions reaching far beyond the materialistic concerns of legalese. The German version of the will, where no religious utterances would strictly speaking have been necessary, nevertheless expresses in pious, almost mystical devotion his willingness to turn over all his worldly affairs to God. The text resorts to biblical teachings and ideas, leaving all answers to existential questions up to God and the hope for salvation in the hereafter. A new voice manifests itself and Heine goes so far as to laud his Hamburg clan and his Uncle Salomon for their reformed Judaism, thereby conforming to the opinions of Salomon's son Carl, to whom these revelations were, after all, addressed. Had cousin Carl ever set eyes on the actual testament, a prayer included in it would have evoked that mysterious Judaic piety so reverently described in Heine's *Zeitgedicht* on the "Neues Israelitisches Hospital zu Hamburg" (DHA 2: 117–18), where he praises his uncle's generous sponsorship of the project as being in keeping with time-honored Jewish tradition.

In order to demonstrate the skillful way in which Heine resolved personal problems by transposing them into a religious context, an extensive quote from the draft version of Heine's testament is necessary. At the outset, he evokes the trauma involved in the official loss of the pension and financial independence promised him by his uncle, which in turn had led to his falsely accusing and offending his cousin Carl. He then refers to *The Merchant of Venice* and plays on phrases and images reminiscent of the Book of Job, which seemingly help him to accept his fate as being in keeping with divine providence as well as biblical and Christian tradition:

> Ich habe diesen Fehler durch langjährige Leiden sattsam abgebüßt, und kann dennoch die Welt nicht verlassen, ohne feyerlich meine Reue darüber auszusprechen. Die Feinde, welche jenen Fehler mittelbar provozirten, haben ihn auch zu meinem Verderben auszubeuten gewußt, und verfuhren dabey mit einer Grausamkeit, die alle Begriffe übersteigt. Ja, ich hatte in dieser Welt Feinde von der blutdürstigsten Sorte, sowohl männliche als weibliche Shylocks, die darnach lechzten, ein Stück Fleisch aus meinem Herzen zu schneiden, und wirklich ein kleines Stückchen daraus geschnitten haben. Ich will nicht sagen, daß ich ihnen verzeihe, aber auch diese Feinde will ich nicht anklagen als die eigentlichen Urheber meines Unglücks: sie waren nur blinde Werkzeuge eines höhern Willens, nur Automaten, deren Drähte droben im Himmel gelenkt wurden.

This is immediately followed by a closing prayer to the almighty Father:

> Nur Du o Gott! bist der wahre Urheber meines Untergangs; jene arme Menschen tragen nicht die Schuld. O Gott! Du wolltest, daß ich zu Grunde ging, und ich ging zu Grunde. Gelobt sey der Herr! Er hat mich herabgestürzt von dem Postamente meines Stolzes, und ich, der ich in meinem dialektischen Dünkel mich selber für einen Gott hielt, und Gefühle hegte und Tugenden übte, die nur einen Gott ziemten — ich liege jetzt am Boden, arm und elend, und krümme mich wie ein Wurm. Gelobt sey der Herr! Ich trage mit Ergebung meine Qualen, und ich leere den Kelch der Erniedrigungen ohne mit den Lippen zu zucken, bis zum letzten Tropfen. Weiß ich doch, daß ich aus dieser Erniedrigung auferstehe, gerechtfertigt, geheiligt und gefeyert. (DHA 15: 215–16)

This tone is rather unusual for Heine, who has apparently come around to regarding doom and salvation as the result of divine chastisement and mercy. His peers are considered mere instruments in this process, and the victim is subjected to these trials and tribulations only to eventually rise in dialogical, reconciled glory. The story of Job is reinstated,[13] thus revealing an element of Heine's late piety that is not readily accessible. In this instance he puts all his trust in the Creator and does not try to undermine His dignity. Doubts and ironic reservations, so liberally expressed elsewhere, are here discretely omitted. Toward the end of his life, Heine therefore seems to have heeded his father's maxim, "Ein gottloser Sohn schadet dem Geschäft." Years before, upon learning that during his philosophy studies in Düsseldorf young Heine had permitted himself some blasphemous quips, Mr. Heine had taken his son aside and given him a dressing down, concluding his sermon with the words "besonders die Juden würden keine Velveteens mehr bey mir kaufen, und sind ehrliche Leute, zahlen prompt und haben auch Recht an der Religion zu halten. Ich bin dein Vater und also älter als du und dadurch auch erfahrener; du darfst mir also aufs Wort glauben, wenn ich mir erlaube dir zu sagen, daß der Atheismus eine große Sünde ist."(DHA 15: 100) Those words mark the abrupt end of Heine's *Memoiren,* and it becomes apparent that Heine junior occasionally shared his father's views on Judaism, deciding that the wisest thing might after all be to "stick to one's religion." Nowhere is this stance better demonstrated than in the German rendering of his last will.

Among the rarely-cited late works are the eighteen stanzas of "Am Himmel Sonne Mond und Stern," the bizarre piety of which is as hard to come to grips with as that of the aforementioned testament. In this case, however, the religious, perhaps even theological perspective goes in an anthropological direction. To give an idea of the curious, yet unmistakably Heinean tone adopted here, let me cite the opening verses:

> Am Himmel Sonne Mond und Stern
> Sie zeugen von der Macht des Herrn
> Und schaut des Frommen Aug nach oben
> Den Schöpfer wird er preisen, loben.
>
> Ich brauche nicht so hoch zu gaffen,
> Auf Erden schon find ich genung
> Kunstwerke welche Gott geschaffen
> Die würdig der Bewunderung.
>
> Ja, lieben Leute erdenwärts
> Senkt sich bescheidentlich mein Blick
> Und findet hier das Meisterstück
> Der Schöpfung: unser Menschenherz.
>
> (DHA 3.1: 408)

The poet thus presupposes that contemplation of the heavens would not be possible without grandiose feats of creation having gone before, but such exaltations, he surmises, are reserved for the truly faithful, while he himself is sufficiently awed by divine creation as manifested in terrestrial and human affairs. Heine's anticlimactic technique thus finds application even in this context. He is not the man to sing of rapture and ecstasy. He need not search for apparitions that go beyond his inner self and his personal experience, but must seek them within the human heart with its exaltations and pitfalls, its abysses and delights. Though the line of argumentation is clad in the guise of a sweet, soft, pious song, it nonetheless retains the radically secular demands made at the beginning of the epic poem *Deutschland. Ein Wintermärchen,* from the politically charged year 1844:

> Ein neues Lied, ein besseres Lied,
> O Freunde, will ich Euch dichten!
> Wir wollen hier auf Erden schon
> Das Himmelreich errichten.

This message eventually concludes with lines that some would still consider blasphemous today:

> Ja, Zuckererbsen für Jedermann,
> Sobald die Schooten platzen!
> Den Himmel überlassen wir
> Den Engeln und den Spatzen. (DHA 4: 92)

Thus, Heine's chief topic is and remains the idea of "heaven on earth," envisaging justice and social peace to the last. This is why until his dying days he maintained a keen interest in the advent of industrialization and the political factions that were taking shape, especially communism, whose future he envisioned with an equal mixture of fear and sympathy. In "Am Himmel Sonne Mond und Stern" his description of the human heart as being a "Welt in Miniatur," complete with awe-inspiring natural spectacles, seasons, forsaken happiness and love, begins in the fourth stanza and continues for a further eleven, followed by four solemn verses to round off the poem. The latter verses are explicitly based on psalms, and their language contains liturgical elements as well as images from the Book of Genesis and Greek mythology, which is eventually dismissed in favor of the hymnal Christian "Hallelujah!" that brings the poem to a close.

Despite coming down on the side of David, the piece still conveys that same ambivalence (a magic word used to exhaustion whenever Heine's work becomes hard to fathom) that is also found in "Es träumte mir von einer Sommernacht" (DHA 3.1: 391–96): that is, the struggle between Judeo-Christian culture and Hellenic tradition, the conflict between "Nazarenertum" — Heine's term for religious asceticism — and the greco-mythological emancipation of the body.

And indeed, Heine had always portrayed himself as a victim of this rupture. It has to be remembered, therefore, that the glorious prostration and praise of the Lord manifest in these lines are little more than an optimistic exercise by means of which Heine aims to counterbalance this unavoidable curse.

Exemplifying as they do the great variety of Heine's late motifs, the skeptical stanzas of "Beine hat uns zwey gegeben" might help illustrate the assertion that Heine's last pieces are as cyclical in conception as the earlier poems of *Buch der Lieder*, *Romanzero* and *Gedichte. 1853 und 1854*. A hint at the way in which Heine's poems complement and mutually augment each other, as though they were conceived as a unity, will suffice. "Beine hat uns zwey gegeben," which appeared for years under the title "Zur Teleologie,"[14] deals with the agenda of divine creation in a manner that for many decades was considered excessively vulgar. Just as "Am Himmel Sonne Mond und Stern" draws parallels between the human heart and the ways of the world in general, so this particular piece examines the functions of human sensory organs and limbs. The two legs, two eyes, two hands, one nose, one mouth, two ears are examined one after the other with respect to their relative purpose and function. The poet enters into a sensitive dialogue with the blonde "Teutolinde," who will not accept that God solved the "problem of efficiency" by means of what Heine calls the "Nützlichkeitssystem" (utilitarian principle), that is, by equipping the human species with either double or single organs. He lets man both urinate and procreate — or, as Heine puts it, make love on the "Hochaltar der Minne" — with the same organ. The language is as explicit as it is ironic, and the poem concludes with melancholic skepticism:

> Alles wird simplifizirt,
> Klug ist alles kombinirt:
> Was dem Menschen dient zum Seichen
> Damit schafft er Seinesgleichen
> Auf demselben Dudelsack
> Spielt dasselbe Lumpenpak.
>
> . . .
>
> Und derselbe Omnibus
> Fährt uns in den Tartarus. (DHA 3.1: 403)

Death is thus portrayed as the eternal leveler, and questions about utility and purpose are rendered pointless.

V. Death and Last Rites

In the draft version of his last will mentioned above, Heine had already evoked final issues and had looked death firmly in the eye. His poem on human teleology ends on a similar note. One must not underestimate that, even in happier times, Heine had never dismissed or repressed those issues and questions that returned to haunt him toward the end of his days. Motifs of the "final voyage" and questions about the purpose of history as well as the destinies of individuals and entire generations already abounded in the *Reisebilder* and in the *Nordsee* poems. Even as a journalist, he had always delved below the surface in order to analyze the causes governing seemingly superficial events, though he always counterbalanced his rhetoric by distancing himself from the subject matter. He waxed ironic only because he took the conundrums of providence, history, and chance seriously, but nevertheless wished to reduce the pain of their tragic escalations by presenting them in as light-hearted a style as possible, such that they might be easier to digest.

The nine stanzas of one of the posthumously published Lazarus poems begin with the line "Die Söhne des Glückes beneide ich nicht" (DHA 3.1: 348–49). In this poem he compares the agonies of imminent death with the carefree lives of those others who make merry at the "Lebensbanquett," only to be stricken down without warning by Death's sickle. Thus they arrive in the underworld without delay as "Fortunas Favoriten," decked out in their state finery and adorned with roses, while the author himself has endured seven years of invalidism, illness, torment, martyrdom, and pain. In the end, he quarrels with God and turns conventional opinion on its head by threatening to convert to Roman Catholicism, so that he might bawl at God in the manner of all good Christians. His is the Promethean ordeal of not being able to die. However, the last four stanzas are addressed to the Judeo-Christian God, and once again his wording is one of striking familiarity. His self-confidence has evidently not been diminished, for he still considers himself "der beste der Humoristen" and must therefore be fully aware of his merits. Yet there is also the prevalent feeling that he will not be able to resist physical defeat for much longer, as evidenced in the lines "Der Schmerz verdumpft den heitern Sinn." A straightforward conversion process embracing the laws and practices of the average religious community went against Heine's nature. His idea of complete terrestrial happiness was the termination of life, but there is no mention of immortality or heaven.

A sonnet entitled "Mein Tag war heiter, glücklich meine Nacht," intended for the Lazarus cycle, was also conceived to uphold a programmatic and indeed deliberate sense of contradiction. It is an artist's poem in the Apollonian vein, its object being the "lyre of poetry." In this instance, Heine does not wish to die but to live on. Two quartets summarize his successes as an author. His life is portrayed as being "heiter" (serene) by day and blissful by night. The masses rejoice and his song exudes "Lust und Feuer," producing a "schöne Glut." Summer is in the air, the harvest is safely stored away in the barn, and he is full of love and affection for the world. The two tercets, on the other hand, evoke his fear of dying, or rather his rejection of death. "Der Hand entsinkt das Saitenspiel" and the glass shatters. Yet again he calls out to God as a dialogue partner whom he may assail with his woes, but even here his farewell to the world does not seem to have a metaphysical dimension:

> O Gott! wie häßlich bitter ist das Sterben!
> O Gott! wie süß und traulich läßt sich leben
> In diesem traulich süßen Erdenneste!
> (DHA 3.1: 353)

By contrast, the ten stanzas of another Lazarus poem, entitled "Ganz entsetzlich ungesund," portray the world as the epitome of vanity and transitoriness, while the stars maintain their distance, abstaining from all things terrestrial:

> Wollen immer ferne bleiben
> Vom fatalen Erdentreiben,
> Von dem Klüngel und Geruddel
> Von dem Erdenkuddelmuddel.
> (DHA 3.1: 355)

The fact that the stars shed "golden" tears of sympathy adds a sentimental touch to the scene. A poem for Mathilde called "Ich war, O Lamm, als Hirt bestellt" (DHA 3.1: 357), which also forms part of his unpublished Lazarus cycle, starts out by describing his prowess as a husband, while the second verse concentrates on his departure as death creeps up to claim him. Heine's rendering of the Christian image of the good shepherd handing back his staff is characterized by an elegiac calm. There is no sign of anxiety or accusation.

To finish, let me cite a few lines from the poem "Es träumte mir von einer Sommernacht," which, together with a few other late pieces, makes up an independent cycle for his "Mouche." In it Heine's attitude toward death and final issues is cast in a more mellow light. Silence and love come together in a "schönen Friedenstraum" that corresponds to the poet's "ungestörten Frieden":

> O Tod! mit deiner Grabesstille, du,
> Nur du kannst uns die beste Wollust geben —
> Den Krampf der Leidenschaft, Lust ohne Ruh
> Giebt uns für Glück das albern blöde Leben!
> (DHA 3.1: 395)

These lines also answer the last remaining questions concerning immortality and resurrection. Just as Heine portrayed these human expectations, in the "Nachwort" to *Romanzero,* for example, as an extra reward one receives for believing in God, here he refuses to make them the focal point of his final deliberations. To the contrary, his self-performed last rites invoke a dreamlike state of death as chaste silence.

—Translated by Sebastian Stumpf

Notes

[1] Compare with the still-valuable Heine biography by Wolfgang Hädecke, *Heinrich Heine: Eine Biographie* (Munich: Carl Hanser 1985). Note page 506, where Hädecke says that Heine, "[hat] in einer Reihe von Gedichten dem Tod ins Auge gesehen wie kaum ein anderer Dichter vor ihm; hart und genau, in manchmal schon prosaähnlichen Versen hat er noch einmal ein Tabu gebrochen, das Tabu der unerbittlichen, unromantischen, unverklärten Darstellung des Todes." Hädecke then goes on to cite Alfred Meißner's comments on this self-depiction of Heine's: "Es ist eine Klage wie aus einem Grabe, da schreit ein Lebendigbegrabener durch die Nacht, oder gar eine Leiche, oder gar das Grab selbst. Ja ja, solche Töne hat die deutsche Lyrik noch nie vernommen und hat sie auch nicht vernehmen können, weil noch kein Dichter in solch einer Lage war." Meißner then adds this interesting comment: "das schreckliche Krankenlager hatte seine Natur auf eine tragische Höhe gehoben, die ihm eigentlich gar nicht eigen war." As an introduction to Heine's writings as a whole, Gerhard Höhn's *Heine-Handbuch: Zeit, Person, Werk* (2nd. ed.; Stuttgart and Weimar: Metzler, 1997) remains unsurpassed.

[2] Cp. Kruse, "Jesuitenlyrik," *Friedrich Spee von Langenfeld (1591–1635): Ein Dichter und Aufklärer vom Niederrhein,* ed. Karl-Jürgen Miesen (Düsseldorf: Heinrich-Heine-Institut, 1991), 143–53.

[3] In his letter dated December 30, 1855, that is, a few weeks before his death, he writes his mother that although the previous year had been "eins der miserabel-

sten," he is always hoping for improvement: "Mit meiner Gesundheit geht es wie gewöhnlich; ich hoffe immer auf Besserung und die Jahre vergehen." He closes with the words: "Du bist meine gute, liebe Mutter und da wir beide unser ganzes Leben hindurch immer brav und redlich gehandelt haben, so haben wir nicht zu fürchten, daß wir in einer anderen Welt wieder von einander getrennt leben müßten" (HSA 23: 473–74). For a medical history, see the extensive work by Henner Montanus, *Der kranke Heine,* Heine-Studien (Stuttgart and Weimar: Metzler, 1995).

[4] Cp. Kruse, "Heinrich Heine — Der Lazarus," *Heinrich Heine: Ästhetisch-politische Profile,* ed. Gerhard Höhn (Frankfurt am Main: Suhrkamp, 1991), 258–75.

[5] On the subject of Heine's "Mouche," see the definitive biographical explanation by Menso Folkerts, "Wer war Heinrich Heines 'Mouche'? Dichtung und Wahrheit," *Heine-Jahrbuch* 38 (1999): 133–51.

[6] See the series entitled *Heinrich Heines Werk im Urteil seiner Zeitgenossen,* which since 1981 has been the official compilation of contemporary German critical writings on Heine's works. It was initiated by Eberhard Galley and Alfred Estermann and continued by Sikander Singh and Christoph auf der Horst. See also its series of French essays on Heine edited by Hans Hörling.

[7] Klaus Briegleb's emphasis on the Jewish undertone throughout Heine's work is justified (*Bei den Wassern Babels: Heinrich Heine, jüdischer Schriftsteller in der Moderne* [Munich: Deutscher Taschenbuch Verlag, 1997]).

[8] See Sander Gilman's work on this connection, for example, "Heinrich Heine und die Krankheit ohne Namen," *Ich Narr des Glücks: Heinrich Heine 1797–1856. Bilder einer Ausstellung,* ed. Joseph A. Kruse (Stuttgart and Weimar: Metzler, 1997), 490–95.

[9] In his introduction to Heine for the Metzler compilation *Realien zur Literatur,* Jeffrey Sammons notes: "Mit Ausnahme einzelner Gedichte ist diese allerletzte lyrische Schaffensperiode Heines von der Forschung etwas vernachlässigt worden" ("Letzte Gedichte und späte Liebe," *Realien zur Literatur — Bd. 261. Heinrich Heine* [Stuttgart: Metzler, 1991], 145).

[10] See the corresponding standard work by Günter Metzner, *Heine in der Musik: Bibliographie der Heine-Vertonungen,* 12 vols. (Tutzing: Schneider, 1989–1994).

[11] See for instance Ernst Pawel's, *Der Dichter stirbt: Heinrich Heines letzte Jahre in Paris* (Berlin: Berlin Verlag, 1997). More important, see the studies by Roger F. Cook, *By the Rivers of Babylon: Heinrich Heine's Late Songs and Reflections* (Detroit: Wayne State UP, 1998), and Arnold Pistiak, *"Ich will das rote Sefchen küssen." Nachdenken über Heines letzten Gedichtzyklus.* Heine-Studien. (Stuttgart and Weimar: Metzler, 1999). And please excuse the author for mentioning his own recent analyses of Heine's later period, which in part appeared in connection with the international Heine boom of 1997 on the occasion of his 200th anniversary: "Die letzte Reise"; "'In der Literatur wie im Leben'"; and "Heines Schmerzen" [both physical and metaphysical].

[12] See the essays by Wilhelm Gössmann ("Die theologische Revision Heines in der Spätzeit," 320–35) and Louis Cuby ("Die theologische Revision Heines in der

Spätzeit," 336–42), both in *Referate und Diskussionen: Internationaler Heine-Kongreß Düsseldorf, 1972,* ed. Manfred Windfuhr (Hamburg: Hoffmann und Campe, 1973).

[13] The Hungarian author István Eörsi concerned himself with this line of interpretative tradition in *Hiob und Heine.*

[14] Cp. Lefebvre, "Heines Gedicht 'Zur Teleologie.'"

Works Cited

Briegleb, Klaus. *Bei den Wassern Babels: Heinrich Heine, jüdischer Schriftsteller in der Moderne.* Munich: Deutscher Taschenbuch Verlag, 1997.

Cook, Roger F. *By the Rivers of Babylon: Heinrich Heine's Late Songs and Reflections.* Detroit: Wayne State UP, 1998.

Cuby, Louis. "Die theologische Revision Heines in der Spätzeit." *Referate und Diskussionen: Internationaler Heine-Kongreß Düsseldorf, 1972.* Ed. Manfred Windfuhr. Hamburg: Hoffmann und Campe, 1973. 336–42.

Eörsi, Istvan. *Hiob und Heine: Passagiere im Niemandsland.* Trans. Gregor Mayer. Klagenfurt, Vienna, Ljubljana, Sarajevo: Wieser, 1999.

Folkerts, Menso. "Wer war Heinrich Heines 'Mouche'? Dichtung und Wahrheit." *Heine-Jahrbuch* 38 (1999): 133–51.

Gilman, Sander L. "Heinrich Heine und die Krankheit ohne Namen." *Ich Narr des Glücks: Heinrich Heine 1797–1856. Bilder einer Ausstellung.* Ed. Joseph A. Kruse. Stuttgart and Weimar: Metzler, 1997. 490–95.

Gössmann, Wilhelm. "Die theologische Revision Heines in der Spätzeit." *Referate und Diskussionen: Internationaler Heine-Kongreß Düsseldorf, 1972.* Ed. Manfred Windfuhr. Hamburg: Hoffmann und Campe, 1973. 320–35.

Hädecke, Wolfgang. *Heinrich Heine: Eine Biographie.* Munich: Carl Hanser, 1985.

Höhn, Gerhard. *Heine-Handbuch: Zeit, Person, Werk.* 2nd ed. Stuttgart and Weimar: Metzler, 1997.

Kruse, Joseph A. "Heines Schmerzen." *An den Ufern jenes schönen Stromes: Kursorische Überlegungen zu Heinrich Heine.* Ed. Joseph A. Kruse, Marianne Tilch, and Jürgen Wilhelm. Düsseldorf: Heinrich-Heine-Institut, 2000. 28–49.

———. "Heinrich Heine — Der Lazarus." *Heinrich Heine: Ästhetisch-politische Profile.* Ed. Gerhard Höhn. Frankfurt am Main: Suhrkamp, 1991. 258–75.

————. "'In der Literatur wie im Leben hat jeder Sohn einen Vater': Heinrich Heine zwischen Bibel und Homer, Cervantes und Shakespeare." *Heine und die Weltliteratur*. Ed. T. J. Reed and Alexander Stillmark. Oxford and London: EHRC, 2000. 2–23.

————. "Jesuitenlyrik." *Friedrich Spee von Langenfeld (1591–1635): Ein Dichter und Aufklärer vom Niederrhein*. Ed. Karl-Jürgen Miesen. Düsseldorf: Heinrich-Heine-Institut, 1991. 143–53.

————. "Die letzte Reise. Heines lyrische wie versepische Paraphrasen über Lebenssinn und Tod." *Differenz und Identität: Heinrich Heine (1797–1856). Europäische Perspektiven im 19. Jahrhundert*. Ed. Alfred Opitz. Schriftenreihe Literaturwissenschaft 41. Trier: Wissenschaftlicher Verlag, 1998. 263–79.

————. "'Die wichtigste Frage der Menschheit.' Heine als Theologe." *Heine-Zeit*. Stuttgart and Weimar: Metzler 1997. 256–72.

Lefebvre, Jean-Pierre. "Heines Gedicht 'Zur Teleologie.' Eine Rede aus Anlaß des Erwerbs der Handschrift." *Heine-Jahrbuch* 31 (1992): 212–23.

Metzner, Günter. *Heine in der Musik: Bibliographie der Heine-Vertonungen*. 12 vols. Tutzing: Schneider, 1989–1994.

Montanus, Henner. *Der kranke Heine*. Heine-Studien. Stuttgart and Weimar: Metzler, 1995.

Pawel, Ernst. *Der Dichter stirbt: Heinrich Heines letzte Jahre in Paris*. Trans. Regina Schmidt-Ott. Berlin: Verlag A. Spitz, 1997.

Pistiak, Arnold. *"Ich will das rote Sefchen küssen." Nachdenken über Heines letzten Gedichtzyklus*. Heine-Studien. Stuttgart and Weimar: Metzler, 1999.

Sammons, Jeffrey L. "Letzte Gedichte und späte Liebe." *Realien zur Literatur — Bd. 261. Heinrich Heine*. Stuttgart: Metzler, 1991.

Werner, Michael, ed. *Begegnungen mit Heine: Berichte der Zeitgenossen, in Fortführung von H. H. Houbens "Gespräche mit Heine."* Hamburg: Hoffmann und Campe, 1973. 2 vols.

Reception in Germany

Heine and Weimar

George F. Peters

> Das Deutsche Volk, einig in seinen Stämmen und
> von dem Willen beseelt, sein Reich in Freiheit und
> Gerechtigkeit zu erneuern und zu festigen, dem in-
> neren und dem äußeren Frieden zu dienen und den
> gesellschaftlichen Fortschritt zu fördern, hat sich die-
> se Verfassung gegeben.
>
> Ich war in Weimar. (HSA 20: 180)

O F THE MANY PUZZLES surrounding Heinrich Heine's political
views, the question of what sort of political system he envisioned
for Germany is perhaps the most perplexing. In two prominent places
in his work, Heine ventures a prediction about Germany's future. In
both cases, his vision is maddeningly ambiguous. He tantalizes the
reader with the expectation that years of keen observation and extensive reporting on the political and social scene in Europe will have led
to an informed judgment about the further course of historical developments. But deliberately, some might say maliciously, he stops short
of making any clear prediction.

In a frequently quoted passage at the end of *Zur Geschichte der
Religion und Philosophie in Deutschland,* Heine does predict one certain event in Germany: revolution. In summing up his discussion of
religious and philosophical developments in Germany from the Middle Ages to Hegel, he formulates the famous thought that the revolution "im Gebiete des Geistes" that commenced with the emergence of
Germanic pantheism and culminates with the idealists will lead, of necessity, to a revolution "im Reiche der Erscheinungen." The metaphor
is compelling: "Der Gedanke geht der That voraus, wie der Blitz dem
Donner." German thunder, he adds, is not very agile and will roll in
somewhat slowly; but it will come, "aber kommen wird er" (DHA
8.1: 118). In typical fashion, Heine spins out the metaphor: the German thunderclap, when it does come, will be the loudest ever heard.
Eagles will fall out of the air; lions in Africa will tuck their tails be-

tween their legs and crawl back into their dens. Then he mixes the metaphor. This German production ("Stück") will make the French Revolution look like a harmless Arcadian romp ("Idylle"). The actors are not yet on the scene. Currently, only little dogs are running around the arena barking and snapping at each other — the metaphor has changed again — but the time will come when a swarm of presumably human gladiators will enter the arena and fight to the death. Heine does not say when this will happen, only that it will, when the right hour is at hand (DHA 8.1: 119).

For a rather extreme flight of poetic fancy, these lines have been the subject of an inordinate amount of serious political reflection. Critics have largely ignored Heine's twofold admission at the outset of the passage that these are the ruminations of a dreamer ("Träumer," "Phantast") and have subjected the images of violent revolution to wildly diverse interpretations, frequently with reference to twentieth-century German history (Harich). The proposition that the profound German revolution in thought is of more consequence than the French Revolution and must, in analogy with the laws of nature, be followed by a revolution in deeds is seductively simple, and the fact that Heine here predicts neither when the revolution will happen nor even which direction it will come from invites a host of speculation. Most critics assume, in the context of Heine's move to Paris following the July Revolution, his acquaintance with Saint-Simonianism, his discussion of Republicanism in *Französische Zustände,* and such poems as "Doktrin" and "Die schlesischen Weber," that Heine is anticipating *the* German Revolution, a revolution on par with the French Revolution. Manfred Windfuhr takes this position when he writes, "Heine endet seine Schrift . . . mit einer Verkündigung der Revolution in Deutschland" (148). For Bodo Morawe there is absolutely no doubt about Heine's belief in the right of a people to revolution "in voller Übereinstimmung mit dem deutschen Jakobinismus" (100). Other critics, however, noting the ominous, threatening tone of the predicted revolution, ascribe uncanny clairvoyance to Heine, namely prediction of "andere politische Resultate der deutschen Ideenentwicklung," the Nazi revolution from the Right (Stauf 24).

The second, equally famous and equally frustrating vision of Germany's future comes in *Deutschland. Ein Wintermärchen.* Here the poetic guise is even more bizarre: the patron saint of Hamburg, Hammonia, transformed into a rum-loving streetwalker, allows her current paramour, the fictionalized Heine narrator of the *Wintermärchen,* a peek into Germany's future. He may read the future of Germany not in the kettle she has just used to brew him some tea, but rather in Karl the Great's chamber pot, which just happens to be standing in the corner (DHA 4: 152). We are prepared for the fact that Heine will not divulge what he sees there. In the previous chapter he has sworn an oath in the name of the Patriarchs, Abraham, Isaac, and Jacob, that he will keep quiet. Hammonia, apparently aware that she is dealing with a poet and publicist, fears, "Doch ach! Du kannst nicht schweigen!" (DHA 4: 150). She has given him a hint about Germany's fate, one that echoes almost verbatim the prognostication in *Religion und Philosophie in Deutschland:*

> Die praktische äußere Freyheit wird einst
> Das Ideal vertilgen,
> Das wir im Busen getragen —
>
> . . .
>
> Der Enkel wird essen und trinken genug,
> Doch nicht in beschaulicher Stille;
> Es poltert heran ein Spektakelstück,
> Zu Ende geht die Idylle. (DHA 4: 150)

Ironically, to view the future, Heine must take an Old Testament oath, and it is only in a moment "angeweht vom Hauche / Der Vorzeit" that he swears, "Nach uraltem Erzväterbrauche," not to reveal the vision of Germany's future that Hammonia will show him.

In one of the most famous passages in the *Wintermärchen,* Heine keeps his word:

> Was ich gesehn, verrathe ich nicht,
> Ich habe zu schweigen versprochen,
> Erlaubt ist mir zu sagen kaum,
> O Gott! Was ich gerochen! — — —
>
> (DHA 4: 153)

Germany's future stinks — that is the political prognostication at the end of the *Wintermärchen.*

Earlier on in both of these works, Heine projects a utopian vision that would seem to express his hopes for a future society. In *Religion und Philosophie in Deutschland* it is the well-known Saint-Simonian message of shared sensual enjoyment: "wir stiften eine Demokrazie gleichherrlicher, gleichheiliger, gleichbeseligter Götter. Ihr verlangt einfache Trachten, enthaltsame Sitten und ungewürzte Genüsse; wir hingegen verlangen Nektar und Ambrosia, Purpurmäntel, kostbare

Wohlgerüche, Wollust und Pracht, lachenden Nymphentanz, Musik und Comödien" (DHA 8.1: 61). At the beginning of the *Wintermärchen,* Heine rejects the Romantic ballad sung by a young girl at the German border and proposes to sing a new and better song, one that glorifies life on earth, life characterized by the same pleasures described in the earlier work:

> Rosen und Myrten, Schönheit und Lust,
> Und Zuckererbsen nicht minder.
> Ja, Zuckererbsen für Jedermann. (DHA 4: 92)

In actuality, the *Wintermärchen* does not fulfill the promise of being a new and better song, at least not in its message of a new society. The Germany that Heine revisits is very much the old Germany. There are no signs at all that the marriage of Europe and Freedom envisioned at the outset of the work is anywhere near imminent. Similarly, in *Religion und Philosophie in Deutschland* the revolution described at the conclusion gives no promise of ushering in a democracy of luxury and well-being for all. Germany's actual future in both works can only be characterized as portentous, violent, and bleak.

Wolf Biermann neatly summarized Heine's paradoxical vision of Germany's future in the *Wintermärchen* — "Zuckererbsen" on the one hand, "Miasmen" on the other — in his opening address at the International Heine Congress in Düsseldorf in 1997: "Entweder so oder so: entweder wir Menschen errichten uns ein Himmelreich auf Erden oder wir geraten in eine irdische Hölle, also der biblische Scheideweg. Das vielzitierte Marxwort dazu heißt: Sozialismus oder Barbarei." But Biermann must regretfully admit that his own and others' youthful enthusiasm for communism as the road leading to Heine's paradise on earth had been sadly misguided. "Heines *Wintermährchen*-Alternative entpuppte sich als eine Scheinalternative. Der Kommunismus erwies sich nicht als des Rätsels Lösung, wie Brecht noch schwärmte" (5).

It is perhaps idle to speculate what Heine would have thought of Germany's political development. There is certainly no critical agreement about which sort of political system he preferred to replace the one system that he abhorred, absolutism. Monarchism, constitutional monarchism, democracy, republicanism, socialism, and communism (in the embryonic form he knew it) all come under scrutiny in his writings. No one alternative is wholeheartedly embraced, none totally rejected. And the one brief article he left describing his view of historical development, *Verschiedenartige Geschichtsauffassungen,* offers little help for predicting the future. Heine rejects both the cyclical and progressive view of history in favor of one that comes down on the rights of the individual in the present, "das Recht zu leben," which means the right to bread and, in turn, the right to revolution (DHA 10: 302).

When this revolution will come is just as uncertain as its nature. In the *Wintermärchen,* Heine first rejects the notion of Barbarossa's triumphant emergence from Kyffhäuser to lead the German revolution. Then, in the harsh light of day — "Der nackten hölzernen Wirklichkeit" (DHA 4: 129) — he reconsiders and calls on the Kaiser to return after all and to restore the Holy Roman Empire, which must surely be better than the current unholy alliance, described as a "Kamaschenritterthum" (130). When Barbarossa should come is unstated, only that it should be soon, prompting a recent critic to propose the novel idea of "Uchronie" to describe Heine's sense of time and history. "Wie der ideale Ort der Utopie nirgendwo liegt, so wird die rechte Stunde der Uchronie für *nirgendwann* erwartet. Das heißt nicht, sie werde nie kommen, es besagt vielmehr, daß sie jederzeit kommen kann" (Kreutzer 38).

Revolution did come to Germany, of course. The first time was indeed soon, soon enough for Heine to experience it. He observed its onset in Paris firsthand in February 1848 and followed its halting evolution in Germany through secondhand reports until it sputtered and died there in 1849. That this was not the revolution Heine had anticipated in 1844 is clear from his own disillusioned reaction, recorded in such poems as "Hans ohne Land," "Erinnerung aus Krähwinkels Schreckenstagen," and "Michel nach dem März," and from the course of events itself. Heine was not surprised that the liberal democratic activists in his homeland failed to instill the French spirit of republicanism into the German people, and was even less surprised that the long-winded parliamentarians in Frankfurt were totally ineffectual in bringing the Prussian king to his knees before the people. With the restoration of the Federation in July 1849, the German Michel wakes from his slumber to find himself, once again, "unter der Hut / Von vier und Dreyzig Monarchen" (DHA 3.1: 240).

Heine did not live long enough to comment on any of the further revolutions in Germany, neither on the "revolution from above" that saw Bismarck channel German nationalism into the formation of the long-awaited German Reich, nor the revolution of 1918–19 that led to the founding of the Weimar Republic, nor the "quiet revolution" that preceded unification of the German republic we know today. But of all these revolutions, the one that comes closest to his predictions of 1844 is surely the explosive series of events that saw the collapse of the authoritarian Reich, the abdication of the Kaiser, and the establishment, for the first time in Germany, of a democracy buttressed by a declaration of human rights. For all its faults, the Weimar constitution contains just those emancipatory principles that Heine championed and that are embodied in the ideals of the French Revolution, *liberté, égalité, fraternité:*

> Artikel 109. Alle Deutschen sind vor dem Gesetze gleich. Männer und Frauen haben grundsätzlich dieselben staatsbürgerlichen Rechte und Pflichten. Öffentlich-rechtliche Vorrechte oder Nachteile der Geburt oder des Standes sind aufzuheben.
>
> Artikel 114. Die Freiheit der Person ist unverletzlich.
>
> Artikel 118. Jeder Deutsche hat das Recht, innerhalb der Schranken der allgemeinen Gesetze seine Meinung durch Wort, Schrift, Druck, Bild oder in sonstiger Weise frei zu äußern. . . . Eine Zensur findet nicht statt. . . .
>
> Artikel 135. Alle Bewohner des Reichs genießen volle Glaubens- und Gewissensfreiheit.
>
> Artikel 137. Es besteht keine Staatskirche.
>
> Artikel 142. Die Kunst, die Wissenschaft und ihre Lehre sind frei.
> (Die Verfassung des Deutschen Reiches)

The constitution was drafted in the town of Weimar for reasons not dissimilar to the one that led Heine to visit there in 1824, Goethe's presence. The spirit of Weimar, so the democratically inclined founders of the Republic hoped, would lend the newborn German state the proper aura of enlightened, non-Prussian humanitarianism. That the republican principles of the French Revolution would not find fertile soil in Weimar might have occurred to members of the constitutional assembly who recalled Goethe's abhorrence of the Revolution and his general indifference to politics, something Heine knew all too well.

It seems likely that Heine would have been skeptical about a parliamentary democracy based on universal suffrage, despite the idealistic rhetoric in the constitution. His negative opinion about the political and social systems in both England and the United States, countries deeply rooted in the principle of human rights, is well known. The fact that the Weimar Republic retained the vestiges of the Kaiser in the form of a president who could appoint and dismiss the chancellor more or less at will, would not, one must think, have surprised him.

Nor can the German Revolution of 1918–19 be considered in any way the explosion of the latent forces of German spiritualism that Heine anticipated in 1844. The lost war and the widespread deprivation of the civilian population, not the transformation of any particular set of ideals into action, spawned the revolution. The hasty proclamation of the German Republic by Friedrich Ebert on November 9, 1918 headed off the efforts of Karl Liebknecht and Rosa Luxemburg to found a socialist republic based on the communist model and led to the assumption of power by a coalition of social democrats and liberals who set out to fulfill the lost promise of the 1848 revolution. The German people, so used to authoritarian rule, found themselves suddenly abandoned by their Kaiser and were, for the most part, clueless as to their political future.

Speculation about what Heine might have thought of the Weimar Republic is an interesting if idle exercise. What the Weimar Republic thought of Heine is another matter. Why, in fact, did the new German Republic, founded as it was on just those principles Heine represented, not embrace this major poet from its illustrious literary past? After all, in the old, now defunct Reich, Heine had been subject for decades to the infamous *Denkmalstreit* that culminated in the fulminant treatise by Adolf Bartels (1906). Anti-Semitic attacks on Heine had sought to marginalize or eliminate him from the pantheon of German literature entirely (Peters 69–126). In the spirit of Weimar and with the freedom of thought, religion, and expression guaranteed in the new constitution, the time was ripe, one would think, for a major rehabilitation of Heine. Writers, intellectuals, literary critics, and publicists all could now turn to Heine as the most prominent and most eloquent spokesman for the new Germany. The decade of the 1920s was dominated by such influential figures as Thomas and Heinrich Mann, Walter Benjamin, Bertolt Brecht, Arnold Zweig, Stefan Zweig, Hermann Hesse, Carl Zuckmayer, Franz Kafka, Heimito von Doderer, and Anna Seghers, all of whom were, despite their individual differences, committed to anti-authoritarian principles, the freedom of the individual, and the right of artistic expression. In Heine they could find a spokesman and ally who stood for the primacy of the artist while defending the rights of the oppressed. By rights, Heine should have found his place in the Weimar Republic.

This did not happen. In the reception history of Heine between 1906 and 1945, the period 1919 to 1933 does not stand out as a period of invigorated critical attention to either the biography or the works. Within this period, in fact, the year 1910–11 is judged to be a pinnacle year of publication on Heine (Prang). To be sure, Heine got his monument in Hamburg in 1926, accompanied by an eloquent plea for the poet's relevance by Alfred Kerr:

> Nach zwanzig schicksalsvollen Jahren schlägt nun die Stunde, wo ein alter Wunsch vieler Deutschen Wirklichkeit wird: die Weihe des deutschen Gedächtnismals für Heinrich Heine — Dichter und lachender Pionier; geboren am Rhein zu Düsseldorf, heimisch zu Hamburg, gestorben zu Paris vor siebzig Jahren; lebend in Schrift und Sang; geliebt und befehdet; und nicht mehr wegzudenken aus Deutschland, nicht auszuschalten aus der Welt. (Kleinknecht 137)

"Und nicht mehr wegzudenken aus Deutschland" — seven short years would prove Kerr's verdict about Heine sadly wrong.

Neither liberals, nor socialists, nor communists, for that matter, seized upon Heine as their champion during the Weimar period. Heine scholarship proceeded apace. A major new edition appeared between the years 1925–1930 (Strich). Numerous studies conducted under the prevalent critical approach of German "Geistesgeschichte" were to prove influential for later scholarship (Loewenthal, Wolff, Belart, Friedländer). But evidence of any widespread attempt to erase the stigma of Heine the Jew, the Francophile, the mannered, frivolous poet, or the talented but superficial journalist is absent. Fundamentally, the German attitude toward Heine did not change.

There are numerous explanations for this curious state of affairs, and it is tempting to posit that, taken in toto, these explanations for why Weimar remained chilly toward Heine support the idea that he would not have cared much for Weimar either. In his 1926 address, Alfred Kerr proudly notes that such cultural luminaries as Max Klinger, Richard Dehmel, Max Liebermann, Engelbert Humperdinck, and Gerhart Hauptmann supported his call for a Heine memorial. "Es waren kaum die schlechtesten der Landsgenossen," he adds (Kleinknecht 138). Yet none of these influential figures went on record in support of Heine by writing essays in his defense. Nor did Thomas Mann, perhaps the most influential and most respected cultural figure of the day. Numerous studies have traced the influence of Heine on Thomas Mann, who left major literary essays on numerous literary figures, including Goethe, yet published only two short notes on Heine. Mann never actively took up Heine's cause, even in the late 1920s, when he began to speak out in support of social democratic ideals in Germany. In a major study of Mann's own reception of Heine, Volkmar Hansen attributes the absence of a public statement to three factors. The first is that Mann wrote most of his major essays on commission and was never asked to speak or write publicly about Heine, which is itself revealing. The second is that when he did begin to engage himself politically after the First World War, he oriented himself to the revered figures of the period, Novalis and Hölderlin, for example, which meant avoiding the Jew and Francophile Heine. The third fact is that he tended to leave intellectual and political matters dealing with the relationship of Germany to France to his brother, Heinrich Mann (Hansen 18–20).

In 1929 Heinrich Mann did, in fact, publish a brief but courageous call for not just the establishment of a Heine monument in Germany, but for a re-evaluation of Heine's importance for the time. For Mann Heine represents "das vorweggenommene Beispiel des modernen Menschen"; he emphasizes the relevance of Heine's journalistic reports for the contemporary world and judges Heine to be among the first to have written social history. He considers Heine's open and realistic depiction of the sensual side of life more appropriate for the present than for his own time. As a Jew, Mann writes, Heine was uniquely able to employ the persuasive power of the German language. He was the prototype of the "European German." Echoing Kerr, Heinrich Mann also concludes that Heine's time had come, "Heinrich Heine hat für sich die Zukunft" (Kleinknecht 141–42).

In proclaiming Heine to be the model intellectual for a new Europe, thinkers like Kerr and Thomas and Heinrich Mann recall Friedrich Nietzsche's dictum that in his writing Heine anticipated "den Europäer der Zukunft" (724). Although Nietzsche had relatively little to say about Heine, and it is unclear what works of Heine he had actually read, his authoritative voice is frequently cited by later critics in support of both Heine's artistry and his cosmopolitanism. Nietzsche names Heine, along with Napoleon, Goethe, Beethoven, Stendhal, Schopenhauer, and Richard Wagner as one of the "deeper and more comprehensive men of this century," one of the "höhere Menschen," as he calls them, who anticipated a Europe of the future, one that would transcend the nationalistic narrowness and boorish decadence of the late nineteenth century (Werner 48).

As impassioned as these calls for Heine's legitimization were, they did not serve to rally intellectuals in the Weimar period to his cause. The failure of German intellectuals to influence the formation of a liberal democratic view of Heine is reflected in two volumes published in the mid-1970s that document Heine's reception in Germany (Kleinknecht, Hotz). The only texts reproduced to substantiate what one of the editors calls "the beginnings of a changed view of Heine" are the statements by Alfred Kerr and Heinrich Mann in support of a Heine memorial, two short pieces by Thomas Mann ("Heinrich Heine, der 'Gute'" and "Notiz über Heine"), the seven-line poem of Hugo von Hofmannsthal, "Zu Heinrich Heines Gedächtnis," and two short poems by Vladimir Mayakovski, "Beziehung zum Fräulein" and "In Heines Manier" — hardly overwhelming testimony to Heine's influence in the new Germany.

In an essay published in 1986, Jürgen Habermas examines the absence of any cohesive stance among German intellectuals after the First World War with regard to the modern relevance of Heine. He argues that despite the influence of the Dreyfus affair, which had dramatically infused intellectual thinking into the political arena in France, no group of intellectuals had formed in Germany before the First World War that coalesced around Heine, whom Habermas calls an early nineteenth-century "protointellectual" (455–56). Even in the Weimar period, the handful of influential writers such as Heinrich Mann and Alfred Döblin who did practice "radikaldemokratischen Humanismus Heinescher Prägung" refused to call themselves intellectuals, preferring instead the quintessential German formulation, "geistige Menschen" (456). Habermas describes how each of four groups in the Weimar period eschewed the status of "intellectuals." First were the nonpolitical writers and "mandarins," such as Hermann Hesse, the young Thomas Mann, Ernst Robert Curtius, or Karl Jaspers, who considered the politicization of the spirit as a betrayal of the truly creative individual. Second were "realpolitische" theorists like Max Weber and the young Theodor Heuss, who feared the injection of incompetent dilettantism into the political sphere by the intellectual. Third was a group of activist writers and artists, such as Kurt Hiller, René Schickele, Carl Einstein, and Ernst Bloch, which did seek to penetrate the political arena but adhered to the elitist view of the nonpolitical thinkers, on the one hand, and the misplaced view of the *Realpolitiker* that participation in political life must mean for intellectuals adoption of a particular party stance, on the other. This latter view then provoked the position of the fourth group, thinkers like Georg Lukács and Johannes R. Becher, who subordinated their role to party doctrine and practiced real political power, seeking, in this process, to eradicate all vestiges of "kleinbürgliche Intelligenz" (457–58).

For reasons that Habermas links to both a misunderstanding of Heine's role as an engaged poet-journalist in Paris and to the fact that in his work he took the radical step of injecting the German Romantic tradition into the modern revolutionary movement, no group of German intellectuals, neither on the Right, nor on the Left, was able to recognize in Heine a potential ally. In Habermas's opinion, this failure represents a singular missed opportunity for the development of an influential intelligentsia in the Weimar period. He concludes that only after 1945 did Heine's self-perceived role as an engaged intellectual begin to serve as a model for a new generation of intellectuals (465).

The failure of German intellectuals to promote Heine's cause may be linked to the fact that his popularity as a poet, which had kept him very much alive on the literary scene in the late nineteenth century despite massive efforts from the Right to banish him, was on the wane. The early twentieth century saw the development of a modernist school of poetry, led by the influential figures of Rilke, Hofmannsthal, and Stefan George and, concomitantly, the widespread adherence to a school of literary criticism oriented toward "Geistesgeschichte," with a marked emphasis on the aesthetic content and form of the literary work. Neither movement was particularly friendly toward Heine. Karl Kraus's 1910 essay, "Heine und die Folgen," which condemns Heine's false use of language, and his inability to "lower his eyes" or to "fall to his knees" in the face of its power, matched the tenor of the times (Kleinknecht 135–36). The traumatic experience of the First World War, expressionism, the reaction to naturalism in literature, and the general skepticism, anguish, and fragmentation that characterized cultural life and formed the basis for modernism combined to render Heine's poetry passé. The new poetry was heavily laden with metaphor; it was formally complex and at times impenetrable in its symbolism; it was esoteric and "weltfremd." And it restored the poet to the position of priest. The sole reason for the poet's existence on this earth, Hermann Hesse exclaimed in 1918, is to act as a holy guardian for the world, a world which is more than just "reality" — it is "eternal" (Habermas 462).

But what of voices on the Left? It is perhaps not surprising that nationalistic and anti-Semitic marginalization of Heine, in the tradition of Menzel, Treitschke, and Bartels, continued in the Weimar period, characterized as it was by the increasing radicalization of the *völkisch* Right. Josef Nadler's persiflage of a literary history, in which Heine is relegated to the status of the homeless "wandering Jew" who was responsible for the "Entsittlichung" of Germany, falls directly into this period (Hotz 131). And if we acknowledge the liberal dilemma that made it problematic for intellectuals to champion Heine (Peters 69–81), that still leaves the large and influential body of nineteenth-century criticism on the Left that engaged itself for Heine. This stream of socialist reception originated in the period of Heine's association with Karl Marx, Friedrich Engels, and Ferdinand Lassalle in 1844 and was channeled into formal literary criticism through the efforts of Franz Mehring, who defending Heine as a "Kämpfer" and "Märtyrer" for the proletarian cause (483), to the degree that Mehring's modern editor states unequivocally that he was the first Marxist Heine scholar in Germany (Mehring 127). In 1893 August Bebel, head of the Social Democratic Party in the German Reichstag, gave a memorable address to the assembled delegates on the future of socialism, which he concluded with the introductory lines from *Deutschland. Ein Wintermärchen* that proclaim Heine's vision of an earthly paradise for all mankind. 1.7 million copies of Bebel's speech were subsequently distributed in Germany (Reese 114).

With the eruption of communist agitation in Germany in 1918, the formation of workers' councils, the near founding of a socialist republic, and widespread if splintered efforts to arouse revolutionary fervor in Germany, Heine, one might assume, would have been given prevalent voice. The opposite seems to have been the case, however. Walter Reese, whose lengthy 1979 study on the socialist reception of Heine remains the most thorough investigation of this topic, concludes, "Heine war in den Klassenkämpfen jener Jahre nur eine nicht einmal unbedingt interessante Beigabe. . . . Die wenigen Zahlen sprechen dafür, daß Heine tatsächlich relativ seltner von den Arbeitern rezipiert wurde als in der Vorkriegszeit" (172). The period started off auspiciously enough, according to Reese, with the appearance of George Grosz's biting visual interpretation of Heine, the painting, "Deutschland, ein Wintermärchen," and the publication in Germany of portions of the long-banned verse satire of Otto Hörth, "Ein neues Wintermärchen," which approaches the verbal brilliance of the original in calling for a revolution to rid Germany once and for all of its "nationalliberalen Gestank" (Reese 169; Grab 148). Yet surveys taken on the reading habits of workers in the 1920s and records of lending libraries in the same period suggest that interest in Heine within the working class declined significantly (Reese 172).

The reason for this decline can be found in the rapidly changing cultural politics within socialist and communist ranks that accompanied Bolshevik revolutionary activity in Russia and throughout Europe. Whereas Mehring and other left-leaning critics had sought to wrest

Heine away from the clutches of liberal bourgeois criticism and to appropriate his legacy for the proletarian cause, attention was now focused on new proletarian literature aimed specifically at enlisting workers for the revolutionary battle and indoctrinating them to the communist cause. Proletarian culture found its outlet increasingly in theater, radio, film, and agitprop. Reese formulates the situation as follows: "In der lauten Agitation jener Jahre, in denen die Köpfe von Straßenkämpfen beherrscht wurden, in denen die künstlerische Szene vom Dadaismus geprägt wurde, konnte literarhistorische Rückbesinnung nur am Rande Beachtung finden." "Heine," he concludes, "wurde nicht diskutiert, allenfalls einmal angeführt" (172–73).

Wolf Biermann cites a personal example of Heine's import for the communist cause during the early 1920s in his Düsseldorf address. His mother, "eine Industriearbeiterin, Mitglied der KPD von Anfang an, Kombattantin im Hamburger Aufstand 1921, illegale Widerstandskämpferin in der Nazizeit," was an avid reader of Heine, *not,* however, of his political prose, but rather his love poetry. The family story has it that Biermann's father wooed his future bride with a red, leatherbound copy of *Buch der Lieder,* and that she was want to read poems from the volume during her breaks at the factory: "Hauptspeise Marx: die billige Broschüre *Lohnarbeit und Kapital* — und dann als Nachtisch Heineverse im fahnenroten Saffian" (7–8).

The German revolution of 1918–19 and the resultant Weimar Republic are now remembered not as the chapter in German history that finally saw the triumph of liberal-democratic forces over blind, militaristic nationalism, but rather as the seedbed of National Socialism and the rise of Hitler to power. Ironically, the "Kamaschenritterthum" that Heine so abhorred was not swept away by the re-emergence of a Barbarossa, but rather by chaotic events surrounding the lost World War. But Barbarossa was lurking in the wings of this "Spektakelstück," as Heine calls it in the *Wintermärchen.* As Ian Kershaw writes in his recent Hitler biography,

> All nationalisms need their myths. In this case, a powerful one was the "Reich myth." The very name of the new nation-state, "German Reich," evoked for many the mystical claim to reinstate the first Reich of Frederick Barbarossa — sleeping, according to the saga, in his holy mountain beneath the Kyffhäuser in Thuringia until the rebirth of his medieval Reich. The new aesthetics of nationalism called for the continuity to be symbolized in the gigantic monument to Kaiser Wilhelm I, mainly funded by veterans' associations, erected on the Kyffhäuser in 1896. (76–77)

The new Barbarossa that awakened Germany's slumbering spirit was Adolf Hitler. And the spiritual forces that Hitler awakened were indeed known to Heine. They were not the liberating forces of Luther and the Enlightenment, however, but rather the dark and dangerous forces lurking in German Romanticism. To cite Kershaw again:

> The central strands of *völkisch* ideology were extreme nationalism, racial antisemitism, and mystical notions of a uniquely German social order, with roots in the Teutonic past, resting on order, harmony, and hierarchy. Most significant was the linkage of a romanticized view of Germanic culture (seen as superior but heavily threatened by inferior but powerful forces, particularly Slavs and Jews), with a social Darwinian emphasis upon struggle for survival, imperialist notions of the need for expansion to the Slavic east in order to safeguard national survival, and the necessity of bringing about racial purity and a new élite by eradicating the perceived arch-enemy of Germandom, the spirit of Jewry. (135–36)

Is this not, one wonders, the odiferous vision that Heine saw in Karl the Great's chamber pot?

It is likely that Heine would have been skeptical of the Weimar Republic and most certain that he would have found Hitler abhorrent. He might not, however, have been terribly surprised. Despite his lifelong effort to forge understanding between France and Germany, Heine was ultimately aware of fundamental differences between the two nations and the two cultures. Hitler and Napoleon are worlds apart, yet they share one fateful similarity, charisma, a political phenomenon to which Heine himself was susceptible. In the case of Hitler, it surfaced in an otherwise unremarkable man and unlocked emotional and spiritual forces that resulted in historical events that match or exceed Heine's prophecy, "Es wird ein Stück aufgeführt werden in Deutschland, wogegen die französische Revolution nur wie eine harmlose Idylle erscheinen möchte" (DHA 8.1: 119).

Works Cited

Bartels, Adolf. *Heinrich Heine: Auch ein Denkmal.* Dresden and Leipzig: Koch, 1906.

Belart, Wilhelm. "Gehalt und Aufbau von Heinrich Heines Gedichtsammlungen." Diss., Bern, 1925. Reprinted Nendeln: Kraus Reprint, 1970.

Biermann, Wolf. "Heine, unsere Zuckererbsen." *Aufklärung und Skepsis: Internationaler Heine-Kongreß 1997 zum 200. Geburtstag.* Ed. Joseph A. Kruse, Bernd Witte, and Karin Füllner. Stuttgart and Weimar: Metzler, 1999. 1–18.

Friedländer, Fritz. *Heine und Goethe.* Berlin and Leipzig: Walter de Gruyter, 1932.

Grab, Walter. *Heinrich Heine als politischer Dichter.* Heidelberg: Quelle & Meyer, 1982.

Habermas, Jürgen. "Heinrich Heine und die Rolle des Intellektuellen in Deutschland." *Merkur: Deutsche Zeitschrift für europäisches Denken* 6 (1986): 453–68.

Hansen, Volkmar. *Thomas Manns Heine-Rezeption.* Heine-Studien. Hamburg: Hoffmann und Campe, 1975.

Harich, Wolfgang. "Heinrich Heine und das Schulgeheimnis der deutschen Philosophie." *Sinn und Form* 1 (1956): 27–59.

Hotz, Karl, ed. *Heinrich Heine: Wirkungsgeschichte als Wirkungskritik. Materialien zur Rezeptions- und Wirkungsgeschichte Heines.* Stuttgart: Klett, 1975.

Kershaw, Ian. *Hitler. 1889–1936: Hubris.* New York and London: W. W. Norton, 1998.

Kleinknecht, Karl Theodor, ed. *Heine in Deutschland: Dokumente seiner Rezeption 1834–1956.* Tübingen and Munich: Deutscher Taschenbuch Verlag and Niemeyer, 1976.

Kreutzer, Leo. "Uchronia oder: die rechte Stunde für Kaiser Rothbart." *"Dichter unbekannt": Heine lesen heute.* Ed. Dolf Oehler and Karin Hempel-Soos. Bonn: Bouvier, 1998. 28–41.

Loewenthal, Erich. *Studien zu Heines "Reisebildern."* Berlin and Leipzig, 1922. Reprinted New York and London: Johnson, 1967.

Mehring, Franz. *Aufsätze zur deutschen Literatur von Klopstock bis Weerth. Gesammelte Schriften.* Vol. 10. Ed. Thomas Höhle, Hans Koch, and Josef Schleifstein. Berlin: Dietz, 1961.

Morawe, Bodo. "Juni 1832: Heine und der Aufstand." *"Dichter unbekannt": Heine lesen heute.* Ed. Dolf Oehler and Karin Hempel-Soos. Bonn: Bouvier, 1998. 81–108.

Nadler, Josef. *Der deutsche Staat.* Vol. 4 of *Literaturgeschichte der deutschen Stämme und Landschaften.* 3rd ed. Regensburg: Josef Habbel, 1932. 4 vols. 1929–1932.

Nietzsche, Friedrich. *Werke in drei Bänden.* Ed. Karl Schlechta. Vol. 2. Munich: 1966. 3 vols.

Peters, George F. *The Poet as Provocateur: Heinrich Heine and His Critics.* Rochester, NY: Camden House, 2000.

Prang, H. "Heine im Schatten Hölderlins." *Neue deutsche Hefte* 2 (1955–56): 472–75.

Reese, Walter. *Zur Geschichte der sozialistischen Heine-Rezeption in Deutschland.* Frankfurt am Main: Peter Lang, 1979.

Stauf, Renate. "Marianne und Germania beim literarischen Tee: Heine contra Mme. De Staël." *"Dichter unbekannt": Heine lesen heute.* Ed. Dolf Oehler and Karin Hempel-Soos. Bonn: Bouvier, 1998. 9–27.

Strich, Fritz, ed. *Heinrich Heine: Sämtliche Werke.* Munich: Georg Müller, 1925–1930. 11 vols.

"Die Verfassung des Deutschen Reiches." University of Würzburg, Lehrstuhl für Rechtsphilosophie. World Wide Web, URL http://www.uni-wuerzburg. de/rechtsphilosophie/hdoc/wrv1919.html.

Werner, Hans-Georg. "Zur Wirkung von Heines literarischem Werk." *Weimarer Beiträge* 19.9 (1973): 35–73.

Windfuhr, Manfred. *Heinrich Heine: Revolution und Reflexion.* 2nd. ed. Stuttgart: Metzler, 1976.

Wolff, Max J. *Heine.* Munich: n.p., 1922.

Contributors

ROGER F. COOK is Professor of German and Chair of the Department of German and Russian Studies at the University of Missouri, Columbia. He has published widely on German literature, film, and cultural history from the eighteenth century to the present, including *The Demise of the Author: Autonomy and the German Writer 1770–1848* (1993) and *The Cinema of Wim Wenders: Image, Narrative, and the Postmodern Condition* (co-editor, 1996). His publications on Heine include *By the Rivers of Babylon: Heinrich Heine's Late Songs and Reflections* (1998). He is currently working on a study of conceptions of Jewish history in the nineteenth century.

WILLI GOETSCHEL is Associate Professor of German at the University of Toronto. He is the author of *Constituting Critique: Kant's Writing as Critical Praxis* (1994) and *Spinoza's Modernity: Mendelssohn, Lessing, Heine* (forthcoming). He is the editor of the edition of the complete works of Hermann Levin Goldschmidt (1993–) and of *The Germanic Review*. He is currently working on a book on Heine and Critical Theory.

JEFFREY GROSSMAN is Assistant Professor of German and a member of the Jewish Studies faculty at the University of Virginia. His first book is *The Discourse on Yiddish in German: From the Enlightenment to the Second Empire*. He has published articles on Walter Benjamin, Herder, Wilhelm von Humboldt, and the Yiddish writer I. L. Peretz. Currently, he is working on literary and cultural appropriation in Heine and the appropriations of Heine in German, English, and Yiddish.

GERHARD HÖHN is an independent scholar and writer living in Paris and former Professor of Philosophy at the University of Caen, France. He has published extensively on German philosophy and political romanticism both in Germany and France. His publications on Heine include *Heine-Handbuch* (1987; 2nd. ed. 1997) and *Heinrich Heine: Un intellectuel moderne* (1994). He has also edited *Heinrich Heine: Ästhetisch-politische Profile* (1991), *Henri Heine: De la France* (1994), and *Heinrich Heine: Nouveaux poèmes* (1998). His current research projects involve Heine and *Vormärz*, and current French and German philosophy (Poststructuralism and the Frankfurt School).

Robert C. Holub teaches intellectual, cultural, and literary history in the German department at the University of California, Berkeley. Among his publications on these topics are books on Heinrich Heine, reception theory, nineteenth-century realism, Jürgen Habermas, recent literary theory, and Friedrich Nietzsche. He has also edited five volumes on various topics from the enlightenment to the present.

Joseph A. Kruse is Director of the Heinrich Heine Institute and Teaching Professor at the Heinrich Heine University, Düsseldorf. He is the author of numerous articles on writers and composers whose manuscripts belong to the archives of the Heinrich Heine Institute, including Karl Immermann, Christian Dietrich Grabbe, and Robert Schumann. He is editor of the *Heine-Jahrbuch* and the Heine-Studien series. His many publications on Heine include *Heines Hamburger Zeit* (1972), *Heinrich Heine. Leben und Werk in Texten und Bildern* (1983), *Denk ich an Heine: Biographisch-literarische Facetten* (1986), and *Heine-Zeit* (1997).

Michael Perraudin is Professor of German and Head of the Department of Germanic Studies at the University of Sheffield. His publications include *Heinrich Heine: Poetry in Context. A Study of "Buch der Lieder"* (1989) and *Literature, the "Volk" and the Revolution in Mid-Nineteenth Century Germany* (2000). He has written articles on Kleist, Eichendorff, Heine, Wilhelm Müller, Mörike, Büchner, Storm, and Heinrich Böll, among others, and is currently working on a study of the early Heine and a range of topics on the *Vor-* and *Nachmärz*.

George F. Peters is Professor of German and former department chair at Michigan State University. He has published monographs on Heine's reception of Goethe and on the history of Heine criticism as well as articles dealing with Heine's adaption and transformation of lyrical models. In addition to literary scholarship, he has published translations and articles dealing with German pedagogy and the state of the profession.

Paul Peters is Associate Professor in the Department of German Studies, McGill University. He has written a study of anti-Semitism and German Heine reception, *Die Wunde Heine,* (2nd ed. 1997), and edited a volume of Heine's writings on Judaism and Jewry, *Prinzessin Sabbat: Heinrich Heine über Juden und Judentum.* (1997). He has also written numerous articles on Heine's poetry, as well as on Kafka, Brecht, and Paul Celan.

ANTHONY PHELAN is Fellow of Keble College and Faculty Lecturer in German at Oxford. He has published a study of Rilke's *Neue Gedichte* (1992), edited *The Weimar Dilemma. Intellectuals in the Weimar Republic* (1985), and has contributed widely to books and journals. His main area of interest is the relation between German Romanticism and the aesthetics of Modernism and modernity. His most recent work has been on Heine, and the present essay is part of a larger project on the critical significance of Heine's reception from Karl Kraus to Helmut Heissenbüttel.

PAUL REITTER is Assistant Professor of German at Ohio State University. He has published articles on Heine, Karl Kraus, Kafka, and on the future of Jewish Studies.

Index